Titles on Politics and Political Economy
Published by James Currey

*The Culture of World Politics**
North–South Relations in a Global Perspective
ALI A. MAZRUI
0 85255 321 8 cased
0 85255 322 6 paper

*Democratic Theory and Practice in Africa**
Edited by WALTER O. OYUGI, E.S. ATIENO
ODHIAMBO, MICHAEL CHEGE & AFRIFA
K. GITONGA
0 85255 327 7 paper

Politics in Sub-Saharan Africa
ROGER TANGRI
0 85255 300 5 paper

Southern Africa

Beggar Your Neighbours
Apartheid Power in Southern Africa
JOSEPH HANLON
0 85255 307 2 cased
0 85255 305 6 paper

South Africa: A Different Kind of War
From Soweto to Pretoria
JULIE FREDERIKSE
0 85255 301 3 paper

None But Ourselves
Masses vs Media in the Making of Zimbabwe
JULIE FREDERIKSE
0 85255 329 3 paper

Endgame in South Africa?
ROBIN COHEN
0 85255 308 0 paper

Race, Class and the Apartheid State
HAROLD WOLPE
0 85255 319 6 paper

A History of Resistance in Namibia
PETER H. KATJAVIVI
0 85255 320 X

South Africa in Question?
Edited by JOHN LONSDALE
0 85255 325 0 cased
0 85255 326 9 paper

Detention and Torture in South Africa
DON FOSTER, WITH DENNIS DAVIS AND
DIANE SANDLER
0 85255 317 X cased
0 85255 318 8 paper

After Apartheid
Renewal of the South African Economy
Edited by JOHN SUCKLING AND LANDEG
WHITE
0 85255 109 6 cased
0 85255 110 X paper

Popular Struggles in South Africa
Edited by WILLIAM COBBETT AND ROBIN
COHEN
0 85255 323 4 cased
0 85255 324 2 paper

*Studies on the South African Media**
Edited by KEYAN TOMASELLI, RUTH
TOMASELLI AND JOHAN MULLER
0 85255 310 2 cased

Sol Plaatje
South African Nationalist 1876–1932
BRIAN WILLAN
0 85255 044 8 cased
0 85255 045 6 paper

*Anglo American and the Rise of Modern South
Africa*
DUNCAN INNES
0 85255 113 4

West Africa

The Nigerian State
Political Economy, State Class and Political
System in the Post-Colonial Era
WILLIAM D. GRAF
0 85255 313 7 cased
0 85255 314 5 paper

Eastern Africa

*Uganda Now**
Between Decay and Development
Edited by HOLGER BERNT HANSEN & MICHAEL
TWADDLE
0 85255 315 3 cased

* *forthcoming*

The Nigerian State

The Nigerian State

Political Economy,
State Class and Political System
in the Post-Colonial Era

WILLIAM D. GRAF

Associate Professor of Political Studies
University of Guelph, Ontario

James Currey
LONDON

Heinemann
PORTSMOUTH (N.H.)

James Currey Ltd
54b Thornhill Square, Islington, London N1 1BE

Heinemann Educational Books Inc
70 Court Street, Portsmouth
New Hampshire 03801

First published 1988

British Library Cataloguing in Publication Data

Graf, William D.
  The Nigerian state: political economy, state class and political system in the post-colonial era.
  1. Nigeria. State, 1960–1987
  I. Title
  320.1'09669

  ISBN 0–85255–313–7 Cloth(James Currey)
  ISBN 0–85255–314–5 Pbk (James Currey)

  ISBN 0–435–08028–8 Cloth (Heinemann)
  ISBN 0–435–08029–6 Paper (Heinemann)

The paper in this book is acid free and meets the guidelines for permanence and durability favoured by
the British Library and the Library of Congress

Typeset in 10/11pt Plantin by Colset Private Limited, Singapore
Printed and bound in Great Britain

for Amanda Rosa Alero Wall-Graf
born 8 May 1979 in Benin City

Contents

List of Tables   ix
List of Figures   x
Prologue and Acknowledgements   xi

1 *Introduction: Premises of Nigerian Politics*   1

   Diversity   1
   Colonial formations and deformations   7
   Polarisation of society   9
   The problem of integration   12
   'Tribalism'   13
   Ethnicity and class hegemony   17

2 *The First Republic*   25

   Political decolonisation   26
   Structural problems   27
   The regionalisation of political life   30
   Political deficiencies   34
   Coup de grace?   38

3 *The Military in Politics*   41

   The first military interregnum   41
   Centralism: the shifting balance of domestic power   47

4 *Indigenisation, Recivilianisation and Elite Formation*   53

   State capitalism and indigenisation   53
   Pressures toward demilitarisation   59
   How, and for whom the 1979 constitution was made   65
   Ideological aspects   71

5 *The Second Republic: Parties and Interests*   77

   Party formation and development   77
   Electoral dynamics of elite rule   85
   Shifting alliances and cleavages   90
   Towards a one-party 'chop' state   94
   Assessment of party rule in the Second Republic   100

6 *Structures and (Mal)Functions of Nigerian Democracy*   115

   Consolidation and legitimation   115

Separated and divided powers 116
The National Assembly 118
The presidency 123
Problems of legislative-executive relations 127

7 *The States in the Federation* 133

Sub-state government in Nigeria 133
Politics of federalism 137
The crucial issues: revenue-sharing and state-creation 139

8 *The Military Returns* 149

Chronicle of the Buhari coup 149
Logic of military intervention 153
Class interests and elite hegemony 156
Transnational dimensions 160
Austerity without development 162
Correcting the corrective 167
Factional shifts within the elite stratum 169
A fragile equilibrium 173

9 *The 'Grassroots' State: Local and Traditional Politics* 180

The special role of local government 180
The 'rationalisation' of traditional rule 186
Dynamics of politics at the basis 189

10 *The State Bureaucracy* 203

Specificity and the Nigerian 'ecology' 203
Structural problems 205
Ideological solutions 207
The judicature 209
Regulating public officers' conduct 213

11 *The Nigerian State and the State of Nigeria* 218

Rentier state in the world market 218
State capitalism at the periphery 224
Whose state? 227
Elites and underdevelopment 229
Excursus on foreign policy 235
Incomplete hegemony 237
Beyond peripheral capitalism? 241

Bibliography 248

Index 276

List of Tables

1.1 Distribution of Nigerian ethnic groups (1963)   6
4.1 Federal Government: military and social expenditures   60
5.1 Summary of 1979 election results: federal institutions by State   86
5.2 Summary of 1979 election results: in the States   88
5.3 Price increases for selected basic commodities   95
5.4 Voters' register: 1979 and 1983   96
5.5 Results of the 1983 Presidential election   101
5.6 Initial results of the 1983 Gubernatorial elections   102–3
5.7 1983 Senate election results   104
5.8 1983 House of Representatives election results   104
5.9 Party control of States   105
5.10 Party consolidation during the Second Republic: the House of Representatives   106
6.1 Percentage distribution of social and occupational backgrounds of House of Assembly members   120
6.2 Percentage distribution of annual income of House of Assembly members   120
7.1 Senate committee recommendations for the creation of new States (January 1983)   144
9.1 Proliferation of local government areas, October 1979–December 1981   190
11.1 Revenues from exports and imports, 1970–83 (Nm.)   218
11.2 Oil's share in Federal Government revenue, 1961–85 (Nm.)   219
11.3 Participation by the Nigerian Government in the oil industry   220
11.4 Some key economic indicators (Nm.)   221
11.5 The directions of Nigerian trade   221

Note

N = Naira which is officially represented as ₦

List of Figures

1.1 Vegetation of Nigeria   2
1.2 Geographic regions of Nigeria   3
1.3 Major ethnic divisions of Nigeria   14
5.1 NPN 'zoning' system   81
5.2 Schematic representation of political party ideological landscape   84
5.3 The parties' ethnic support bases   89

Prologue and Acknowledgements

A decade ago, Tilman Evers, in his pioneering attempt at formulating a theory of the state in the Third World, argued for a materialist theory of the peripheral state incorporating the external and internal interrelationships between state(s) and society(ies), and focussing on politics, not as 'a mere object of economics', but as the subject of analysis 'with its own social bodies, its own laws and contradictions, its own means and instruments and its own history' (Evers, 1977:15). It was not only that a theory of the Third World state had not been developed, Evers argued, but that even the fundamental preconditions for such a theory were lacking, namely, historical analyses of concrete individual cases of underdeveloped states whose variety and diversity had not been shaped and analysed into identifiable patterns and tendencies.

Evers' dual 'specificity' argument – of the political and of the individual case study – has since re-emerged whenever the issue of the peripheral state has been addressed on the basis of materialist premises. If Miliband and Badie and Birnbaum have made the case for an analytical concern with the primacy of the political in the study of the generic capitalist state,[1] then a number of scholars have advocated the need for concrete studies of particular peripheral states as a prelude to any general theory. Among the latter, Bernstein and Campbell have argued for 'more rigorous and refined analyses of the prospects and limitations of particular conjunctures of struggle – the concrete analysis of concrete situations' which, they hope, might contribute to a 'knowledge of Africa that is adequate to its profoundly contradictory realities'.[2] Joel Samoff and Harry Goulbourne[3] also make a case for concentrating on 'historical specificity' in coming to grips with any theory of the African state, while Richard Joseph rightly speaks of 'a willingness to confront the untidy reality of the Nigerian political economy'.[4] And for Clive Thomas, 'there can be no abstract study of the state and politics' in the Third World; rather 'the specific nature of each and every state form and the concrete conditions of its politics bear directly on the conclusions of any general theoretical inquiry'.[5]

With a view to these injunctions and prescriptions, I have eschewed what, given the nuances and complexity of the phenomena under discussion, has been a strong inclination to force the 'untidy reality' of the Nigerian state into a preformulated paradigmatic framework. I have instead attempted to approach the 'specificity' of the Nigerian development inductively and diachronically, rather than deductively and synchronically. This approach is a concession to and confirmation of the fact that there are now several paradigms and approaches – notably world-systems theories, peripheral class analyses and Marxist state debates – more capable of illuminating certain aspects of the state in the Third World than was the case when pluralist, structural-functional or even modernisation theories represented the dominant paradigms for the study of African social phenomena. One is reminded (again following Samoff) that, in this context of successive paradigms, such shifts are at bottom themselves part of a political process and relate to the constellations of power and conflicts at a particular historical moment. Nevertheless, right at the centre of the multiplicity of conflicting and contradictory paradigmatic interpretations of 'development' and prescriptions for overcoming under-development lie certain abiding problems which, however deduced, essentially remain unsolved and which therefore compel an ongoing and self-correcting process of theory-formation.[6]

To adopt an inductive-diachronic methodology is not, however, to offer an apology for some form of veiled eclecticism. The critical approaches just alluded to can be subsumed into a general political economy framework which is capable of integrating, comprehending and interpreting the complex reality of the postcolonial Nigerian state. The political economy framework can best be regarded as a paradigm-in-becoming. Without entering into the intricate and at present largely fruitless debate about what political economy is, and is not, I will simply describe how it infuses this study. Following Drache and Clement, political economy is definable simultaneously as a (Marxian-inspired) tradition, a (multi-disciplinary) field of study and a paradigm (of the links between economics and the social, cultural, ideological and political orders).[7] The political economy framework derives its impetus initially from an awareness of the limitations of 'conventional' social science methodologies which, fragmented into 'disciplines' and frequently serving dominant interests, have produced findings aptly described as ahistorical, banal and hence conservative.

As early as 1958, Barrington Moore Jr. warned against the 'decline in the historical perspective':[8]

> The use of a formalist deductive tradition in search of laws has been accompanied by an increasing static bias in much contemporary social science . . . The search for categories that apply without reference to time or place easily introduces a static bias unless we are extremely careful to notice the historical limitations of our generalizations.

The present study attempts to account for this temporal dimension by examining the succession of political formations in the postcolonial state. It moves from the colonial transformation of traditional society (chapter 1) to the First Republic (chapter 2), the first succession of military governments (chapters 3 and 4), the Second Republic (chapters 5, 6 and the substance of 7) and the current series of military regimes (chapter 8). The general discussions of local and traditional rule (chapter 9) and of the state bureaucracy (chapter 10) are also integrated into a diachronic perspective. Only chapter 11 attempts to deal with the 'total' theoretical concern. By organising most of the analysis within this chronological framework, each succeeding set of political structures can be seen as a temporary coalition of forces and classes, internal and external – that is, a specific conjuncture – which lends itself to description and analysis and, when interrelated to other stages and developments, permits insights into the dynamics of the Nigerian socio-economic formation over time. In other words, periodisation and thematisation reinforce and complement one another and so contribute to an enhanced analytical perspective.

Another essential element of the political economy framework, as developed here, is that of commitment. In this, I share Peter Waterman's view that 'conventional' social science approaches to African studies too frequently run aground in triviality, conservatism and irrelevance. 'In this sense,' he submits, 'any work which ignores the superficial and epiphenomenal, which uncovers basic structures and root problems, can and should be considered radical.'[9] Admittedly, all scholarship is in some measure 'committed'. But the radicalism of political economy is premised, to a greater or lesser extent, on a desire to change an undesirable reality. That desire may stem from an awareness of mass poverty or class exploitation, or from a belief in the mutability of the structures of domination and oppression that characterise social relations. Hence critical political economy does have the special capacity to formulate and analyse socio-economic phe-nomena from the perspective of the oppressed and exploited social classes and peoples. It does not ask how to make a given system of domination more functional or palatable; it examines the operation of that system, exposes its beneficiaries, defines its *raison d'être* and – explicitly or implicitly – proposes alternatives to it.

For these reasons, class conflict emerges as a crucial analytical focus of the political economy orientation. Indeed, Terisa Turner sums up (1985b:8) her political economy perspective as 'the analysis of the formation and interaction of social classes, historically and on a world scale.' Again and again, as this study progressed, elite interests and behaviour emerged as the crucial explanatory variable, through the various forms of regime over time, for such diverse phenomena as election rigging, economic depend-ence, party formation, the deformation of traditional rule, the pre-emption of local governments, the kaleidoscopic formulas of federalism and the federal character, the deficiencies of the state bureaucracy and parastatals, intra-military power struggles, general strikes, peasant uprisings, and much else. Thus, merely to anticipate a few findings elicited by the political economy methodology, the process of decolonisation amounts to the transfer of political power to a successor elite, the alternation of civilian-military ruling forms appears as a series of factional shifts within the elite stratum, the implementation of liberal-democratic structures is a means of effecting elite consoli-dation, and the 'federal character of Nigeria' is a device for positioning elite segments for access to the trough of state largesse.

Since class formation and conflict are mainly functions of the specific mode and relations of production, the diverse, ostensibly temporally limited aspects of postcolonial developments must be incorporated into a broader theory of the Nigerian state. This is the subject of the concluding chapter. While the specificity of the Nigerian state self-evidently derives from the particular constellation of forces and classes within the national boundaries, the theory of the postcolonial Nigerian state must be located, as Samoff posits for the African state generally, at the 'intersection of external and internal dynamics, particularly in the operation of a world capitalist economy and in class conflict both at the world system and nation-state levels.'[10] The development of the theory of a peripheral state with its external linkages and depend-encies and its internal structures and dynamics – which can only be accomplished within the political economy framework – leads to the conceptualisation of the state as a category of class power, namely, as the structural power of an (external and internal) capitalist class standing in a fundamentally antagonistic relationship to labour. The peculiar nature of class power in the Nigerian state is captured, in chapter 11, with the notion of a state class.[11]

The preceding discussion in some measure explains the choice of title of this book. 'Political economy' describes both the object studied and the means of studying it. 'State class' defines an elite whose dependence on, and collaboration with, the external elites and whose particularist domination of the local state explain much about Nigeria's underdevelopment. 'Political system' refers to both the primacy of politics in the peripheral state and to the respective 'shells' through which political power is exerted. And the 'Nigerian state' subsumes the linkages and interconnections of politi-cal, economic and social developments within a specific conjuncture. If it is recalled that about one in four black Africans or one in two West Africans is a Nigerian, that Nigeria is the world's ninth most populous country and sixth largest oil exporter, and that the country's aggregate output of goods and services or GDP (at least in periods of oil-centred prosperity) is greater than that of the rest of black Africa combined, then it is evident that the study of the 'Nigerian state' is of central relevance to the African condition more generally and to the evolution of a theory of the peripheral state on the foundation of 'concrete individual cases'.

Finally, I want to acknowledge at least some of the help and encouragement that I have received in conceiving, researching and preparing this book.

Gavin Williams, Terisa Turner, Bill Freund and Bob Shenton – whose works on Nigeria have influenced mine – have all read and commented on parts of it. Their stimulating (and unsparing) criticisms and insights have enhanced the pleasure that writing it has been. The fact that none of them has read the completed manuscript, and that I have not always heeded their suggestions, of course exonerates them from any culpability for its deficiencies.

I would also like to record some longstanding debts to my colleagues in Nigeria who, in various ways, have furthered one Oyinbo's understanding of the Nigerian political economy: Sam Egite Oyovbaire, Yolamu Barongo, Claude Ake, Oyelele Oyediran, Omo Omoruyi, M. Angulu Onwueojogwu, Wang Metuge, Okwudiba Nnoli, Olatunde J. B. Ojo, Ray Ekpu and Mae King-Akesode.

The annual conferences of the Canadian Association of African Studies and the Canadian Political Science Association have, over the past four years, provided a tolerant forum for me to advance, in more or less coherent form, many of the arguments and concepts contained here. In particular, I have learned much from comments offered by John Cartwright, Julius Ihonvbere, Obafemi Taiwo, Doug Anglin, Richard Joseph, Anthony Kirk-Greene, Michael Stevenson, Linda Freeman, Eboe Hutchful, Tim Shaw, Jim Silver and Claudia Wright. Talks that I have been invited to give to the African Students' Associations at the Universities of Toronto, York, Waterloo and Guelph as well as to the Walter Rodney African Studies Seminar at Boston University – then organised by Bill Hansen and Brigitte Schulz – have, more than other fora, compelled me to clarify several of my positions and have thus enhanced the 'political' content of my work on Nigeria.

The impetus to write this book evolved while I was at the University of Benin; my institutional anchor during its preparation has been the University of Guelph. The latter has admirably managed, in the face of fierce government underfunding of higher education, to maintain the institution of the teaching/research assistant. As a result, this study has been assisted by the fine supportive work of Matt McCormick, Joanne Marshall, Andreas Pickel, Sandra Couch, Faye Mercan and Isaac Bashorun. Isaac, whose B.A. and M.A. studies have roughly coincided with the progress of this book, has been an invaluable source of current information and ongoing discussion on developments in Nigeria as well as a guide to certain linguistic and conceptual aspects of Nigerian politics. He, and Joanne, helped to conceive and draft many of the maps and tables in chapters 1, 2 and 5.

A SSHRC research grant, administered by the Office of Research of the University of Guelph, helped to finance my 1983 fieldwork in Nigeria. Infrastructural support provided by the Department of Political Studies through Chairperson O. P. Dwivedi and by the College of Social Science through Dean John Vanderkamp has been crucial. Beyond this, the 'moral' support of my chairperson and my dean has been both warm and consistent.

Further, I want to thank the staffs of the Nigerian Institute for International Affairs, the University of Benin Library (especially Joan Omoruyi), the University of Lagos Library, Boston University Library and African Studies Centre, the *Daily Times*, the *Nigerian Observer*, the now defunct *Nigerian Hope* (notably its co-publisher, Augustin Ebueku), the Nigerian High Commission, Ottawa (Habib Elabor in particular), and especially the University of Guelph Library (Lorne Bruce, Bernard Katz and Pauline Bartol, among others). Susan Sommerauer, Lorraine Black and Donna Murray have applied their excellent word-processing skills to put together the original manuscript from a heterogeneous variety of drafts and fragments.

Parts of chapter 3 are derived from my *Elections 1979: The Nigerian Citizen's Guide to Parties, Politics, Leaders and Issues* (Lagos: *Daily Times* 1979), while other parts of it, and most of chapter 4, are developed from my 'Political Economy, Political Class and Political System in Recivilianized Nigeria', Working Paper No. 47, Boston University African Studies Centre, 1981, and from my 'African Elite Theories and Nigerian Elite Consolidation: A Political Economy Analysis' in Yolamu Barongo (ed.), *Political Science in Africa: A Critical Review* (London: Zed Press, 1983). A similar case was made in 'Nigerian Elite Consolidation and African Elite Theories: Toward an Explanation of African Liberal Democracy' in *Verfassung und Recht in Übersee*, No. 16, 2nd quarter 1983. Chapter 8 incorporates material first presented as 'The Nigerian New Year's Coup of December 31st 1983: A Class Analysis' in *Journal of Black Studies*, No. 9, 1985. Some of the electoral data in chapter 6 first appeared in my section on Nigeria in *New African Yearbook* 1980. Chapter 9 is essentially identical to my 'Nigerian "Grass-roots" Politics: Local Government, Traditional Rule and Class Domination', in *Journal of Commonwealth and Comparative Politics*, Vol. XXIV, No. 2 (July 1986); certain suggestions made by the *JCCP*'s editor, Richard Crook, and its anonymous reviewers, have been incorporated into the article and chapter. And several points made in chapters 5, 6, 7 and 8 were first formulated in *Globe and Mail* articles published between 1982 and 1986. In all cases I am obliged to the respective editors and publishers for providing me with the initial forum, and for their kind permission to incorporate the material into the present work.

The transformation of a rather less wieldy manuscript into a more concise book has been facilitated by the professionally competent and sympathetic support of James Currey and his publishing house. The comments of his two anonymous reviewers have prodded me to make certain valuable corrections and clarifications of substance, while the sustained and insightful editorial work of Margaret Cornell has much enhanced the book's readability.

W. D. G.

Notes

1. See respectively, Ralph Miliband, *Marxism and Politics*, London, 1977, chapter 1; and Bertrand Badie and Pierre Birnbaum, *The Sociology of the State*, Chicago, 1983, pp. 59–60 and 61–2.
2. Henry Bernstein and Bonnie Campbell, 'Introduction' to H. Bernstein and B. Campbell (eds), *Contradictions of Accumulation in Africa*, Beverly Hills, 1985, pp. 7 and 8.
3. Respectively, Joel Samoff, 'Class, Class Conflict and the State in Africa', *Political Science Quarterly*, Vol. 97, No. 1 (Spring 1982), p. 115; and Harry Goulbourne, 'Some Problems of

Analysis of the Politically Backward Capitalist Social Formations' in H. Goulbourne (ed.), *Politics and State in the Third World*, London, 1979, pp. 12–18.

4. Richard Joseph, 'Class and State in Nigeria: Implications for Civilian Rule', Working Paper, Boston University, Walter Rodney African Studies Seminars, April 1981, p. 4.

5. Clive Y. Thomas, *The Rise of the Authoritarian State in Peripheral Societies*, New York, 1984, p. xviii.

6. On this, see Alfred Schmidt, 'Strategien zur Überwindung von Unterentwicklung: Einführung in die Diskussion uber Probleme und Lösungsansätze', in A. Schmidt (ed.), *Strategien gegen Unterentwicklung: Zwischen Weltmarkt und Eigenständigkeit*, Frankfurt and New York, 2nd edn., 1978, pp. 9–11.

7. Daniel Drache and Wallace Clement, 'Introduction' to their *The New Practical Guide to Canadian Political Economy*, Toronto, 1985, pp. ix–x.

8. Barrington Moore, Jr., 'Strategy in Social Science', in his *Political Power and Social Theory: Six Essays*, Cambridge Mass., 1958, pp. 136–7.

9. Peter Waterman, 'On Radicalism in African Studies', in P. C. W. Gutkind and P. Waterman (eds), *African Social Studies: A Radical Reader*, London and New York, 1978, p. 14.

10. Samoff, *op. cit.*, p. 107.

11. A term adapted from Hartmut Elsenhans; see the discussion in chapter 11 below.

1

Introduction: Premises of Nigerian Politics

This introductory chapter attempts to organise and develop some of the central leitmotifs of the Nigerian political economy on the basis of a broad range of data drawn from the country's history, economy, sociology, ethnology and even geography. Its focus is thus essentially a diachronic (and admittedly in some measure subjective) study of more or less 'given' conditions which both constrain and present the special challenges and opportunities for contemporary Nigerian politics. The chapter's guiding assumption is that the past – critically and systematically examined – can be resolved into a series of patterns or themes which facilitate an understanding of the sprawling and otherwise confusing reality of modern Nigeria. The (tentative) conclusions – the premises of Nigerian politics – may usefully be regarded as a series of propositions which will link up with and underpin arguments to be advanced in subsequent chapters.

It must be stressed that they represent nothing more than hypotheses to be discussed, qualified, scrutinised and, ultimately, verified or falsified. Since this chapter attempts to collate and interpret a wide spectrum of more or less well-known material – i.e. assumes a certain amount of previous knowledge on the reader's part – it should be read in conjunction with other relevant studies listed in the Bibliography.

Diversity

Most interpretations of modern Nigeria indicate that the country is anything but homogeneous. Such terms as 'the conglomerate society', 'unity in diversity', 'the vertical–horizontal mosaic', 'the multi-national state', and 'the geographical expression' represent conceptual attempts to come to terms with this. Before proceeding to examine other social and historical problems, it is worth investigating the essential factors making for diversity, and then considering whether, and to what extent, this diversity has affected political economy and political life.

Depending upon the set of statistics one chooses to use, between 80 and 120 million – let us say 100 million[1] – Nigerians inhabit a land area of 356,669 square miles (923,773 square kilometers), extending from East to West across a distance of from 600 to 700 miles (900–1,200 kilometers) and about 650 miles (1,050 kilometers) from North to South. Upon this vast territory, a multi-faceted and many-tiered mosaic has built up over many centuries. At times the pieces seem to coalesce into distinguishable patterns;

but just as often they appear disjointed, inchoate and hence difficult to comprehend. In what now follows an attempt will be made to distinguish the salient features, rather than to dwell upon the separate pieces, of this mosaic.

A useful point of departure might be geography. An initial differentiation can be made between the North and South, along the East-West axis formed by the Upper Niger and Benue River valleys. While this distinction admittedly originates in the colonial North–South divide, it remains perhaps the most important one politically.

The North. The vast Sudan-savanna-scrubland to the north of the Niger–Benue valleys is largely a broad stepped plateau, ranging from the flat, monotonous Sokoto Plains in the west to the wide plains and sloping countryside of the Chad Basin in the east. The Northern High Plains of the centre is the dominant geographical subregion of the North. Here stepped plains and undulating surfaces with domed hills criss-cross the area, relieved by the 4,000-ft Jos Plateau with its cooler temperatures and, in places, quasi-European vegetation. Along its northern borders semi-desert conditions prevail. But for the most part, the land is fertile and productive, although irrigation and manuring must be employed extensively. Since there are two quite distinct annual seasons, rainy and dry, a degree of agrarian diversification has evolved. Crop rotation is practised and mixed crops are produced, in particular cereals. With few natural enemies (such as the tse-tse fly in the South), domestic animals thrive here; large herds of cattle and goats, some horses, and, in the extreme North, camels, are kept.

Thus the North is largely open and accessible and contains few natural barriers to trade and migration. This is especially true of the region facing the Sahara through

Figure 1.1 *Vegetation of Nigeria*

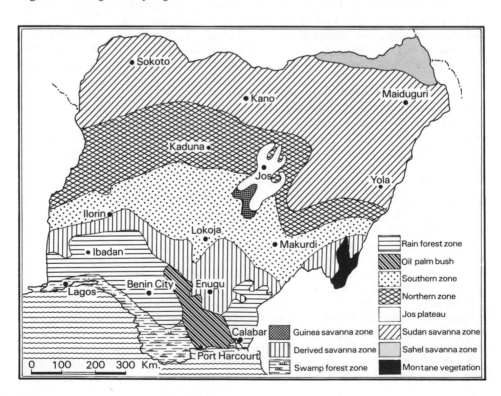

which, in the course of centuries, Arab traders and Islamic proselytisers have entered, bringing with them lasting influences on social organisation, religion and cultural values. The Muslim–Sudanic culture, adopted with modifications by the Hausa–Fulani, centres around the large Northern cities and the broad network of emirates in the rural areas. As in other predominantly Islamic states, the political structure has largely evolved in accordance with religious principles. For example, most of Nigeria's pre-colonial centralised kingdoms and states were established in the North – Daura, Katsina, Zaria, Kano, Kanem–Bornu. Centrally directed, with a well-developed system of administration, hierarchical and multi-national, these political units long ago achieved an advanced division of labour and a discernible unity of purpose.

But Northern conditions also encouraged the parallel evolution of a kind of social organisation which is anything but centralised: the nomadic, cattle-rearing groups of the so-called pastoral Fulani (to distinguish them from the sedentary Fulani who, since at least the fifteenth century, have been integrated with the Hausa).

The South. Nigeria's Southern territories – the coastal rain forests and low coastal region – are in many ways the antithesis of the North. If the North is relatively open, uniform and homogeneous, the South presents a picture of diversity, variegation and heterogeneity.

There are five distinct geographic regions in the South. The low plains of the southwest bordered by the Gulf of Guinea, which seldom rise above an elevation of 100 feet, are mostly swampy land areas interspersed with creeks and lagoons. These are backed by gentle plains rising to the north with dense, lush tropical vegetation. The

Figure 1.2 *Geographic regions of Nigeria*

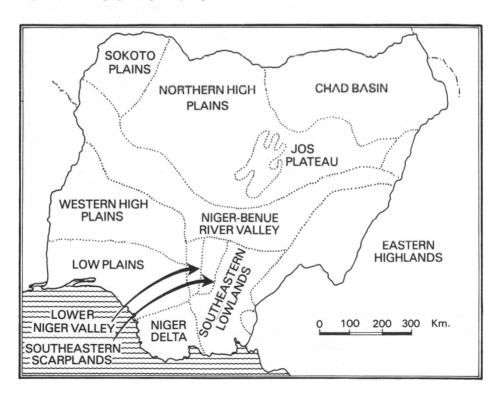

northern part of the low plains is ideally suited to cocoa production. The Niger Delta area, a formation created by the cumulative result of centuries of sedimentary deposits, stretches about 80 miles from its apex at Aboh town into the sea and covers an area of some 10,000 square miles. It is a series of (inhabited) islands of solid ground surrounded by mangrove and freshwater swamps. From Aboh northward to Lokoja at the confluence of the Niger and Benue rivers – a distance of perhaps 185 miles – runs the Lower Niger Valley, a broad alluvial plain which is intensively farmed during the dry season and largely inundated by floods in the rainy season. Immediately eastward is an eroded plateau area, containing the Udi and Igala plateaux and the Awka–Orlu Uplands, and commonly referred to as the Southeastern Scarplands. The last geographic region of the South, the Southeastern Lowlands, is much like the low plains area: lush, nearly impenetrable vegetation broken by mangrove swamps. It contains an oil-palm belt east and northeast of the Niger Delta and a sparsely populated Cross-River Basin east of the scarplands where transportation and communications are quite difficult.

The 'big picture' which emerges of the Nigerian South, then, is one of formidable natural barriers – swamps, thick forests, rivers and streams, and plateaux – which historically in some measure probably inhibited free intercourse among peoples. These impediments are enhanced by heavy, almost year-round rainfall which can render roads and pathways impassable for several months, and by the presence of the deadly tse-tse fly which hinders the use of beasts of burden for transport and land cultivation, as well as the rearing of cattle and sheep for domestic use. Cassava, yam and maize, in addition to oil palms in the East, cocoa in the West and rubber in the Mid-West, have been cultivated here.

Given the problems of transportation and communication in this physical environment, it is not surprising that in the South a large number of relatively small and isolated ethnic communities evolved. Social organisational forms developed in accordance with these physical parameters. The predominant ethnic group in the East, the Igbo, grew along the lines of semi-isolated kinship communities; until the twentieth century there were some 200 such communities with populations ranging from a few hundred to 20,000, each with its different customs and, in most cases, separate dialect. Other major ethnic groups of the East, such as the Ibibio, Anang and Efik, were similarly loosely organised into what anthropologists call segmentary lineage systems. The same applies to the Ijaw of the Niger Delta area. Analagous patterns prevail in the West, i.e. the area west of the Lower Niger and south of the Upper Niger. The Yoruba, as the numerically largest ethnic group, also developed a partly decentralised, partly centralist form of social organisation, with individual units centred around urban capitals and compact settlements. Despite relative isolation from each other, the Yoruba groupings managed to sustain a measure of cultural unity through common loyalties, such as reverence for the Oni of Ife and the possession of pan-Yoruba tribal deities.

Admittedly, a few centralised kingdoms developed in the South – Nri, Agbor, Ife and, most notably, Benin – but these were the exceptions to a general pattern of non-centralised societies which prevailed throughout the region.

The Middle Belt. Between North and South, indeed separating them, is an area of deciduous forest region with hills, low plateaux and quite open woodland. The (colonial-coined) metaphor of the belt is most apt, since this region's central or unifying feature is the Niger–Benue River Valley, extending in an East–West band from the Cameroonian border to the Republic of Benin. The Upper Niger is a relatively open valley underlain by sedimentary rocks. The erection of the Kainji Dam just above Jebba has flooded an 85-mile stretch of the valley and created Kainji Lake. Southward from the Upper Niger are the Western High Plains or Plateau of Yorubaland, covered with savanna parkland and grass. The Benue Valley is somewhat broader than the Upper Niger and paralleled along most of its length by erosional low plains.

Just as the Middle Belt's physical characteristics are a transition between the dense, humid South and the open, drier North, so its ethnic inhabitants' forms of social organisation contain 'Northern' and 'Southern' characteristics. Apart from the Ilorin Yoruba, most of the Middle Belt peoples historically moved from the North or the South to escape domination or persecution by their numerically larger neighbours. All became agriculturalists. The Tiv, inhabiting the middle Benue River Valley and enjoying a reputation as fiercely independent, have evolved a non-hierarchical social structure and a participatory pattern of decision-making best described as a form of direct democracy. The Nupe of the Niger Valley, on the other hand, have adopted, or been induced to adopt, many of the organisational traits of the Northern emirates along with a now-assimilated Fulani leadership caste. Precolonial 'government' in Nupeland was thus centralised, stratified and restrictive of popular participation.

This 'regionalisation' into a North and South, with the latter bisected by the Lower Niger into an East and West, and a broad Middle Belt separating the regions,[2] goes some way toward outlining the basic contours of the Nigerian mosaic. From this perspective, the individual overlaying and overlapping component elements can be better examined.

Language differences have been called the greatest single divider of peoples. Conversely, the existence of a common language is said to be essential to 'national solidarity' and the political stability of a state. In Nigeria there are more than 100 indigenous languages and many more dialects, so that as many as 380 modes of communication may be currently in use in the country. (As in the case of population, estimates differ substantially.)[3] The most common Northern language, Hausa, belongs to the Afro-Asiatic family of languages, while the Kanuri speak a Sudanic language. If the Southern and Middle Belt languages all belong to the Niger–Congo linguistic family, the Kwa substock predominates in the former and the Benue–Niger substock in the latter. The North acquired a substantial written language, while in the South communication was historically primarily oral, although two pre-colonial written languages did evolve there. Despite a high incidence of bi- and even tri-lingualism in border areas, no one *indigenous* language is understood by more than one-third of the population. In this context, English – introduced by the colonial administration and originating in a quite different socio-cultural context – has come to serve as the principal medium through which Nigerians (or at least those with more formal education) from different parts of the Federation communicate with each other. Thus the problem of language is twofold: the existence of many indigenous languages hampers inter-ethnic understanding, detracts from a feeling of national identification and remains a constant latent source of friction; and the use of English unites the national elites and sets them apart from non-elites, while the multiplicity of indigenous languages helps to keep the latter divided and outside the political mainstream.

Differences of language are of necessity associated with ethnic differences. *Ethnic plurality* is indeed a prominent feature of the Nigerian conglomerate society. The – highly controversial – 1963 census identified well over 200 ethnic groupings, and other estimates suggest a figure of between 250 and 380. Three ethnic groups numerically dominate their respective regions: the Hausa–Fulani in the North, the Igbo in the East and the Yoruba in the West. Between them they make up some two-thirds of the national population. Six other ethnic groups – the Edo, Tiv, Ijaw, Kanuri, Ibibio and Idoma – constitute a further 26% or so. The remaining 8% range in size from one thousand to over one million. Each group, despite historical links, has its own history and traditions, its own geographic territory, usually its own language and culture, and its special kinship and familial loyalties. What is more, many ethno-cultural groups may have stronger affinities to contiguous groupings outside the national frontiers than to other groups inside the country, thus creating certain centrifugal tendencies. The Yoruba of Benin Republic, for example, are related to the Western Nigerian Yoruba; both the Fulani and Hausa of the Northwest look to the Fulani and other pastoral peoples in Niger and Mali; and the Kanuri have ties with the peoples of Northern Cameroon and the Republic of Chad.

Religion is a further defining characteristic of diversity. The North, interacting with Arab invaders and traders over many centuries, is for the most part Islamic. The South, with its proximity to the coast, has been largely Christianised. Christianity and Islam have attracted approximately equal numbers of Yoruba and Christianity has predominated among most other southern peoples, while in the interstices of these two dominant religions, most particularly in the Middle Belt, traditional religions are widely practised. Some 44% of all Nigerians are adherents of Islam, while perhaps 22% or more are Christians and the rest belong to traditional religions. Though, in the past, religiously motivated conflicts have affected political life (normally as a result of the advance of one or other proselytising religion: Islam or Christianity), contemporary Nigeria is remarkably tolerant of differing religious beliefs, more so in the South, less so in the North. It is quite common, particularly in Yorubaland and parts of the Middle Belt, to find adherents of different denominations living side by side; indeed, not infrequently one individual may simultaneously practise two or more faiths.

Table 1.1 *Distribution of Nigerian ethnic groups (1963)*

Group	% of Population
Hausa-Fulani	29.5
Kanuri	4.1
Tiv	2.5
Nupe	1.2
Yoruba	20.3
Edo	1.7
Ibo	16.6
Ibibio	3.6
Ijaw	2.0
All others	17.5

Source: Etienne Van de Walle, 'Who's Who and Where in Nigeria', *Africa Report*, no. 1, January 1970. For reasons already alluded to, these statistics should be viewed as mere approximations.

Urban–rural differences are evident nation-wide, as a fifteen-minute drive from the centre of Kano, Ibadan, Sokoto or Benin City will readily show. About 75% of Nigerians live in the country, that is, in villages and townships having a population of less than 20,000, whereas more than one-fifth – a percentage that is rapidly increasing – inhabit the urban areas which are heavily concentrated in the East, West and North, notably Ibadan, Lagos, Enugu and Kano. Although rural–urban migration and urban–rural kinship networks help to mitigate such differences, it is still true that urban dwellers, by and large, have life experiences substantially different from those of their rural fellow countrymen and women.

Colonial formations and deformations

The last two sets of differentiating criteria – religion and urban–rural differences – suggest a still more fundamental source of diversity in Nigerian political life: *differential impacts of colonialism*.

Colonial rule may of course be examined and analysed from a great number of perspectives. But in the first instance it was a manifestation of nineteenth-century capitalism, namely imperialism. As such it was intended to produce profits, i.e. it was established in order to extract a surplus from the areas under its sway. It normally did this under the aegis of the metropolitan state which supplied, *inter alia*, a military machine to maintain law and order, a bureaucratic apparatus to administer the areas under its control, and a series of infrastructures, especially in transport and communications, to facilitate extraction of the colony's minerals or crops to the mother country. New religions and belief systems were also introduced into indigenous societies, generally with the aim of creating a greater identity between coloniser and colonised, thus making the fact of exploitation more palatable all round.

Nigeria as a territorial state evolved gradually, under British administration, from the establishment of the Crown Colony of Lagos in 1861, through a series of extensions and incorporations, to the Amalgamation by Lord Lugard in 1914 and the 1939 division of the Southern provinces into an Eastern and Western Region. Thus the territory of present-day Nigeria was defined, not on the basis of its peoples' shared historical, economic or social experiences, but merely by the arbitrary amalgamation of a number of disparate ethnocultural units which happened to occupy contiguous land areas that were then under British colonial administration. Today, the ruthless, often brutal, methods of British conquest of the Nigerian peoples, and the latter's prolonged resistance to it, are often forgotten or downplayed.[4]

The modality of British colonial administration was designated as 'indirect rule'. Essentially, this meant the superimposition of a 'higher' or 'national' layer of political authority – the colonial government – upon the various indigenous emirates, kingdoms and tribal chieftancies. Indirect rule was styled as an optimal division of labour. On the one hand, the colonial rulers were supposed to attend to foreign affairs, the development of national institutions – such as the legislative councils and civil service – and the management of the macro-economy. On the other hand, it fell to the emirs, obas and chiefs (where these existed) to carry out judicial and policing tasks, raise local revenues, administer the social units under their domain and in general carry on the 'development' process determined by the higher authorities. In this way, the traditional society was supposed to advance gradually and effortlessly towards modernisation, development and ultimately independence and self-rule.

The underlying motive of colonialism was thus to ensure the effective and unchallenged exploitation of the colony to the benefit of British finance and industry, and indirect rule was intended as the best means of accomplishing this end. Uniting the subject peoples, say by providing mass education and training or by instituting forms of equal participation in profit-making or governing, would, from this point of view, have been positively dysfunctional. Indirect rule actually throve upon and derived its effectiveness from the perpetuation of inter-ethnic and inter-regional differences. For the traditional rulers' authority rested largely upon their ability to maintain intact their ethnic-group cohesiveness, tribal customs, and distinctiveness from adjacent groups. Indirect rule tended to reinforce the most conservative aspects of traditional political organisation while shutting out pre-colonial tendencies towards supra-ethnic group co-operation. Thus, S. E. Oyovbaire (1979:83) posits 'structural factionalism' as a persistent feature of Nigerian national political life, and declares that:

Colonial rule was hardly more than a scaffolding, a superstructure over numerous pre-colonial social orders having varying degrees of independence from, and inter-dependence upon, each other. The pre-colonial political cultures of authority of these social orders also varied enormously among themselves. All Colonial rule did in the context of national unity was to 'amalgamate and divide' for its own purposes of domination and exploitation.

In the absence of a coherent, progressive colonial policy, colonial rule cannot be said to have had a uniform impact on Nigeria. Rather, the quality and extent of its impact varied according to each area's importance to the colonial economy and the nature of the respective groups' pre-colonial political culture.

Across the Muslim North, for example, indirect rule was quite functional and effective (in terms of colonial purposes) for it merely involved the imposition of one more layer of authority upon an already hierarchical, authoritarian, centralised and many-tiered system of governing. But among the Yoruba in the West, who had evolved a kind of limited constitutional monarchy derived from a broader cultural heritage and subdivided into units based upon family, lineage and clan, colonial rule inflated the chiefs' powers and backed these with force. Whereas traditionally the Yoruba chiefs had had to 'earn' their right to govern through such valued qualities as wisdom, fairness and efficiency, and could be de-stooled if they contravened these norms, they were ensconsed by colonial might and shielded against any popular pressure from 'below'. The effects of this process were often corruption, irresponsible rule and enhanced authoritarianism. In the East the dilemma of indirect rule was even more palpable; since the segmented family groups of Igbo seldom had an institution of chieftancy, the colonial administrators had to resort to creating it, and so a whole new ruling class of 'warrant chiefs' came into being. Of course, such chiefs seldom enjoyed the legitimacy and popularity of more autochthonous rulers and thus relied in large part upon the coercive powers of the colonial administrators – who to be sure, were also dependent on them – for their continued authority.

What has been said about indirect rule so far points to a fundamental defect in British colonial policy in Nigeria: while it was founded in order to serve and promote the capitalist interests of the mother country, its continuation in power largely depended on the co-operation of local authorities whose power was rooted in pre- or non-capitalist forms of social organisation. Thus, wherever indirect rule applied (Kay, 1975:38):

> The outcome was a curious paradox: the establishment of a series of capitalist states with deep roots in non-capitalist societies which they were forced to protect as the foundation of their power. But at the same time they also represented a social force that systematically under-mined these societies. For the existence of merchant capital – and to exist it had to accumulate – led inevitably to the spread of commodity production.

One effect of this contradiction was to undermine pre-colonial socio-economic structures, while at the same time failing to transform society so as to enable it to cope with the requirements of the new capitalist order. In those areas of the country of interest to foreign companies, the integrated self-sufficient village community was eroded by its conversion to crop or mineral production for consumption or processing elsewhere, within the framework of the capitalist cash nexus. In this process the peasant converted his land, labour-power and produce into commodities which, intended for sale in a distant overseas market, had very limited relevance to the context and needs of the community from which they were extracted. Simultaneously, colonial capitalism loosened the bonds of communal and familial obligations while converting the people into economic actors responding to market forces.

Traditional patrons – chiefs, emirs, noblemen – either adapted to the exigencies of the new economy or yielded a good portion of their authority to groups more inclined towards collaboration. In the West, for instance, the British promoted the 'election' of 'educated' individuals to political posts:

> notably Adesoji (later Sir Adesoji) Aderemi, an educated produce buyer, to the most ancient Yoruba throne as Oni of Ife. In Ibadan, wealthy Muslim traders and educated Christians entered the lives of chiefs with the encouragement of the colonial rulers, who wished them to take over the reins of local administration from the geriatric scions of warrior families, who succeeded to higher offices by seniority. They in turn resented the attempt to place men of commoner origins above them, and provoked a series of crises from 1936 to 1951 over the advancement of such upstarts to the most senior titles.[5]

The traditional rulers' *raison d'être* – namely their organic links to their communities and their social responsibilities towards their subjects – was thus further called into question, and the chiefs' role increasingly became that of enforcer and autocrat, backed by the colonial regime's law, administration and coercive power.

This examination of the different impacts of British colonial administration, though necessarily cursory, does help in locating the origins of two persistent and salient sources of internal socio-economic conflict: the segmented and sectoralised economy, and a society divided into 'haves' and 'have-nots', or more precisely, *an elite and a mass*.

Polarisation of society

The segmentation and sectoralisation of the national economy, given the exploitative means and ends of colonialism, was all but inevitable. Each region, according to its natural factoral endowments and/or convertibility to colonial purposes, produced crops or minerals of a greater or lesser exploitable value. The North's contributions were groundnuts, cotton and tin; the West produced huge quantities of cocoa, while that part of it which in 1963 became the Mid-West, produced rubber and rubber products; and the East was a large reservoir of palm oil products. Had they been integrated into a national economy geared to the needs of the Nigerian peoples, these products collectively would almost certainly have contributed towards the development of a symmetrical and well-balanced economic structure. But they were not. They were in fact developed for further processing and/or consumption in the coloniser's home economy. Thus the economy of each producing region was adapted and integrated, not with its adjacent producing economies, but with that of Great Britain and through this link, with the world capitalist economy. There was no plan for national integration, but many extractive regional 'plans', centred around plantation or mining enclaves and aimed at enhancing the sponsor's own economy. Segmentation of this kind gave rise to a dual process of 'unequal development'. (a) Intra-state development was unequal, since each colonial enclave developed at its own pace, a pace determined by the demand for its principal product or products and the corresponding infrastructures which they required; railways, roads, and telegraph lines were not erected to further any coherent national development plan, but rather led from the rubber, groundnut and palm oil plantations to Lagos, Port Harcourt and other coastal ports for onward shipment to the colonial metropole, and (b) an 'unequal exchange' developed between the raw-materials-exporting colony and the capital and technology exporting coloniser; in such relationships, as is well known, the former is invariably disadvantaged and usually exploited.[6]

Very little of the surplus value generated by colonial enterprise in Nigeria was actually returned to the national economy. Apart from services and facilities needed to enhance the productivity and hence profitability of the export industries – transportation, communications, law and order institutions, limited training of low-level manpower – little investment was made in the economic infrastructures which could have promoted more even and thorough development: universal primary education, higher education, import-substitution industries, technology transfer, health and welfare services and the like.

Too frequently, uneven development patterns followed ethno-geographic boundaries and were co-determined by pre-colonial social organisation. For example, the South with its proximity to the sea, its largely segmented or acephalous social units and its multiplicity of religions and ethnic groupings, was relatively amenable to influences from abroad. Christianity, Western-style education, use of English, new forms of administration and social organisation, and European economic structures all took root more rapidly and thoroughly in the South than elsewhere. The North, by contrast – physically removed from the urban colonial centres and with its long Islamic tradition which, combining church and state, amounted to a theocracy, its own language, religion and centralised administration – was far more impervious to Western ways. In combination with the sectoralised economy, these factors conspired, as it were, to prevent the growth of mass education, the implanting of new belief systems, the 'rationalisation' of economic life and the balanced development of capitalist economic activities which are supposed to be indicators of 'modernisation' and 'development'. Much the same applied to the Middle Belt and other peripheral areas which contained few crops or minerals of interest to colonial capitalism. The long-term result, of course, was a structural economic imbalance and hence inequality of opportunities among the country's multiple ethnic communities and social classes, a situation which mirrored the economic priorities and policies of the colonial state.

A pronounced social class cleavage exists in Nigeria between the elite and the mass. Admittedly there are several further social subcategories within each of these groupings, as will be discussed later. But this elite-mass distinction, it can be argued, is the most fundamental and persistent trend in the country's social structure. To discover why this is so, it is necessary to look again at the nature of colonial rule and its effects on the social structure.

Under the colonial administration, the 'national' elite or ruling class consisted primarily of foreigners, falling into roughly two categories. First, the educated expatriate elite whose positions were derived from advanced training and expert qualifications; these included administrators, functionaries, missionaries, military officers, policemen and other specialists. Second, the business elite – the representatives of overseas concerns and those who set out to make their fortunes under colonial protection.

In this scheme of things, aspiring Nigerian elites remained either (a) localised, as in the case of indirect rulers backed by the colonial policy of indirect rule, or (b) subordinate, as in the case of those recruited for lower-level administrative positions in the colonial bureaucracy or foreign-owned businesses. This latter group emerged in force in the latter period of colonial rule and in a sense were inherent in the logic of an expanding colonial capitalism which needed more and more persons to perform 'modern' functions in the expanding economic order. The British colonial administrators, lacking European manpower reserves which would have been furnished, say, from a white settler population, were forced to train 'indigenes' for minor administrative positions or for rank-and-file soldiering and policing. Business concerns were interested in ensuring a ready supply of clerks and semi-skilled workers. And cash-crop and mining concerns required some trained personnel.

These needs were reflected in the objective of imperial education policy which, according to a 1925 statement of the Advisory Committee on Native Education, was to 'raise the standard alike of character and efficiency of the bulk of the people' (Coleman,

1963:114). This was entirely compatible with the interests and goals of the churches and missions who saw as their task, apart from the conversion of the indigenous population to their religions, the provision of basic education for the many and advanced or university training abroad for those who showed special promise or could afford it. Church-sponsored education resulted in the Westernisation of a small group of Nigerians who, as Coleman points out, evolved into a self-conscious group isolated in some measure from the larger society: 'Conversion to Christianity, knowledge of and preference for English, imitation of European behaviour, and postschool employment in an urban milieu all helped to isolate the educated African from his traditional environment.' Demonstrating further that traditional African education was group-centred rather than individualistic as in the West, Coleman concludes that (ibid.:115): 'The resulting incompatibility between African tribal life and Western education made reintegration into the tribal community very difficult.'

However, contrary to theories which suggest the formation of an entirely new class of indigenous administrators and traders somehow separate from and antagonistic towards traditional rulers, it is apparent that the chiefs, emirs and obas and their kin, as the mediating agency between the colonisers and the people, were best placed to capitalise on the opportunities afforded by colonial rule. Their sons and (sometimes) daughters were sent to mission schools or for education abroad – though admittedly persons of humbler origin (even ex-slaves) frequently underwent Western training, but even then mostly at the behest of traditional rulers. They or their kin staffed the administrative positions opened to indigenes. They engaged in plantation farming, mining and trading – albeit in a subordinate role – and in this way accumulated comparatively large amounts of capital and expertise. Of course only a minority of traditional rulers and their kin actually entered the colonial capitalist economy in this fashion; and not only traditional rulers' families achieved positions in the administration or in business. But these general patterns of early elite formation have continued through time and help to explain the origins of Nigeria's elite classes. They also seriously qualify the persistent myth that Westernisation revolutionised, rather than merely accelerated, traditional patterns of social predominance.

The major criteria of pre-independence elite formation can therefore be summarised as wealth, education and traditional authority. Embryonic Nigerian elites, despite their ethnic, political, religious and sectoral differences, had, and still have, in common, high incomes. Westernised life-styles, advanced education, special privileges such as private schools and trips abroad, and enhanced life prospects; and possession or enjoyment of these things is what distinguishes them from the 'masses'. They also share in common – given national economic dependence on foreign capital and know-how and a corresponding absence of internally generated sources of wealth and power – the fact that they must cohere around the state apparatus. For the state, under colonialism (and neo-colonialism), was the principal employer, by far the largest source of finance and therefore the vehicle for the most rapid accumulation of wealth, status and power. More will be said about this later.

Thus the distance between the ruling classes of Nigeria and the masses was immense, even prior to independence. Yet it was this elite which guided the nation as a whole into the post-colonial era. Their goal in shedding the British administration was merely to replace it. Relatively well placed in the bureaucracy or in control of local or regional power centres, the Nigerian elite realised well in advance that the top positions in all the leading institutions would accrue to them with the departure of the colonial masters, and they therefore negotiated independence by degrees, with the least possible disruption of the colonial institutions. Under the circumstances, the nationalist movement could not be mobilised through a popular revolutionary struggle nor motivated by unifying ideological slogans of 'equality' or 'social justice'. Instead, independence largely amounted to a negotiated settlement – a gentlemen's agreement – between the colonial elite and the emergent Nigerian elites. The wishes, involvement or long-term interests of the masses scarcely played a role in the movement, except insofar as mass support for political independence was used to legitimate the transfer of power to the Nigerian leaders. This may account for the popular phrase about Nigeria having produced not political martyrs, but successors. It may also help to explain the absence of a national ideology – a Nigerian equivalent to *uhuru* or *ujamaa* – to guide the national liberation movement and unite the population behind shared goals.

Independence, then, entrenched the ruling structure produced under the colonial regime and further sharpened the already well-developed distinction between the elites and the masses. Even in periods of dire national distress, the elites have managed to maintain their ascendancy. For example, during the Civil War:

> The Ibo elite inside Biafra behaved just as they (or the Yoruba or Hausa elite) had done in Nigeria. Throughout the war, they had special houses, large cars, adequate food and all the other privileges inherited by Nigerians from the British governing officials. There was never any special taxation to help pay for the war, any rationing or any attempt to share out scarce supplies with those starving in the refugee camps.[7]

The masses, on the other hand, remained, as before, those 'who get the least of what there is to be had'. As already suggested, about three-quarters of the population live in the rural areas and many of these are among the world's poorest people. The urban mass is slightly more diversified. Petty traders, often living a marginal existence, may from time to time take on wage employment. The great mass of unemployed, mostly immigrants from rural areas, survive by occasional paid labour or by semi-legal activities such as touting, portering and the like. A large army of domestic servants, frequently junior relatives of more highly placed persons, supports the urban structure. And a class of urban workers is growing along with the industrial and manufacturing concerns which employ them.

As among the elites, so among the masses, there are many distinguishable subgroupings according to status and function. But what gives these 'masses' a commonality is the fact that they own less, eat less well, inhabit inferior dwellings, have less security, obtain less education and enjoy a markedly less full material life-style than their elite fellow countrymen. (One important qualification should, however, be inserted here, which will be discussed more thoroughly later: any 'gap' theory of elite-mass relations grounded in conditions prevalent in advanced capitalist societies is mitigated in the African context by the existence of an informal network of patronage – and corruption – which links the political elite to lower-placed members of their ethnic group, clan or kinship unit, thus helping to overcome problems of maldistribution which elsewhere are partly dealt with through public agencies and political institutions.)

The problem of integration

The mere facts of physical–territorial barriers, ethnic plurality, separate historical experiences, different customs and languages, uneven levels of development and social class cleavages are not *in themselves* necessary causes or facilitators of conflict and competition. Indeed, the ostensible centrifugence of these interacting elements can equally be viewed in terms of centripetence, that is, of a fundamental unity in all this diversity.

For example, economic competition has been depicted as a series of segmentations originating in economic diversification and differential rates of growth. And this is largely the case. But it is this very diversity which at the same time contains a potential for supra-regional co-operation. Separately, Northern groundnuts, cotton and tin, Western cocoa, timber and rubber, and Eastern palm products have historically been subject to fluctuations according to climate, world-market prices and a variety of other factors. Collectively, these regional products augment and supplement each other, thus constituting a potentially balanced, symmetrical economy relatively secure from unexpected natural disasters or market vagaries. In fact, since the turn of the century no single commodity – until the discovery and exploitation of oil, about which more will be said later – accounted for more than one-fourth of export earnings, and eight commodities consistently made up about four-fifths of such income. Moreover, the sheer size and complexity of the internal market, as P.C. Asiodu has written (1967:167), has been 'the greatest incentive, the most important stimulus to industrial development in Nigeria'. Not in spite of, but rather because of, diversity, the unified whole, at least in terms of economic development, *can* be greater than the sum of its parts.

Yet harmony, co-operation and 'unity' have manifestly not characterised social and political life in post-independent Nigeria. No effective formulas have been found to bring ethnic competition, class conflict, social diversity and the like into a 'higher', productive synthesis. Most adult Nigerians have directly and poignantly experienced protests, riots, even massacres, civil war and coercive military rule, and thus know at first hand the results of faulty integration.

In a neo-colonial capitalist socio-economic order whose primary function is to preserve elite hegemony, the stability of the political system is directly related to the degree to which it is integrated. Integration implies a process of consolidation and co-ordination of the many sub-units of society, economy and polity. One of the most enduring definitions of integration – if one sets aside the structural-functional theory in which it is imbedded – is furnished by Rosberg and Coleman who see it as 'a broad subsuming process' consisting of two main dimensions: (a) political integration, which occurs when the gap between the elite and the masses is reduced and a participant political community created, and (b) territorial integration, involving a reduction in cultural-regional tensions and the establishment of a homogeneous territorial political community.[8] Surely, a further dimension should be added: (c) economic integration, to ensure that a solid economic foundation exists upon which inter-class solidarity and broad political participation can grow, and to reduce inter-territorial and inter-cultural antagonisms. Again, this separation of political, territorial and economic integration can be achieved only at the level of theory; in practice these aspects are interrelated and interdependent.

'Tribalism'

Wherever the Nigerian political system has most dramatically experienced breakdowns – constitutional crises, political immobilism, *coups d'état*, civil war, etc. – this has always occurred within a context of inter-ethnic controversy. The phenomenon of *ethnicity, ethno-nationalism* or, as it is popularly termed, *tribalism*,[9] is thus a focal point of national politics. 'Tribalism' has been defined by Chief Awolowo (who equated it with 'regionalism') as (1966:90):

(i) morbid adherence or loyalty to one's region or tribe to the exclusion, prejudice and detriment of other regions or tribes;

(ii) discriminatory practices designed to favour one's region or tribe at the expense of, or to the prejudice or detriment of, other regions or tribes;

(iii) inciting one's region or tribe against the other regions or tribes; and

(iv) exploiting one's popularity or standing in one's region or tribe for unworthy ends.

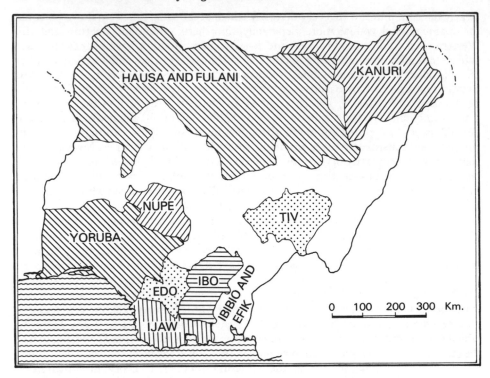

Figure 1.3   *Major ethnic divisions of Nigeria*

Another, more recent definition of ethnicity emphasises its quality of exclusiveness (Nnoli, 1978:7):

> Ingroup–outgroup boundaries emerge with [ethnicity] and, in time, become marked, more distinct than before, and jealously guarded by the various ethnic groups. Acceptance and rejection on linguistic–cultural grounds characterise social relations. These are expressed inevitably through interethnic discrimination in jobs, housing, admissions into educational institutions, marriages, business transactions or the distribution of social welfare services. This factor of exclusiveness is usually accompanied by nepotism and corruption. Merit is sacrificed on the altar of ethnic chauvinism and solidarity.

Ethnicity, however defined, has unquestionably been a dominant factor in Nigerian political life. (Whether or not it still is, is a subject which will be discussed in later chapters.) Taking ethnicity as a starting point, one may examine a whole range of factors contributing to problems of stability and integration in Nigeria: nationalism, unbalanced regional development, distribution of scarce resources and, in particular, class conflict.

Historically, the outstanding feature about pre-colonial inter-ethnic rivalry within the boundaries of contemporary Nigeria is that – apart from occasional tribal wars and slave-taking raids – it did not exist, at least not in the forms suggested by the above two quotations. Relations among the ethnic formations were, by and large, at least regulated,[10] and indeed none of the many original Nigerian languages has a concept equivalent to the English 'tribalism'. What today is deplored as 'tribalism' seems to be a phenomenon which only emerged with colonialism and has achieved its fullest development since independence.

During the colonial era, a number of processes of differentiation were at work to create or enhance disparities among Nigeria's ethnic groups, including:

(i) Proximity to colonial administrative centres, 'enclave' areas of the extractive economy, or coastal ports. Groups positioned nearest the colonial power were more frequently exposed to European education/training, other missionary activities, the money economy and the wage-labour system.

(ii) Population size. The numerical superiority of the Hausa–Fulani, Igbo and Yoruba assured them a dominant position in the North, East and West respectively, quite apart from their individual assets or capacities.

(iii) Possession of material or natural resources. The quantity and quality of raw materials located in an ethnic group's territory, and the relative ease with which they could be extracted, in large measure co-determined the group's rate of exposure to 'modern' influences. Thus Nigerians situated near Western cocoa-producing areas, Eastern palm oil plantations and Northern tin-mining regions were almost inevitably drawn into the colonial political economy.

(iv) Nature of the pre-colonial socio-political culture. If the centralised, self-contained Muslim communities of the North were relatively resistant to foreign penetration and the adoption of foreign ways while remaining internally highly stratified, the segmentary or acephalous societies of the South, with their greater emphasis on what in the literature is usually labelled individualism and personal achievement, and their lesser degree of social stratification, were more receptive to the kind of social change needed for integration into the colonial-capitalist economy and society. In many cases, ethnic-group images evolved by the colonial administrators contributed directly to this differentiation. The Yoruba, for example, were thought to be good clerical personnel, and large numbers of them were recruited as clerks into the lower echelons of the colonial civil service. Similarly, the Tiv were supposed to make good soldiers, the Itsekeri merchant middlemen, and so on; and in general, recruitment policies and preferences conformed to these stereotypes.[11] The Northern region, whose socio-political organisational forms the British administrators seemed to admire – or at least more readily comprehend – was the recipient of a number of favours from the departing colonisers. Also in the North, the colonial administrators frequently reversed the process of demonstrably successful integration of Southern immigrants into the local communities, relegating the newcomers instead to separate *sabon garis* (strangers' quarters) and otherwise emphasising those factors which set the peoples apart from each other.

Indeed, the colonial policy of 'indirect rule' was predicated among other things upon the assumption that the colonised peoples (or 'tribes') were fundamentally and qualitatively different from one another. Commonalities among groups – 'African personality', similarities of social organisation, cultural interconnections – were never considered as possible sources of unity. Instead, an awareness of separate identity or ethnicity was consciously fostered and perpetuated. To be sure, this policy of 'divide and rule' was highly functional in terms of colonial interests, for it placed a formidable ideological and psychological barrier in the way of the evolution of a mass-based, supra-regional and unified anti-colonial movement. In particular, ethnicity, by creating 'tribal' rather than national power bases, helped to divide and fragment the educated elites, who of course constituted the leadership and motive force of the independence movement.

Indirect rule also corresponded with the sectoralised enclave economic structure. Within the colonial enclaves, a kind of 'modern' economy – characterised, for example, by wage-labour, money exchange, rationalised production processes, injection of advanced technology and new infrastructures – came into being, while outside them, the 'traditional' subsistence economies carried on much as before, though increasingly subject to spill-over effects from the new economic imperatives. Ethnic awareness and, eventually, assertive ethno-nationalism largely received their initial impetus in the colonial urban centres and areas of extraction, for the following reasons:

(i) Exposure. The development of the colonial political economy, with its growth in Europe-oriented supra-regional trade, its commoditisation of many agricultural products, its increase in migrant wage labour both on the farms and in the cities, and its greater social mobility, set in motion processes of migration and interaction on a scale hitherto unknown in the 'Nigerian' area. Particularly in the colonial enclaves and towns, where opportunities for work and trade were greatest, people were intensively exposed to members of many different ethnic groups, with their 'foreign' customs, beliefs and languages. In many respects these relations were precipitate and forced, so that:

> Paradoxically, the most important problems of integration facing the nation seem to result from the imposition of economic intercourse with each other upon the various groups of people who just happened to fall within the borders of Nigeria, and who would have otherwise have remained separated for much longer.[12]

(ii) Socio-economic competition. Far from being 'natural' or amicable, this initial inter-group intercourse occurred in a situation of extreme competitiveness. Drawn into the impersonal colonial–capitalist economic milieu which was characterised by extreme disparities of wealth and privilege, subject to low or subsistence wages, and often forced to endure wretched working and living conditions, migrants to the colonial enclaves immediately found themselves in competition for a whole range of essential, and scarce, social resources: money, jobs, education, training, housing, the entire spectrum of social services, and even the right to vote. Given the newness, to them, of the capitalist economy, the absence of a developed class consciousness, and the impossibility of organising social-class defence groups under the conditions of colonial administration, transplanted members of ethnic groups often sought the solidarity which was psychologically and sociologically necessary within ethnic group associations, voluntary communal organisations and patron–client linkages based primarily on ethnicity. Since such groupings were then automatically in competition with others for the relatively few valuable resources, and since the competing units were ethnically perceived, ethnicity evolved in place of class consciousness.

(iii) Insecurity. Any situation of extreme insecurity tends to produce a state of mind conducive to hostility, ingroup–outgroup identifications and general alienation from one's surroundings and place of work. In colonial Nigeria, enclave dwellers tended to react in this way to the situation of extreme exploitation, anomie and physical dislocation in which they found themselves. The stabilising psychological factor enabling them to come to terms with this situation was ethnicity: a projection of apprehensions, resentments and frustrations on to other groups, combined with a feeling of community and security deriving from intra-ethnic-group solidarity.

Ethnicity and class hegemony

Bearing in mind what has been said in the preceding sections about the segmentation of the Nigerian economy, the cleavage of society into an elite and the masses, and the differential rate of development of its manifold ethnic groups, a key inference can now be drawn, namely, that *social class, ethnicity and political power are actually different facets of the same complex phenomenon*. As Robin Cohen has rightly suggested (1972:244), there exists a high degree of 'congruence between inter-class and inter-ethnic relationships', and this congruence rests upon the fact of stratification, or 'the principles that regulate the distribution of social advantage'. In other words, the phenomenon of 'tribalism' can and must be regarded in terms of its socio-economic context and functions.

The pre-independence elite, it will be recalled, was almost entirely beholden to the colonial power for its position of relative pre-eminence. Western education, foreign administrative or technological skills, colonial-capitalist-produced profits, a constantly increasing number of chieftancies and emirates – all emanated directly or indirectly from the colonial administration or foreign business monopolies. However, this indigenous elite was still confined to relatively subordinate positions in the economy and society, and hardly played a role at all in national or regional politics, though its role at the local level was of course crucial. The achievement of independence could eliminate the colonial upper stratum literally overnight, thus opening up the top jobs and all their attendant perquisites to well-placed Nigerians. For them – as has been suggested above – the struggle for independence amounted to a struggle for succession to colonial power and privilege, the right to replace one elite with another, rather than, say, a struggle for socio-economic transformation.

Nevertheless, even this carefully circumscribed struggle necessitated substantial mass involvement and participation, since only 'the people' could lend it the aura of legitimacy and popular support needed to convince the colonial power to effect the handover. Popular support for independence did not only derive from a widespread desire for 'liberation' and 'self-rule'; it was also purchased with promises of a better way of life and more material abundance after the departure of the British – promises which could be kept only if the system of rewards and distribution was drastically modified. Any such modifications would of course have been inimical to the interests of the successor elites, whose overriding concern was to preserve the *status quo* as intact as possible with themselves in its commanding positions. In other words, the masses who had been mobilised and politicised on behalf of a *universal* goal – national independence – now had to be either depoliticised or, as it were, 're-politicised' in the service of *particularist* ends – elite domination. One way of accomplishing this with the least possible resistance on the part of those who would gain less than they had been promised was to employ the – colonially generated – spectre of ethnicity. This point will be taken up again later.

From the discussion so far two things may be inferred about the Nigerian 'bourgeoisie': (i) As an essentially non-productive successor elite removed from direct ownership of the means of production, it was compelled to look to the state apparatus as its primary source of elite formation and consolidation. (ii) As a non-revolutionary class lacking a historical *raison d'être* beyond its own consolidation, it had to seek out and deploy *ersatz* ideologies in order to retain a mass following and to forestall social reform. Here 'tribalism' – the objective conditions for which had already been created – presented itself as most opportune. These two imperatives will be considered in their interrelationship: *as a dialectic of ethnicity and class struggle*.

Colonial statism, organised according to the principle of indirect rule, had consciously sought to prevent the formation of a national bourgeoisie. It created instead a series of regionalised and tribalised bourgeoisies who could be managed according to the strategy of divide and rule. Economic power, thus diffused, could not coalesce into a permanent political power capable of challenging the sole 'national elite', namely the colonial administration. Hence the Nigerian bourgeoisie was rendered incapable of fulfilling the historical role played by its European counterparts: the development of a national economy and national forces of production.

Instead, Nigeria's post-independence elites of necessity gravitated towards the state in order to use it to achieve economic and social power. For, unlike earlier European and North American elites, post colonial Nigerian elites were merely the recipients of a socio-economic system and state structure created by and for the metropolitan power. In order to re-deploy it – rather than transform it – in their own interests, they had to seize control of the system's centre: government, civil service and military. This solution became all the more compelling, since the constraints of the colonial socio-economic structure had retarded the evolution of those groups which might have constituted a counterweight to a statist elite: there evolved few organised working-class movements, few business associations, and still fewer agencies to defend rural interests.

The inter-class relations prevailing in neo-colonial capitalist African states such as Nigeria, in other words, may be seen in terms of an inversion of the Marxian concepts of base and superstructure. If in advanced capitalist countries political power derives in the main from economic structures and relationships, the equation in neo-colonial capitalist countries is reversed:

> It is rather political power (which here also means administrative and military power) which creates the possibilities of enrichment and which provides the basis for the formation of an economically powerful class, which may in due course become an economically dominant one.[13]

Possession of political power or access to government funds thus represented the *sine qua non* for the good life: status, security, honours, benefits and, above all, wealth. Since wealth was largely a function of government office, politics centred around competition for top positions, and political activities were geared to gaining access to state power and the allocation of revenue and the patronage connected with it. Successful appropriation of state resources, achieved by the manipulation of marketing board surpluses, capitation taxes, export levies and a variety of other devices, could enrich the successor elites, enhance their security of tenure, and lead them to seek power by all means available.

These contradictions of the post-independence elites might have been mitigated, however, (i) had political independence been accompanied by economic independence, and (ii) had the dominant classes been able to constitute themselves into a coherent and self-aware stratum. But the Nigerian bourgeoisie, for the reasons explained above, had no real interest in overcoming the inherent structural dependencies and defects of colonialism, so that (a) neo-colonial capitalist relations persisted, thus perpetuating the elites' dependence on foreign capital and technology, and (b) the successor elites, lacking a real, dynamic, mass-based and progressive function, turned to latent, regressive and colonial-induced tribalist appeals.

Setting aside for a moment the implications of neo-colonialism, the resort to ethnicity introduced a series of contradictions into the political life of all post-independence regimes, military or civilian, with which each successive ruling elite has been compelled to come to terms.

First contradiction: Conflicting loyalties within the elite class itself between the need to acquire a share of the state power at the centre and pressures emanating from local or regional bases of mass support. In the segmented 'national' society, each elite's power base was confined to 'its' regional or ethnic-group support. Yet the survival and development of Nigeria in the form of a nation-state depended on the evolution of efficient, integrative, 'national' institutions at the centre capable of adequately balancing and incorporating disparate needs and claims. Furthermore, access to the decisive powers of patronage and distribution could be gained only via the central institutions – the more so under military governments, the less so under civilian regimes. In this situation the emergence of 'national' leaders and parties was all but impossible, and the federal government, under the First Republic, became essentially a loose, potentially antagonistic coalition of particularist elites based upon mutual advantage.

If the process of 'nation-building' was thus contingent upon the several elites' willingness and ability to concur on essential programmes and development plans, the demands of their various constituencies for immediate tangible rewards – government contracts, new projects, better roads and other infrastructures, positions in the bureaucracy, scholarships, etc. – subjected them to a cross-pressure to divert federal resources to the allied and/or kinship groups whose support they needed to stay in power. Such diversions, within the context of scarcity, had to be accomplished at the expense of other elites' constituencies. Elite coalitions at the centre therefore tended to be factious, divisive and highly competitive. Where ruling groups realise that the extension of their power and influence are *de facto* limited by the ethnic, linguistic or geographical composition of their reservoir of popular support, they will logically seek to maximise that support in order to further their bargaining basis within the national or regional coalition, with the ultimate goal of dominating it. In the absence of a well defined class consciousness, or of a charismatic leader with an appeal transcending region or ethnic group, ethnicity presents itself as the most effective and readily available ideological appeal to mobilise and retain as many of one's constituents as possible. Of this phenomenon, Yolamu Barongo writes:

> What is usually regarded as 'tribalism' by Western writers is no more than a reflection of the underlying conflicts among groups over the allocation and possession of material resources. In competing for resources ethnic or 'tribal' identity and solidarity are merely used by the elite members of ethnic groups as means of mobilizing groups for corporate action against other groups, usually for the purpose of achieving personal interests of the elites such as political power, jobs and other material rewards.[14]

The natural corollaries of these complementary processes of elite factionalism and ethnic politics are stalemate, immobilism and hence ossification of political life.

Second contradiction: The need for intra-elite solidarity versus actual or potential intra-elite conflict. From the foregoing it is evident that the Nigerian elites are structurally both united and divided in a number of ways. Similar life-styles, enjoyment of privileges and proximity to the centres of state power were (and are) characteristic of all of Nigeria's various elites.

But these elites also shared a basically insecure and unstable position. Since their power base was segmented, and complete domination of society and economy by any one faction therefore out of the question, exclusion from power on the basis of shifting coalitions or even military *coups* was an omnipresent spectre. This was especially so in the regionalised and decentralised constitutional structure of the First Republic, as the next chapter will show. Exclusion, however, would mean loss of all the advantages already mentioned. Thus 'the major activity of the ruling groups' may be seen as 'an attempt to redress the insecure position they find themselves in', and the principal means was utilisation of public resources to cement intra-elite cohesion (Cohen, 1972:248).

For the moment the neo-colonial elites may be analytically separated into sub-elites of politicians, the 'intendant' class (to be described below) of civil servants and administrators, soldiers and a commerical–national bourgeoisie of traders, contractors, land speculators, independent professionals, etc. Solidarity among these disparate groups developed, on the one hand, from their utility to each other, and on the other from a common awareness that their self-enriching activities must be carried on, through the political machinery, to the detriment of the broad majority. Thus contracts were awarded to ruling-party supporters, contractors contributed to parties or individual politicians, civil servants were large shareholders in contracting companies, government-owned banks financed the ruling parties and granted loans to party stalwarts, public corporations became syndicates for patronage dispensation, policies such as 'Nigerianisation' of the civil service or 'indigenisation' of foreign-owned businesses brought promotions and wealth only to a tiny elite, government projects were used to create opportunities for private investment, and virtually all transactions involved obligatory payments of 'dash' all round. All members of the elite stratum used their proximity to the state to further their own accumulation, and the wealth thus generated – and invested in shares, real estate, consumer goods or squirreled away in banks at home or abroad – went a long way toward ameliorating their chronic feelings of insecurity.

On the other hand, however, the elites could hardly afford to alienate themselves from their mass ethno-regional support. The connection was sustained partly through patronage (which was limited), partly through charisma and personalisation of politics (which did tend to be effective at the communal level), but primarily through calculated ethno-nationalist appeals:

> A symbiotic relationship develops between politicians who wish to advance their own positions, and their 'people', who fear political domination and economic exploitation by a culturally distinct group allegedly organized for these ends. A politician thus gains a tribal power base by successfully manipulating the appropriate cultural symbols and by articulating and advancing his people's collective and individual aspirations (which he himself probably helped to arouse).[15]

Third contradiction: Communal *versus* national dissonances *within* individual members of the elite. Not only must elite members reconcile external pressures from their supporters on the one hand and their class interests on the other; they must also come to terms with the subjective, psychological conflicts within themselves deriving from their ethno-cultural origins, which may clash with their largely European education and their objective role in the 'modern' political system. The Nigerian sociologist, Onigu Otite, describes the resultant 'dialectical situation' in this way (1975:128):

> Drawn from various ethnic groups, the new elites generally possess common characteristics obtained through educational, political and economic socializations and achievements. The new elites are more influential and pre-eminent and are more advantaged than the other members of their ethnic groups in many areas of life. Yet, they share largely the norms of their respective ethnic groups and their behaviours attune to their various cultural systems. In this respect, the new elites are not much different from the rest of the society whose cultural symbols they share. Thus, in spite of their common socialization and education, members of the new elites continue to regard ethnic ties as important . . . Therefore, conflicts that occur between ethnic groups also have a strong tendency to divide elites on ethnic lines.

Such anomalies not only apply to the more narrowly political elites, they cut right across the entire upper stratum. The intendant classes, for example, whose professional ethos includes efficiency, impartiality and rationality, are nevertheless often imbedded in traditional systems of reciprocity, involving the giving of gifts and favours, nepotism in hiring or contracting practices, and the like. Much the same applies to the business and comprador elites whose efforts to make profits within a neo-colonial capitalist economy may be impeded by familial obligations, kinship ties and other claims originating in the non-capitalist sectors of the economy.

Fourth contradiction: The need for stability and progress versus the fundamentally destabilising nature of elite behaviour as manifest in ethnic politics. Stable government, and with it, an effective spoils-distribution system and growing wealth and prosperity, are evidently all in the long-term interests of the political class. Yet their appeals to ethnic sentiments and resentments, by fragmenting and dividing society, prevented the realisation of these aims. The political elites as a class became the crucial agency of fragmentation, both in the First and Second Republics. To recall the late Professor Dudley's terms, they failed to respond to their foreseen role as 'conflict managers' and degenerated instead into 'conflict generators' or 'the chief proponents and purveyors of parochialism and particularistic values' in Nigerian political life (1973:35).

The point raised earlier, about the organic interconnection between power, class and ethnicity, has thus been made. From it, certain conclusions now present themselves concerning the social functions of the ideology of ethnicity.

'Tribalism' is, above all else, an ersatz ideology. It is profoundly conservative, indeed reactionary and regressive, for it appeals to latent, inward-oriented sentiments rather than to real social relations and urgent socio-economic issues. By propagating an image of ethnic groups locked in inexorable – because biologically pre-ordained – competition for scarce resources, the ruling classes have been able (a) to explain away the fundamental fact of a society divided into 'haves' and 'have-nots', thus preventing the less privileged classes from organising effectively in their own interests, (b) to obscure the ongoing intra-elite struggle for state power and the state's resources, a struggle whose outcome is bound to be detrimental to society's collective interests, and (c) to vindicate the whole post colonial capitalist socio-economic order of which they are the principal beneficiaries, by 'explaining' huge gaps in the distribution of resources and pervasive inequality in terms of ethnic competition and making these appear as part of the natural order of things. Okwudiba Nnoli describes the situation in this way (1978:13):

> By diverting attention away from imperialist exploitation and the resultant distortion of African economic and social structures, ethnicity performs the function of mystification and obscurantism. Consequently, it helps to perpetuate imperialism, and militates against the imperative of revolutionary struggle by hampering the development of a high level of political consciousness by its victims.

Ethnic politics, thus utilised by the political class to conceal other intra-societal antagonisms, such as class struggles and maldistribution, contains its own debilitating and dysfunctional dynamic. If class struggle – whose emergence the elites had to prevent at all costs – calls into question the legitimacy of the prevailing socio-economic system *within* the polity, then communal conflict is the more invidious, for it challenges the boundaries and continued existence of the nation-state itself. Secession and/or civil war are its logical ultimate outcomes.

With these considerations it can be inferred that the several 'premises of Nigerian politics' set out in this chapter are dialectically interlinked and interdependent. The discussion has revealed that given diversities of language, culture and geography are not in themselves causes of fractiousness and malintegration, but on the contrary also represent potential sources of a higher 'unity in diversity'. Rather, these problems seem to stem from an absence of symmetry, or from a process of 'unequal development' between

- well developed and less well developed regions,
- 'traditional' and 'modern' communities,
- diverse and distinct ethnic groups,
- metropolitan and rural areas, and in particular
- the elite and the masses.

The dialectical link between stability and development is apparent from Manfred Halpern's definition of stability as 'an intrinsic capacity to *generate* and *absorb* continuing transformation'.[16] The malformations introduced by colonialism, combined with the comprehensiveness of the development process, virtually ensure sporadic, unequal 'growth without development' biased in favour of particularist interests. Solutions to this systemically dysfunctional development are generally advanced by structural-functional and Eurocentric theorists, both in Africa and elsewhere, in terms of the need for solid institutions capable of continuous 'conflict management' and effective 'nation-building'. Such theories of course fail to address not only the problem of *cui bono* from such development but also the influences generated by the international capitalist order. So long as these conditions prevail, however, 'development' will maintain only a tenuous relationship with 'stability', and 'modernisation' will merely involve the modernisation of underdevelopment.

For a very long time, development theorists believed that 'modernisation', by creating 'new' behavioural patterns and new foci of loyalties on the part of individuals in society, must necessarily break down ethnic barriers and suspicions and substitute in their stead a modern, homogeneous political culture. However, the Nigerian experience has put paid to any such determinist notions, demonstrating instead that development processes, when channelled in the service of particularist interests, in fact may exacerbate inter-ethnic conflict. Prior to colonialism, the ethnic groups of present-day Nigeria dwelt in relatively harmonious interaction. Regular and systematic competition among them first occurred within the colonial enclaves and urban areas, and produced the first manifestations of ethnic conflict. This contact, seen in terms of competition for scarce resources, not only increased ethnic group awareness, it often also enlarged the subjective boundaries of ethnic affiliation. Thus, for example, neither the Yoruba nor the Igbo existed as self-aware entities before the colonial era; only colonial economic competition provided the impetus for a broader identification.[17] The era of the most rapid development under colonialism, the 1930s and 1940s, was also the era in which the great ethnic communal associations were formed: the Lagos Igbo Union which ultimately became the Igbo State Union, the Yoruba self-help association or the Egbe Omo Oduduwa, the Ibibio Welfare Union, the Urhobo Progressive Union, and many others. These associations were formed not in the ethnic groups' traditional territories but in the colonial cities and enclaves where economic competition was keenest, uprooted rural emigrants sought security and a familiar frame of reference, and social mobilisation was at its most advanced. At the same time, however, the wider ethnic association did not necessarily transcend primary identifications, and while Igbo or Yoruba might form communal associations to press their claims in the larger economic struggle, they might just as frequently be divided along the lines of Bendel Igbo versus Onitsha Igbo, or Ondo Yoruba against Oyo Yoruba, and so on.

Independence, by eliminating at a stroke the class of ostensibly impartial colonial administrators, greatly intensified the scope for ethnic competition. New positions and rewards were now within the grasp of those elites, who tended to foment ethnic resentments in order to enhance their bargaining positions at the centre. Added to this was the fact that regional imbalances induced by the colonial extractive economy persisted and in most cases became more pronounced. These imbalances generally coincided with ethnic group boundaries, thus reinforcing inter-ethnic competition and creating a further source of instability: the wealthier regions feared that the poorer regions – which in Nigeria happened to be the most populous regions – would use their political power to force a redistribution, while the poorer regions resented their status which they tended to see as the outcome of ethnic politics.

Nor does integration into the so-called modern sectors of the economy necessarily erode ethnic group affinities. This has already been shown to be true of the educated elites. Melson and Wolpe observed that Nigerian workers too, in strike actions in 1945 and 1964, developed a high degree of social class solidarity which 'transcended' ethnic group membership. Yet ethnic and communal sentiments among the same workers again came to the fore in the 1964 elections. From this they concluded that the process of 'modernisation' need not, as had been assumed, erode communal identities. A co-existence of these two sets of references was thus possible within one and the same individual (Melson and Wolpe, 1972:31):

> In effect the retention of communal points of reference enables industrial man to receive the best of two worlds – the collectivism inherent in the functionally diffuse ties of language and culture, and the individuation requisite to effective performance in the modern commercial and industrial milieu. We are suggesting . . . that the essence of modernity may lie not in the transition from particularistic to universalistic forms, but rather in their compartmentalization.

Thus the problem of ethnicity/communalism, seen in its socio-economic context, well illustrates the multi-dimensionalism and interdependence of the processes of generating development and achieving integration. Not only must the Nigerian polity find adequate solutions to the many specific problems of each process, it must also and above all find ways to combine these solutions into a broader, more comprehensive, overarching political strategy. This is perhaps *the* central 'premise' of Nigerian political life. And it almost certainly implies substantial socio-economic transformations of a kind which would directly attack and undermine the constellation of ruling interests within the country.

Notes

1. Population enumeration in Nigeria has always been problematic. The controversies surrounding the 1954, 1963 and 1973 censuses were popularly linked with revenue allocation and hence politically charged. Indeed, the Military Government was forced to 'annul' the 1973 poll. Semi-official estimates, based on projections from the 1963 figures, show a population of about 80 million. But the 1977/8 voter registration yielded a registered voting population of some 47.7 million, while that of 1983 produced 65.3 million voters. On the extremely conservative assumption that half the population were too young to vote in 1983, the total population could be construed as being not less than 130 million. If these estimates were considered to be reliable, however, they would indicate several things: (a) that between 1979 and 1983, annual population growth had shot up 13% from its 2.5% rate between 1960 and 1979, (b) that within a decade Nigeria's population would surpass that of the USA, and

(c) by the end of the century more than one of every two Africans would be Nigerians – developments which Tunde Obadina ('The Numbers Game', *National Concord*, 19 August 1983) terms 'too fantastic to be true'. As he points out, this would also hopelessly undermine existing national development plans and all government social and economic policies. The political dimensions of population inflation are further discussed in chapters 6, 7 and 8. For a balanced discussion of the technical and planning implications of the population problem, see R. B. Davidson, 'How Many Nigerians?', *West Africa*, 20 August 1979, pp. 1503–5.

2. It is important, however, to realise that North and South, East and West, and Middle Belt reflect colonially set administrative–exploitative boundaries which by no means describe 'natural' pre-colonial units. Each of these arbitrary divisions resulted, for instance, in the separation of various Nigerian peoples; and trade routes certainly did not stop at these points.

3. In fact, estimates of the number of languages spoken range from 250 to 500; see Allan 1978, p. 402.

4. On this see Crowder, 1971a.

5. Gavin Williams, *The Nigerian Civil War*, manuscript written for the Open University, 1983, p. 28.

6. The scope of this book unfortunately precludes any systematic exposition of the concepts of unequal development and unequal exchange, as well as the various dependency theories to which they are related. Some of these are discussed further, in the Nigerian context, in chapter 11.

7. John MacKintosh, 'Foreword' to Oyinbo, 1971, p. xvff.

8. J. S. Coleman and C. G. Rosberg, *Political Parties and National Integration in Tropical Africa*, Berkeley and Los Angeles, 1964, pp. 8ff.

9. It should be recalled, however, that the notion of tribalism is a profoundly ideological–racist conceptualisation whose origins are found in colonial policy towards the 'natives'. For this reason the term must be treated with caution. Cf. Mamdani, 1976 (esp. p. 3). Further see Mafeje, 1971, pp. 253ff and Nnoli, 1978, pp. 111ff.

10. The patterns of interaction among pre-colonial social units in West Africa have been examined by Robert S. Smith who concludes that 'in large parts of West Africa before the partition of the region among European powers, international relations in peace and war were carried on in a more or less recognizable fashion, and, to go a little further, in a coherent and rational manner which showed itself capable under favourable conditions of leading to political, economic and technical improvements in society' (1976, p. 187).

11. These stereotypes, moreover, were more or less explicitly conditioned by contemporary racism. For instance, British colonial administrators saw the Fulani as 'members of a higher race distinct from the indigenous Negroid peasant population. They admired the achievements of Fulani civilization. The physiological traits of the cattle Fulani in particular, such as their slim, tall builds, fair skin, finely arched noses and occasionally straight hair – all these suggested Caucasian or Hamitic influences. Similarly, their legends about their origins seemed to point to North Africa or Egypt, and thus "confirming" the new rulers' assessment of the Fulani, an assessment based on social prejudices'. Wirz, 1982, p. 36.

12. Abubakar Koko, 'National Ideology and Nigerian Integration', M. Turkur (ed.), *Nigeria in Search of a Viable Polity*, Zaria, 1977, p. 82.

13. Ralph Miliband, *Marxism and Politics*, London and Oxford, 1977, p. 109.

14. Yolamu R. Barongo, 'Ethnic Pluralism (in Nigeria) and Democratic Stability: The Basis of Conflict and Consensus', paper presented to the 5th Annual Conference of the Nigerian Political Science Association, 3–6 April 1978, mimeo, p. 9.

15. Richard Sandbrook, *Proletarians and African Capitalism: The Case of Kenya 1960–72*, Cambridge, 1974, p. 11.

16. 'The Revolution of Modernization in National and International Society', in R. J. Jackson and M. B. Stein (eds), *Issues in Comparative Politics*, New York–London–Toronto, 1971, p. 39 (italics added).

17. As pointed out in 'Introduction' to Smock and Bensi-Enchill, 1976. See also next chapter.

2

The First Republic

A central premise of Nigerian politics, as stated in the previous chapter, is that there was nothing inherently fractious about the pre-colonial Nigerian polity. Even given the illogical, colonial-imposed territorial boundaries, a number of preconditions were present which, differently understood and acted upon, *might have* contributed toward a unified, stable and symmetrically evolving Nigerian nation-state. Economically, the regions with their different resources and products, *could have* complemented, rather than competed with, each other. Ethnically, *no one group* was in a position to dominate all the other groups (at least not until the regionalisation of the country, which will be discussed in this chapter). In general, a substantial number of factors were present which *might have* shaped the great diversity of Nigeria into a broad, integrated and functional whole.

But colonialism eclipsed these possibilities and established instead a system of rule whose effects were felt in a multitude of ways in the post-independence economy and society. Colonialism's historical role was not so much that of *creator* of the forces and conditions tending to fragment the Nigerian nation-state, as it was that of *manipulator* and *exacerbator* of those diverse factors which differentiated the country. The very political boundaries set by the colonial administration were arbitrary and scarcely related to the subject peoples' historical experiences. The system of indirect rule absolutised regional and ethnic differences, while colonial capitalism, for reasons of its own internal logic, sectoralised and regionalised the national economy. The results were inter-ethnic competition, the formation of a dependent successor elite, continuing dependent development, and hence the creation of the major preconditions for neocolonialism following formal independence.

Yet such tendencies obviously worked against the objective need for the balanced development of the 'new' Nigerian political economy. Any political system adopted for Nigeria must be structured in such a way as to enable it to do a number of things: accommodate ethnic diversity, facilitate integration, effect relatively equitable distribution, reduce regional disparities in socio-economic development, create permanent political institutions and a 'national' political culture, and develop a reservoir of voluntary compliance on the part of most citizens, to name but a few. One would expect that such a political system would develop from Nigeria's specific socio-historical conditions and – perhaps following a period of revolutionary struggles or domestic trials of strength between contending forces – reflect the country's own needs and aspirations.

Nigerian independence, however, was not preceded by any such mobilising and unifying struggles – it has already been argued that Nigeria's first set of post-colonial rulers represented a 'successor elite' – with the result that the balance of social forces had to be worked out *after* independence under the strictures imposed by a governing system that was anything but autocentric and integrated. To understand how and why

25

Nigeria's First Republic (1960–66)[1] was structurally flawed from the outset and readily yielded to a military *coup*, therefore, it will be useful, first of all, to examine the terms and conditions under which power was handed over by the colonial administration. This will be followed by an exposition of the principal structural defects of the new liberal–democratic system, which in turn will enable the discussion to move into the area of political conflicts and the socio-economic forces which underlay them.

Political decolonisation

The period of preparation for colonial withdrawal (or decolonisation) began in Nigeria much later than is commonly supposed. A number of writers have noted the 'tutelage' aspect of colonial rule (legislative councils, indigenous advisers to governors, district officers, etc.) and inferred from it that the decolonising process began even before the First World War. In fact, Nigerian self-rule, as more recent research reveals, was never seriously contemplated by the colonial administration until well after the Second World War – after nationalist agitation in Nigeria, and other parts of Africa and of the colonised world compelled the colonial powers to place decolonisation near the top of their political agenda. For this reason, in the words of Professor Babatunde Williams (1968:55):

> Seen from the standpoint of their architects and designs, none of the colonial constitutions can be regarded as Nigerian. In large measure, all conformed to the prototype colonial constitution which had a non-democratic character with three main features, namely a morally homogenous legislature in which there was no serious division on policy issues, the subordination of the legislature to the executive and the absence of party organization as a factor in the governmental process. Thus they were all designed as instruments of administration and provided for some consultations of selected audiences to the extent that this accorded with the end of administration.

Not until 1946/7, with the enactment of the Richards Constitution – so-called, like almost all Nigerian constitutions before 1960, after the then colonial governor – did the British begin to deal with the fundamental political contradiction arising from the existence of a central, bureaucratic and national tier of government (colonial unitarism) on the one hand, and a remarkably diversified and disparate series of local or provincial ruling systems – the byproducts of indirect rule – on the other. The Richards Constitution's solution was the superimposition of federalism upon the nation-to-be. Following a 1939 administrative fiat, the Western and Eastern Regions were created for the first time, incorporating groups of former administrative divisions. The Northern 'Region' of course antedated amalgamation. Since the Regions were the constituent parts of the centre and the administrative units were linked to the Regional governments, a more or less direct connection was established between native authorities, local governments, etc. and the national or federal government.

While Richards thus helped to promote institutionalised contact – and *ipso facto* conflict – among the various territorial and ethnic groups, and did attempt to find a solution to the problem of particularist versus national orientations, the institutions and solutions chosen proved to be inadequate for the goals envisaged. Each Region was given its own House of Assembly and was permitted to deliberate on Regional matters in consultation with the colonial Regional Governor. No comparable machinery existed at the centre. Therefore, the Regional assemblies, which were supposed to be harbingers of national unity by creating three systems of 'unity in diversity' at the subnational level, antedated the same process at the national level, thus in effect becoming agencies for the assertion of Regional interests as *against* the centre, and in this way setting in motion the process of the *regionalisation of politics*.

Admittedly, the subsequent MacPherson Constitution of 1951 did belatedly attempt to set right some of Richards' dysfunctional effects. It attempted to establish a broader consensual basis by including a wider ethno-territorial Nigerian representation in its preparation. Then it created a central government and a quasi-federalist structure in an attempt to 'nationalise' political institutions. But the centre remained weak: representation in the unicameral federal legislature was apportioned according to Regional population, which thus produced an *automatic preponderance of Northern delegates* in that body. (Proposals by the East and West for 'unit representation', i.e., a fixed number of seats from each Region in the national parliament, were rejected by the colonial administration.) The Regional legislatures, moreover, elected members of the national parliament from among themselves – meaning in fact that the Regional delegates to the federal legislature would be chosen from the majority party in each Region; and these parties were, by then, dominated by each Region's ethnic majority. Since no one party could transcend its Regional base, each of the parties as a matter of priority had to attend to its Region – if necessary to the exclusion of the centre. Federal government was therefore essentially a *loose coalition of Regional powers*, and 'opposition' was whichever Regional party happened to advocate a policy different from the other two. In any case, the appointment of the executive was still the preserve of the (British) Governor-General.

The 1954 Lyttelton Constitution enlarged and extended the system of federalism and above all gave the Regional governments access to separate revenue sources. Henceforth, deputies to federal and Regional parliaments were elected directly, from separate constituencies. The drift away from colonial unitarism was all but cemented as residual powers were accorded to the already semi-autonomous Regions, at the centre's expense, and provisions were made for separate public services, judiciaries, marketing boards and Governors replacing the former Lieutenant-Governors, all resulting, of course, in the further regionalisation of politics. By 1957, Nigeria's first Prime Minister, Abubakar Tafawa Balewa, was operating within the framework of Lyttelton. The Robertson Constitution of 1958 added some structural refinements to the constitutional edifice: a bicameral legislature and a judiciary with powers, *inter alia*, to pronounce on constitutional matters and on inter-regional and federal-regional disputes.

It was this agglomeration of colonial constitutions with its, to some extent, jerry-built and *ad hoc* provisions that, with minor modifications, became Nigeria's Independence Constitution of 1960. Special provisions were made to entrench the more important sections of the constitution – for example, liberal rights, federalism, powers of the highest officials and the creation of new Regions – by making the amendment procedure subject to two-thirds majorities in both legislative houses and presupposing the assent of at least two of the three Regions.

Structural problems

In retrospect, it can be seen that the 1960 Independence Constitution as well as its 1963 successor Republican Constitution (which merely substituted an indigenous head of state for the British monarch) established a governing structure whose origins and development lay outside the Nigerian socio-historical experience. In many ways, it was an *'imposed' constitution*, a kind of extension of the British state structure.

Its salient structural features may be described as (i) adoption of the 'Westminster Model' of parliamentary cabinet government, (ii) modified, however, by a centrifugal federalism which accorded considerable, probably decisive, powers to the Regions.

(i) *The 'Westminster Model'*. It was, no doubt, inevitable that Nigeria's first government system should be patterned after that of the United Kingdom, since no substantial socio-economic reforms were planned, and the Nigerian successor elite by and large felt some affinity toward the former colonial power. Sir Tafawa Balewa, on becoming Prime Minister, declared, (1966:5):

> Our association with the people of the United Kingdom has been a happy one and there has always been tremendous goodwill on both sides. Their system of democratic government has now become part of our own heritage and we should be wise to maintain our institutions on the British model.

The correspondence between the two was, therefore, extensive. The parliamentary system, unlike the presidential system of the Second Republic, fused the legislature and executive, with the latter, in theory, drawn from and responsible to the former, with a consistent, though generally alternating, parliamentary majority party or party coalition. The Nigerian constitutions, on the other hand, were federalist, and the particular form of federalism adopted for this extremely heterogeneous society, in fact, created what turned out to be insurmountable barriers to the formation of a majority party, or even a stable majority coalition.

The First Republic also established a dual executive at the pinnacle of government, i.e., a ceremonial head of state (1960: the British monarch and her local representative; 1963: an indigenous figure elected indirectly by both Parliament and Senate at a joint meeting) whose term of office was five years,[2] in addition to a chief executive (Prime Minister). That the dual executive is less suited to the African context than to the 'old' Commonwealth countries has been amply demonstrated in the past two decades. In ex-Commonwealth Africa at independence, all the new states, apart from Botswana and Zambia, adopted the Westminster model of a fused legislature and executive, and the British sovereign – or an indigenous monarch, as in Swaziland or Lesotho – as cere-monial head of state. One by one, during the subsequent decades, all these states – by a series of parliamentary reforms, constitutional conferences, referenda, *de facto* develop-ments, popular pressures, creation of one-party states or military interventions – have acquired presidential-type systems with strong executives. A partial explanation of this tendency undoubtedly lies in the nature of colonial government which deprived its subject society of the institution of the 'above-party' or 'non-political' head of state – which is crucial to the successful operation of the Westminster model – since that office was occupied by the colonial administration itself (Oyinbo, 1971:9):

> So long as the British were present they acted as a referee for whom an indigenous substitute could never be found, obscuring the inevitable power struggle which alone would produce a political equilibrium. They were also a pressure group in favour of arrangements which they understood and which they could expect might best favour the future security of their interests.

In the absence of a history and political culture supportive of a division of executive and ceremonial power, the 'new' African states, now lacking the colonial overlord and referee, tended toward strong executive-type governments. In Nigeria, every step in the decolonising process towards centrifugal federalism, regionalisation and 'tribalisation' of the post-colonial constitutional structure rendered more difficult the institu-tionalisation and popular acceptability of a supra-party head of state or, indeed, of all national figures and offices. Moreover, important political issues which the colonial administration had suppressed or simply ignored had to be dealt with by successor Nigerian regimes. Problems of local government efficiency and reform, of staffing regional and federal bureaucracies, and of settling disputes for succession to traditional rulerships forced the new government into partisanship from the outset. Thus the mere act of transferring sovereignty from British to Nigerian rulers laid bare many structural problems of the Westminster model which had, hitherto, remained dormant, and set off a process of constitutional transformation whose result can be seen in the succession of military and civilian governments since 1960. Ten years after the collapse of the First Republic the formulators of the 1979 Constitution would reject the Westminster model with these words:

> The separation of the Head of State from Head of Government involves a division between real authority and formal authority. The division is meaningless in the light of African political experience and history. The tendency indeed of all people throughout the world is to elevate a single person to the position of ruler. In the context of Africa the division is not only meaningless, it is difficult to maintain in practice. No African Head of State has been known to be content with the position of mere figurehead . . . The system has resulted in a clash of personalities and of interest, a conflict of authority and an unnecessary complexity and uncertainty in governmental relations. The system presupposes a non-political Head of State, but the lesson of African experience with the system is that if non-political Heads of State are not already in existence, mere constitutional provisions alone will not bring them into being.[3]

(ii) *Centrifugal federalism*. The sheer size and diversity of Nigeria, particularly after a half-century of indirect rule, precluded any total transference of the unitary Westminster model to the ex-colony. The homogeneous nature of British society, its consensual political culture and its advanced degree of industrialisation – the latter achieved partly at the expense of the colonies at the periphery – ensured the 'proper' operation of parliamentary government there. None of these conditions was present in post-independence Nigeria. The British, therefore, in consultation with the Nigerian successor elite, determined to superimpose on the Nigerian state a system of federalism which, like federalist governments elsewhere, would permit a degree of autonomy and scope for self-development of the multiplicity of sectoral and ethnic groups, while, at the same time, connecting and holding together these pluralist forces in a common set of interests and conflict-regulating institutions, thus binding them in voluntary and self-interested association to the national central government. Federalism, in other words, was the structural expression of the notion of 'unity in diversity'.

The question was: what kind of federalism? Despite numerous objections and protests, particularly from minority group representatives, the British decided, essentially, to base the Nigerian federal system upon the constitutional arrangements which had evolved, largely *ad hoc*, from Richards to Robertson. This meant, more than anything else, the enshrining of *regionalism as the guiding principle*.

British thinking on this issue was partly determined by a 1958 Minorities Commission Report which (reflecting the colonial-successor elite consensus) reasoned that dominant-ethnic-group parties would form in each Region, but would have to collaborate with minority-ethnic-group parties in other Regions in order to gain power at the centre. Hence, those minority-group interests which might be submerged in Regional, one-ethnic-party-dominated governments, would at least be accounted for in the central government in Lagos.

Constitutional theory, however, did not correspond to social reality. The federalist system imposed upon Nigeria rested on at least four – absolutely decisive – wrong assumptions, namely:

(a) *That no one Regional government would be sufficiently powerful to dominate the entire federation.* Yet this is precisely what happened in the case of the North, which possessed about two-thirds of the country's land area and more than half its population.

(b) *That each Region would develop a multi-party system.* The fact of numerical predominance by one Region would certainly have been mitigated had there been several contending political parties there. But virtual single-party rule in the North (as in the East and West), as actually happened, would mean that a party (the Nigerian People's Congress, NPC) based on an ethnic group of an estimated 16 million (Hausa–Fulani) could first dominate a region of some 30.8 million, which in turn could potentially govern the entire nation practically on its own strength of numbers. The federalist system was not adequate to ensure minority interest representation either at the Regional or federal level.

(c) *That the constitutional machinery at the centre was sufficiently well structured to create effective national governing institutions.* Such an assumption was, at best, naive, for the Regional governments had antedated the federal government by at least a decade and had got a substantial 'head start' over it. On independence, they possessed coherent bureaucracies, including their own judiciaries and public corporations, which, in the East and West at least, had been Nigerianised long before the federal civil service, as well as virtually self-contained economic systems – the result of colonial sectoralisation – including revenue-generating marketing boards, powers of industrial location, direct links with the international economic system, and powers of control over local governments and chieftaincy matters. On top of all this, they were accorded residual powers by the Independence Constitution, which thus gave them a marked advantage in federal–regional jurisdictional disputes.

(d) *That there would be no discrepancy between political and economic powers,* or, if there were, that the new federalism could balance and integrate these powers.

The failure in this respect is well illustrated by contemporary (and not absolutely reliable) statistics concerning regional revenues and personal taxes. In 1961 total regional revenues (excluding federal allocations) were just over 125 m., of which 58.5% was from the West, 25.7% from the East and only 15.7% from the North. Percentages of the national aggregate of personal taxes collected from the regions in the same year were 67.7% West, 27.2% East, 9% North. These are corroborated by educational enrolments: the North, containing more than half the national population, in 1965 had a primary-school population which was 10% of that of the country as a whole. Similar tendencies were evident in higher education where, in the same year, Northerners made up only 8% of the total student population, while the East, Lagos and the West constituted 48%, 5% and 39% respectively.[4]

The regionalisation of political life

Thus Nigeria's Independence Constitution in fact reflected and exacerbated, rather than mitigated and regulated, the manifold centrifugal tendencies and forces in society and economy.

The regionalised political structure reproduced itself in several areas:

(i) *Communal foundations of politics.* Ethnic associations came to constitute the basic social units of political interest – representation and activity. Initially founded as kinship unions to help family members in multi-tribal areas find work, pay for burial or naming ceremonies, or deal with their new employers, these groups grew during the 1930s and 1940s into great cultural sections of Igbo or Yoruba or – lesser in scope – Hausa interest associations. (Indeed the Yoruba and Igbo were now made aware, for the first time, of their respective common cultural ties; previously their reference group had been primarily clan or kinship groups.) These communal associations assumed a number of important functions – wage negotiations, articulation of demands for welfare, interest representation of occupational groups, and the like; all *vis-à-vis* the colonial administrators – functions which in other countries, for different historical reasons, had been performed by trade unions, farmers' associations and business interest groups. But the latter forms of interest organisation were stifled in Nigeria by the effects of the colonial system: workers were few in number and not thoroughly integrated into the wage-labour economy, most farmers remained formally outside capitalist agriculture, and indigenous business was relatively powerless since most large and medium business concerns were foreign-owned and staffed. (Nearly all banks were foreign-owned, while almost three-quarters of all firms with a capital of over $70,000 were owned by non-Nigerians (Nafziger, 1977:56).

(ii) *Political party formation*. In view of the conspicuous absence of countervailing interest groups, then, ethnic and cultural associations emerged as the principal organisational bases of new political parties during the period of decolonisation. Given the regionalised structural framework of politics, it is difficult, in retrospect, to imagine any other possible outcome. For the initial thrusts toward a kind of Pan-West African or at least all-Nigerian nationalism which were evident in, for example, the West African Students' Association (based in London, 1925–45), the groupings around Herbert Macauley's Nigerian National Democratic Party, and the Nigerian Youth Movement (from which emerged leaders such as H. O. Davies, Ernest Ikoli and Nnamdi Azikiwe), had no real organisational or mass social base outside Lagos. Thus, as decolonisation was effected within regional parameters during the late 1940s and throughout the 1950s, the Nigerian Youth Movement disintegrated along communal lines and was transformed into a Pan-Yoruba organisation, while Azikiwe and the Igbo members left and constituted their own party.

In a process which James Coleman has aptly termed 'the regionalisation of nationalism' (1960:319), 'the ethnic associations became the nuclei of 'national' party political formation *in their respective Regions*. From the Jam'iyyar Mutanen Arewa (Hausa Cultural Organisation) emerged – with active British assistance – the Nigerian People's Congress (NPC) as the dominant Northern party and the vehicle for Hausa–Fulani rule. The Federated Igbo State Union engendered the National Council of Nigeria and the Cameroons (later National Council of Nigerian Citizens: NCNC) in the East, the sole party among the 'Big Three' to tap a mass basis drawn from more than one ethnic group. And the Yoruba self-help organisation, Egbe Omo Oduduwa, was instrumental in forming the major Western party, the Action Group (AG).

The minority parties too, were formed on the basis of ethnic-group associations, and the desire for an organisational safeguard against majority domination was a powerful additional motive. In this way the Middle Zone League (MZL), the Nigerian Elements Progressive Union (NEPU) and the United Middle Belt Congress (UMBC), among others, were formed in the North, while the South produced the Calabar-Ogoja-Rivers State Movement (COR), the Niger Delta Congress (NDC) and the Mid-West State Movement (MSM).

With the parameters of popular support thus defined by ethnic group membership, the political parties set out to maximise their respective group's support. Ethnicity provided the ideological mortar which held together the disparate elements that constituted these communally based parties. Under its banner each party could be seen as upholding its group's interest against all other groups. And, under its umbrella, the political class could consolidate its support and develop its networks of patron–client relationships to ensure its own continued self-aggrandisement.

Ethnic politics was thus characterised by vague ideological appeals based on tribal membership, a conglomeration of promises of rewards to the multiplicity of sub-groups, and the personalisation of politics. Party leaders were stylised as preservers and defenders of ethno-nationalism, while their efforts to increase support, including election campaigns and party propaganda, disseminated ethnicity even into the remote rural areas thus implanting communal thinking (and conflict) into all members of the group. Such patterns, once established, tended to persevere over time.

(iii) *One-party sub-states*. The First Republic was thus beset by a threefold structural contradiction; political party formation on the bedrock of ethnic group solidarity and exclusiveness; a constitutional framework which reposited predominant political power with the sub-national units; and a federal organisation of government at the centre. Of these, Regional supremacy was decisive and its effects on political life were profound and enduring.

First, those politicians and parties in control of the Regional governments were simultaneously the principal beneficiaries of economic development. For in the Regions were situated the lucrative colonial-founded Marketing Boards, described by Robin Cohen (1972:239) as 'one of the most glittering prizes of nationalist politicians', which were empowered to purchase export crops from the peasants at fixed prices and sell them abroad for maximum return. They also controlled the issue of licences permitting individuals and companies to participate in the purchase of produce. All in all, the marketing boards were crucial in financing all forms of public spending: the surpluses they produced 'were the source, directly or indirectly, of about 95 % of the £46 million made available between 1946 and 1962 to the publicly-owned development boards and corporations'; and these mainly Regional bodies 'were responsible for about one-tenth of all public investment spending in that period'.[5] As Claude Ake points out (1976:3–4), all this is indicative of economic exploitation *without* the institution of wage labour. The 'state' – the political class – employed 'its' state monopoly to direct peasant economic activities – activities which, prior to the discovery of oil, accounted for almost 60% of the country's Gross Domestic Product. The surplus value thus generated accrued to the middleman-state and through it was passed on to the top officials, their clients and their parties. Thus, their political functions were at least as central as their economic functions, though of course inseparable from them.

Also in the Regions, the overwhelming part of agricultural and commercial credit was dispensed by statutory boards and banks controlled by the Regional governments. And according to the derivation principle adopted in 1954, the most substantial import and excise duties collected by the federal government were distributed to their Regions of origin. Mining revenues were divided equally between the federal government and their originating Region. Furthermore, income tax was levied by the Regions, and the Regions could borrow funds from abroad on terms and conditions negotiated by them without federal government mediation. In this context, the open-door and dependent economy operated largely within the Regional political framework so that business and politics were intertwined and interdependent to a remarkable degree. Complex linkages of patronage, donations, personnel interchange and the like therefore evolved.

The nexus has been described by Barbara Callaway,[6] who starts from the assumption that the marketing boards represented the 'key to the power system of the First Republic'. Marketing board surpluses were deposited in Regional banks and lending institutions which extended credit to the regionally-based businessmen. The latter were, of course, expected to throw their financial and political weight behind the political party in power. Marketing boards also financed various loan and development corporations which undertook a variety of projects in co-operation with business groups. Such corporations were directed by administrators appointed by the party in power, and those interests to whom loans and other support were given were constrained to back the regional government. Naturally, none of these groups would have any interest in overturning the regionalist *status quo*.

Now each Region was 'automatically' dominated by a single party – the NPC, the NCNC and the AG – which in turn was dominated by a single ethnic group – the Hausa–Fulani, Igbo and Yoruba respectively. (These general tendencies held despite strong NCNC showings in parts of the West and despite a number of centrifugal forces in the North which qualified somewhat the monolithic image it projected to the outside.) Minority groups in each Region, who also, by and large, had formed their own parties or at least ethnic associations, had essentially two choices: (a) to go into opposition, thus facing exclusion from the Regional system of patronage and rewards, or (b) to merge or co-operate, in a subordinate position, with the dominant party in order to obtain for their elites and ethnic group at least a 'piece of the action' as well as to avoid the ostracism and persecution which was the normal fate of oppositional minorities. In most cases the solution adopted was (b).

The dominant Regional parties were at the same time vitally interested in incorporating, or at least gaining the allegiance of, as many minority groups as possible, since their object was to maximise their Regional power base in order to enhance their bargaining power at the centre. For, despite the focus of power in the Regions, capturing federal power still held out the prospect of controlling the national government and with it the national economy and the key position in federal–regional negotiations, as well as access to still more opportunities for patronage and privileges.

Here again, the explanation for these contradictory tendencies lies partly in the structural pathology of the First Republic. The regionalised parties could only hope to gain a commanding position in the central government by way of coalitions and working agreements with other Regional parties. This was true even of the NPC which, with its numerical majority, could only dominate the lower house but *not* the regionally weighted Senate (where the South, including Lagos, controlled 40 of 56 appointments) *nor* the civil service whose personnel consisted pre-eminently of better educated Southerners. In addition, the North felt constrained to maintain an ally in the South in order to forestall any alliance of the two Southern Regions. Hence, the Regional parties' influence at the national level depended more than anything else upon their ability to consolidate and mobilise their Regional bases of support. The NPC, for example, could not hope to win all 312 seats in Parliament, but it could at least attempt to win all 174 *Northern* seats. Similarly the AG could attempt to fill all 62 *Western* seats, the NCNC each of its possible 73 *Eastern* seats.

Thus the dominant Regional parties tried, by all conceivable means, to entice, cajole and intimidate minority ethnic groups into supporting them. As the minorities were integrated in varying degrees into the ruling structures of the dominant parties, the Regions developed into *virtual one-party sub-states*, with an internal stratification system based on the various groupings' proximity to power. At the apex were the respective dominant ethnic groups, below them the allied minorities, and at the bottom the minorities in opposition. To some extent, over time, the Regional loyalties built up in this way became strong enough to erode, or at least suppress, ethnic loyalties, so that the dominant parties began to be able to employ Regional (i.e., supra-ethnic) sentiments to legitimate their own rule. This tendency appeared more pronounced in the North, with its strong traditional class distinctions, where a feeling of 'One North' did partially overcome certain ethnic divisions. Thus when the 1966 *coup* was carried out, the

Northern population widely interpreted it as a blow against the 'North' rather than against the Hausa–Fulani.[7] Even the Tiv, who were consistent political foes of the NPC, were still more opposed to Igbo influence in the Northern Region, and participated in the 1966 massacres of Igbo resident in the North.

Political deficiencies

In a very real sense, then, the First Republic was locked, from the first elections onward, into a structural framework of practically unmitigated regionalism and winner-take-all politics. Those elections, the last held under colonial government auspices, were said to have been relatively fair (except for abuses emanating from the administrative and legal institutions already subject to political pressures, such as the Native Courts and Native Administrations (Post, 1963:439).) The results could have been predicted on the basis of demographic (and ethnographic) statistics: the dominant party in each Region, buoyed by the power and influence accruing to it from several preceding years as the ruling party, captured the majority of its Region's seats.[8] The results demonstrated that no party was able to transcend in any substantial way its ethno-regional social bases. Not only did this confirm the already evident absence of any 'national' parties, it also dashed Southern parties' hopes of making inroads into the North in order to compensate for the lesser number of Southern seats assigned by the constitution to the federal parliament. True, the AG, which was then – prior to the creation of the Mid-West Region – the most supra-Regional party, did manage to gain 25 Northern seats (as well as 14 Eastern seats), while the NCNC/NEPU did capture 8 seats in the North. But almost all of these seats won by the major parties outside their own Regions were among minority groups.

Enforced intra-Regional consensus was brought about, above all, by the manipulation of the constitutional machinery to favour the most powerful interests and party in each Region. Subversion of the electoral laws and electoral machinery was one way in which this was accomplished. In line with the principle of centrifugal federalism, elections were the responsibility of the Regional governments which, dominated by single parties, were able to organise and conduct them virtually at will. Not surprisingly, charges of election rigging, thuggery and intimidation punctuate the history of the First Republic, particularly in its final phase. Electoral laws, too, were used to discourage the opposition, for instance, by increasing the amount of deposits required for each election, by raising costs of the conduct of queries into the results (election petitions), by increasing from one-eighth to one-fifth the minimum percentage of the popular vote needed by a defeated candidate in order to recover his or her deposit, and by making a fair court hearing with respect to these issues all but impossible.[9] Indeed, the state apparatus could be used in many ways to entrench one-party Regional government: control over the appointment, salary level and deposition of traditional chiefs; distribution of patronage to supporters and the withholding of it from opposition groups; over- or under-assessment of individuals for taxation purposes; withdrawal or cancellation of trading licences; dissolution of local government councils; or deployment of the police and other state officials to harass or intimidate minority groups and arrest their leaders. These pseudo-legal methods were, of course, augmented by quite illegal ones such as bribery, 'hooliganism' and 'thuggery'.

Opposition was equated with treason. When, for example, the UMBC leader and Tiv spokesman, J. S. Tarka, refused to collaborate with the Sardauna and his NPC, the Tiv Division was grossly neglected by the Northern Regional government and Tarka himself arrested and charged with treason just prior to the 1961 Regional elections.[10]

At the centre, many of these Regional tendencies were in fact replicated. The structure of the First Republic necessitated a Northern-dominated coalition at the federal level, since the North was by far the largest Region, though not quite strong enough to rule alone. After considerable negotiations the NCNC joined forces with the NPC, and the AG was left as the sole significant opposition party. But again the pressures of winner-takes-all politics were too great to support a permanent, respected and 'loyal' opposition. For while the ruling coalition proceeded to monopolise all the top positions (Azikiwe became Governor-General, Sir Abubakar Tafawa Balewa the first Prime Minister) and avenues of patronage for itself, the AG began to disintegrate under the dual impetus of its desire for a share in the windfalls which would have been available to it as a part of the ruling coalition, and of constant harassment and persecution by the ruling parties. Again, the inadequate constitutional-structural framework precluded the formation of a broad and productive tension between government and opposition and created instead a permanent regionalised conflict between the central government and the Western Region which affected every area of political activity.

Thus, at its 1962 Jos Congress the AG split into a 'radical' wing under Chief Obafemi Awolowo, leader of the federal party, and an 'accommodationist' grouping under Chief Akintola, Premier of the Western Region. Naturally, the NPC/NCNC leaders preferred to deal with Akintola, whose stand on the Anglo-Nigerian Defence Pact, for example, was not different from theirs, and who, unlike Awolowo, wanted to collaborate with the central government while prudently refraining from extra-Regional politics. Using the (partially engineered) May 1962 Western Region parliamentary crisis as a pretext, the Prime Minister suspended the Western government, detained a number of AG leaders, and set in motion a commission of inquiry into corruption (the Coker Commission) which exposed an incredible degree of corruption and malfeasance in the Western Region (though undoubtedly no more extensive than that in the other Regions). Awolowo and some 30 others were brought to trial on charges of plotting to overthrow the government.

These developments demonstrated clearly the process of *political justice* which was marshalled successfully and repeatedly by the wielders of state power against actual or potential opposition. Just two years after independence, one of the country's 'founding fathers', the major opposition leader and chief spokesman for one of the component units of the federation, was made to stand trial for conspiracy and treasonable felony. Among the co-accused were politicians who already were, or later became, prominent in political life: Samuel G. Ikoku, Anthony Enahoro, Lateef Jakande and Joseph Tarka. Even the Chief's constitutionally guaranteed right to a choice of legal counsel was violated when the Ministry of Immigration refused to admit his British lawyer, Mr F. E. N. Gratien, into the country – a decision upheld by both the High Court of Lagos and the Supreme Court.[11] Awolowo was subsequently convicted and sentenced to ten years' imprisonment, reduced on appeal to seven years.

Sedition, incidentally, became a favoured charge against opponents of the federal government. Dr Chike Obe, leader of the minuscule Dynamic Party and a member of the House of Representatives, was also sentenced in April 1961 as a result of the publication of his pamphlet *The People: Facts That You Must Know*. The offending passage read:

> Down with the enemies of the people, the exploited of the weak and oppressors of the poor . . .
> The days of those who have enriched themselves at the expense of the poor are numbered.
> The common man in Nigeria can today no longer be fooled by sweet talk at election time only
> to be exploited and treated like dirt after the booty of office has been shared among the
> politicians.[12]

The beneficiaries of all these measures were the federal government and the NPC. The AG's disintegration was complete: some members joined the NPC, others defected, and the party's total strength in the House of Representatives was reduced to 13 from an original 75. A series of by-elections and the addition of seven seats for Northern Cameroun presented the NPC with an absolute majority in the House. Eventually 'normalcy' was restored to the Western Region and Akintola, now heading a renamed United People's Party, and in collaboration with the NCNC, ruled his Region in a manner amenable to the federal coalition. Later in the year Akintola's UPP, with its 41 seats, merged with the Western NCNC and its 44 seats to form the Nigerian National Democratic Party (NNDP) which ruled the Western Region for the rest of the First Republic. Meanwhile the Mid-West Region – where the AG had always attracted about 50% of the popular vote so long as it remained part of the Western Region – had been created from the eastern part of the Western Region. All of its seats (save one) were, as intended, won by the NCNC who were now in control of the two Regions.

However, what initially appeared to be a straightforward victory of the two coalition parties began to develop – or was perceived in the South to begin to develop – into a threat of outright Northern hegemony. This apprehension was fed by several developments which strained at the already deficient structural and socio-economic formations. First came the May 1962 census. Believing that not only each Region's political strength, but also revenues, amenities, welfare allocations, scholarships, etc., would hinge on population numbers, political and communal leaders urged their people to be 'counted in'. As a result, the first count showed that the East's population had ostensibly increased by 71% since the 1952/3 census, the West's by about 70% and the North's by 30%. Of course, the Western and Eastern figures were found to be 'grossly inflated', and a 'verification' of Northern statistics carried out in December 1962 indicated a ten-year population increase of 80%. Thereupon the Prime Minister ordered a completely new census, held during 1963, which produced similar results: this time the North's population went up by 67%, the East's by 65% and the West's by almost 100%. Even more significant than these astronomical rates of population increase was the bottom line: that, of 55.6 million Nigerians, nearly 30 million were resident in the North. This revelation ended Southern hopes, nourished since the 1952/3 census, that an all-Nigerian head count would finally reveal a greater Southern population, and with it bring more seats in parliament, more federal appointments, more scholarships, and increased revenue allocation. Over the objections of the Eastern leaders, the Prime Minister, with the support of the now-docile Westerners (including the Western wing of the NCNC who would soon break away from their Eastern parent party), declared the 1963 census valid and final.

By 1964, then, Nigerian ruling groups had established a kind of ethno-regionally based party cartel which survived tenuously on an intra-elite agreement to eliminate opposition groups, exclude the masses and apportion wealth and power among the competing top groups. As Gavin Williams has written (1976:43): 'The ethics of business penetrated politics, the ethics of politics penetrated business; the ethics of the gangster penetrated both.' In this situation, however, the limits of outright ethnically-grounded class rule became apparent. For one the NPC–NCNC coalition at the centre in essence represented only 46% of the population – i.e., the Hausa–Fulani and Igbo – so that minority groups and their leaders were increasingly alienated from a political system in which they could only hope to play a secondary or indeed tertiary role. They saw national resources and opportunities channelled through ethno-regional funnels into areas and to the benefit of social groups over which they had practically no control. Second, more and more of the powerless began to regard government as merely the instrument of class rule. As the political class throve and grew immensely wealthier, even while the living conditions of the majority remained static or declined, a popular resentment of government and the governing class began to evolve, and a general feeling of malaise and disillusionment with the order of things set in.

This embryonic consciousness helps, for example, to understand continuing mass support for the AG, despite the fact that backing it was not likely to bring tangible rewards. Walter Schwarz writes (1968:153): 'The purged, chastened and depleted Action Group had become the first major political party in independent Nigeria to be identified with the underdog.' And about this time, the AG began to evolve a radical-socialist platform which tended to see politics from the point of view of the ruled and which spoke of class struggle and social change. The programme was significant not for its long-term effects on the party itself – for it was neither consistent nor stood any chance of realisation – but because it was the first and only time, both in the First and Second Republic, when a major Nigerian political party committed itself to an apparently anti-capitalist programme.

The broad social malaise also translated, more significantly, into the 1964 general strike. For one brief historical moment, all the fragmented and disparate organisations of the labour movement were able to combine into a Joint Action Committee (JAC) under the popular labour leader, Michael Imoudou. The immediate issue was higher wages, which were promised in the Morgan Commission Report, but which the federal government was slow in publishing, to say nothing of granting. The strike, which began on 31 May and officially ended on 13 June, brought masses of workers in all Regions out into the streets for higher wages and better conditions. Under pressure, these were conceded by the government, though not in the amounts proposed by the Report. Certainly the tangible returns of the strike action were not in themselves of great significance, since prices of food and staples immediately went up, and many semi-redundant workers, particularly in smaller firms, were dismissed while work was intensified for those who remained. But the strike's symbolic value was considerable: not only had the labour movement managed to consolidate itself for a class action, but in the process the walls of ethnicity, for a brief moment, had come down and something like a class struggle was waged by Nigerian workers. Labour had arrived as a force in politics, at least for the duration of the First Republic. And the events demonstrated that the increasingly isolated federal government, lacking a broad popular base, could not hold up against sustained mass pressure from below.

In this context of social conflicts and power shifts, the NPC–NCNC alliance at the centre began to come apart, and gradually, with the approach of the December 1964 elections, gave way to new party alignments which more accurately reflected the evolving domestic balance of power. The NPC, by now the only real political force in the North, foreswore its alliance with the NCNC for a variety of reasons, which included the increasing Igbo presence in the Northern civil service and professions, resentment at the NCNC's party pro-labour behaviour during the general strike, and apprehension at the growing *rapprochement* between the NCNC and other extra-coalition parties. The NCNC for its part was bitterly resentful at anti-Igbo measures in housing and civil service hiring policies in the North, as well as the outcome of the census in which, they felt, the East was intentionally underrepresented.

Thus each of the coalition partners went in search of more amicable alliances. A *Northern-conservative coalition* came about with the combination of Akintola's NNDP in the West and the NPC in the North into a Nigerian National Alliance (NNA). This arrangement was more to the liking of the Sardauna, since the NNDP, lacking a solid popular base in its own Region, was entirely dependent on the federal government and hence the NPC. The NNA was quickly joined by the main non-Igbo opposition party in the East, the Niger Delta Congress (NDC), and the Dynamic Party. Meanwhile, a *Southern-progressive coalition*, which partially overcame the economic-political power dichotomy reflected in the initial 1960 coalition, developed as the NCNC and AG joined forces. Incorporating the Northern Elements Progressive Union (NEPU) under Amino Kano and the United Middle Belt Congress (UMBC) led by Joseph Tarka – which two parties had already merged into a Northern Progressive Front – the new grouping emerged as the United Progressive Grand Alliance (UPGA).

Thus the desire to win the elections produced two supra-tribal (yet tribally defined), supra-regional (though regionally grounded) and nation-wide coalitions, the NNA and UPGA, who were bitter and intransigent rivals for power. The zero-sum quality of political life became even more apparent now, since the one's loss really did amount to another's gain. In order to win, the UPGA, with only a 'safe' Mid-Western and Eastern basis, had to break into the NPC and NNDP-controlled areas in the North and West and increase its popular support there. The NNA, of course, was determined to prevent any such developments and instead aimed to maximise its votes in the Northern and Western areas under its control.

The story of the 1964 election campaign and the polling itself has often been recounted.[13] It is one of tribalism and petty jingoism, of smear tactics and corruption, thuggery and violence, rigging and 'unopposed returns', even kidnapping and murder. There was an attempted boycott by the NCNC to protest against registration and procedural irregularities, and an avalanche of official protests from all sides. An initial hesitation by the (Igbo) President to reappoint the (Hausa–Fulani) Prime Minister was prompted by the apparent illegality and immorality of the campaign and election. Indeed, the President considered for a time calling in the military, until it was pointed out to him that his title of Commander-in-Chief was only a ceremonial one and did not confer the right to command military operations. At the end of it all, the trend toward regionalism was considerably enhanced: the NPC strengthened its hold over the North, the NCNC predominated in the Mid-West as it did six weeks later in the East (where no polling had taken place as a result of the boycott) and in the West the NNDP (and thus NNA) won 36 seats, the United Progressive Grand Alliance (in spite of its boycott) 6. Thus the AG within the UPGA was unable to re-assert its regional hegemony. The UPGA failed utterly to make inroads into the North, and received only 4 Tiv seats there. The final count was NNA 197 seats, UPGA 108, Independents 5. Nevertheless, the NNDP and other UPGA elements were able to minimise their losses by entering into the new 76-member cabinet (!) with 11 appointments each.

Coup de grace?

It is never easy to establish precisely at which point a degenerating liberal democracy is transformed into a qualitatively different governing form. Nigeria's First Republic presents a particularly difficult case in this respect. Some writers claim that liberal democracy never in fact existed at all, since the political structures imposed on Nigeria in no way related to the people's shared past and future aspirations; thus from the outset democratic *forms* merely masked the *content* of neo-colonial class rule. John Oyinbo's epitaph to the First Republic reflects this view. 'It is wrong,' he argues (1971:175), 'to think that democracy has failed in Nigeria. What has failed are the democratic institutions of an alien culture and history.' Still others point to the fact that the liberal-democratic *institutions* persevered until the military *coup* of the night of 14–15 January 1966 which for them marks the end of Nigerian democracy.

What is evident is that, by the 1964 elections at the latest, both the institutions and spirit of liberal democracy were gravely undermined and in many cases unable to function. Within each Region, the organs of the state were deployed to crush all opposition and dissent, to facilitate distribution of the social product into the pockets (and foreign bank accounts) of the ruling groups, and to violate the liberal rights of individuals and minorities. The principle of federalism was abused in order to achieve the same ends within the federation. Politics operated according to the Darwinian maxim of survival of the fittest. Here the jungle metaphor was most apt, since the First Republic served to strengthen groups and individuals who exercised power in society and to suppress those who did not. Towards the end, therefore, a clear majority of Nigerians were alienated from and dissatisfied with liberal democracy and began increasingly to think in terms of alternatives.

Events after the 1964 elections merely reinforced such longings. The Western Regional elections, scheduled for November 1965, in essence replicated the 1964 power struggle. Both the NNA and UGPA had a vital stake in the outcome of the election, which it has been said (Schwarz, 1968:178), 'proved, literally as well as metaphorically as far as the First Republic was concerned to be an election to end all elections'. For the UPGA it presented a last opportunity to forestall Northern hegemony at the centre by gaining mastery over the entire South – a not unreasonable undertaking since the NCNC already controlled two Regions, and the West under Akintola's somewhat isolated and unpopular NNDP seemed vulnerable to an NCNC–AG offensive. Again the NNA was placed on the defensive and forced to resort to enhanced tribalist appeals and manipulation of political institutions in order to hold its power position.

This time election malpractices were even more flagrant, and bribery and corruption were literally flaunted in the open. The ostensible NNDP 'victory' hardly mattered to anyone, amid charges and countercharges, popular disillusionment with the entire democratic process, riots, a series of crime waves and a virtually total breakdown of law and order. The deployment of army units – among whom were many UPGA adherents – only exacerbated the situation. By mid-January, events were clearly beyond the power of both Regional and federal politicians, while strong repercussions were being felt in the other Regions.

The First Republic was now manifestly bankrupt. Practically every sector of society was in some measure disaffected and disillusioned: labour, farmers and peasants, many civil servants and professionals, the poor, the middle classes, the minority ethnic groups, even majorities not currently at the centre of power and, not least, the military. Centrifugal federalism was the conduit for the looming Hobbesian war of all against all: Northern population power against Southern economic power, the North and West against the Southeast (and before that, the North and East against the West) for control of the central government, the East against the West for civil service posts and hegemony within the South, and in each Region majority rule versus minority rights, and 'haves' versus 'have-nots'.

It is not at all surprising, therefore, to learn of the profound lack of popular regret which ensued when a military *coup* of 14–15 January 1966 ended the lives of the Sardauna of Sokoto, Sir Tafawa Balewa, Samuel Akintola, as well as a number of prominent (and mostly Northern) army officers, and replaced the First Republic with a military government.

Notes

1. In common usage the First Republic refers to the period from Independence to the first military *coup* on 15 January 1966, and will be referred to in this way throughout the book. But it should be noted that for the first three years of its existence Nigeria was in fact a Dominion with the British monarch as its formal head of state and an indigenous Governor-General formally appointed by her. Only on 1 October 1963 did it officially become a republic with its own President.

2. Dr Nnamdi Azikiwe was the sole incumbent of both the Governor-Generalship and the Presidency. His five-year term of office as President was, of course, interrupted by the January 1966 *coup* which also ended the First Republic.

3. *Report of the Constitution Drafting Committee*, Vol. 1, xxix, 1976; on this problem in general see also Selassie, 1974, chapter 2 and Nwabueze, 1974, *passim*.

4. Bamisaiye, 1971:98. To be sure the total picture changed during the First Republic, so that in 1965 '32.9% of the tax was from the East, the North had jumped to 29.9% and the West plummeted to 37.2%. The corresponding revenue from all sources, excluding the federal allocation, (had) actually declined in real terms in the West. The percentages are East 31.7%, North 29.7% and West 38.6%' (Bamisaiye, 1971, pp. 98, 100, 102).

5. Douglas Rimmer, 'Development in Nigeria: An Overview' in William Zartman (ed.), *The Political Economy of Nigeria*, New York, 1983, p. 37.

6. Callaway, 1975, p. 111ff. The rest of this paragraph follows her argument. Further see Sklar and Whitaker, 1966.

7. On this see Post and Vickers, 1973.

8. The results of these and all preceding Nigerian elections are neatly summarised in Sklar, 1963, p. 35.

9. For a more comprehensive discussion of all this, and for charts relating to election deposit increases and costs for queries into election results see Ayoade, 1978, pp. 13a and 14a.

10. Nor was this the first state persecution of Tarka. For details see M. J. Dent, 'A Minority Party – the UMBC' in Mackintosh, 1966.

11. Just five months later – and as part of the same trial – Chief Anthony Enahoro's counsel, Dingle Foot was also barred from entry after the Chief himself had been extradited from the UK.

12. Quoted by M. I. Jegede ('The Supreme Court's Attitude towards some Aspects of Individual Freedom and the Right to Property' in Kasunmu, 1977, p. 111), who also provides an excellent discussion of the juridical aspects of this, and other, sedition cases.

13. See, e.g., the accounts given by Mackintosh, 1966, Schwarz, 1965. Ostheimer rightly speaks of 'electoral warfare of extraordinary brutality' (1973, p. 58).

3

The Military in Politics

Nigeria's Second Republic was, in more ways than is commonly realised, the creation of the post-1966 military government. In a series of actions (and reactions) extending over thirteen and a half years, the military leaders laid the groundwork for the liberal–democratic government which followed. This is as true of the enactment of ethnic conflicts and the inflation of corruption as it is of the creation of a new balance of federalism and the imposition of the formally liberal-democratic governing institutions. And by extension it is also true, in some measure, of the pathologies and structural defects of the Second Republic which led to its overthrow by the military on 31 December 1983.

The first military interregnum[1]

The Nigerian military in power has never aspired to do more than 'correct' the political system in order to restore order, discipline, stability and unity to economic and social life. This was the declared intention of all four regimes in the first period of military rule (1966–79) as well as of the more recent military governments under Buhari and Babangida (since 1984). Its style and substance have thus rightly been described as 'a kind of symbiosis of bourgeois constitutionalism and military–civilian emergency power' (Hutchenreuter, 1980:134). The courts, the civil service, the police, the public corporations and private business were all permitted – indeed encouraged – to carry on 'business as usual', subject only to occasional commands or decrees which were invariably declared to be in the 'national interest'. The Nigerian state under military government was thus anything but 'revolutionary' or 'totalitarian'.

The legal foundation of military rule, The Constitution (Suspension and Modification) Decree No. 1 of 1966, abolished the national parliament and Regional legislatures, empowered the federal military government to make laws for the 'peace, order and good government' of the country, and vested supreme legislative as well as executive power in that body. Subsequent decrees somewhat modified the formulas of federalism and the modalities of rule, but the underlying principle of military supremacy was maintained until 1 October 1979 and has re-emerged again since 31 December 1983.

At first glance, the ease with which the military has been able to assume supreme political power is astounding. Quite literally overnight, this minuscule (10,500 men in 1965), relatively inexperienced (80% of its officers had no more than four years in service), poorly educated (66% of combat and non-combat officers had no more than secondary education before being commissioned) and young (62% were between 20 and 24 years old) entity[2] overthrew the First Republic and eliminated many of its most prominent leaders. In fact the *coup* itself was engineered by a group of five majors; the military hierarchy merely accepted and took over the *fait accompli*.

However, a second glance suggests that the army's strength was not the decisive factor, but the weakened and decayed condition of the First Republic. The preceding chapter has underlined the sectional–factional disputes and the erosion of popular support of the republican regime. To this must be added the institutional weaknesses of the postcolonial society discussed in the last chapter. The military was one of the very few organised, functionally specific groups in Nigerian society, the sole one, apart from the police, in possession of arms, and hence a 'natural' successor organisation to the discredited political class.

The first military government under Major-General Johnson Aguiyi-Ironsi, an Igbo, was therefore generally favourably received. Even those federal cabinet members who had not been killed during the *coup* seemed to support the General initially. Although he perceived Nigeria's central problem as that of 'national unity', his solution was – fatally – wide of the mark. The *coup* instigators managed to kill the premiers of the Northern and Western Regions, the Federal Prime Minister and a number of top army officers who were mainly Northerners, but they notably failed to dispose of the two Igbo premiers and Igbo officers, including, of course, Ironsi himself. Neither were the 'January Boys' – the majors who had set off the *coup*, four of whom were Igbo – brought to trial nor did Ironsi appear to include any non-Igbo in his inner circle of confidants.

All these developments did nothing to allay Northerners' growing apprehensions about what they feared (not without reason) was a campaign to extend Igbo hegemony into the military, civil service, education and commerce. Thus when on 24 May Ironsi, in a nation-wide broadcast, unilaterally proclaimed the creation of a unitary republic, the transformation of the former Regions into mere territorial units now to be called provinces, the establishment of a unified national civil service and the banning of political and tribal organisations for two years,[3] the North balked. Student demonstrations in favour of Northern secession broke out in May. Many Igbo living in the North were harassed and killed, and their property looted or destroyed in the course of the infamous May riots.

Finally, in July, Northern officers successfully brought off a second military *coup*, killing in the process General Ironsi, Brigadier Fajuyi (the Western military governor), a number of other Igbo officers and soldiers, and some civilians. After this second *coup*, senior Northern officers were unable to control their own ranks and during a four-day period practically all Igbo army officers stationed outside their own Region were (often brutally) murdered.

It became evident that the July *coup* represented the North's successful attempt to assert, or reassert, its control over the army and, through it, the nation. The decision as to who would lead the revamped military government, however, was not so readily apparent. The senior surviving military leader, Brigadier Ogundipe – a Yoruba – was simply passed over. Murtala Mohammed, a dynamic but rather impetuous Northerner, nearly prevailed with his proposal for secession by the North. But in the end the 31-year-old Army Chief of Staff, Lieut.-Colonel Yakubu Gowon, a member of the Middle-Belt Angas tribe and a graduate of Sandhurst, emerged as head of the re-formed military government. Significantly, the only challenge to his appointment came from the Eastern military commander, Lieut.-Colonel Chukwuemeka Ojukwu, who asserted that he was prepared to recognise only Ironsi, if still alive, or Ogundipe as supreme commander.

Like Ironsi before him, Gowon was immediately confronted with the urgent problem of finding a solution to the questions of crumbling federalism and a return to civilian rule. (It is worth noting that military government in Nigeria has always been popularly regarded as a 'necessary evil'. Consequently all the military heads of state have been under considerable pressure to be seen to be taking positive action towards re-instituting civilian rule and to furnish the public with specific timetables for it.)

Gowon took immediate steps to marshall support for his military government. He renounced all plans for a unitary governmental structure and made the first of several pledges for a phased return to civilian rule. He also released from custody a number of prominent politicians, among them Chief Obafemi Awolowo and Chief Anthony Enahoro. Then he convened a series of advisory groups, 'leaders of thought', and consultative assemblies to deliberate and advise on the nation's future. These all crystallised in mid-September as the Ad Hoc Constitutional Conference to which each of the Regions sent delegations.

The issue of national cohesion again loomed large at that Conference. Just before it opened, a series of reports of terrorism and violence against Igbo in the North, and of counter-violence against Northerners in the South, was widely disseminated. The Conference's protracted deliberations on an acceptable formula for maintaining the federation were prematurely ended with the news of renewed massacres in the North and of retaliatory actions in the South.

Not surprisingly, these events resulted in a massive polarisation of the population. Perhaps a million Easterners returned from the North to the Eastern Region, to be joined later by some half-million more from the Western and Mid-Western Regions. In October Ojukwu ordered all non-Easterners out of his Region, stating that he could no longer be responsible for their safety. And in November he refused to participate further in the constitutional discussions in Lagos.

When a last-ditch meeting between Gowon and Ojukwu in Aburi, Ghana in January 1967 failed to produce any agreement – but rather resulted in a monumental misunderstanding – between the two men on the subject of a revised federalism, secession appeared inevitable. In April, the Eastern Region ceased paying federal taxes and took over control of all federal utilities. On 27 May the Eastern Consultative Assembly, at Ojukwu's instigation, empowered him to declare the formation of a separate Biafran nation. Gowon, in an astute but no longer timely counter-move, decreed a substantial change in the federal structure: in place of the former four Regions, twelve States were now called into existence. In particular, the reform divided up the Northern Region into six States, thus assuaging Southern apprehensions about a 'monolithic' North and meeting the demands of minority Northern ethnic groups; and it separated the Eastern Region into three States, thereby isolating the Igbo from other minority groups in the East. On 30 May, at 2.00 a.m., Ojukwu summoned diplomats and journalists to the State House in Enugu where he proclaimed the new Republic of Biafra. Though more than a month passed before actual fighting broke out, the Nigerian Civil War was, effectively, in progress.

This is not the place to give an account of the Civil War. Many excellent and comprehensive studies have already been carried out, notably by Anthony Kirk-Greene (1971), John de St. Jorre (1972) and Zdenek Cervenka (1971). But the central issue of the war was essentially the same as that of pre- and post-colonial politics: national cohesion. The war was fought largely to determine whether or not Nigeria would continue as a federation according to Gowon's twelve-State scheme, or would split into its component parts in a confederal system, as Ojukwu wanted. The outcome, after two and a half years and between 500,000 and 1,000,000 deaths, represented an enforced military solution to the perennial problem of the proper balance of federalism and the role of elite groupings therein.

If the Federal Military Government did not exactly provide a textbook lesson in how to conduct a *war* – stories of inefficiency, indiscipline among the ranks, lost opportunities and the like were rampant – it did in some measure demonstrate how a lasting *peace* could be made. In a series of magnanimous gestures, Gowon, quoting Abraham Lincoln, spoke of 'binding up the nation's wounds', declared an amnesty to all who had fought on the Biafran side, and announced that since there had been 'no victors and no vanquished' no medals would be struck or presented in this campaign. The Biafrans, now again citizens of Nigeria, were relieved when no (organised) reprisals were taken against them, and the fear of imminent 'genocide' proved to be nothing more than a propaganda device. The spirit of reconciliation and unity in the formidable task of rebuilding and reconstruction, remarkably, seemed to infuse the popular consciousness.

The post-war situation, with its new constellation of possibilities and problems, in the end proved too much for the Gowon regime. Initially, however, those problems amenable to swift, surgical solution were tackled with dispatch in line with Gowon's well-known three Rs slogan: Reconstruction, Rehabilitation, Reconciliation. The military government decimalised the currency, effected a change in the traffic system from left-hand to right-hand driving, decreed a long-overdue national census for 1973, legislated the further indigenisation of certain classes of enterprise, and established the National Youth Service Corps, a kind of non-military conscription system for graduates. Gowon also altered the previous system of revenue allocation, by means of channelling oil and other revenues through the Federal Treasury, in order to distribute the vastly increased national income more evenly among the individual states.

The preservation of the territorial state, the process of national reconciliation, the sudden windfall of oil revenues, a popular awareness of being part of the scheme of things, a burgeoning business sector – all of these factors created an auspicious situation for a rapid return to civilian rule. After all, the military had always claimed to be a guest in power, a mere corrective regime necessitated by the failures of the 'corrupt' and 'venal' politicians of the civilian government. And indeed much of the military's popular acceptance (or legitimacy) was attributable to its self-proclaimed transitional tenure in power, deriving its vitality from a self-image of a 'hard-headed and practical approach' which was at the same time 'symbolic of the revolutionary tradition.' (Garba, 1979)

Again and again the military had reiterated its intention of handing over to duly elected representatives of the people once it had attended to the unsolved problems. Thus on Independence Day 1970 Gowon announced firm plans for a return to civilian rule by 1976. According to his nine-point programme, however, the following conditions had to be fulfilled prior to any such transition: re-organisation of the armed forces, implementation of the National Development Plan and repair of all war damage, elimination of corruption from national life, settlement of the question of more States, preparation and adoption of a new constitution, introduction of a new formula for revenue allocation, conduct of a population census, formation of 'genuinely national' political parties, and election of state and national governments.

The opportunities afforded by the situation called for bold, dynamic and immediate measures. Gowon's plan for recivilianisation could only be realised if steps were taken to bring about the necessary preconditions. We now know that, with the civil war over and the process of reconstruction begun, the Gowon regime was beset by inertia and torpidity, with the result that a number of persistent problems were never solved, no steps were taken toward demilitarisation, and eventually the regime, like its civilian predecessor, foundered in a morass of inaction, corruption and inefficiency. How did this happen?

One of the principal inertia-producing factors was the military itself. The post-civil war army, bloated with a troop strength of nearly a quarter of a million, was a persistent drain on federal funds. Poorly equipped, inadequately housed, badly trained, and frequently undisciplined, the oversized army was a problem to military and civilian leaders alike. Between 80 and 90% of the military budget was consumed by salaries alone. The obvious solution was partial demobilisation. From the army's point of view, monies set free in this way could be put into re-equipping and modernising its obsolete force. But the release of large numbers of ex-soldiers into the economy would undoubtedly induce a rise in unemployment, greater demands on public welfare services and an increase in crime, particularly armed robbery (which in any case increased dramatically after 1970).

Post-January 1966 events, moreover, once and for all put paid to the popular image of the army as a force for national unity. Far from being a cohesive, united, 'corrective' instrument, the Nigerian military proved to be a reflection of the ethnic and social tensions which had plagued the country since independence. The first *coup*, for example, was intended to suppress the ethnic–tribal rivalries and overwhelming regionalism that had crippled the civilian regimes. But the subsequent ethnic differences which were reproduced within the army resulted, in the course of the second *coup* and later massacres, in more intense violence than anything produced under the civilian regimes. Once the initial *putsch* had been executed, the precedent of violent military action as a means and extension of ethnic politics was well established and in a sense legitimated. Military organisations by nature have few conciliatory (or 'feedback') mechanisms beyond that of internal discipline. Once that discipline is shaken, for example by a *coup*, its cohesive force is sapped and few restraints remain to check a headlong flight into violence and counter-violence. As Martin Dent rightly suggests (1972:386), moreover, the military is merely one institution within the larger society whose conflicts and tendencies it mirrors:

> If the regioanl tensions in the body politic itself are very acute and if the means of the coming to power of the military increases those tensions and brings them into the army itself, then, far from the army uniting the body politic, the body politic may divide the army. We are left with a situation where the officers of a certain tribal group become but the armed wing of a tribal political group.

Similarly, the army's claim to the right to exercise political power also rested on its ostensible ability to eliminate corruption and preserve law and order. But under military rule, especially during the later years of the Gowon administration, corruption became more widespread and more flagrant (albeit less visible) than had ever occurred under the civilian government.[4] And again the Igbo massacres in the North, partly incited and carried out by soldiers, as well as the many crimes committed by the military during and after the war, and the susceptibility of many officers to bribery and corruption, hardly vindicated the military leaders' claims to be a supra-political moral force in national life. It was, furthermore, military officers who had actually instigated the civil war and who were instrumental in prosecuting it.

All these problems – demobilisation, corruption, actual and potential inter-ethnic rivalry – go some way toward accounting for the inaction of the military government under Gowon. If demobilisation were accomplished at the apparent expense of any ethnic group, the issue of tribalism–regionalism might again flare up. Moreover, there was no scheme for the re-integration of the released soldiers into civilian life. Many newer soldiers and younger officers who had benefited from the opportunities for rapid upward mobility during the war were opposed to any cuts or threats of cuts whatsoever.

In any case no clearly defined role for the army in peacetime under a civilian regime had been laid down, so that there could be no guidelines for a reorganised (and reduced) army. In this situation many military men were receptive to former President Azikiwe's proposals of 1970 and 1972 for the creation of a 'dyarchy' or power-sharing arrangement between civilian and military leaders – proposals which in various forms have found their way back into the political discussion since the 1983/4 New Year's *coup*.

At the very pinnacle of the military government, corruption and dissoluteness seemed to be most pronounced, with the State military governors and higher civil servants apparently colluding in a pact to divide the spoils of government and the economy among themselves and their kin. The 1974 scandals surrounding the Governor of Benue-Plateau State, Joseph Gomwalk, and that State's representative on the Federal Executive Council, Joseph Tarka, were only one prominent example of this trend.

The regime's malaise extended into a number of other vital areas. The 1973 census, widely discredited because of irregularities and inflated figures, was neither scrapped nor validated; and since it was directly tied to the question of federal revenue allocation, smouldering ethnic rivalries again threatened to ignite over the division of the national fiscal 'cake'. In education, the government announced that universal primary education (UPE) would be available by 1976, but it then took little action aimed at realising this goal. The issue of creating more States was discussed, but no specific means for consultation and evaluation preparatory to passing the necessary legislation were ever provided. There were increasing shortages of essential commodities, notably petrol. Port congestion became a hopeless bottleneck, particularly after the arrival of two million tons of cement under the most suspicious of circumstances. The future location of the new and urgently needed federal capital was not decided, nor even a committee appointed to start action on it. Huge salary increments which followed publication of the Udoji Report tended to benefit higher civil servants while bypassing middle-rank public servants and workers in the private sector. One result was some industrial unrest. Another was inflation which reached 50% within a few months of the awards.

By his protracted inaction, Gowon, it seemed, was exacerbating the very problems which he had declared must be solved prior to recivilianisation in 1976. When on 1 October 1974 he announced an indefinite postponement of the promised return to elected civilian rule, therefore, most sectors of the population – including the divided and potentially unstable army – were thoroughly dissatisfied.

It is hardly surprising then, that the bloodless *coup* of 29 July 1975 which removed Gowon, was met with widespread manifestations of relief and elation. Only one military commander took steps to support Gowon, but his efforts came too late. The new regime was headed by Brigadier Murtala Mohammed, with Brigadier Olusegun Obasanjo as Chief of Staff, Supreme Headquarters and Brigadier Theophilus Danjuma as Chief of Staff, Army.

The new government acted rapidly and decisively. Its targets, of course, were the abuses and omissions of the preceding regime. The former State governors were dismissed and a series of inquiries instigated into their corrupt practices. The structure of military government was modified so that the new State governors were responsible directly to Supreme Headquarters and no longer operated State governments as their personal fiefdoms. The reformed military government then became the central agency for eliminating inefficiency and corruption from public life. Some 10–11,000 civil servants, including not a few well-known upper-echelon figures in the universities, police, statutory corporations, judiciary and state administration, were retired or dismissed. Tribunals at various levels uncovered serious irregularities in administrative practices, hiring policies, contract-awarding procedures and revenue allocation. Even in the army, all officers above the rank of Brigadier were retired, and plans were formulated to reduce the number of enlisted personnel from 250,000 to 100,000. By 1979 the army's strength had in fact dropped to some 180,000.

Measures were taken to unblock the constitutional impasse that had developed. The 1973 census was simply declared invalid and revenue allocation, State creation, etc. were instead based on the – also somewhat dubious – 1963 census. A five-man advisory committee weighed the evidence and listened to some 200 proposals before recommending the creation of twenty States. The government then decided on nineteen States, and the new units were declared final. Further reforms were effected in the sphere of local government (see chapter 9). A committee on the establishment of a federal capital also reported back to the military government, and a binding decision was made in favour of the more centrally located Abuja. Public Complaints Commissions were set up at State and national levels to hear and deal with citizens' complaints against government actions or policies. A second Indigenisation Decree in 1976, augmenting that of 1972, further hastened the conversion of selected foreign-owned enterprises into (relatively few) Nigerian hands. Action was also taken to reform (and discipline) trade union organisation and create a single trade union congress in place of the former localised and fragmented organisations. Even in the area of foreign affairs, the dynamism of the new regime was evident. In place of a rather 'low-profile' and pro-western approach to world affairs, the 'new' Nigeria rapidly became a leading advocate of African unity, a prominent opponent of racism and neo-colonialism and increasingly a leader of African non-alignment in the East-West controversy.

When an abortive *coup* in February 1976 felled Murtala Mohammed, it was widely agreed that in six months his government had achieved more, and greater, accomplishments than the three preceding governments. The *coup* was not generally supported; on the contrary, subsequent public action indicates that during his brief regency Murtala Mohammed had become a popular leader. Even the post-1983 military government has acknowledged him as a model and inspiration. In the event, the *coup* leaders, Dimka, Bisalla, *et al.* were executed. The new Head of State, Lieut.-General Obasanjo, with his chief of the Supreme Military Council, Brigadier Shehu Yar'Adua, carried on Mohammed's policies with no more than minor modifications, though perhaps with less élan and zeal.

Chief among these policies was the military government's political programme for a phased, carefully co-ordinated return to civilian rule and the establishment of a constitutionally based liberal democracy. The programme, which is described at greater length in the next chapter, included the formation of a Constitution Drafting Committee to write a new constitution and a Constituent Assembly to amend and ratify it, public consultation at all stages, local government council elections, the readmission and close regulation of political parties, universal adult election of federal and State politicians, and the return to civilian rule 'not a day later than October 1, 1979', as Murtala Mohammed had pledged.

Centralism: the shifting balance of domestic power

The internal structure of Nigeria's first military interregnum was relatively straightforward, and need not be dwelt on here. Corresponding to the organisation of the military hierarchy itself, it was relentlessly centralist both in spirit and in substance. No doubt this tendency also reflected popular reaction against the centrifugal federalism which had characterised the First Republic. And the 30-month civil war, with its pressures toward corporate solidarity and unity of command, certainly enhanced the centralism of the country's governing bodies.

By means of a series of decrees and *de facto* developments after the 1966 *coups*, all the powers of the leading political institutions – legislature, executive, civil service – were formally arrogated by the Head of the Military Government. On the face of it therefore the military, like military governments elsewhere, appeared to have eliminated all countervailing institutions and to have centralised powers under itself. But in fact both the great diversity of Nigeria and the pluralist forces within society did compel the military government to develop a partial division of labour and specialisation of function which came to resemble a system of quasi-separation of powers and quasi-federalism, since unmitigated centralist rule, in the Nigerian context, was practically impossible – as the Ironsi regime quickly discovered when it attempted to impose unitary government on the country.

Thus the Supreme Military Council (SMC) incorporated the military governors of the 12 States (in addition to the service heads), which amounted to a scheme of geographical representation or quasi-federalism. The same body also functioned partially as a 'legislature' inasmuch as it turned into a 'sounding board' for local interests prior to the passage of relevant legislation normally introduced by the military leaders of the SMC. At the same time, the Federal Executive Council (FEC) which included civilian commissioners, operated analogously to an executive branch of government, since it was charged with the carrying out of numerous decrees. The FEC was, of course, endowed with certain deliberative functions as well, so that it also operated in many ways like a legislature. The judiciary, which in 1966 was subordinated to the SMC, regained its independence by a 1970 Decree promulgated by the federal military government. Except for limited military incursions concerning specific issues, it retained its relative autonomy throughout the rest of military government rule.

At the State level too, from 1967 on each government had its own State Executive Council under a military governor, but also including civilian commissioners. Decree No. 32 of 1975 then set up the National Council of States composed of essentially the same membership as the FEC, but like it, allowing for a varying number of civilian appointees. Again, as a concession to federalism and pluralism, its powers were advisory with respect to economic and social matters pertaining to the States and to the co-ordination of States' needs in federal development plans.

Moreover, since the military government had eliminated the political class from the leading positions, or had reincorporated individual members in such subordinate capacities as commissioners, advisers and ambassadors, and since its political goals were anything but revolutionary, it was compelled to raise the civil service to a position of 'junior partner' in the business of governing. In many ways the alliance between the soldiers and civil servants was a 'natural' one, since both groups occupied a similar social–structural position as members of the 'intendant' classes, and as such tended to share certain attitudes and orientations, such as career-mindedness, hierarchical organisation, 'non-political' ethos and a proclivity towards a national outlook. If the Nigerian military, like military regimes virtually everywhere,[5] had to turn to the civil servants to find the administrative personnel, expertise and at least a modicum of the responsive capacity which it lacked, the bureaucrats, under the military aegis, stood to extend the scope of their authority and power, and to draw closer to the centres of income generation and distribution, thus in some measure moving into the vacuum left by the proscribed politicians – but simultaneously taking on many of the latter's problems, as will be demonstrated below. And where the military–civil service structures could not furnish the responsive capacity or 'feedback' once provided by political parties and politicians, the military often turned to 'corporatist' institutions to articulate *some* class interests: the Nigerian Employers' Consultative Association (NECA), the Nigerian Chamber of Commerce and Industry (NCCI), the Nigerian Institute of Management (NIM) and – far less frequently – the trade unions and farmers' associations. As may be inferred from this list, a third and increasingly important partner entered the military–civil service coalition: business. Its role will be discussed in the following chapter.

Centralist by organisation and outlook, relatively unimpeded by local or regional claims and pressures, frequently guided by ideals of nationalism or national greatness, and standing to advance their own careers considerably, the military–civil service coalition set about 'correcting' Nigeria's factional, divisive and therefore dysfunctional development by means of far-reaching and comprehensive – but not revolutionary – programmes of consolidation and centralisation.

(i) *Politically*, the creation of 12, then 19, States in place of the former four Regions, on the one hand, offered most minority groups formerly under the hegemony of one of the three major ethnic groups the prospect of socio-cultural autonomy, thereby increasing their loyalty to, or at least greater acceptance of, the federal government. On the other hand, it broke down the ethno-regional power blocs and, coupled with greater revenue control at the centre, ensured that each of the States – administered by military governors and civil servants responsible to the federal government – would in effect remain client States of the federal government, forced now to look to the centre for leadership, economic planning and overall development. At the same time, the States' former independent law-making powers, as embodied by the old concurrent legislative lists, were arrogated by the centre.

(ii) *Administratively*, the proliferation of States set off a rapid growth in the civil service establishment. Absolute numbers of civil servants, already swollen by the post-independence Nigerianisation of the bureaucracy, expanded still further with (a) the expansion of the 'politically relevant' population, which increased the quantity of demands placed on the system, and (b) the extension of the civil service into remote and rural areas in line with the policy of development administration. The civil service machinery was made to reflect the principle of federal supremacy. A sustained effort was undertaken to recruit leading personnel into the federal service, which was now considered primary. Among other incentives, the federal bureaucrats were offered higher salaries and better conditions of service. For the first time, Nigerians from all over the federation were attracted into the national civil service in large numbers: Southern-based civil servants who saw the federal apparatus as the best avenue to enhance their career prospects, since it was expanding more than twelve times as rapidly as the State bodies, and 'progressive' Nothern bureaucrats who saw in the federal penetration into the North a source of new opportunities for advancement as well as a means of undermining the power of encrusted traditional authorities and thus of accelerating the process of development. The military government established several special national councils to provide consultation on and co-ordination of activities related to works and health, housing, agriculture, finance and personnel and establishments. And a number of intergovernmental administrative institutions – for example, the Nigerian Council for Science and Technology, the Medical Research Council, Agricultural Research Council, Natural Resources Research Council – were 'created ostensibly to provide avenues of Federal-State consultation and cooperation but actually to provide additional pressure points for integration and federal dominance' (Olatunde Ojo, 1976).

(iii) *Educationally*, primary and secondary schooling were made part of the concurrent list in 1973, thus, as has been shown, effectively bringing them under federal control. Institutions of higher education were at the same time made an exclusively federal area of competence.

(iv) *Economically*, finally (and most important), the central government from the late 1960s on became more and more the principal generator, collector and distributor of funds. First, the prosecution of the war necessitated a re-orientation of the economy. To achieve greater efficiency and enhanced self-sufficiency, it was necessary to centralise and streamline the economic–administrative apparatus which, for its part, was thus enabled to undertake a number of vital reforms such as increased import-substitution, protectionism, restrictive trade measures and the adoption of new policy priorities. This amounted to a fairly comprehensive, albeit initially *ad hoc*, programme of state intervention in and control of the essential sectors of the economy which, though initiated as a measure of expediency, proved to be unexpectedly effective in terms of enhanced efficiency and generation of surplus capital.[6] The legal–administrative foundations for the aggrandisement of federal economic powers were furnished in 1970 with the suspension of section 164 of the Republican Constitution which required the federal government to consult with the Regions before altering fiscal arrangements. Subsequent unilateral reviews of federal-State revenue arrangements in 1975 and 1978 resulted in further central gains at the expense of the States.

The end of the civil war roughly coincided with the beginning of the massive extraction of oil in and around the Niger Delta area. If by 1971/2 oil revenues accounted for about half of all government revenue, by 1975/6, following the first OPEC price escalation, they made up about 93% of export earnings (Williams and Turner, 1978:153), a percentage which has since held more or less constant. Total federal revenues were collected by the central government and distributed, according to varying formulas, to the States, so that by 1977/8 the centre was disbursing some 37.6% of the States' total revenues and in 1978/9 a peak of 94.6%.[7]

With these developments, the federal government could scarcely avoid – even had it sought to do so – becoming the focus of national economic activity. Independent State sources of revenue-raising were eroded as economic power accrued to the centre. Separate State powers of taxation and levying customs/excise duties, automatic revenues based on derivation, and other income sources once conducive to economic regionalisation were systematically abolished and such revenues diverted to the federally controlled distributable pool account. Noteworthy here was the 1973 conversion of the marketing boards – once a staple source of Regional income – into federal agencies no longer concerned with generating surpluses for Regional government use, but now with promoting agrarian production and productivity and with encouraging more equal regional development. Similarly, the percentage of royalties payable to the States on the basis of the principle of derivation was reduced from 45% to 20%. Thus there was a massive increase in the quantity of federal revenues – over fourteenfold in a single decade, 1970–80 – and a corresponding rise in the amount of federally collected revenue, from N282 m in 1967/8 to N6,100 m in 1976/7. This absolute increase in federal income was augmented by a relative one: prior to 1967 under the four Regions the percentage of national revenues retained by the central government was 65%, but with the advent of 12 States it rose to 72%, and held more or less constant at 71% after the creation of 19 States in 1976.[8]

The development planning process also had to be systematised and centralised. In place of individual Regional or State plans, there was now a single Federal Plan, formulated by a Central Planning Office in Lagos, working with the State Planning Offices and the National Economic Advisory Council, and collaborating with other consultative bodies such as the Joint Planning Boards, the Federal Executive Council, etc. This intricate planning machinery has been analysed carefully by T. O. Odetola (1980) and other writers. It aimed (and aims) at collating and co-ordinating the work of professional planners from both federal and State governments (Central Planning Office) with that of bureaucracies, unions, the professions, commerce and the universities (National Economic Advisory Council) in order to advise government planners and other civil servants engaged in overall plan scrutiny and federal-State collaboration (Joint Planning Board). The entire apparatus, of course, was (and is) subject to final approval of, and receptive to initiatives by, the highest political bodies, namely the SMC and FEC prior to 1 October 1979, and again since 1983/4, and the Federal Executive during the Second Republic.

The state's economic role thus became more extensive and intensive, entering into such key spheres as banking, insurance, imports, tin and coal mining, foreign exchange and basic production, and especially into those areas in which Nigerian entrepreneurs lacked experience and/or financial power. In particular, the state moved rapidly into the 'structure-forming' spheres of the economy, namely those crucial branches of industry with a high capital intensity and gradual capital circulation. This concentration on the basic industries demonstrates the anticipated role of state capitalism as a motor for economic development with the objective of creating an independent industrial base characterised by extensive import substitution and sustained attempts at technology transfer.

These aspects of the evolution of Nigeria's political economy – centralisation of economic control, development planning and an active state role in industrialisation – define the context of the central functions of military government in the development of the political economy and in elite formation. These will be discussed in the next chapter.

Notes

1. Whether in fact it is military rule or civilian rule that must be classified as an 'interregnum' is an issue that may be deferred until chapters 8 and 11; the use of the term here merely follows popular usage.
2. All statistics from Billy J. Dudley, 'Military Government and National Integration in Nigeria', in Smock and Bentsi-Enchill, 1976, p. 36.
3. On Ironsi's proposed structural changes, see Decree No. 34 of 1966. For commentary and analysis see Dudley, 1982, p. 87.
4. Dudley, 1982, provides details of irregular self-enrichment by members of the state elite: Governor Joseph Gomwalk of Plateau State, Governor S. O. Ogbemudia of Midwest State, State Administrator Ukpabi Asika of Enugu (later East-Central) State, and Governor Usman Faruk of Sokoto State. He also (pp. 119–20) writes that: 'the disclosures before the Assets Investigation Panel showed, for example, that at the time the military governors were thrown out of office following the July 1975 coup, the average commercial property holdings of each of the (then 12) governors was some eight houses ranging in value from N49,000 to N120,000 and no fewer than seven of the high-ranking members of the military – including the last military Head of State, General Obasanjo – retired or was retired from the army to start a new career in large-scale farming. All acquired their farming estates while the military was in power. The bulk of the commercial property holdings of the regime managers, interestingly enough, were in the middle-class residential areas of the main urban centres. The Rent Decree

of 1976, which was aimed at controlling rents in the urban areas, actually led to an increase in rent, an increase of between a third and a half, in these areas. As most of the residents in such housing were public servants who therefore had their rents highly subsidised by state agencies – the various governments, para-statals and universities – the effect of the Rent Decree was simply to legalise the transfer of public funds – in the form of rent subsidies – from the state's coffers into the pockets of those who held the reins of political power.'

5. G. Edward Feit, *The Armed Bureaucrats*, Boston, 1973, pp. 2ff.
6. On this, see, *inter alia*, Aboyade and Ayida, 1971.
7. Olatunde J. B. Ojo, 'The Changing Balance of Centre-Periphery Relations', in W. D. Graf (ed.), *Towards A Political Economy of Nigeria: Critical Essays*, Benin City and Cambridge–New York (forthcoming), here quoted from manuscript, p. 39.
8. Federal Republic of Nigeria, *Report of the Technical Committee on Revenue Allocation* (2 vols.), Lagos, December 1977, Vol. I, p. 20.

4

Indigenisation, Recivilianisation and Elite Formation

State capitalism and indigenisation

The combination of wartime rationalisation and centralisation of the economy, and the revenues generated by the oil bonanza, led, in the decade following the civil war, to a qualitative transformation of the Nigerian political economy. It was a period characterised above all by an increasing, and increasingly active, state involvement in the economy particularly in the interrelated processes of industrialisation and indigenisation, an era which Peter Waterman calls 'the period of peripheral capitalist industrialization'[1] and which I. V. Sledzevski terms 'a special stage in the development of state capitalism in Nigeria'.[2] Both authors are attempting conceptually to come to terms with the fact that the Nigerian economy since 1970 has gone beyond its neo-laissez-faire, open-door phase – or, as Waterman puts it, the 'robber baron phase of regionalized, tribalized and centrifugal commercial capitalist competition' – into a new stage of state-sponsored, but still dependent (or 'peripheral') industrialization, along the capitalist road to development and within the framework of a more genuinely 'national' economy.

However, the state's role ought not to be misinterpreted as some variety of state socialism, much less as evidence of a 'mixed economy'. Rather, state economic intervention has been a conscious means of, first, generating continued economic growth and, second, appropriating the surplus value for the elite. Since the former has absolute priority – because the latter, private appropriation, is its consequence – the state occasionally must impinge on the interests of this or that sector of the bourgeoisie. But this is only a manifestation of state capitalism's *raison d'être*: the co-ordination and, if necessary, the overriding of particularist elite interest is in the long-term collective or hegemonic interests of the elite class as a whole. In order to ensure this necessary growth, the state first assumes control over the most dynamic sectors of the economy (oil). It then creates or extends the infrastructure of extraction (transport, communications), while simultaneously eroding independent State sources of revenue-raising (abolition of separate taxation, derivation, and in particular marketing boards) and integrating all sectors and regions by means of a comprehensive process of national planning (Five Year Plans) combined with revenue allocation by the centre which helps to overcome destabilising regional imbalances. The private appropriation of the surplus thus generated follows quasi-automatically by the passive technique of failing to change the existing class structure and system of rewards allocation.

This interrelationship between state capitalism and private appropriation suggests the close connection between economic boom and the emergence, during the 1970s, of a more coherent, rationalised system of elite interaction. For one, the factionalisation of the First Republic and, in particular, the civil war had demonstrated that uncontained intra-class struggles – comprador versus national bourgeoisie, traditional versus modern claims, and the regionalised/tribalised war of all against all – threaten the survival of the very fount of accumulation itself: the Nigerian state. 'It is as if the class needed to fight a war', Olufemi Taiwo writes, 'to realize how much its members have in common and have a duty to protect and expand'.[3] Second, the massive increase in State revenues accruing in this period from the burgeoning oil economy not only expanded the absolute size of the proverbial national cake, thus making elite access easier all round, but also made the accumulation process more uniform, predictable and hence 'rational', thus reducing the tensions among formerly competitive elite factions.

If the fundamental class cleavage – elite versus masses – therefore did not change substantially during the first military interregnum, the relative strengths of the various groupings who make up the ruling classes did. Seen from Timothy Shaw's 'radical perspective', the succession of more or less violent intra-military personnel shifts in 1966, 1975 and 1976 – and by extension recivilianisation in 1979 and the *coups* of 1983 and 1985 – was merely 'reflective of fractional shifts within the local bourgeoisie and constitute(d) stages in the evolution of social forces in this particular part of the semi-periphery' (1980:80).

The dominant alignment of social forces from January 1966 to October 1979 has been aptly described as a 'triangular elite alliance'[4] of the military, the civil service and various business groupings. Within this constellation, the military were, and remained, by far the politically dominant elite group: the more so under Ironsi's centralised regime and Mohammed's post-purge recivilianising government, the less so under Gowon who incorporated more civil servants and ex-politicians into the ruling group. For it was the military elite who laid down political and economic goals and enforced them, who controlled and manipulated society's other institutions, and who – with its members receiving an average salary eight times the national average, with its many benefits and improvements, with its troop strength of a quarter of a million, and with its 25% and more share of the national budget – was the greatest single beneficiary of military government.

The civil service, for reasons already suggested, was also essential to a military government bent on reforming the economy and society. Szymon Chodak underlines the point in a more general way:[5]

> The bureaucratic elite is important as a stratum in many respects. Lack of support of the civil servants, as was especially evident in the case of Kwame Nkruma's rule [in Ghana] can incapacitate political leadership. Nothing works if the civil servants do not do their job since the institutions composing the organization of the modernized part of African socio-economic life are no less than in other countries of the contemporary world a part of an administered society. Organized groups with enough power to exert pressure on the civil service to subordinate their activities to the needs of the society are practically absent. The governments, whether civilian or military, regardless of their official proclamations, depend, in the final instance, on civil servants' support which they have to elicit by all available means. The civil servants are also the main market for consumer goods, whether imported or produced locally. Hence, both the political elite as well as the subordinate population depend on this stratum.

In many respects, the younger, middle-level civil servants, along with many professionals, academics and military officers, had constituted a marginal faction of the elite, perhaps even a partial counter-elite during the First Republic, since they had been largely excluded from the system of rewards and relegated to a subordinate, service capacity. The advent of military government presented these civil servants with a welcome opportunity rapidly to enhance their status and income.

The role of business in this scheme of things, as already suggested, was initially that of a subordinate grouping, tied as it was to the more narrow political class of locally or regionally based politicians and their clientele of traders, contractors, land speculators and the like – the main propagators of 'tribalism' and regionalism. This is not to suggest that the latter groups were excluded completely from the ruling circles. Only their *relative hegemony* declined, so that they became junior partners in the elite coalition under military rule, rather than codetermining principals. Many of the old politicians, for example, retained government posts as civilian commisioners or as members of consultative bodies such as Gowon's 'leaders of thought' or as co-opted members of State cabinets. And certainly many sectors among the 'national' business bourgeoisie carried on much as before. But the nature of the comprador classes did change somewhat: as the civil service's powers grew in proportion to state intervention in the economy many middlemen, whose function had been to 'mediate' between foreign interests and local political leaders, were now made redundant, since ' "statist" compradors were increasingly able to exclude them and in effect replace some triangular relationships with bilateral ones' (Turner, 1976:9). Only when the civil service and military had interpenetrated with, and/or transformed themselves into, a business class, did business become a stronger faction in the elite coalition.

The increased pre-eminence of the intendant classes was significant in a number of ways. For one, class *formation*, rather than class *conflict*, is the more salient form of class action in any analysis of the Nigerian ruling class in this period, as Richard Sklar reminds us.[6] The peculiar forms of class-formation struggles under the military government are frequently misinterpreted as inter-generational conflicts, Sklar argues, but what is at work is really an *intra-class* struggle. The sub-class of politicians and related business groups, who happen to be of an older generation, had been largely regionalised and particularised by the nature of their power base, as chapters 1 and 2 have shown. The bureaucratic-technocratic-military sub-class, who happened to be younger on average, derived their power positions from membership in institutions – civil service, military, universities, etc. – which were based on an ethos of rationality, impersonality and universality (i.e. were 'national'). There was also an important North–South dimension at work here: the odd political class, dominated at the federal level by Northerners, gave way to the new intendant classes who, on account of the educational history of the country, consisted mostly of Southerners.[7] Furthermore, as Sklar points out the rising classes were distanced by education and outlook from the masses, and increasingly had to realise that, even though discredited and divided, the old political classes had an important role to play in the maintenance of popular support and legitimacy of the ruling order – not unlike the traditional rulers (see chapter 9).

All these fractional developments and shifts within the Nigerian bourgeoisie may be interpreted in terms of intra-elite struggles and the need to 'nationalise' (as opposed to 'particularise') the economy and polity, insofar as channels were needed to enact disputes among the various elite groups, who now looked increasingly to the system's centre for the realisation of their interests and goals, rather than to local or regional sub-systems. This tendency was reflected in the evolution of state capitalism, the increase in federal powers and the influx of oil revenues during the 1970s. The new institutions of federalism, for example, even as they established the machinery for 'national integration' (especially of the various elite groupings) also benefited the intendant stratum. With reference to the proliferation of States, Okwudiba Nnoli demonstrates that their particular interests were and are well served:[8]

> (W)ho benefits from the establishment of these states? Certainly not the farmer or worker, but the bureaucrats who become permanent secretaries overnight, the university dons who achieve professorial status irrespective of merit because of new universities located in their states, the university dons, lawyers, and doctors who become commissioners, chairmen of public corporations and directors of various institutes and broadcasting services, and the contractors and businessmen who monopolize official contracts in their states of origin.

State capitalism – the conversion of publicly created profits into private gains, *as if* the state sector were privately owned – is also the context of the much misunderstood and misrepresented state policy of economic nationalism or 'indigenisation'. Indigenisation, or the state-decreed transfer of ownership, management and control of commercial and industrial enterprises from foreign into Nigerian hands, is part of a state-capitalist strategy of development, and is supposed to parallel in the economic sphere what national independence achieved in the realm of politics; hence the widespread notion of economic nationalism.

A general commitment to indigenisation was first anchored, by the military elite, under pressures from the reforming local business elite, in the Second National Development Plan and the policy has been executed through the Nigerian Enterprises Promotion Decree (NEPD) of February 1972, later intensified by Decree No. 3 of 1977 following on the report of the Industrial Enterprises Panel. The policy represented a conscious attempt to increase the state's leading role in the economy by taking a direct hand in production, especially in large-scale, long-term investments, by buying shares in some industries while aiding individual Nigerians to purchase shares in others, and by participating directly in industrial development – all this, in the words of the Decree 'in order to ensure that the economic destiny of Nigeria is determined by Nigerians themselves'.

The strategy of indigenisation consisted, and consists, mainly in compelling foreign concerns, within an overall framework of national development planning, to sell off a proportion of their Nigerian operations to indigenous businessmen, civil servants, the general public and – as a last resort – the States and the federal government. The extent of indigenous control mandated is dependent upon the perceived capacity of local personnel to take over. Thus the ratio varies (in terms of the 1977 Decree) from 100% Nigerian ownership/control of retail trade, light manufacturing and most low-technology service firms (Schedule 1) through at least 60% participation in more technology-intensive manufacturing and fiscal sectors such as insurance (Schedule 2) to a minimum 40% ownership of shares in high-technology manufacturing and industry. A number of objectives underlay this strategy, among them the desire of Nigerian commercial and manufacturing interests to reverse the foreign domination of certain sectors of the economy, the experience of the civil war which showed that foreign economic interests do not always coincide with Nigerian political interests, and the 'demonstration effect' of similar developments in other African states.[9] In particular, indigenisation exemplifies express state policies aimed at furthering the interests of the indigenous forming bourgeoisie.

The notion of indigenisation, in the context of capitalist development, however, ought not to be interpreted literally, for it does not aim at a consistent 'nationalisation' – defined here as a transfer from foreign to Nigerian ownership – of the economy. What is intended is, in effect, the transformation of the distributive rather than productive sectors of the economy to a different or 'higher' level of dependency. The country's unabated need for foreign investment and technology transfer was underlined by each succeeding military government. If General Gowon in 1973 spoke of 'attracting more investment in sectors of the economy where Nigerians are not yet able to rely on themselves',[10] then Brigadier Garba, Foreign Minister under the Mohammed/Obasanjo regime, assured foreign and indigenous capitalists that 'all we are trying to do is blend indigenous enterprise and capital with foreign capital, technology and management in such a way as to ensure fairness to foreigners and Nigerians alike'.[11]

Indigenisation can therefore be seen less as an attempt to use state power to overcome the substantial structural problems which persist in the economy – regional imbalances in the distribution and utilisation of human and natural resources, huge urban–rural and upper class–lower class income differentials and discrepancies between the public and private sectors[12] – than as 'an attempt to secure a certain position for growing elite or private entrepreneurs whilst at the same time preserving the dominant place for foreign capital elsewhere in the industrial sector'.[13] Thus indigenisation has fostered an 'indigenous "capitalism" within a framework of continued dependence on foreign enterprise in many sectors' (Collins, 1977:127).[14] This point will be addressed later.

The 'nationalisation' of selected sectors of the economy cannot be equated with the 'socialisation' of the economy in general. Indigenisation is part of an overall programme of *elite accumulation within the parameters of the given socio-economic order*. It is not, and has never aspired to be, a programme of social and economic redistribution and trans-formation geared toward the resolution of the structural contradictions alluded to above. In particular, it reflects the necessity for state intervention to strengthen indigenous capital *vis-à-vis* foreign capital and to compensate for the weakness or inexperience of local capitalists. It is true that, from colonial times onward, the government has owned or controlled large sectors of the economy, primarily in the infrastructure and other non-profit–generating areas, and this phenomenon has led some economists and ideologists to speak of a 'mixed' economy. But when one considers that public investment – particularly massive public investment since the onset of the oil boom – has been overwhelmingly governed and shaped by private interests and that the crucial profit-producing sectors are mostly in private hands, the notion of a partly socialist, partly capitalist 'mixed' economy is a misleading one. The Nigerian road to development has been and remains an unambiguously dependent–capitalist one. The imbalances thus perpetuated – between foreign and indigenous economic control, between the elite and the masses, and between the wealthier and poorer regions – collectively constitute considerable obstacles to further development.

The fact that the takeover of, or achievement of equity in, foreign enterprises has been accomplished by the state *on behalf of* private capital has meant that those elites closest to the state machinery who either own capital or have access to the – largely state–owned – lending institutions are by far the greatest beneficiaries of indigenisation.[15] But the transfer of ownership/control to Nigerians has not increased productivity or economic performance; it has only led to the evolution of a kind of 'drone capitalism'[16] even more dependent upon the state and foreign capital.

The social classes whose fortunes are so interwoven with this economic structure have been aptly called an 'auxiliary bourgeoisie' (Collins, 1977:141) existing in the bureaucratic, managerial and commercial sectors. This auxiliary bourgeoisie consists, first, of Nigerians who have bought shares in the large public companies (Schedule 2, 1972; Schedules 2 and 3, 1977). Upper-level civil servants in particular, with their better access to credit and information and their direct links with foreign companies, have become the 'cadre of the emergent share-owning class'. Second, leading Nigerian executives of foreign-owned companies have also acquired large share-holdings in public companies – often through stock options and special bonuses – especially in the companies which employ them. They are joined by, third, a number of large-scale businessmen and relatively wealthy professional people – but seldom by top military personnel, who tend to prefer the 'quick-gain' sectors such as contracting (Collins, 1977:143). A fourth auxiliary category derives from Nigerians employed in the smaller foreign private companies which were not made public corporations and hence not subject to direct government surveillance. The social antecedents of these share-owners are somewhat more heterogeneous and include 'top civil servants, professionals, big businessmen, some military officers, traditional rulers' families, former politicians, state commissioners and employees and distributors of companies selling the shares'. Consequently Paul Collins rightly sees as one of the major effects of indigenisation 'a tightening nexus between government and foreign capital', which he describes as follows:

> On the one hand important sections of the bureaucratic and managerial bourgeoisie have been coopted as shareholders, while on the other chosen members of the commercial bourgeoisie have secured a niche in the alien-dominated distributive network and therefore tied in, as satellites, through the latter's monopoly of supplies and credit. The state must now protect even more the interests of foreign capital in which the local bourgeoisie has a stake.

It is thus evident that indigenisation's primary social function is to enhance the position of the national and comprador bourgeoisie; indeed it helps to consolidate these factions of the Nigerian elite. It is *neither productive nor redistributive*. Here again, therefore, a universal principle (economic nationalism) fronts for particular elite interests. What was formally a programme to reduce national economic dependency and establish a state-backed indigenous bourgeoisie has been transformed into a more complex and in many ways more irreversible nexus of dependency. Transnational corporations and Nigerian elites have in fact conspired – especially during the Second Republic, as will be demonstrated below – to circumvent both the letter and the spirit of the indigenisation programme. To follow Thomas Biersteker's incisive study,[17] strategies evolved to bypass the Decrees include (i) retention by the foreign partner of the right to choose and adapt the technology used, (ii) fragmentation of enterprise ownership among many Nigerians (market allocation of shares) as opposed to bloc ownership of 40% of the shares by the participating transnational corporation, (iii) negotiation of special arrangements and exemptions for foreign companies: special schedules, complete exemptions, etc., particularly in industries like oil, with little international competition, (iv) fronting or 'placing of Nigerians in positions of apparent ownership or responsibility . . . as cosmetic fronts to provide legitimacy', (v) various practices aimed at subordinating, co-opting or corrupting the Nigerian partners: grooming of a comprador elite, non-productive but well-paid positions for Nigerian managers, selection of board members from different ethnic groups to forestall unified opposition, simple bribery etc., and (vi) 'unilateral violation of the law . . . by only partly complying with or by totally ignoring . . . indigenisation requirements'. Bierstecker concludes not only that indigenisation has deepened Nigerian dependence, but that it has done so more and more on the strength of Nigerian investments. He formulates the process as follows:

> Essentially, indigenization has shifted the financial risk burden of new and existing investments onto Nigerian investors without any appreciable increase in their control over the enterprises. Rather than import capital or obtain it from local sources, on their own, transnational corporations have been provided with capital from Nigerian shareholders or partners.

And,

> indigenization inevitably encourages investments in transnational corporations. There are no counter incentives for investments in indigenously controlled enterprises, hence the program undermines the basis of accumulation by a national capitalist class. Although some pockets of local accumulation exist, a risk-averse, profit maximizing Nigerian investor will buy shares in foreign owned and dominated concerns. Indigenization thus encourages a comprador role for local business in a society already plagued by strong comprador tendencies. Accordingly, indigenization may have contributed to a *decrease*, rather than an increase, in Nigerian control of the economy.

What is evident from the growing body of critical studies of Nigerian indigenisation, therefore, is that although some degree of Nigerianisation of personnel (especially in the categories of personnel management, legal advice, public relations and clerical work; but *not* in production, engineering and finance)[18] and ownership has been achieved, the indigenisation of *control* is as remote a prospect as ever. Thus, until technological and managerial dependence, as well the relegation of the Nigerian elite to the sphere of distribution and circulation have been overcome, indigenisation will no doubt continue to deepen and extend the process of dependency.

In any case, economic nationalism must be seen in terms of its legitimating function, as a kind of consolation for the real reforms that cannot be implemented within the framework of elite domination. Like ethnicity, like political nationalism, it is an *ersatz* ideology. While in fact vindicating and hence entrenching the socio-economic *status quo* and justifying the exclusion of the non-propertied classes, it presents the illusion of a genuine, progressive and participatory economic order[19] aimed at accelerating development and economic independence. It is as though the salient problems of self-sufficiency and development were nothing more than a question of the nationality of the owners of the means of production. This still-unresolved contradiction – between ideological egalitarianism and *de facto* elite-formation – led, among other things, to a clash between certain developmental goals set by the Second and Third National Development Plans, i.e. between the goal of a 'just and egalitarian society' and that of 'a land of bright and full opportunities for all citizens'. In terms of access to economic opportunities, indigenisation, by favouring owners of capital, negates economic egalitarianism while proclaiming the existence of a broad range of opportunities for all citizens. The contradiction (and a logical solution to it) is defined by O. Aboyade:[20]

> The public sector take-over of the ownership and control of foreign enterprises, on the other hand, could have simultaneously achieved both objectives (mentioned above) and, as a starting point, also help in achieving the other three of the now famous five national objectives. Part of the recent doubts and confusion can be traced to this incongruous, if not ludicrous, situation of a people (or rather their government) trying to pursue socialist ends with capitalist instruments.

Pressures toward demilitarisation

Seldom do parties, organisations or individuals who hold political power surrender it voluntarily. In the case of the Nigerian military it is especially important to probe behind its ostensibly voluntary disengagement from politics in order to discover the real interests and motives leading to recivilianisation, because understanding why and how the military egressed from its political power position should also provide some insight into the question, which is crucial to any analysis of the Second Republic: what caused the military to intervene again? Why, then, did the men in khaki hand over to the men in *agbada* in the first place?

First, the military's pre-eminent position was structurally undermined over time. Lacking any system-transforming 'mission', by nature unresponsive to popular opinion and demands, and internally cross-pressured as a result of its accession to political power, the military – every military government from 1966 to 1979 – was under a strong compulsion to 'return to barracks' after its immediate post-*coup* 'corrective' objectives had been accomplished. Once the Gowon regime had reasserted 'national unity' through the successful conclusion of the civil war, the creation of a new system of federalism and the centralisation of power, and had laid the groundwork for a more functional national capitalism, it lost its historical *raison d'être* and had to face a rising opposition from within. For it had no effective conflict–resolving capacity, lacked the dynamism necessary for mass mobilisation to promote further development, and above all its existence set limits on the rising and/or re-emerging capitalist classes' opportunities for expansion and profit–realisation – opportunities afforded by the military's 'corrective' actions and measures.

Second, conflict within the military itself developed largely out of the dual constituency of the leadership, namely, the interests and objectives of the 'politicised' group of military governors, cabinet members and others directly involved in government – never more than 100 officers at any one time – and the great majority of the ranks who remained outside the political system looking in. Once the initial problems of intra-military ethnic balance[21] had been (violently) solved and each ethnic group more adequately balanced at each rank-level, corporate cohesion was not an overriding problem during the civil war period. Fighting the war and providing more benefits and amenities to the military ensured solidarity in the short term. Both in absolute and relative terms, the military's material gains were immense in the period from the civil war to recivilianisation (see Table 4:1).

Table 4.1   *Federal Government: military and social expenditures*

	Defence		Education		Health	
	Nm.	N Per Capita	Nm.	N Per Capita	Nm.	N Per Capita
1971/2	285.89	3.24	5.16	0.06	15.43	0.17
1973/4	420.16	4.71	12.21	0.14	19.97	0.23
1975/6	1166.69	13.26	295.23	3.35	69.77	0.79
1978/9	597.85	6.79	779.36	8.85	81.0	0.92

Source: Recurrent and Capital Estimates of the Government of the Federal Republic of Nigeria.

But during peacetime the 'political' officers became progressively alienated from their original military constituency as they were integrated into the ruling class and engaged in the latter's self-aggrandising and often corrupt practices (10 of the 12 State governors under the Gowon regime were eventually found guilty of gross misappropriation of funds), while the non-governing military both deplored the resultant declining prestige of the army and not infrequently themselves engaged in intense competition for lucrative political appointments. Those excluded from power were also factionalised into pro-disengagement groups (for example, combat officers and soldiers who had no particular political skills and who adhered to the military ethos handed down by the former colonial officers) and anti-disengagement groups (for instance, those who had not yet had a share of power and its rewards; the instigators of the anti-Murtala *coup* of February 1976 are a case in point). Furthermore, an ethnic dimension could also be discerned in intra-military factionalisation: officers from the larger ethnic groups tended to advocate civilianisation, since many believed that their peoples stood to gain most from a return to civilian rule, whereas minority-group officers had gained in relative terms from military rule and were often apprehensive about a new civilian government dominated by the Igbo, Yoruba and Hausa.

Thus, far from their popular image as a united moral force operating 'above politics', the Nigerian military was, in fact, rent by a number of fundamental internal cleavages. An important example was the issue of troop reduction already alluded to. Virtually all officers agreed that manpower ought to be reduced in order to free monies for the replacement and modernisation of equipment or the provision of better amenities and higher salaries for a reduced number of soldiers. But the wholesale discharge of troops would certainly exacerbate employment problems, and the dismissal of too many rank-and-file soldiers belonging to one or two ethnic groups – and most of the ranks were Middle Belters or Northerners – could have set off another round of intra-military ethnic conflicts. The latter spectre was a particularly daunting one because of the vehemence of soldier-against-soldier conflicts, which has been underlined by Martin Dent:[22]

> Of the 300 or so officers with regular commissions in January 1966, something like 60 have been killed by their brother officers in the course of carrying out coups or executed following unsuccessful coups.

This example serves to underline Jackson and Rosberg's general observation that:[23]

> In practice, most African armies are less like military organizations and more like political establishments: they are infected by corruption, factionalism, and patterns of authority based not only on rank, role or function, but also on personal and ethnic loyalties. The ability of African armies to deal with internal conflicts is dubious.

Third, conflicts were also produced within the governing coalition of military officers and civil servants. As the bureaucrats moved into policy-making, rather than policy-executing positions, they too had become 'politicised' and highly visible. As in the case of the military, the civil service also developed an internal contradiction between those who desired to maintain the politically neutral, efficient and rationalised organisation, and those who sought an even greater voice in political decision-making and with it a greater share of government 'outputs'. In the absence of popularly chosen political mediating agencies, the civil service, as it moved towards increasing political involvement, came into direct conflict with the military itself:[24]

> The increasing visibility of the civil service and the perception among elites and non-elites in Nigeria that the civil service was a political actor made the civil service more vulnerable to the housecleaning that a new military leadership undertook in 1975. The civil service was now part of the political fray and thus fair game. As some civil servants feared, the political activity of the civil servants weakened the civil service as an institution. Some high level servants who were closely linked with the Gowon regime were not tolerated by the Mohammed regime. Low level civil servants and high level ones too became convenient scapegoats for a military regime itself vulnerable to charges of corrupt practices.

Fourth, antagonism within the broader elite stratum also developed. Those groups who, although now an integral part of the socio-economic elite, did not enjoy a corresponding share of political power – in particular, the class of large entrepreneurs and indigenous managers of transnational corporations – now sought to rectify this imbalance between economic and political power, to compensate for the top civil servants' inside track in the indigenisation race and to gain access to other sources of state largesse. Moreover, as the post-war political economy expanded in the ways discussed above, it required a broader basis of participation and decentralisation of resource allocation, as well as adaptable institutions to contain and resolve intra-elite conflicts. The Gowon regime, however, beholden as it was to a relatively narrow-based clique of top military governors, civil servants, army officers, permanent secretaries and civilian and military commissioners, could not realise such reforms, since doing so would have undermined the power base upon which it rested. It is not so much that the form and substance of military government were somehow inimical to the interests of the political-business groups. On the contrary, collaboration was extensive, protracted and by and large mutually advantageous. But military authoritarianism could not regulate and legitimise intra-elite affairs as efficiently and reliably, it was thought, as liberal democracy could. Sklar puts this phenomenon in more general terms:[25]

> Normally authoritarian regimes consolidate the power of dominant classes. They are resented and rarely provide for orderly changes in governmental organizations and personnel. On the contrary, authoritarian rule virtually guarantees that political changes will be eruptive and costly to privileged classes which renders it distasteful and expendable to dominant classes that can maintain themselves in power by other means. Demands for liberal and limited government in many African countries reflect the rejection of authoritarianism by bourgeois classes that are steadily consolidating their power.

The old political classes, with their greater responsiveness to popular regional and sectoral needs, increasingly appeared a desirable alternative to the more and more remote military government. Pressures for the return to power of these groups could not be abated even by overt attempts to 'buy off' the bourgeoisie with indigenisation measures or with massive increases in public (1974) and private (1975) sector employees' salaries and emoluments.

Fifth, something like a mass basis for popular participation in public decision-making emerged more and more clearly as the limits of the military–civil service's reform capacities became increasingly evident over time. The existence of such popular pressures was crucial in explaining the choice of a liberal–democratic form of post-military government. For without them, the consolidating military–civil service-political–business elites might well have at least considered alternative forms of regulating their evolving class hegemony, for instance some form of authoritarian federalism or even dyarchy. The desire for liberal–democratic forms probably emanated most insistently from the growing lower-middle and middle classes – that stratum of middle-level civil servants (especially teachers), independent professionals such as lawyers, doctors and engineers, university dons, managers and technocrats in the private sector – who constituted a rising class of well-educated (often abroad), critical and ambitious individuals whose upward mobility and further progress were blocked by the relatively top-heavy socio-economic structure. For this group, the implementation of liberal–democratic governing and administering institutions offered not only a kind of national (as well as international) parity, a means of being heard, and a more rational system of government, it also held out rapid occupational advancement, new positions in state (and State) organs, and hence unprecedented opportunities for promotion and self-improvement.

Their goals in this respect coincided with those of the political-business class just described as well as, in some measure, with those of organised labour which also stood to gain, it was thought, from a general democratisation of labour-capital bargaining and enhanced rights for the Nigerian labour movement. The convergence of all these class aims – representing, let it be recalled, a numerically rather small yet qualitatively essential percentage of the population – created a practically irreversible clamour for a liberal–democratic organisation of government and in practice eclipsed other alternatives.

If to these interrelated contradictions and pressures – intra-military conflicts and intra-bureaucracy cleavages, civil service-military and civil service-business rivalries, growing ossification of the conflict-resolving capacities of government in the face of mass pressures for a share in decision-making – one adds factors of gross misman-agement (port congestion, botched 1973 census, inflation, deficient infrastructures), corruption (cement scandal, events in Benue–Plateau State) and a general weariness of military rule among the population, then the reasons for the third military *coup* in 1975 and the subsequent course of recivilianisation are apparent. The Mohammed/Obasanjo regime, a self-styled 'corrective' transitional government, set out to inject efficiency, honesty and therefore resiliency into Nigerian political life. Within the parameters of these objectives, the regime was remarkably successful. It was able to resolve, or at least allay, a number of intra-elite contradictions by setting a firm timetable for military withdrawal from politics, while at the same time increasing the army's pre-eminence within the ruling coalition. The latter goal was largely achieved by the expedient of a thorough purge of the bureaucracy, by further reducing the State governments' powers in favour of heightened centralism, and by embarking on an anti-corruption, pro-discipline crusade throughout the nation.

Entirely committed to its self-image as a transitional regime, the Mohammed/Obasanjo government undoubtedly enjoyed a legitimacy and indeed immense popu-larity, which paradoxically derived largely from its firmly proclaimed intent to make itself redundant. By effecting recivilianisation, the military government was of course paving the way for a *greater rationalisation of the elite structure*. The army stood to resolve most of its internal tensions while remaining one of the major ruling groups, with its privileges intact; the civil service could withdraw from its overtly political role and con-solidate its gains; the bourgeoisie could regain a substantial share of political power; and a new group of professional politicians, organically linked to the latter two groups, could re-enter the elite coalition. As intended, the liberal–democratic political apparatus was designed as a conflict-enacting and regulating agency whose aim was 'to rationalize the purchase of state favor and the conversion of public resources to private advantage, not to eliminate it'.[26]

In view of the military's vested interests in and commitment to the maintenance of neo-colonial capitalism, it is understandable that the civilian successor regime should have displayed marked affinities with it. For, as is well known, departing military governors will seldom transfer power to civilians whose socio-economic antecedents and political outlooks are too dissimilar to their own, since they will be concerned about policy reversals, loss of perquisites, probes or even possible trials, retributive acts, etc.[27] No doubt such concerns were multiplied by the appearance in Ghana and Liberia, during the terminal stage of military disengagement in Nigeria, of the rank-and-file *putsches* led by Flight Lieutenant Jerry Rawlings and Master Sergeant Samuel Doe. Thus the military aimed at shaping and influencing the transition to civilian rule at every important stage.

For example, the Head of State, convening the constitution-making body, virtually prescribed a presidential structure, a system of federalism, public accountability, a multi-party system and, in general, a liberal–democratic constitutional order,[28] while proscribing the adoption of 'any particular philosophy or ideology' from the constitu-tion. Similarly, the February 1976 creation of seven new States and the 1975/6 local government reforms represented military pre-emption of decisions which, strictly speaking, ought to have been taken within the new civilian governmental process, meaning also within the terms of reference of the Constituent Assembly. Particularly noteworthy here is the pivotal mandate bestowed on the Federal Election Commission (FEDECO) with respect to political party formation and the conduct of the elections. FEDECO's powers went far beyond mere technical arrangements to include the careful screening of all candidates. 'In other words', Claude Phillips writes (1980:14), 'a quasi-authoritarian body designed to ensure orderly and democratic elections soon acquired the power to determine who would enter the contest'. Then FEDECO interpreted the provisions of the Electoral Decree[29] (which required it to register political parties) to mean that it (FEDECO) also had the right to refuse such registration. According to Phillips (1980:14), this right

> stemmed from (section 78 of the Decree): 'No association by whatever name called shall function as a political party unless *it is registered as a political party by the Electoral Commission and* – (a) the names and addresses of its national officers are registered with the Electoral Commission.' (My emphasis, because the italicized words have been omitted in Section 201 of the Constitution.)

As Phillips rightly noted, the extraordinary powers were supposed to be a one-time transitional measure, and:

> It is likely that the Commission will never again have the same authority it wielded during the period 21 September 1978 to 1 October 1979, since Section 208 of the Constitution grants to the National Assembly the authority to confer on FEDECO such powers over parties as the former may deem necessary.

(Although essentially correct, Phillips' observations failed to account for the predominance of party power in determining FEDECO's actions; see chapter 5.)

Another dimension of military-sponsored recivilianisation was an attempt – in retrospect pathetic – to impose formal legal solutions on abiding socio-economic problems. For instance, the collapse of the First Republic had demonstrated that unbridled class conflict in the form of 'tribalism' threatens the structure and boundaries of the state itself. For this reason both military and civilian elites consistently opposed its re-emergence. General Obasanjo warned at the height of the recivilianisation exercise: 'Political recruitment and subsequent political support which are based on tribal, religious and linguistic sentiments contributed largely to our past misfortune. They must not be allowed to spring up again.'[30] The appeal was echoed by the five 'licensed' political parties, the mass media and the university dons. A number of provisions aimed at overcoming – or at least channelling – ethnic politics were anchored in the 1979 Constitution, for example, requirements that political party support must be nation-wide, that ethnic discrimination in any form be outlawed, that the federal cabinet include at least one member from each State, and that the personnel composition of all public agencies, save the armed forces, reflect 'the federal character of Nigeria'.

The obverse of military pre-determination of the basic institutions and ruling constellations of the Second Republic was its policy of active and often severe *repression* of forces and movements which fundamentally threatened the emerging system. The much vaunted 'tolerance' and 'pluralism' of the military regime – exemplified, for instance, by the relative independence of the press and judiciary – did not apply to social class formations or groupings considered to be in basic opposition to the neo-colonial capitalist order. The trade unions were 'rationalised' and subordinated to the political institutions. Students and academics, whom the military leaders viewed with considerable suspicion, were discouraged from political activities via the National

Universities Commission, established in 1974 to advise the military government on academic affairs. Public officers (meaning primarily dons) and students were constitutionally prohibited from forming party branches, holding meetings or using university facilities for partisan political purposes. Whenever students protested *en masse*, as during the April 1978 demonstrations against increases in boarding fees, the military showed itself capable of the most ruthless offensive against what was perceived as fundamental opposition. Following those events – during which, this writer is convinced, far more students were killed than has ever been made public – the military government appointed a commission which recommended discharging two university vice-chancellors, a number of student union leaders and several 'dissident' intellectuals.

Of course, repression on this scale and in this style undermines the very stability it is intended to preserve, as the groups and issues concerned are forced underground, where they develop into radicalised oppositional cells. The military, as already stated, lacks the sensitivity and feed-back mechanisms to cope with such challenges, and therefore is pushed further toward recivilianisation as an alternative to still more violent, legitimacy-eroding repressive measures.

Hence recivilianisation was the, perhaps only, means of (temporarily) resolving the multiplicity of contradictions which had built up under military government. But right from the military handover at 10.36 a.m. on 1 October 1979, a persistent question of Nigerian politics became: would the military intervene again and, if so, under what conditions and with what effects? The question was ultimately answered on 31 December 1983, and that answer is the subject of chapter 8.

How, and for whom the 1979 constitution was made

Murtala Mohammed, in his 1975 Independence Day speech, prescribed five stages in the constitution-making process:

(i) appointment of a constitution-drafting committee to prepare the first draft of a new constitution by September 1976;

(ii) establishment of new States and reorganisation of the local government system, on the basis of which a partially elected, partially appointed constituent assembly could be called into existence;

(iii) deliberations on, and amendments to, the draft constitution by a constituent assembly before October 1978; subsequent dissolution of the body;

(iv) acceptance by the Federal Military Government of the completed constitution and its enactment, by decree, into law; and

(v) coming into force of the new constitution: dissolution of military government; assumption of office by elected civilians on 1 October 1979.[31]

And this was essentially the way in which the process unfolded.

The Constitution Drafting Committee or CDC was established in September 1975 and began work in October. Chaired by the prominent lawyer and ex-minister of the former Western Region, Chief Rotimi Williams, the CDC consisted of 49 'wise men' (initially 50 until Chief Awolowo declined). The Federal Military Government's terms of reference to the CDC were set rather broadly and permitted the Committee some latitude. The military, Murtala Mohammed stated, were committed to a federal government system, a free and democratic government, guaranteed basic human rights, political stability, and constitutionalism. Hence, the future constitution should be framed so as to: (i) eliminate cut-throat political competition based on a system of winner-take-all; as a corollary, it should eliminate electoral malpractices; (ii) discourage institutionalised opposition to the government and instead develop consensus politics and government based on a community of all interests rather than the interests of particular sections of the country; (iii) firmly establish the principle of public accountability for all holders of public office; (iv) eliminate over-centralisation of power in a few hands, and as a matter of principle, decentralise power wherever possible, as a means of diffusing tension.

These principles might be realised, the Head of State continued, by means of: (i) genuine and truly national political parties, the number of which should in some way be limited; (ii) an executive presidential system of government in which the president and vice-president would be directly elected and reflect the federal character of the country; (iii) an independent judiciary, guaranteed by the constitution; (iv) corrective institutions such as corrupt practices tribunal and public complaints bureau; and (v) constitutional limitation on the number of further States to be created.[32]

To facilitate its work, the CDC subdivided into six subcommittees to deliberate on: national objectives and public accountability; the executive and the legislature; the judicial system; the economy, finance and the division of powers; citizenship, fundamental rights, social security, political parties and the electoral system; and public services, armed forces and police. A seventh subcommittee, composed of all twelve lawyers on the CDC, was constituted as a legal drafting committee. The CDC also invited submissions from the general public, and eventually received about 400 written briefs, proposals and drafts to aid it in its deliberations. The publication of the CDC's two-volume Report in September 1976 marked the real beginning of the long process of public debate and deliberation on the new constitution, whose basic parameters had, as just shown, already been set. The *CDC Report* was widely circulated and became the subject of discussion in the media, national academic conferences of political scientists, economists and public administrators, of local fora and even of several books and anthologies. Of course, few of these were accessible to peasants and workers who, it will be argued presently, had little influence in the constitution-making process.

The Constituent Assembly's role was twofold. It was charged, first, with scrutinising and re-examining the Draft Constitution, amending individual articles where necessary, rewording and touching up different passages. And second, its (implicit) task was to legitimise the decisions made by the smaller, non-elected CDC.

The Constituent Assembly (CA) began work in December 1976 under the chairmanship of Sir (Justice) Udo Udoma, and completed it in June 1978.[33] As just mentioned, it made no fundamental changes in the CDC proposals. Nevertheless it left its impression in the form of detailed amendments, more tightly worded clauses and the like. For example, it changed the size of the majority required in the legislature in order to effect amendments to the constitution, and further entrenched the chapter on fundamental rights. It restricted the state's powers to impose involuntary detention. It also improved the procedure for impeaching government officials, notably the President, and limited somewhat the latter's considerable emergency powers. It went on to alter the formula for electing the President and State Governors to ensure a broader base of support for these top elected leaders. It even inserted a clause in effect outlawing future military *coups*!

By the very fact of its being mostly elected, the Constituent Assembly represented a kind of pre-parliament. Indeed, most of its members were to feature prominently in the political parties and government agencies of the Second Republic. In the hands of such a body, the highly volatile and political nature of constitution-making was bound to generate conflict. Two of the most contentious issues were the establishment of a separate Federal Sharia Court and the formula for the creation of more States, both of which invoked memories of the factional and regional aspects of politics in the First Republic.

During the final phase of its evolution, the constitution again passed through the hands of the same body that had initially set it in motion: *the Supreme Military Council.* In September General Obasanjo announced seventeen amendments made by the military, including revised fiscal arrangements for the judiciary, deletion of provisions for the possible future incorporation of foreign states into the Federation, rejection of any ethnic quota system in the armed forces, altered procedures for removing Chief Justices etc. More important, the military added provisions for the possible future use of Hausa, Yoruba or Igbo, in addition to English, as the National Assembly's language of business. It also entrenched several items in the constitution: the Land Use Decree, the National Youth Service Corps, the Public Complaints Bureau and the National Security Organisation. Moreover, public officers holding executive positions and members of the legislature were prohibited from engaging in private enterprise or holding foreign bank accounts. Persons convicted of bribery, corruption or malfeasance after January 1966 (rather than October 1960) were not eligible to contest public office. Thus it was left to the SMC to resolve and amend some of the more contentious articles remaining after the CA's deliberations.[34]

One interesting and as yet little investigated SMC amendment has to do with the guarantee of the right to own or hold private property and the payment of compensation for expropriations of such property by the government. Both the CDC and the CA had expressly included provisions in the draft constitution for the right of private property and the payment of *adequate* compensation in the event of compulsory acquisitions (to be determined, if need be, by the High Court). The relevant formulation anchored by the SMC in the 1979 Constitution, on the other hand, stated only that no movable property or any interest in an immovable property could be acquired compulsorily in any part of the country except in the manner and for the purposes prescribed by a law which, among other things, (a) required the prompt payment of compensation therefor and (b) gave to any person claiming such compensation a right of access, for the determination of his interest in the property and the amount of compensation, to a court of law or tribunal or body having jurisdiction in that part of Nigeria.

From this, it may be inferred that compensation for expropriated property need not be 'adequate' and could therefore be politically determined by the legislature, and also that therefore no absolute guarantee of private property was contained in the constitution. No doubt, this final constitutional act by the military was intended in part to facilitate the operation of the Land Use Decree, which was also constitutionally entrenched (see chapter 9). And certainly, the military did not consider the private property issue sufficiently important to mention it in General Obasanjo's speech, of 21 September 1978. But so long as these clauses remained constitutionally anchored, they embodied a threat to the owners of private property and the nucleus of a possible future strategy of socialist change, particularly in the event of the military's return to power.

For this and other reasons, the post-military state elite found it expedient to dilute these principles. When, for instance, the Lagos State government in the Second Republic decided to abolish private primary schools, the State Chief Justice, invoking the guarantee of personal liberty in the Nigeria bill of rights (also constitutionally entrenched), noted that 'the state is enjoined to protect the right of every citizen to engage in any economic activities outside the major sectors of the economy as may from time to time be declared by a resolution of each house of the Nigerian Assembly' (quoted in Nwabueze, 1982b:534). Here again the *liberal right* of 'free choice' was held to supersede the *fundamental objective* of equal adequate educational opportunities.

On 1 October 1979 the Constitution was made into law by means of an enabling decree, the newly elected civilian government stepped into office, the military withdrew to barracks and the Second Republic began its legal existence.

When constitutions are made, insights are also provided into the constellation of social and economic forces prevailing within the country concerned. Although these charters of government are promulgated on behalf of 'the people' – like laws executed 'in the name of the people' and proclamations invoking 'the people's will' – they must also be considered in terms of the particularist interests and goals which they entrench. In less developed countries, particularly those whose development strategy is capitalist (or state-capitalist) and where therefore large income differentials, severely restricted access to the structures of power and privilege, unequal regional and sectoral development, and a high degree of actual or potential class conflict tend to exist, constitutions generally are less representative of any nebulous 'popular will' than of very specific class interests. Starting from these assumptions, the Nigerian constitution-making process can now be examined from the perspective: by whom and for whom was it undertaken?

Much has been made of the notion of popular participation in the process of constitution-making. The preamble to the 1979 Constitution asserts that 'we the people of the Federal Republic of Nigeria . . . do hereby make, enact and give to ourselves the following constitution'. No doubt, when compared with the arbitrary and occasionally authoritarian decrees handed down over time by the Supreme Military Council, the constitution stood as a relatively democratically produced and legitimised document. But an examination of the composition of the CDC and CA, as well as of the goals and principles which they invested in the constitution, reveals Nigerian constitution-making to have been less an act of 'the people' than the formulation of a *provisional intra-elite consensus*.

The CDC, for example, was an appointed group of experts which was never intended to be representative of the population. According to the then Head of State, only a limited geographic representation (at least two members for each of the then 12 States) was sought, as well as token (not proportional) ethnic-group representation. The sole woman member of the two bodies was a businesswoman elected to the CA. Beyond this, 'expertise' or 'eminence' in relevant academic disciplines or spheres of society were the deciding criteria of selection. The composition of the CA, to be sure, was somewhat broader. Of its 230 members, 40 were *ex officio* or other appointments of the federal military government. The remaining members were chosen indirectly through a system of electoral colleges based largely on local government units[35] – 95 on the basis of geographic representation or 5 per State (an embryonic Senate?), and 95 on the basis of representation by population (House of Representatives?).

Two representative imbalances resulted from this selection system: a *geographical* imbalance weighted in favour of the smaller States, so that a citizen from, say, Rivers or Lagos was three to four times 'more' represented than a citizen from one of the larger States such as Oyo or Kano,[36] within the CA. Overall, the North was considerably under-represented vis-à-vis the South. Within the CDC too, representation had also been skewed in favour of urban, male intellectuals from the upper social classes.

The second representative imbalance was *sociological*. Both the CDC and CA were made up of leading members of the ruling classes. What has been said of the CDC applies *mutatis mutandis* to the CA, namely, that its members derived 'exclusively from among the elements of the national bourgeoisie: lawyers, medical practitioners, businessmen, administrators, university dons and company directors'.[37] At least 14 of the 49 CDC members had been prominently involved in political party activity in the First

Republic and four of its seven subcommittees were chaired by these politicians. A large number of members had also served as consultants and administrators under the federal military government. And within the CA, 120 of its 230 members were lawyers.[38] Since the CDC comprised rather more members of the intelligentsia (some 26 were, or had been, university teachers and/or administrators), while the CA's membership was largely derived from the business-commercial class, it may be inferred that the agreement between these groups represented the elite consensus which was supposed to sustain the liberal–democratic forms of the Second Republic. (The consensual basis of the First Republic, by contrast, was the 'political class' [Dudley, 1982:161]). Neither body included a worker, peasant, artisan, employee or market woman among its membership, and only the CA admitted a token student representative. If one considers that certainly not less than 90% of the Nigerian population may be subsumed under the latter six social categories, then the unrepresentativeness of these two constitution-making bodies is self-evident. The absence of representatives from these groups must have deprived the new constitutional order of some important perspectives. For example:[39]

> The Nigerian working-class movement has veterans with several decades of dedication to the cause of workers and vast political experience. The Nigerian peasantry also have cooperatives and farmers' associations which have not in any way been silent on the aspirations and interests of the peasantry . . . the exclusion of the Nigerian workers and farmers from the constitution-making process becomes indeed revealing when it is recognized that simultaneously as the CDC was being constituted, the labor movement was under a governmental probe which ultimately led to an as yet unexplained ban on the most militant labor unionists with well known left wing connections.

Demonstrating the pronounced upper-class composition of these 'pre-parliaments' is one part of the argument. The second part is to show how and why the CDC and CA operated logically and consistently in that class's interest. First, however, some qualifications must be made. The two bodies cannot be seen solely and exclusively as 'agents' of the ruling classes, nor did they deliberately and unanimously proceed to override the other classes' interests while entrenching their own. Three developments militate against any such oversimplified explanation of this rather more complex phenomenon:

(i) Both bodies contained a minuscule left-wing opposition whose espousal of radical and to some extent anti-capitalist positions may be seen as evidence of the (indirect) interest representation of the non-bourgeois classes. Two dissenting members of the CDC, Drs Osoba and Usman, wrote in their Minority Report that the CDC majority displayed 'basic commitment, sometimes thinly disguised and sometimes blatantly expressed, to the consolidation and perpetuation of the neo-colonialist capitalist social and economic order in Nigeria'.[40] Segun Okeowo, head of the subsequently banned National Union of Students, and by virtue of that position a member of the CA (but later imprisoned and suspended from that body in connection with the student demonstrations of April/May 1979), argued that the draft constitution represented a 'perpetuation of class distinction and . . . of what we call bourgeois constitutionalism'.[41]

(ii) Similarly, the formation of a purely single-class will was mitigated by the 'federal character' of delegate selection to the CDC and CA – a highly significant factor in Nigeria where, in the past, ethno-regional differences have tended to be confused with the class struggle.

(iii) And further, the extensive and frequently acrimonious debates, particularly those in the more representative CA, which occasioned protests, petitions and even a walk-out by 92 of its members, and its adjournment without a vote on at least two controversial issues, are evidence of the lack of any overt issue solidarity among Nigerian constitution-makers.

Some insight into the differentiated class composition and nature of the constitution-making bodies may be gained by recalling that CA members were both united and divided on a number of issues. The CA was more or less unanimously agreed that socialism, social reforms and socio-economic change should be kept out of the constitution; that the provisions of the Land Use Decree should be qualified with reference to the rights of private property; that no concrete measures should be taken to extend popular ownership of stocks and shares in 'indigenised' corporations; that elected public servants should be permitted to maintain foreign bank accounts; and that government and civil service agencies should display a 'federal character' in their personnel composition. But, on the other hand, some issues were the subject of protracted and vehement debate: the creation of a Federal Sharia Court of Appeal; the question of whether to ban politicians previously convicted after October 1960 or January 1966; and the creation of more States. Notably absent from the deliberations was a third category of issues: those which were ignored or omitted. Thus the CA never came to grips at all with the problems of neo-colonialism and economic dependency, maldistribution among the social classes, and the ways and means of realising the 'Fundamental Objectives and Directives of State Policy'.

A tentative explanation of these ostensibly inconsistent orientations may be advanced with the model, suggested earlier, of *intra-class* versus *inter-class conflicts*. It has already been demonstrated that politics is necessarily a vital preoccupation of the elite groups. Hence any policy or measure which would undermine the socio-economic foundations of elite-formation had to be excluded. The neo-colonial capitalist order, above all other things, had to be maintained as intact as possible. Any sustained proposals for achieving economic independence or a redistribution of the social product could not, therefore, be entertained. In particular, it was necessary to prevent the so-called masses from gaining an increased degree of economic and thus social and political participation. A future political force consisting of peasants and workers alone, for example, would represent a substantial challenge to the system of power and privilege, not necessarily as a result of any revolutionary programme which it might advance, but simply because advocating its elementary interests – housing, education, higher wages, social security, etc. – would generate strong pressures for socio-economic transformation.

This is the area in which the notion of *inter-class struggle* helps to account for upper-class solidarity vis-à-vis actual or potential demands from below. With the aid of this concept, the CA's attempt to nullify the Land Use Decree is more comprehensible: this decree was eventually anchored in the constitution, not by the largely elected 'representatives of the people', but by the Supreme Military Council. In this context, the propagation of the ideology of a 'mixed economy' and the failure to render enforceable the catalogue of socio-economic rights (to be discussed in the following section) also become transparent. So, too, does the decision to allow public officials to maintain foreign bank accounts, since (one may assume) virtually all the members of the political elite either had, or hoped to have, funds stored abroad – a fact which has been amply documented by the revelations following the December 1983 *coup*. Here again, it was left to the departing military regime to ban this practice by constitutional provision.

A political system which consciously excludes popular mass participation need not have a sterile or atrophied political life. On the contrary, such a system must, for reasons of its continuing legitimisation, be at pains to create the semblance of meaningful political alternatives. The well-publicised controversies surrounding the 'Sharia issue' (i.e., whether or not to create a new Sharia Court of Appeal),[42] the creation of more States, and the banning of corrupt politicians are evidence that the CA was much more than a 'gentlemen's club'. However, these issues were 'safe' ones inasmuch as any possible outcomes could not jeopardise the elites' leading position in society. Here *intra-class conflict* could be allowed to take its full course. Thus the Sharia controversy may be best regarded as a struggle for pre-eminence between the Northern bourgeoisie (who were under-represented in the CA) and the Southern bourgeoisie. The disputes surrounding the cut-off date for banning politicians previously convicted of corruption hinged on whether certain individuals, notably Chief Awolowo, would be permitted to take part in politics again, and as such represented an attempt to settle some long-standing intra-elite quarrels. Likewise, the clamourings for more States were largely an attempt to establish additional 'secure' constituencies for those political formations which hoped to come to power in them (see chapter 7).

Of course, apart from these elite motives, the public interest may also be served by the outcomes of such intra-class conflicts as the banning of corrupt politicians from political life. It has rightly been suggested that:[43]

> Ironically, it is only when an issue involves intra-elite differences that the masses stand a chance of getting a fair deal for then the interest of the winning group at the time may coincide with the public interest.

Ideological aspects

No less than dynamic revolutionary movements, conservative and narrowly based ruling orders require a credible and acceptable ideology, or at least a collection of pseudo-ideological tenets, in order to ensure voluntary compliance (or 'legitimacy') on the part of the majority of citizens. The forming Nigerian national bourgeoisie found a twofold formula to vindicate its class rule in the Second Republic, namely, *postulating the 'mixed economy' as a national ideology, and asserting socio-economic rights while at the same time relegating them to the realm of remote goals.*

Concerning the issue of a national ideology in general, the CDC's subcommittee on national objectives and public accountability came out unequivocally for a unified and unifying belief system.[44] It went on to discuss the substance of this national ideology in terms of Nigeria's specific problems and needs, namely, the unjust and unequal distribution of wealth in society, the co-existence of many potentially antagonistic ethnic groups and the overriding need for national unity and development. The presence of these factors, the subcommittee concluded, necessitated the adoption of socialism.[45]

However, for reasons which will be discussed below, the main body of the CDC had to prevent these radical proposals from being realised. Nevertheless, in view of popular resentment against certain aspects of capitalism and currents favouring socialist solutions, it was not able to reject the subcommittee's report outright. Instead, it had to find a formula which, while ostensibly conceding the rhetoric of socialist demands, would effectively defuse them in substance and at the same time ideologically vindicate the continuation of the capitalist economic order. This task was, of course, facilitated by the Military Government's injunction to the CDC, mentioned earlier, against the 'adoption of any particular ideology'. The military further bequeathed to the emergent civilian ideology-formulators a certain propensity to submerge potentially contentious issues by means of idealising and absolutising formulas which, at bottom, reinforced and legitimated the *status quo*. For instance, Chief of Staff Yar'Adua was quoted in July 1976 as having claimed that:[46]

Ideology or no ideology, we have said that as a military regime we consider ourselves a passing phase: we think we are essentially corrective (and) do not think it is right to enforce ideology as such . . . We want the people to have, to select, to elect exactly what type of government they want . . . Our policy is 'Nigeria first in everything.' So if you are insisting that we must have an ideology . . . call it Nigerianism.

The CDC resurrected the notion of the 'mixed economy' – which had been more or less in use since the early days of the 'open-door' phase of economic development – to perform these functions. The 'mixed economy' resembles its counterparts in other places in the world – the 'welfare state', the 'social market economy' or the 'third way' – inasmuch as it, like ethnicity or economic nationalism, is an *ersatz* ideology. When socio-economic change is pressing and a large part of the population are aware of this fact, but when simultaneously such change would threaten the existing system of power and privilege as well as the position of an entrenched elite within it, then demagogic formulas must be concocted and propagated which, while giving the appearance of dynamism and progressive movement, do not in fact compel any substantial alterations in the *status quo*.

Thus the champions of the 'mixed economy' start from an abstract notion of some form of 'pure' capitalism so as to 'prove' that the variant of state capitalism in Nigeria deviates from this model because of state ownership of some sectors of the economy and the existence of nominal welfare benefits. They then conclude that the given socio-economic system somehow incorporates the most desirable elements of capitalism and socialism, or indeed achieves a 'higher' or 'optimal' synthesis of the two. In view of all this, any radical–socialist transformation, it is argued, would upset this hypothetical equilibrium between individual initiative and egalitarian redistribution. The predominant group within the CDC asserted that:[47]

> in point of fact the Nigerian economy is 'socialist' in certain areas of the economy whilst in other areas individual initiative and ownership is permissible. In other words, Nigeria has never hesitated to assume full ownership or control of sectors of the economy whenever it is necessary in the national interest to do so. At the same time Nigerians have always encouraged and protected individual ownership and initiative in those sectors of the economy where it is felt that public ownership or control is not in the national interest.

The CDC also argued that socialism was merely an ideology 'conceived in a foreign political climate' which, unlike capitalism, was incapable of achieving rapid development and an abundance of goods or indeed basic food and shelter for the people. This was so because 'it is not possible to pursue simultaneously the aims of rapid development and income equality'.[48] It is not difficult to refute this assertion on a factual level, for historical evidence shows clearly that capitalism, first in the form of colonialism, then of neo-colonial dependency, is far from an 'indigenous' economic system.

The 'mixed economy' itself can also readily be shown to be an exercise in ideological obfuscation. It is a well-established principle that state intervention in and ownership of selected sectors of the capitalist economy, particularly in countries proceeding on the capitalist road to development, are both desirable and functional. This point has been made above. Control of state power by the national bourgeoisie is an effective device for actively promoting class interests while subsidising the 'losses' incurred in non-profit-generating sectors and minimising the risks which would be attendant upon business ventures in a more 'purely' capitalist economy. A genuinely 'mixed' economy, therefore, cannot be defined in terms of *degree* of state ownership alone, but especially in the light of its *direction* and *objectives*.[49] As a minimum, it would have to aim at a qualitative transformation of the economic society (Yugoslavia) rather than merely describing the extant economic structure.

Indeed, the notion of a 'mixed economy' is most expedient, from the point of view of a conservative legitimating ideology. Since every national economy in the world is in fact somehow 'mixed', the term can justify any economic system at any time – colonial capitalism, the post-independence open-door economy, or the highly state-interventionist, oil–dependent economy. For the same reasons, the mixed economy can be made compatible with any form of government from authoritarian dictatorship to liberal (or even socialist) democracy, and with any combination of domestic and foreign elite interests. Okwudiba Nnoli sees it as an ahistorical denial of Nigeria's colonial and neo-colonial history which absolutises dependency and internal class conflict, and concludes that (1981:59): 'The Nigerian bourgeois, mixed-economy adherents are wilfully truncating and distorting the country's history, itself a part of an unmistakable history of capitalist development in Africa.'

It is thus relatively easy to demonstrate that the 'mixed economy' as ideology is intrinsically untenable. This matters less, however, than the fact that it is espoused by large numbers of people, particularly those in a position to co-determine the course of economic development – which indeed is the more relevant measure of any ideology's effectiveness. Once the ideology has gained wide acceptance, or at least when it is no longer opposed by a large, aware, and critical sector of public opinion, it then lends itself to the justification of certain policies or actions aimed at preserving the existing socio-economic order. In the case of Nigerian constitution–making, it led to the separation of socio-economic rights from civil liberties.

Civil liberties (or liberal rights) have a long and firm tradition in Nigerian constitutions and constitutionalism, and the framers of the 1979 Constitution also provided for, and legally guaranteed the individual's right to life and liberty, the dignity of the person, the right of free speech, freedom from arbitrary arrest, religious freedom, freedom of movement, etc. – and, not least, the right to private property. The CDC subcommittee on national objectives and public accountability proposed also to elevate socio-economic rights – right to work, right to adequate food and shelter, right to education, right to a minimum wage, etc. – to the same level as liberal rights. The subcommittee, in other words, sought not only to anchor the principles themselves in the constitution, but also the means of realising them. It therefore proposed to make the principles justiciable to the extent that individuals might apply to the courts for a declaration as to whether a state organ or authority were performing in accordance with this constitutional mandate. The guiding rationale here is evident: that socio-economic rights are a precondition for the effective exercise of liberal rights, for example, that the right to adequate food and shelter antedates any freedom of movement or freedom of conscience. Or, in the words of Bade Onimode:[50]

> In particular it is fraudulent to give a country with an about 80 per cent illiteracy rate freedom of expression in official English without offering them (sic.) a right to formal education. Similarly, bourgeois 'right to life' and 'right to dignity of human person' are plainly deceptive in a country where people have to beg to eat or starve to death, sleep on the streets, suffer the deprivations of unemployment without assistance and similar deprivations and affronts to human dignity.

In a manner entirely analagous to the substitution of the 'mixed economy' for concrete formulas of social reform, the CDC then set about appropriating for the draft constitution the aura of legitimacy deriving from its ostensible espousal of progressive socio-economic principles while simultaneously removing these principles from any possibility of realisation. The subcommittee's 'directive principles of state policy' became, in the draft constitution itself as well as in the 1979 Constitution, 'fundamental objectives and directive principles of state policy'. True, the revised version retained most of the socio-economic rights proposed by the subcommittee. But, as the respective subtitles suggest, it transformed them from a binding constitutional mandate into a mere declaration of future intent. This metamorphosis was achieved by positing that socio-economic rights, unlike liberal rights, were only realisable once the facilities had been established for them.[51] Socio-economic rights therefore – and again, unlike liberal rights – were said not to impose limitations on governmental powers and thus could not be made justiciable.

What is at issue here is no simple shift of emphasis or minor alteration of phraseology. The mere assertion of lofty and emotive principles, such as socialism, social justice or socio-economic rights, without, however, any provision of the *specific* and *concrete means* of realising them, amounts to their neutralisation or negation. Moreover, any empty invocation of such principles for demagogic purposes does them a considerable disservice and makes their ultimate realisation more problematic. The 'socialism' articles in the 1979 Constitution were primarily rhetorical in intent. No machinery was created for enforcing them or for obtaining redress for their non-implementation. And no state authority was actually bound to do anything about realising them. Nor, given the basically conservative interest structure of the Second Republic, was any measure ever taken in that direction.

A broad conceptual attempt to grasp the ideological processes at work here has been made by Claude Ake with his theory of 'defensive radicalism'. In order to preserve the *status quo* in political formations such as Nigeria, the upper classes are constrained to make rhetorical concessions to the demands of the lower classes without actually implementing policies leading to their realisation. Such concessions may be termed defensive radicalism:[52]

> Defensive radicalism is a progressive force. Paradoxically, while it allows the bourgeoisie to buy time, it develops the consciousness of the people, reveals the contradictions of the social order, and intensifies the class struggle. It develops the consciousness of the masses because the rulers' objective interest demands that their defensive radicalism be given the maximum visibility. The process of giving this visibility necessarily entails the propagation of the values and the ideologies of the class enemies of the regime. The regime achieves the requisite visibility by propagating ideas and creating expectations which cannot be satisfied in the context of the existing order. It intensifies the class struggle by developing the consciousness of the masses and by revealing the contradictions of the system. Defensive radicalism has a dynamic all its own.

That this ideological propensity continued into the civilian era was illustrated by a statement by former Vice-President Alex Ekwueme, who was reported as having warned that the gap between rich and poor would have to continue for some time, before narrowing at some future date. The move in the direction of egalitarianism would not come about through 'ideological sermonising' but 'by the development of a humanistic and enlightened approach engendered by our communalistic heritage'.[53] Any concretisation or quantification of such elevated ideals was, of course, out of the question. In this context, Stanley Macebuh aptly wrote that:[54]

> Having failed to buttress our political adventure on a firm base of ideological passion, we appear to have found a curious substitute in moralism, which may be good for the soul, but hardly has any useful effect on the health of the body politic.

Notes

1. Peter Waterman, 'Capitalist Development, Labour Control Strategy and the Working Class Movement in Nigeria', (being part of a larger study, in preparation, on *The Wage-Labour Relationship in Nigeria*), in W. D. Graf (ed.), *Towards a Political Economy of Nigeria*, Benin City and Cambridge, forthcoming, here quoted from manuscript, p. 3.
2. I. V. Sledzevsky, 'Entwicklungsprobleme des Staatskapitalismus im Nigeria der siebziger Jahre', *Asien-afrika-lateinamerika*, Vol. 2, No. 7, 1979, p. 277.
3. Olufemi Taiwo, 'Reading Ideologies in Constitutions: A Marxist Analysis of the 1979 Nigerian Constitution', paper presented to 14th Annual Conference of the Canadian Association of African Studies, Antigonish, N. S., 9–12 May 1984, mimeo., p. 5.
4. As suggested by Williams and Turner, 1975 and Terisa Turner, 'Commercial Capitalism and the 1975 Coup', in Panter–Brick, 1978, pp. 166ff.
5. Szymon Chodak, 'Social Stratification in Sub-Saharan Africa', *Canadian Journal of African Studies*, Vol. 7, No. 3 (1973), p. 414.
6. Richard Sklar, 'Ethnic Relations and Social Class', in Sanda 1976, p. 153.
7. David B. Abernathy, 'Education and Integration', in Melson and Wolpe, 1972, p. 400ff.
8. In a paper presented to the Fourth Annual Conference of the Nigerian Political Science Association, 1977, p. 31.
9. See Collins, 1975, p. 141.
10. Quoted in *ibid.*, p. 143.
11. 'Address to the Nigerian National Union of Great Britain and Eire, 26 September 1976', Lagos, Federal Ministry of Information Late Press Release No. 1207.
12. As outlined by F. Olu Okediji, 'Indigenization Process and the Quality of Nigerian Capitalism', in Nigerian Economic Society (ed.), *Nigeria's Indigenization Policy: Proceedings of the November 1974 Symposium*, Ibadan, 1974, p. 69.
13. Collins, 1975, p. 144.
14. Further see Collins, 1976, p. 493ff.
15. As suggested by E. O. Akeredolu-Ale, 'Some Thoughts on the Indigenization Process and the Quality of Nigerian Capitalism', in Nigerian Economic Society, *op. cit.*, p. 69.
16. *Ibid.*, p. 68.
17. Biersteker, 1983, pp. 193–202; further see Collins, 1977, pp. 134–7.
18. On this see *West Africa*, 5 March 1979, p. 391.
19. See, e.g., Onoge, 1974, pp. 57–60.
20. 'Indigenizing Foreign Enterprises: Some Lessons from the Nigerian Enterprises Promotion Decree', in Teriba and Kayode, 1977, p. 380.
21. As Dudley points out (1982, pp. 39–40), the pre-civil war military resembled a three-layered cake with Igbo and Yoruba at the top, the far Northern groups in the middle (i.e., captains and lieutenants), and the Middle Belters at the base.
22. Martin Dent, 'Corrective Government: Military Rule in Perspective', in Panter-Brick, 1978, p. 131.
23. R. H. Jackson and C. G. Rosberg, 'Why Africa's Weak States Persist: The Empirical and the Juridicial in Statehood', in R. Matthews, A. Rubinoff, J. Stein, *International Conflict and Conflict Management: Readings in World Politics*, Scarborough, Ontario, 1984, p. 199.
24. Henry Bienen with Martin Fitton, 'Soldiers, Politicians and Civil Servants', in Panter-Brick, 1978, pp. 52–3.
25. Richard L. Sklar, 'The Nature of Class Domination in Africa', *Journal of Modern African Studies*, Vol. 17, No. 4 (1979), p. 552.
26. P. Collins, G. Williams, T. Turner, 'Capitalism and the Coup', in Williams, 1976, p. 191.
27. On this see Welch, 1974, p. 231 and his 'Praetorianism in Commonwealth West Africa', *Journal of Modern African Studies*, Vol. X, No. 2 (July) 1972, p. 213. See also, following Welch, Dare, 1974, pp. 297f and 1981.
28. This may be inferred, *inter alia*, from Murtala Mohammed's address to the Constitution Drafting Committee's opening session, 18 October 1975, reproduced in *Report of the Constitution Drafting Committee Containing the Draft Constitution*, Lagos 1976, Vol. I, pp. xli–xlii (henceforth: *CDC Report*).

29. Decree No. 73 – Electoral Decree 1977, Extraordinary Supplement to *Federal Republic of Nigeria Official Gazette*, No. 61, Vol. 64, Lagos, 29 December 1979.
30. *East Africa*, 2 October 1978, p. 1937.
31. For details of the speech see, e.g. *New Nigerian* and *Daily Times*, 2 October 1975.
32. 'Address by the Head of the Federal Military Government, Commander-in-Chief of the Armed Forces at the Opening Session of the Constitutional Drafting Committee on Saturday, 18th October, 1975', *CDC Report*, Vol. I, pp. xli–xliii.
33. On the CA's work see 'Changes in the Constitution', *West Africa*, 4 and 11 September 1978, pp. 1729–31 and 1788–9.
34. For a statement explaining the military government's motives in making these amendments, see General Obasanjo's address to the nation, 21 September 1978, reproduced in *New Nigerian*, 22 September 1978.
35. For details of the 1976 local government elections, see chapter 9.
36. See 'Candido', *New Nigerian*, 19 April 1978.
37. O. Onagoruwa, writing in *Business Times*, 1 June 1976: reproduced in: *The Great Debate: Nigerian Viewpoints on the Draft Constitution*, Lagos 1978, p. 25.
38. According to Mohammed Haruna's column in *New Nigerian*, 22 May 1978.
39. 'The Politics of Transition to Civilian Rule in Nigeria: The National Bourgeoisie Comes of Age', *Positive Review*, No. 1/1978 (undated), p. 8.
40. Quotations from the Minority Report here extracted from Marenin, 1978, pp. 9ff.
41. *Proceedings of the Constituent Assembly. Official Report*, 2 November 1977, column 138.
42. See Draft Constitution, Para.180 (1) C.
43. Haruna, *op. cit.*, p. 7.
44. *CDC Report*, vol. II, p. 35.
45. *Ibid.*, p. 36.
46. Quoted in Herskovits, 1977–8, p. 185.
47. *CDC Report*, Vol. I, p. xiii.
48. *Ibid.*, p. xiv.
49. Cf., Eskor Toyo, 'The Mixed Economy as Fundamental Objective', paper presented to the 1977 conference of the Nigerian Political Science Association, reprinted in: *Political Issues in the Draft Constitution*, Zaria, 1978.
50. B. Onimode, 'The Citizen and the Draft Constitution' in: *Quarterly Journal of Administration*. Special Issue on 'Aspects of the Draft Constitution,' vol. XI, no. 4 (July) 1977, p. 256.
51. *CDC Report*, Vol. I, p. xv.
52. Claude Ake, 'The Congruence of Political Economies and Ideologies in Africa' in Gutkind and Wallerstein, 1985.
53. *New Nigerian*, 16 February 1980, p. 1. (Admittedly, it is not possible to determine from the reporting whether the quotation is direct or indirect.)
54. Stanley Macebuh, 'A Textbook of Democratic Politics', *Sunday Times*, 3 December 1978.

5

The Second Republic: Parties and Interests

Today Nigeria is a working democracy in a prospering but inegalitarian society. Its new democratic institutions will certainly survive current strains. (Kraus, 1982:136)

[The military handover represents] . . . a bright new page in modern African, and especially Nigerian postcolonial history. (Joseph, 1981:78)

An important lesson of the [1983] elections then is that the Nigerian voter, faced with a choice between bread-and-butter – or 'chop' – issues, and so-called tribalism–ethno-centrism, opts overwhelmingly for the former. That collective verdict . . . is making the system a 'national' and 'functional' one[1].

William Graf

This, and the following chapter, as well as important parts of the rest of the book, attempt to depict, analyse and comprehend the role of the Second Republic in the evolution of the Nigerian political economy and its institutional expression, the post-colonial state. As the irony contained in the above quotations suggests, this is no simple task, not even with all the advantages of hindsight. The hardly lamented collapse, on 31 December 1983, of the formally liberal-democratic structures established by the 1979 Constitution, it may be argued, finally put paid to the vague conglomeration of notions about 'modernisation', 'nation-building' and 'social engineering' that underlay the recivilianisation and elite-formation process[2]. *Structurally*, the Second Republic, with its minutely calibrated system of checks and balances, its technically well-thought-out federalism, its extensive mandate to law-makers, law-executors and law-adjudicators, its codes of conduct and its federal character, was, even in retrospect, a practically flawless creation. But in terms of *content* – its ability to respond to the development imperative described in Chapter 1, its consonance with the needs and aspirations of the majority, its correspondence with its own history and social composition – it was manifestly inadequate, particularly once the commanding positions had been ceded to the newly consolidating civilian elites. Nowhere were the substantial deficiencies of the formally democratic Nigerian state more evident, or more significant, than in the operation of the party system.

Party formation and development

In attempting to locate the 'specificity' of the party system of the 1979–83 interlude, one must recall the ambiguous relationship between the military and civilian elites analysed in the preceding two chapters. On the one hand, the military was propelled by its own internal contradictions and its sense of mission to withdraw from political leadership and formally democratise the state. But, on the other hand, it had to ensure that the successor regime would refrain from impinging on its corporate interests and would operate the state in the hegemonic interests of the elite class as a whole. This ambiguity was reflected, *inter alia*, in the distrust, even apprehension, on the part of the military leaders that prevailed in the waning months of military government. In December 1978, Brigadier Yar'Adua summoned all the political party leaders to dissuade them from personal attacks on each other, inflated promises and departures from the democratic 'rules of the game'[3] – itself a revealing metaphor. Subsequently, General Obasanjo hinted that he saw little difference between the old and new politicians; they were all 'sweet-talkers' and susceptible to corruption.[4] Again in March 1979, the parties' presidential candidates were summoned and reminded to follow the rules of the democratic game.[5]

For all its reservations, however, the military elite was forced to recognise that 'modern' elite-accommodating democracy *is* effectively party democracy and that the transfer of power would have to be accomplished via the mediation of ostensibly 'free' elections and party competition. Constitutional provisions, the Electoral Decree and, as a last resort, direct military intervention were intended to shape and constrain the party system and delimit the range of possible electoral choice.

Thus the definition of what constitutes a political party was tautly formulated. Both the Decree and the constitution distinguished between a party and an association. Whereas an association was seen as a group of people acting together for any common purpose (ethnic, social, cultural, occupational or religious), a party was defined as a vote-gathering association 'whose activities include canvassing for votes in support of a candidate for election to the office of President, Vice-President, Governor, Deputy Governor or member of a Legislative House or Local Government'. Political parties alone were permitted to canvass for votes or contribute funds to the election of candidates. This definition, of course, effectively excluded the candidacy of independents or non-party members, since individuals as such were prohibited from campaigning openly or soliciting votes. It also precluded the formation of a social-class-based party of the kind that might have evolved – as once in West Europe – out of associations representing urban workers, middle classes or even peasant groups. For instance, as Richard Joseph has argued (1981), 'the proscription of any formal association between trade unions and political groups or of any financial contribution from the former to the latter will gravely undermine the prospects of any left-wing, not to mention socialist, party for some time to come'. In a word, therefore, *the emergence of organised countervailing power was precluded by fiat*.

Indeed, just as the Second Republic itself was a conscious creation (or imposition?) 'from above', so the party system was intended to organise various factions of the elite class and exclude 'disruptive' elements. The process of party formation was biased from the outset towards the establishment of elitist parties headed by comparatively well-known figures. The few months that were fixed between the lifting of the ban on political activities and the final registration date meant that already prominent and/or wealthy figures with a reservoir of voters, workers, active supporters and a nucleus of a party organisation were much better placed than associations who had to acquire all these 'from scratch', for example by developing a mass basis or mobilising less wealthy, less organised groups. Alone the cost of setting up 19 state party offices was estimated at not less than N1 m. (Ofonagoro, 1979:26).

By the same token, the *status-quo* associations were much better able to meet the technical requirements of 'engineered democracy'; especially those relating to the material requirements imposed by regulations respecting the 'federal character' of Nigeria, according to which any 'licensed' party had to have its headquarters situated in the federal capital and establish branch offices in at least two-thirds of the States with effective penetration into most of the local government areas. The old politicians' contacts with the state elite, 'indigenised' business and other sources of funding enabled them to establish the required facilities – or to bypass these requirements – more readily than the groups aspiring to form 'new-breed' and socialist parties. Thus, the five licensed parties were all headed by members of an elite stratum prominent during the First Republic and since then active, in various ways, in high-level positions under the military government and in the national economy. On one level, that of legitimation, this phenomenon produced a popular perception that no substantial differences existed between the party systems of the First and Second Republics.[6]

But on another, structural, level, any reversion to regionalist, winner-takes-all politics was precluded, it was thought, not only by the new federalist political relations, the centralised economy and the regulations respecting the federal character, but also, positively, by provisions requiring intra-party democracy, open finances and state subsidies to the parties according to their electoral success, and negatively, by prohibition of ethnic biases, electoral malpractices, corruption, etc. Above all other things, national political power was only attainable by means of electoral success in a majority of States; and for this each party would have to aim at achieving a 'national spread' of votes. Although the class bases of the 'new' parties were fundamentally unchanged from the First Republic, their ethno-territorial sources of mass support would necessarily have to be much broader, thus precipitating certain new strategies and tactics on their part.

This concept of class continuity seems to possess considerable power in explaining the flaws of the party system of the Second Republic. The interests of the re-emergent political elites were well served by restrictions on the number and quality of new parties, since this effectively limited politics to system-supporting policies and proposals. Similarly, ideological alternatives were also circumscribed. Section 204 of the 1979 Constitution, following from Section 174 of the CDC's draft constitution, prescribed that party goals and programmes should conform with Chapter II of the Constitution which set out the basic goals of the liberal-democratic state. More appropriate to a one-party state, these rules bound all parties to the existing neo-colonial capitalist order, and ensured substantial ideological correspondence among them. In this context one must underline Sam Egite Oyovbaire's description of the political party system as having an 'obvious non-intellectual bias' and 'organizational aridity',[7] as reflected in the choice of party labels ('great', 'national', etc.) or in the similarity of party programmes and pronouncements, all of which represented catalogues of promises and intentions and hence appeals to voters' self-interest.[8] Ideologically, therefore, and despite the contrary views of a number of observers, the parties displayed a high degree of convergence. All were bent on[9]

> wooing the voter with promises of basically the same goodies. All are offering free medicare, free education, cheaper and better housing, pipe-borne water in all the villages and cities, more Made in Nigeria goods, jobs for every man and woman, self-sufficiency in food production through mechanised agriculture, better and cheaper transportation, etc.

Given these systemic factors, the parties could hardly be equal even to the basic 'modernising' task of mass mobilisation and democratisation. Apart from producing the legitimacy needed for elections and intra-elite disputes (for example, State elites versus federal elites), popular mobilisation and participation in the general interest (however defined) would have been dysfunctional. The party-political system aimed mainly at *elite interest-mobilisation* and at 'rationally' sharing out the social product among that elite class. In the absence of (consciously excluded) countervailing forces, the party system would amount to a mechanism for regulating access to the trough of state patronage and resources, that is, to a search for political offices barely mitigated by 'broker' or 'intermediating' parties. In this respect, the comparison with political life in the immediate post-colonial period could scarcely be more palpable.

These tendencies can be better illustrated with a brief account of the genesis and early development of the major political parties in the Second Republic. Although similar descriptions of party formation already exist,[10] it is necessary to reiterate a number of points here in order to prepare for the arguments that follow.

Within a party constellation of contending elite factions and anti-revolutionary pragmatism, hegemony would most likely go to the party best able to 'replicate within itself the fundamental structure and principles of the postcolonial Nigerian state' (Joseph, 1981:83). *The National Party of Nigeria* (NPN), which initially was often wrongly seen as a mere reincarnation of the old NPC, emerged as the party best able to incorporate and articulate the structural, class, and ideological realities of post-military government. Though the NPN's origins and dominant leadership cadres can be located among the same Northern, Hausa-Fulani forces that sustained the old NPC – the Sokoto Emirate, Barewa Old Boys' Association, Ali Akilu Memorial Fund (Kirk-Greene and Rimmer, 1981:33) – it set out early on to broaden its support base, via the 'Committee of 111' pro-Sharia members of the Constituent Assembly and its successor, the National Movement (Williams, 1982:149–52), into a conglomeration of regional and ethnic interests. The concept of interests here is most revealing, for the NPN's diverse ethno-regional composition was complemented by a consistent class make-up that, reflecting the elite-consolidating process described in the preceding chapter, established a 'pattern of trans-ethnic bargaining and accommodation' (Diamond, 1981:36) in the overall interests of its founding classes. These included not only prominent Northern politicians from the First Republic, but many leading figures who had previously opposed Northern domination but who now, in the context of a revised federalism, saw their interests well served in this 'natural alliance' of 'heavyweights', 'juggernauts', 'big men', and 'men of timbre and calibre' in Nigerian society: Tiv leader Joseph Tarka (formerly UMBC leader), Anthony Enahoro (of the old AG), Kingsley Mbadiwe (ex-NCNC), M.K.O. Abiola (business), and Maj.-General (Ret.) Adebayo (former military). To these came professionals, business groups, wealthy former military men and – though not always explicitly – traditional rulers, especially in the North. What bound these groups into a political alliance was a profound desire to conserve and consolidate the prevailing socio-economic order and their newly regained pre-eminent position within it. According to contemporary press accounts, the well endowed 'founding fathers' of the party donated N5 m. on the spot to the party at its first convention, thus instantly creating an alternative party appellation: Naira Party of Nigeria.

This loose collection of elitist groups, coupled with the party's trans-ethnic mass appeal, distinguished the NPN from all the remaining parties with their centralised, personalised leaderships and limited ethno-regional support base. As with much else about the NPN, the party was able to convert these potential drawbacks to its own advantage. First, it institutionalised its national character by adopting, in all essentials, the zoning system proposed by the Constitution Drafting Committee as a means of regulating the presidential elections[11]. The scheme is important, not only as a political party tactic, but for what it suggests about the federal character and the realities of party politics in the Second Republic. As Figure 5.1 shows, the CDC proposed that representation in federal and, *mutatis mutandis*, State agencies be achieved by dividing the nation into four zones, two in each of the 'North' and 'South' – thus recognising the main postcolonial lines of political cleavage in the country. Translated into NPN organisational policy, the principle meant that party leaders were chosen so that the main national positions were divided up among the zonal representatives: the Presidential candidate from Zone 1, Vice-Presidential candidate from Zone 3, the Party Chairman from Zone 2, and the President of the Senate from Zone 4. After their terms of office had expired, in theory, the next series of candidates was to have been chosen from different zones. This policy not only ensured the minimisation of intra-party ethnic or sectional conflict, it also contributed to making the NPN the only really national – in the sense of geographical spread – party contesting the 1979 and 1983 elections. Significantly, all the other parties were sooner or later compelled to attempt to adopt an analogous *de facto* process of intra-party leadership selection.

Figure 5.1 *NPN 'zoning' system*

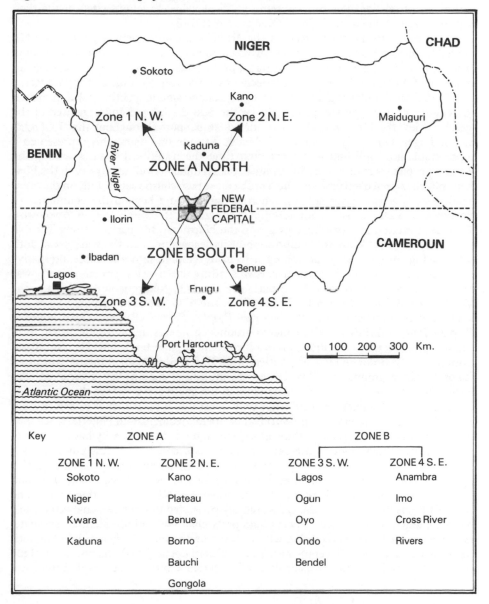

Second, and partly as a result of this zoning arrangement, the NPN was able to engage in a more representative leadership selection process, and each of the ten aspiring presidential candidates was constrained to muster his own support at the first party convention. The choice of Shehu Shagari in an open vote – but not by a majority[12] – thus appeared as the outcome of a 'national' and 'democratic' process.

And third, the party's underlying strategy of adapting to Nigerian society-as-it-is guided and shaped its political tactics. As a political association, its main objective – like the other parties, but more unreservedly – was to gain political power. Once in possession of it, it would attempt to provide essentially 'more of the same' – more development, more facilities, more benefits – but without any change in the socio-economic order. Indeed, the party has rightly been criticised as elevating patron–client relationships to a supreme political value, as summarised in the then popular slogan 'You Chop - I Chop' (Koehn, 1981:27–8).

By contrast with the slower start of the NPN, the *Unity Party of Nigeria* (UPN), headed by former AG leader Obafemi Awolowo, announced its formation within hours of the lifting of the ban on politics. It had a preformulated programme (essentially an amalgam of Awolowo's writings and speeches over the years[13]), a list of party leaders, a broad, dedicated following of supporters especially among youth, and a prepared strategy for gaining political power. By far the best disciplined and organised of the 'new' parties, the UPN quickly consolidated its support throughout the 'LOOOB' States: Lagos, Ondo, Oyo, Ogun and Bendel. On the one hand, this represented a considerable accomplishment; for the first time the traditional fissures among the Yoruba peoples (as manifest in, for instance, the Akintola–Awolowo rivalry in the First Republic) had been overcome and the Yoruba mass base consolidated. But, on the other hand, the UPN was never able to penetrate significantly beyond the boundaries of Yorubaland to gain the supra-ethnic support enjoyed by the NPN. Despite Awolowo's overtures toward minority ethnic groups in the Northeast, the party's strong Yoruba-centricity, the very 'Western' composition of its leadership, and the widespread anti-Awo feelings in other areas prevented it from developing into a credible alternative elsewhere in the country. In particular, Awo's failure to evolve a supra-ethnic party was reflected in the loss to other nascent parties of the AG's 'old reliables' – Tarka in the Middle Belt, Anthony Enahoro in Bendel State and S. G. Ikoku in Anambra State.

The nucleus of what became the *Nigerian People's Party* (NPP) and *Great Nigerian People's Party* (GNPP) initially cohered around an interesting and tendentially progressive premise: that a coalition of minorities could counter traditional Hausa–Fulani, Yoruba and Igbo domination of political life. The predominant thinking within its major founding group, the Club 19 (an assemblage of mainly 'anti-Sharia' MCAs, former NCNC politicians and other notables in the South and East; see chapter 4), was that a coalition of minorities could not only constitute a parliamentary majority but would be the best guarantor of the survival of liberal democracy in Nigeria, since they could not form a homogeneous ethnic bloc-party and would necessarily have to operate on the basis of continuous intra-party compromises and a balancing-out process.[14] However, Club 19, in a search for funds and organisational support, quasi-naturally hit upon Club 400, a similarly oriented association of younger MCAs, financed by and beholden to Alhaji Waziri Ibrahim, a Kanuri and one of Nigeria's wealthiest men. The early NPP was therefore, like the UPN, rapidly converted into the personal vehicle of a powerful leader, who insisted on being both party chairman and presidential candidate. However, as the NPN succeeded in winning over important (mainly anti-Igbo) minorities in Rivers and Cross-Rivers States, and as Waziri opened 'his' organisation to Igbo support (for example, the Organization of Nigerian Unity, a caucus of former Zik supporters) without simultaneously seeking further ethnic balance in the West and North-West, the coalition of minorities gave way, at the party grassroots, to a focus on an Eastern (Igbo) and Northeastern (Tiv, Kanuri) bloc strategy. This being the case, the surprise entry into the NPP of Nnamdi Azikiwe, former NCNC leader and ex-president of the First Republic, precipitated a split between those – mainly former NCNC members like Ogunsanya and Olu Akinfosile – who adhered to the Igbo-based bloc strategy and therefore supported 'Zik', and those who concurred with Waziri Ibrahim's refusal to step down from either of his two party posts. The former became a reconstituted NPP, the latter the GNPP. The two parties entered the Second Republic with virtually identical ideologies and platforms; and the minority-coalition idea was effectively lost.

The fifth party, the *People's Redemption Party*, led by the late Aminu Kano, emerged from the outset as a bundle of contradictions. In some respects the lineal successor of the old NEPU with its traditional suspicion of the emirate aristocracy, it also attracted many new elements such as S. G. Ikoku of the old AG, and Michael Imoudu, the radical trade union leader. Founded in some measure as a breakaway of the NPN when the latter failed to provide Aminu Kano with a position 'worthy of his stature', and joined later by a group of more or less radical intellectuals, the party framed part of its platform in such terms as anti-imperialism and anti-capitalism even while officially adhering to Aminu Kano's vague ideology of 'democratic humanism'. Aspiring to be a universal leftist party, it never managed to extend its support base beyond Kano and parts of Kaduna States. It harboured within itself a dominant accommodationist wing (Aminu Kano, S. G. Ikoku) and a militant, increasingly assertive radical wing (Imoudu, Abubakar Rimi, Balarabe Musa), a crucial factor in the subsequent party split to be discussed below. Initially more 'pure', populist and oriented to the *talakawa* (Northern common people) masses, the party in time, as it absorbed wealthy businessmen, landowners and elements of the Northern middle classes, increasingly developed in the direction of a catch-all mass party.

As this brief summary of individual party formation demonstrates, ideological considerations scarcely played a role in elite mobilisation except insofar as token packages of promises were required to rally mass support. With the partial exception of one faction of the PRP, it is justifiable to speak of an ideological convergence of the Nigerian party system right from the outset, one which reflected the ideological hegemony of the elite classes. Catalogues of promises cannot be equated with ideologies. If not enunciated within a framework of ends and means, they amount to mere demagogic devices. Eddie Madanugu therefore asserts (1982:86):

> If a party tells us that it is going to mechanize agriculture, we are right to doubt it unless the party tells us simultaneously that it is going to stop the importation of luxury goods in order to be able to finance the importation of agricultural machinery . . . If a party tells us that it is going to double the national minimum wage, workers will be right to dismiss the promise unless the party simultaneously promises to reduce the wages and incomes of some other people, since the national income cannot be multiplied at will . . . If a party tells us that it is going to ensure full employment, we shall be justified to have a big laugh unless the party simultaneously tells us that it is going to nationalize key sectors of the economy since no government can indefinitely enforce employment in businesses it does not control.

In this context, it is worth adding that, had it not been for personal ambitions and personality clashes among individual party elite members and factions, as well as the ethnicity factor, all the preconditions for a one-party, or at most two-party patronage-oriented system were present. The nucleus of the PRP, for instance, was a leadership unwilling to assume a subordinate position in the NPN. There is also compelling evidence that Zik's decision to head the NPP was based on a strategy of bargaining from a position of relative strength, i.e. from the leadership of a party consolidating Igbo voting power and thus extracting maximum benefits from a subsequent alliance with whatever turned out to be the dominant party. On this, Professor Omoruyi posits a Zik–Nwobodo (the latter a central NPP figure and subsequently Governor of Anambra State) gatekeeper function 'mediating the relationship between the Igbo and the Nigerian society'. The Owelle (Zik's honorary title) was said to foresee an ultimate NPN-NPP fusion into an NPNP (National Party of Nigerian People).[15] The post-election alliance between the NPN and NPP – to be discussed presently – would tend to bear out Omoruyi's thesis. If the NPP could co-govern with the NPN, then presumably so too could the GNPP with its virtually indistinguishable programme. This leaves only the UPN. Its somewhat stronger focus on more material enablements (for example, immediate and 'free' universal primary education) and the polarising effect of Chief Awolowo no doubt would have made a merger more difficult, but not inconceivable, since the UPN was also primarily concerned with outputs. The rush of defections and 'decampings' in the latter days of the first electoral period, also to be described below, suggested the ease with which party loyalties could be transferred and 'ideologies' exchanged.[16]

All this would seem to qualify both Joseph's (1981:81, 85) and Diamond's (1982:635–6) division of the five parties into centre-right and centre-left categories, to say nothing of Dudley's scale (1982:194), which looks like this:

PRP	UPN	NPP	GNPP	NPN
LEFT		CENTRE		RIGHT

A more appropriate depiction might therefore be:

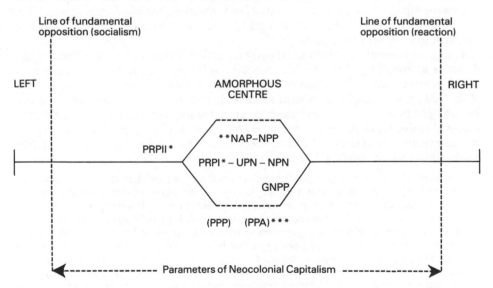

*PRP I = Kano/Ikoku faction
 PRP II = Rimi/Imoudu faction
**NAP = Nigerian Advance Party; admitted 1982 by FEDECO
***PPP/PPA = quasi-party formations; see explanation next section

Figure 5.2 *Schematic representation of political party ideological landscape*

where 'left' is taken to mean, as a minimum, advocacy of material enablements, more popular participation in political life and opposition to neo-colonialism and neo-colonial capitalism; and where 'right' represents the goal of restoring colonial and/or pre-colonial conditions. By these criteria, then, all five parties operated securely within the ideological *status quo*. What distinguished them from one another was the respective ethnic, sectional, sectoral and territorial factions of the elite that they represented.

Electoral dynamics of elite rule

The 1979 elections set in motion the dynamics of elite rule that were to dominate the Second Republic. Staged sequentially at one-week intervals between 7 July and 11 August 1979, the elections fixed the relative strengths of the various elite factions and groupings. For our purposes, it is not necessary to recreate the campaign or analyse the – notoriously suspect, in any case[17] – results and percentages. Tables 5.1 and 5.2 and Figure 5.3 summarise these, while a whole body of literature is occupied with the intricacies of the elections themselves.[18] But the elections did produce the basic party political constellation of power that prevailed throughout almost all the Second Republic, and it is this constellation in its several dimensions that explains much about the modalities of elite rule and patterns of bargaining under the recivilianised regime. Of these dimensions, the federal-state distribution of political power proved to be salient.

Federally, the NPN's self-image as being *the* national party proved to be prophetic. As the tables demonstrate, the party received a consistent one-third or so of the popular vote in all national elections, thus winning the presidency, 36 of 95 Senate seats (from 12 different States) and 168 of 449 National Assembly mandates. In 90 of the 95 Senate contests, the NPN finished either first or second. Moreover, this electoral support was far more widely spread ethnically and territorially across the federation than that of any of the other parties. It also won seven governorships in States ranging from South-eastern Cross Rivers to Northwestern Sokoto. And it gained House of Assembly seats in 17 of the 19 States. No other party even approached this distribution. The results of the presidential elections were even more suggestive. Shagari was elected President with a total of 5,688,857 votes or roughly one-third of the total popular vote. Awolowo, the runner-up, was not quantitatively far behind with his 4,915,857 votes. But their respective spreads represented the crucial variable. Shagari received a quarter or more of all the votes recorded in each of 12 States as well as 20% of the Kano vote; or, put another way, in 18 out of the 19 States he was either the first or second popular choice for the presidency. Awolowo, on the other hand, drew some 4.3 million votes alone by mobilising massive support in four States: Lagos, Ondo, Ogun, and Oyo, with just half a million additional votes coming from the remaining States, principally from Bendel.

But *sub-federally*, namely at the State level, traditional ethno-regional patterns were clearly reasserted as a 'countervailing' tendency. Twelve State governorships went to the opposition parties, which also collectively constituted a majority in both federal houses. These patterns demonstrate that voting in the Second Republic was still ethnically based. Indeed, the correlation between political party preference and ethnic group affiliation was irrefutable: throughout all five elections, the more ethnically homogeneous the individual State, the greater the degree of voting solidarity accorded to 'its' party and candidates. Thus Ogun, Ondo and Oyo States returned only UPN senators, deputies, and governors. (So did more heterogeneous Lagos, most of whose non-Yoruba inhabitants probably abstained, had their votes rigged away or returned to their home areas to vote.) These States gave the party leader, Chief Awolowo, 92.6%, 94.5% and 86% of the presidential vote respectively. Similarly, the States of the Igbo

Table 5.1 *Summary of 1979 election results: federal institutions by State*

State	Registered Voters	Total Votes Cast	Presidential % Total Votes By Party GNPP	UPN	NPN	PRP	NPP	Total Votes Cast	Senatorial % By Party GNPP	UPN	NPN	PRP	NPP	Total Votes Cast	House of Representatives % By Party GNPP	UPN	NPN	PRP	NPP
Anambra	2,606,663	1,209,038	1.67	0.75	13.50	1.20	82.58	953,546	1.45	1.15	22.03	2.05	73.32	1,108,771	3.06	1.7	22.90	1.35	71.01
Bauchi	2,096,162	998,683	15.44	3.00	62.48	14.34	4.72	709,518	26.47	4.08	45.57	17.94	5.94	807,210	24.40	3.35	59.7	8.5	4.09
Bendel	2,400,174	669,511	1.23	53.23	36.19	6.73	8.60	709,703	5.99	46.57	37.25	0.29	9.89	903,140	3.37	41.1	47.3	0.24	8.05
Benue	1,636,371	538,879	7.89	2.57	76.39	1.35	11.71	470,359	9.88	3.17	70.79	0.53	15.63	513,359	11.60	2.7	68.9	1.4	15.5
Borno	2,945,925	710,968	54.04	3.35	34.71	6.52	1.35	519,884	53.54	4.26	35.51	6.06	0.63	736,327	53.01	4.3	35.4	6.3	1.01
Cross River	2,464,184	661,103	15.14	11.76	64.40	1.01	7.66	620,496	26.39	12.64	49.97	—	10.99	729,667	21.7	12.9	53.2	0.42	11.8
Gongola	2,308,355	639,138	34.09	21.67	35.52	4.34	4.35	636,673	35.04	19.59	31.92	10.64	2.80	668,381	35.5	21.3	34.6	4.5	4.10
Imo	3,490,484	1,153,355	3.00	0.64	8.80	0.89	86.67	1,018,743	9.88	0.92	13.92	0.85	74.42	1,162,689	8.94	6.9	19.21	1.22	69.2
Kaduna	3,455,047	1,382,712	13.80	6.68	43.12	3.66	4.72	1,040,874	22.38	8.17	38.51	26.77	4.17	1,256,780	20.2	6.9	39.6	28.8	4.41
Kano	5,226,598	1,220,763	1.54	1.23	19.94	76.41	0.91	966,613	3.66	1.43	24.21	70.70	—	1,045,154	2.52	1.033	22.5	73.9	—
Kwara	1,108,029	354,605	5.71	39.48	53.62	0.67	0.52	314,882	10.28	46.04	49.00	0.20	0.47	340,692	9.7	40.6	49.2	0.24	—
Lagos	1,829,369	828,414	0.48	82.30	7.18	0.47	9.57	534,102	2.71	80.24	6.48	0.48	10.09	595,149	0.95	88.8	9.5	0.53	0.18
Niger	1,051,160	383,347	16.50	3.69	74.88	3.99	1.11	270,187	26.16	4.95	64.95	3.32	0.32	299,712	20.2	4.3	71.04	3.3	1.09
Ogun	1,663,608	744,668	0.53	92.11	6.23	0.31	0.32	461,954	0.67	87.68	11.49	—	0.16	612,454	0.30	90.9	8.7	—	—
Ondo	2,573,960	1,369,547	0.26	94.51	4.19	0.18	0.86	563,449	0.86	89.00	8.81	0.04	1.28	824,759	0.31	91.6	6.8	0.12	1.19
Oyo	4,534,779	1,396,547	0.57	85.78	12.75	0.32	0.55	978,247	1.15	77.45	20.48	—	0.91	1,011,233	1.05	78.2	19.8	0.30	0.69
Plateau	1,748,868	548,405	6.82	5.29	34.73	3.98	49.17	454,198	8.91	4.32	34.08	4.19	48.50	584,167	9.13	3.88	32.6	3.16	51.2
Rivers	1,675,934	687,951	2.18	0.33	72.65	0.46	14.35	310,469	15.20	6.49	49.43	0.73	28.15	491,264	11.49	5.2	58.5	0.9	23.9
Sokoto	3,818,094	1,348,697	26.61	2.52	66.58	3.35	0.92	1,024,768	37.16	3.33	55.77	3.73	—	1,250,647	36.40	2.1	59.8	1.71	—

heartland, Anambra and Imo, presented Dr Azikiwe with their solid support. Kano State opted overwhelmingly for Malam Aminu Kano; and the Kanuri areas of Borno State voted primarily GNPP. Although the NPN did receive a broader voting spread, as just indicated, it too consistently registered 70% or more of the popular vote in Benue, Niger and Sokoto States. These trends were still more pronounced at the State level. The UPN secured control of the LOOOB States: in Lagos and Ogun 100% of the Houses of Assembly, 99% of the Ondo House and 93% of Oyo. In Anambra 85% of State assembly seats went to the NPP and 88% in Imo. In Kano State the PRP gained 89% of the House seats, while in Borno the GNPP won 81%. In all these cases, the dominant party also won the governorships, thus producing (or in some measure re-producing) what I have called one-party sub-states (see chapter 2). By contrast, such ethnically heterogeneous States as Bendel (UPN 56.7%, NPN 36.7% of Assembly seats) and Gongola (GNPP/UPN alliance) reflected greater balance in their State legislatures. It is therefore noteworthy that the sole non-ethnically based party, the Nigerian Advance Party, which was only licensed in 1982, could not obtain more than 1% of the vote in the 1983 elections. Indeed, a careful study of pre-1966 and post-1979 voting patterns does indicate that the correlation between ethnicity and voting preference remained virtually unchanged, and this observation has been used as evidence of an unregenerate tribal consciousness among the Nigerian electorate.

Yet such precipitate conclusions have to be qualified, and the qualifications themselves provide important insights into the nature of formal liberal democracy in Nigeria.

For one, the absence of substantial political alternatives undoubtedly acted as a disincentive to vote for other than what was perceived to be the dominant party of one's State. Faced with five fundamentally similar parties, with practically interchangeable programmes that largely amounted to catalogues of unco-ordinated promises, and all composed of wealthy notables at the top, 'rationally acting' voters simply opted for the party which most represented their own ethnic affinity. Experiences of the First Republic had shown that ethnic solidarity might at least bring some tangible rewards. This argument was of special relevance in the minority States where, as Olatunde Ojo posits, the high votes for the NPN were attributable to 'cool calculations of economic and political interests'.[19] Since the NPN everywhere rested on the local power of 'big men' and 'favourite sons', and since these local notables were convinced that the party could both maintain political stability and ensure an appropriate allocation of state outputs, they were well able to carry their States for the NPN.

Second, the new structures of federalism had in fact been designed to accommodate ethno-sectional tendencies. The structural aspects of this machinery are dealt with in chapter 6. But as far as party-political alignments are concerned, the new federalism permitted the ethnic minorities in the old Middle Belt or on the Niger Delta some measure of autonomy. For example, the old Regions had merely compressed them into appendages of the larger ethnic groups which dominated the respective Regions; now, however, the various minorities in Cross-Rivers, Rivers Plateau, Benue and Kwara could assert their independence from perceived majority domination. For these reasons, the Cross-Rivers, Rivers and Bendel votes can be interpreted as essentially an anti-Igbo vote; the Gongola, Borno and Plateau results can be seen as anti-Hausa–Fulani; in Kwara a strong anti-Yoruba tendency among the Igala and Igbirra is evident; and the Kano *talakawa* could proclaim their separateness from the dominant Hausa–Fulani oligarchy in the North. Much of the NPN's success – and virtually all the PRP's success – can be attributed to their ability to attract support from such minorities.

Table 5.2 *Summary of 1979 election results: in the States*

State	Total No. of Seats	State Assemblies					Governor/Party
		GNPP	UPN	NPN	PRP	NPP	
Anambra	87	1	—	13	—	73	Nwobodo/NPP
Bauchi	60	9	—	45	2	4	Ali/NPN
Bendel	60	—	34	22	—	4	Alli/UPN
Benue	57	6	—	48	—	3	Aku/NPN
Borno	72	59	—	11	2	—	Goni/GNPP
Cross River	84	16	7	58	—	3	Isong/NPN
Gongola	63	25	18	15	1	4	Barde/GNPP
Imo	90	2	—	9	—	79	Mbakwe/NPP
Kaduna	99	10	3	64	16	6	Musa/PRP
Kano	138	3	1	11	123	—	Rimi/PRP
Kwara	42	2	15	25	—	—	Atta/NPN
Lagos	36	—	36	—	—	—	Jakande/UPN
Niger	30	2	—	28	—	—	Ibrahim/NPN
Ogun	36	—	36	—	—	—	Onabanjo/UPN
Ondo	66	—	65	1	—	—	Ajasin/UPN
Oyo	126	—	117	9	—	—	Ige/UPN
Plateau	148	3	—	10	—	34	Lar/NPP
Rivers	42	1	—	26	—	15	Okilo/NPN
Sokoto	111	19	—	92	—	—	Kanjiwa/NPN
Total	1347	157	333	487	144	226	

All this suggests a number of somewhat changed political imperatives in the Second Republic. Since no one party could by itself achieve a majority at the federal level, compromise and coalition-building would be necessary. But given the larger number of sub-federal units and the much more differentiated interplay of ethnic units, such compromises and coalitions would be shifting, fluid and rather unpredictable. To reduce the uncertainty which this situation entailed, therefore, all parties would be under pressure to emulate the national spread of the NPN, either by transforming themselves into supra-ethnic groups (which, given their limited ethnic mass bases, was most unlikely), or by allying with, merging into, co-opting or otherwise enlisting the support of other parties. Seen in terms of nation-building and institution-building theories derived from Western social science, such developments were highly desirable, since they pointed the way to 'institutionalised bargaining' and perhaps to a 'competitive' two-party system.

However – and this point has had to be made several times in this book so far – the fit between such theories and Nigerian reality is rarely an adequate one.

With its successful presidential candidate, its electoral plurality and its national spread, the NPN was, of course, the only political formation able to establish a governmental coalition at the federal level. This it achieved, after considerable negotiations, by concluding a working alliance with the NPP, which for its part had mainly been created as a bargaining unit, as the preceding section has argued. Almost exclusively an alliance of convenience, the NPN-NPP Accord (not unlike the erstwhile NPC–NCNC alliance) was founded not on lofty principles or strategies of fundamental change, but on a series of tangible conditions intended to bring advantages to the two partners' leaderships. For the NPN, the Accord provided the majority support initially essential – until the powers of patronage and office could supply a substitute – for proposed

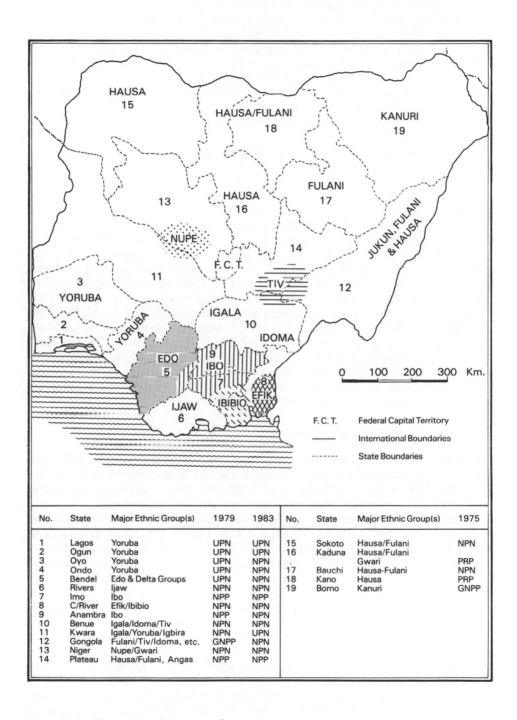

No.	State	Major Ethnic Group(s)	1979	1983	No.	State	Major Ethnic Group(s)	1975
1	Lagos	Yoruba	UPN	UPN	15	Sokoto	Hausa/Fulani	NPN
2	Ogun	Yoruba	UPN	UPN	16	Kaduna	Hausa/Fulani	
3	Oyo	Yoruba	UPN	NPN	.		Gwari	PRP
4	Ondo	Yoruba	UPN	NPN	17	Bauchi	Hausa-Fulani	NPN
5	Bendel	Edo & Delta Groups	UPN	NPN	18	Kano	Hausa	PRP
6	Rivers	Ijaw	NPN	NPN	19	Borno	Kanuri	GNPP
7	Imo	Ibo	NPP	NPP				
8	C/River	Efik/Ibibio	NPN	NPN				
9	Anambra	Ibo	NPP	NPN				
10	Benue	Igala/Idoma/Tiv	NPN	NPN				
11	Kwara	Igala/Yoruba/Igbira	NPN	UPN				
12	Gongola	Fulani/Tiv/Idoma, etc.	GNPP	NPN				
13	Niger	Nupe/Gwari	NPN	NPN				
14	Plateau	Hausa/Fulani, Angas	NPP	NPP				

Figure 5.3 *The parties' ethnic support bases*

legislation, ministerial appointments and the like in both federal legislative houses. In exchange, the NPP exacted the speakership of the House of Representatives, the deputy presidency of the Senate and eight Cabinet posts for itself, as well as an assurance that the government would act speedily to remove certain controversial issues left over, as it were, from the civil war, such as chronic underdevelopment of the former Eastern Region and the problem of 'abandoned properties' in the non-Igbo areas.

This bipartisan agreement was, however, extremely tenuous and fragile from the outset, and this for a number of reasons: (i) The NPN, in itself a highly patronage-oriented party, was under constant pressure to divert state contracts, appointments, scholarships and other state resources to its own supporters and leaders, thus denying the NPP commensurate shares of federal largesse. (ii) The fundamental assumption underlying the Accord, namely, that the executive needed a continuous working legislative majority, was only partially correct, as the next chapter will explain. This assumption was no doubt rooted in the structurally different conditions of the First Republic; but once the initial ministerial appointments had been confirmed and the first legislative programme put in place, the President was in fact able to function comparatively well without recourse to a legislative majority. (iii) The NPP, increasingly pressed into the junior partner role, for instance by being excluded from inner-governmental decision-making bodies and by receiving insufficient patronage to sustain its following, more and more refused its support for certain crucial bills such as on revenue-sharing. (iv) Meanwhile, the NPN like a magnet was able to draw individual support from the four other parties, mostly senators and mainly from the NPP, GNPP and PRP. Invoking the national interest and the dangers to democracy, the party was thus able to persuade, co-opt or buy off a number of legislators who, though constitutionally prohibited from 'carpet-crossing' could sustain the government merely by refusing to oppose NPN policies or bills. Thus on 6 July 1981 the NPP gave notice of its intention to dissolve the Accord, to which the NPN replied that no notice was necessary and that dissolution could be effected immediately.

Shifting alliances and cleavages

The collapse of the NPN–NPP working arrangement triggered a twofold development that dominated inter-party relations for the rest of the Second Republic. On the one hand, the NPN, on the strength of its wealth, influence and power position, persevered in its strategy of winning over individuals and groups from the other parties. In February 1981, for instance, three GNPP senators (including the party's Senate Leader and Deputy National Chairman, Mahmud Waziri) were expelled from their party for voting with the NPN on the Revenue Allocation Bill (Diamond, 1983:51). And when in December 1979, PRP second-in-command S. G. Ikoku agreed to co-operate with the NPN in Kaduna State 'in the interests of stable government', the protests of the PRP radicals generated the beginning of the party's subsequent split, as will be explained later. The NPP itself was debilitated by a series of defections to the NPN, beginning with National Vice-Chairman, Matthew Mbu, and two other prominent party leaders in Cross River State and extending to two of the party's federal ministers who refused to follow the NPP into opposition. In particular, the loss of the party's former vice-presidential candidate and then Minister of External Affairs, Dr Ishaya Audu, was symptomatic of this trend.

On the other hand, the four parties excluded from federal power were now constrained to attempt to offset the NPN's national predominance by seeking a co-ordinated oppositional alliance. Individually, none of them could 'transcend' its ethno-sectional basis of mass support. But by means of expanding the grouping of 'Nine Progressive Governors' into the 'Twelve Progressive Governors', the GNPP, UPN, NPP and PRP leaderships envisaged a united-front strategy of sustained opposition to the NPN, and hoped to jerry-build a majority coalition out of this working arrangement.

The 'Nine Progressive Governors' had, of course, represented an initial oppositional grouping to the dominant coalition. Right from Chief Awolowo's court challenge to Shagari's election on the basis of the famous twelve and two-thirds States formula, through the UPN-GNPP-PRP rejection of presidential liaison officers and their challenge to the government's deportation of the GNPP majority leader in the Borno House of Assembly, Alhaji Shugaba, to their resentment at federal control over the mass media,[20] the Nine Governors, with the UPN Governors as their central driving force and Awo as their mentor and leading personality, had relentlessly criticised government policies and constituted a rallying-point for the various oppositional currents. Effectively excluded from a share of federal political power and all the material incentives associated with it, the nine governors and the parties they represented had met regularly to explore ways and means of establishing a countervailing political force and of exacting an appropriate share of federal 'outputs' for the areas under their control.

The entry of Azikiwe's NPP into the anti-NPN alliance produced two significant effects on the latter. First, the axis of primary political conflict in the Second Republic now clearly became a federal-State one. The Twelve Progressive Governors constituted a majority of the States and realised that their ability to operate as a counterweight necessarily rested on their control of State power. For this reason, they were constrained to retrench and shore up their basically localised sources of support (for example, by overwhelming intra-State opposition and/or by manipulating 'their' Local Government Councils and traditional rulers (see chapter 9), as well as by focusing on emotive issues such as revenue-allocation), even while, paradoxically, searching for a federal coalition capable of ousting the NPN from its power position. This reproduced in a somewhat altered form the old contradiction between particularist bases of support and the need to seek national power. Second, the presence of Azikiwe posed, in practically unresolvable terms, the question of the leadership of the opposition forces. Hitherto Awo and the UPN, with their tactics of uncompromising, strident opposition and their quantitatively greater mass support, had quasi-automatically emerged as the coalition's leading force – despite occasional recalcitrance displayed by Waziri Ibrahim. But Zik, like Awo, was a strong public personality with a large mass following. Both men, then in their seventies, had held high positions in the First Republic and under military government, both were able spokesmen for their ethnic group (with whom they were absolutely identified) and both were extremely ambitious personally. Moreover, both to some extent embodied and even articulated long-standing ethno-regional animosities and rivalries, so much so, in fact, that the loyalties they inspired could by no means guarantee that their respective followers would accept the negotiated leadership of one or the other of these 'big men' of Nigerian politics.[21] For these reasons, the forming opposition in the Second Republic could not coalesce into a unified, supra-ethnic force; it remained a two- or three-headed creature of expediency.[22]

Although the Twelve Progressive Governors were able to produce a common oppositional front on some matters directly affecting State powers – the 1981 Revenue Allocation Bill and the apparent federal restrictions on State television autonomy – they were quite incapable of countering the 'magnet' effect accruing to the NPN with its powers and sources of patronage which rested on control of the central government. Thus, on the one hand, a palpable polarisation of party politics occurred as, in Larry Diamond's words 'the middle ground in Nigerian politics disappears, political feeling intensifies, the rhetoric of conflict becomes more extreme, trust between opposing forces diminishes, and the political stakes rise with each new contest'.[23]

On the other hand, the forming opposition was continuously undermined partly by individuals' succumbing to the president's invitation to support a 'broad-based government of national unity', and partly by internecine conflicts and rivalries within the parties themselves. In general, the smaller and more ethno-regionally based the respective party was, the more susceptible it was to these basic imperatives.

The GNPP expellee faction, just alluded to, quickly declared their intention to co-operate with the national government and rejected party leader Ibrahim Waziri's alleged attempts at pushing the GNPP into an alliance with the UPN. What followed was a rapid and irreversible process of factionalisation characterised by an outbreak of the 'You Sack Me, I Sack You' syndrome within the party,[24] and culminating in almost total disintegration. For our purposes, it is not necessary to recount the shifting alliances and manipulations within the party at this time. What is of interest, however, is that the GNPP fractured into at least three groupings. (i) The core of the expellees, led by party General Secretary Nduka Eze, First Deputy National Secretary Kola Balogun and second Deputy National Chairman Dr Ben Nzeribe, after counter-expelling Waziri Ibrahim, eventually joined the NPN. (ii) The Mahmud Waziri faction of expellees was joined by still further expulsions of GNPP Senators (ultimately seven out of eight). If these manoeuvres effectively separated the party's federal representatives who were loyal to Alhaji Waziri, subsequent events in Gongola State achieved the same end at the State level. There, Governor Abubakar Barde's participation in the PPA and PPP (to be discussed below) resulted, at Waziri's instigation, in his expulsion from the party.[25] (iii) This left at increasingly isolated National Chairman, Ibrahim Waziri, in partial control of the remnants of the party organisation as well as of an indeterminable number of Gongola State and National Assembly members. Given FEDECO's refusal to recognise any breakaway party fragment, however large, the only question remaining for the GNPP after mid-1982 was: how would its various factions eventually re-align themselves?

The PRP was subject to similar strains and stresses. In fact, it managed to reproduce within itself a series of cleavages entirely analogous to those evolving in the larger political system between state power and States' power. The PRP 'national' party leadership (Aminu Kano and Ikoku) had opted for a policy of 'accommodation' with the NPN in what was said to be the 'national interest'. But the party's two State governors in Kano and Kaduna, who moreover represented the more radical-socialist tendency therein, had been consistent and vocal members of the Nine, then Twelve, Progressive Governors. As the NPN actively began to seek out new allies, in particular by persuading, inducing or co-opting individuals and groups from other parties, the PRP leadership under Ikoku – Aminu Kano fell ill and was abroad for medical treatment for much of this period – entered into serious negotiations with the ruling party. This apparent *rapprochement* with an NPN that was perceived as the traditional enemy of the party's mass base among the *talakawa* gave rise to general intra-party resentment, especially when the national directorate passed a resolution forbidding the two PRP Governors (Abubakar Rimi of Kano and Balarabe Musa of Kaduna) to participate in the Progressive Governors' activities. The two governors refused to comply on the grounds of State autonomy and ideological consistency. The controversy was summed up by an intra-party panel headed by national publicity secretary, Uche Chukwumerije:[26]

The mere idea of any Accord with [the] NPN, which is seen by [the] generality of PRP supporters as a reincarnation of their historical oppressor, NPC, and the manner in which the negotiations were handled generated distrust . . . [the impression was given] that the leadership was determined to drag the party into the Federal Government at all costs.

When the two governors were first suspended, then expelled, from the party (together with several allied members of the National Assembly) they retaliated by convening a convention in December 1980 to expel Kano and Ikoku and elect Rimi as national secretary and labour leader Michael Imoudu as party president. As in the case of the GNPP, the question of who represented the 'authentic' PRP was urgently posed. Again, FEDECO declared for the originally licensed party leadership, while the two State party organisations as well as 38 out of 47 federal PRP House members and five out of seven Senators went with the 'breakaway' faction. Paradoxically, the 'national' accommodationist group subsequently was reduced to a State-based rump after abandoning its claim to be a federal party, while the 'radical' oppositional group, which was based on the States' rights principle, was forced to seek out a national alliance. After Aminu Kano's death, Ikoku resigned from the party in August 1982 and joined the NPN Government as Special Adviser to the President on National Assembly Affairs, and most of the other accommodationists were rewarded with government sinecures. After the 1983 elections, the PRP Governor of Kano, Alhaji Sabo Bakin Zuwo, was content to head a strictly regional State-oriented party even while pledging loyalty to the President and vowing never to be 'confrontational'. The new party leader, Alhaji Hassan Yusuf, indicated his willingness to participate in the national government after the 1983 elections.[27] The radicals, on the other hand, with most of the party legislators and elected officials behind them, yet with no prospect of formal recognition, had to find other institutional affiliations before the 1983 elections.

In this context of fragmentation of the smaller parties, on the one hand, and consolidation of the larger ones, on the other, it is possible to perceive from about mid-1982 onward, *a fundamental re-alignment of the party system* in the face of the 1983 elections.

As the elections approached, the problem of how, on what terms, and under whose leadership to unite the disparate opposition forces, became increasingly pressing. As argued above, in a primarily chop-oriented party system, the party in control of state power exerts a powerful consolidating effect on the rest of the political system, while the ethno-regionally constituted opposition forces lack the coherence and will that, say, a common ideology or set of ideals would furnish. Failing these, the unity of the opposition revolves mainly around the issue of access to state munificence. At the same time, however, this very secular and material concern provides an incentive to overcome – if not transcend – the particularistic bases of party formation and support.

Thus the Progressive Governors moved fitfully towards a party alliance which, following an initial meeting in 1981 in Benin City, consolidated itself as the Progressive Parties Alliance or PPA at a Maiduguri 'summit meeting' in March 1982. This 'Gang of Four' opposition parties – UPN, NPP, GNPP (pro-Waziri) and PRP (Rimi–Imoudu faction) – was handicapped from the outset by all the problems just alluded to. Yet, on the surface of things, it retained a strong potential. It formally controlled majorities not only in the two federal houses but also in eleven State Assemblies and, of course, the twelve State executives. If it could agree on even a minimal strategy of non-competition for its members' electoral districts – and assuming electoral results similar to those of 1979 – then its prospects of unseating the NPN were by no means bleak. Indeed, its central concern (and only notable success) was to apportion federal offices among its members, the formula for which was reached at its November 1982 Lagos meeting.[28] The one office which could not be parcelled out, however, was the presidency; and the failure to find agreement on this suggested the alliance's central weaknesses. First, the presence of at least two forceful, antagonistic personalities prevented either from 'subordinating' himself to the other. And second, even if Zik or Awo had been chosen, large sectors among the 'loser's' following would certainly have defected from the alliance, for reasons already discussed. Not surprisingly, therefore, at least six PPA meetings called to resolve the leadership question produced a substantial amount of bargaining, scheming and plotting, but no leadership candidate. By the end of 1982 all four parties had nominated their own presidential candidates, thus ensuring that no common candidate could emerge for the 1983 elections. In any case, the PPA never saw itself as forming a united party; it was and aspired to be only a loose association of separate parties aiming at a negotiated share of state power. But even this minimal framework was increasingly jeopardised as the dominant parties, UPN and NPP, often competed with one another to absorb the unattached factions of the PRP and GNPP,[29] and Waziri Ibrahim withdrew from the association, alleging 'deceit, incompatibility, treachery and back-biting'.[30]

Partly as a reaction to PPA immobility, and partly to establish a vehicle for the unrecognised factions of the PRP and GNPP, an attempt was made to constitute a Progressive People's Party (PPP) in May 1982 – albeit *within* the PPA – a rather more militant and tactically more coherent amalgam of the Rimi–Imoudu PRP, the Shettima Mustapha segment of the GNPP and, after some hesitation, the NPP. Although these moves were perceived by the UPN as akin to betrayal, thus further undermining the PPA, the PPP applied for, but was denied, recognition as a political party, mainly on the grounds that its members remained members of their respective parties (Diamond, 1984:908).

The inability of the PPP to gain recognition did, however, provide a pretext for the 'homeless' PRP and GNPP groupings to fuse with the NPP, thus reducing the intra-PPA cacophony to two principal and more easily regulated voices and sets of ambitions and making the NPP – under the now undisputed leadership of Zik – into a more supra-ethnic catchment party than it had been in 1979 and endowing it with a more 'progressive' image.

Towards a one-party 'chop' state

This far-reaching reshuffling of the party system, it must be recalled, took place within a stagnating economic environment. The 1980/81 oil glut, combined with rampant mismanagement and corruption – to be analysed in subsequent chapters – had resulted in declining state revenues, a shrinking balance of foreign exchange, chronic shortages of essential imports (especially food), and rising social tensions in the form of strikes, religious unrest and resurgent ethnicity. The situation has been depicted as follows:[31]

> During the slightly more than four years of civilian rule, foreign currency reserves plunged from $8 billion to less than $1 billion. External debt spiralled from roughly $4 billion to $15 billion. By the time of the coup, Nigeria was believed to be more than six months and $5 billion in arrears on short-term payments to creditors and suppliers. What was smuggled abroad probably equalled or exceeded those arrears. What the government paid to ghost workers may have represented a third or more of the debt it accumulated under civilian rule.

Here, many of the same factors that had contributed to the NPN's electoral strength also sapped its ability to deal effectively with the crisis. As a supra-ethnic association of 'heavyweights' and local/ethnic notables held together by links of patronage and mutual advantage, it was under continuous pressure to 'deliver' to these party stalwarts. In a situation of constant growth and surplus, this strategy had worked effectively. But in times of a shrinking 'national cake', the party's pay-off capacity could only be maintained at the expense of the other sectors of society. As the gap between the party elite and the generality of society thus increased and grew more visible, overall system legitimacy was undermined to a degree that would have been inconceivable had the party officials been seen to be sharing in the 'national sacrifice'. The *National Concord* of 15 July 1983 thus defined Nigerian politics as 'government by the rich, for the rich and in the name of the people'. Even while politicians continued to consume flagrantly, raise their personal emoluments and live in an unprecedentedly lavish style (see next chapter), the population were subject to worker 'retrenchments', higher taxes, declining services and inflation. Table 5.3 shows the price increases for a few basic commodities from 1980/81 to election time 1983.

Table 5.3 *Price increases for selected basic commodities*

Commodity	1980/81	July 1983
Gari (one kerosine tin)	N15.00	N25.00
Vegetable oil (one gallon)	3.00	7.50
Pepper (milk tin)	.50	1.00
Mellon (milk tin)	.50	1.20
Tomato paste (small tin)	.30	.80
Yam flour (one kerosine tin)	5.00	10.00
Palm oil (one kerosine tin)	9.00	32.00
Rice (sack)	30.00	100.00
Bread (loaf)	.20	.50
Sugar (St. Louis)	.30	.75

Source: The Guardian (Lagos), 16 July 1983.

The consequent rise in labour-government tensions (May 1981 general strike: strikes by electrical workers, construction workers), peasant discontent (Bakalori Dam protests in late 1981), popular protests in the form of ostensibly religious unrest (Maitatsina incidents in 1981 and 1983 Kano riots) were hardly assuaged by Shagari's proclamation of an 'Ethical Revolution' – which to a surprising extent would be echoed in the Buhari regime's 'War Against Indiscipline' (see chapter 8) – aimed at restoring internal unity, peace and stability by emphasising the idealistic, non-materialistic bonds holding Nigerian society together, and hence at rolling back the 'social malaise' threatening to overtake the country.[32] Yet in the absence of political will or capacity to address the root problems of the Nigerian political economy, ethical revolutions, patriotic appeals, a resort to law and order or the proclamation of various national campaigns were the only available substitutes for political action.

Given these circumstances, a worsening of relations between the parties, particularly between the NPN and the variegated opposition, was the logical outcome. The general atmosphere of confrontation and violence in the larger society was reflected, and in many respects amplified, within the party system. More and more, party thugs were employed to subdue opposition. Armed factions of parties clashed in several States, killing and injuring hundreds of supporters.[33] Rumours of assassination attempts, plots and conspiracies abounded. Most of the federally and State-owned media degenerated into mere producers of propaganda for the respective ruling party.

All these tendencies entered into, and were inflated by, the 1983 election campaign. First, the operation of the electoral machinery did not augur well for the conduct of free and fair elections. Not only did FEDECO, now headed by former Bendel State Chief Justice Ovie-Whiskey, refuse to register the majority factions of the PRP and GNPP – actions which worked to the advantage of the NPN, as already suggested; it only licensed one further party, the Nigerian Advance Party (NAP). With Tunji Braithwaite as its leader and a rather fuzzy notion of 'scientific pragmatic socialism' as its programme, the NAP did not appear to meet any of the major criteria for party formation described at the beginning of this chapter. Then it was announced – without explanation – that the order of elections would be changed from that of 1979 so that the presidential elections would be held first rather than last. Since the altered sequence clearly stood to aid the incumbent party by setting a 'bandwagon effect' in motion, it was widely perceived that FEDECO's action had been taken at the behest of the NPN.

Table 5.4   *Voters' register: 1979 and 1983*

States	Registered voters		
	1979 (1)	1983 (2)	% Change
Anambra	2,606,663	3,532,053	+ 35.5
Bauchi	2,096,162	2,684,354	+ 28.1
Bendel	2,355,023	3,154,672	+ 34.0
Benue	1,636,371	2,400,525	+ 46.2
Borno	2,945,925	3,587,715	+ 21.8
Cross River	2,464,184	3,365,672	+ 36.6
Gongola	2,299,012	2,965,022	+ 29.0
Imo	3,490,484	4,521,089	+ 29.5
Kaduna	3,455,047	6,688,450	+ 93.6
Kano	5,226,598	7,639,281	+ 46.2
Kwara	1,108,029	1,313,712	+ 18.6
Lagos	1,829,369	2,232,800	+ 22.0
Niger	1,051,160	1,277,090	+ 21.5
Ogun	1,663,608	1,853,511	+ 11.4
Ondo	2,573,186	3,058,918	+ 18.9
Oyo	4,534,779	5,145,377	+ 13.5
Plateau	1,748,868	1,541,990	– 11.8
Rivers	1,608,409	3,008,821	+ 87.1
Sokoto	3,806,214	5,124,819	+ 34.6
F.C.T.		208,947	–
Total	48,499,091	65,304,818	+ 34.6

Source: Adapted from Nigerian Television Authority Study, as reproduced in *Daily Times*, 20 July 1983.

The final voters' register did not appear until less than a week before the first election. Apart from hundreds of thousands of inaccuracies, the register listed some 65.3 million voters (see Table 5.4), which, if accurate, would indicate a total population of at least 130 million, on the conservative assumption that roughly half the population are minors. The 1979 register – itself thought to be inflated – had contained about 47.7 million voters. The 1983 register thus indicated a population increase of about one-third within a four-year period! Moreover, the greater part of the population 'growth' took place either in NPN-dominated States or in Kano, where the NPN had a vital stake in a PRP victory, and Kaduna, where the party hoped for a massive win. In fact, the inflated register reflected widespread multiple registration and registration of minors, and these registrations could then be cast by party agents voting in several places on polling day.

As well as its failure to hold these malpractices in check, FEDECO could also be indicted for many administrative shortcomings. As an observer of the 1983 elections, the present author witnessed – and the Nigerian press reported – how polling officials turned up late or not at all, how ballots or ink or other supplies were missing, how voters were treated discourteously and sent from station to station to try to find their names on the register and how observers from certain parties (who had a legal right to be present) were refused access to the polling centres. *The Punch* of 12 May 1984 concluded that 'virtually all FEDECO officials were paid agents of a political party', and that the police behaved 'like political thugs'; it spoke of a 'conspiracy' against the people and a serious 'crisis of confidence' in the political system.

A second and perhaps still more significant tendency – not unconnected with the technical problems just discussed – related to the process of intra-party candidate selection for the elections. The series of party primaries and other nomination procedures from late 1982 onwards produced a number of stunning developments, especially for those accustomed to viewing the Nigerian party system in terms of party allegiance and modernisation-theory paradigms rather than as intra-elite competition for access to sources of 'chop'. Since, it was thought, the outcomes of the 1983 elections could be more or less predicted on the basis of the 1979 results (especially in the 'one-party' States), and since the holding of political office was now a guaranteed and proven means of self-enrichment and status acquisition (particularly in a time of austerity when other means were less effective, or at least contingent on political success), party offices and nominations became sharply contested prizes. Engaging in this competition could be costly: depending on State, party and relative certainty of getting elected, a party candidacy for, say, State legislator might involve an up-front 'donation' to the party of ten to twenty thousand naira;-gubernatorial or National Assembly candidacies could cost ten times as much.[34] In addition to purchasing nominations, aspiring candidates also employed small armies of 'supporters', agitators, 'front men' and thugs to marshall intra-party support – groups which could subsequently carry on the same activities during the official campaign. The losers of these contests often besieged the party with petitions and calls for revision; when these measures failed, they 'went public', thus filling the media with (further de-legitimating) attacks on their party and its leaders, as well as the party system.

As a last resort, unsuccessful candidates transferred their support to another party – often two or three times – in a search for political office elsewhere. In this way, the phenomenon of the *political decampee* not only became a characteristic feature of the 1983 campaign, it also demonstrated once and for all the secondary (or even tertiary) role played by party labels, political principles and ideologies in the party system. The decampee was the ultimate manifestation of 'chop' politics in the Second Republic. Although this discussion would not be well served by a detailed account of all the instances of transfer of party loyalty during this period, a brief analysis of some of the main developments will help to round off the earlier description of shifting party constellations as well as to illustrate the growing predominance of materialist issues in the last election campaign of the Second Republic.

As a general tendency, the NPN, as the chief holder and dispenser of political patronage, emerged as the chief beneficiary of the decamping process. Even where the NPN could not ensure a victory for all its candidates at the polls, federal contracts, party offices, import licences and other favours were welcome consolation prizes. As President Shagari proclaimed at the launching ceremonies ('Gboko 83') of the NPN's 1983 campaign:[35]

The NPN umbrella is large enough to accommodate everybody. We stand for One Nation, One Destiny. We are tolerant and democratic, open and accommodating. Our doors are wide open. Let them join us or get set for defeat. I say to them. If you cannot beat the NPN join the NPN.

Of those who responded to the NPN leader's call, the decampees from the Yoruba-centred UPN were among the most interesting. Their defections were tangible evidence of the success of the NPN's strategy of capturing well-known 'heavyweights' with a ready-made following rather than attempting to create a mass basis on the strength of party policies or ideals. Thus in Oyo State, former deputy governor Chief Sunday Afolabi and former commissioner Chief Busari Adelakun – who were defeated in their respective bids for the governorship and deputy governorship on a UPN platform – declared for the NPN at a special rally held in Ibadan in April 1983. The NPN then appointed them members of its national executive council and ensured their nomination for the desired offices, which they subsequently 'won' (see below). In Ondo State too, Akin Omoboriowo, ex-deputy governor, decamped to the NPN on losing out in the contest for the UPN gubernatorial nomination. As a leader of the State's major sub-ethnic group, moreover, his defection may have promoted a certain 'retribalisation' – or perhaps 'differentiation' – within the hitherto united Yoruba front in the UPN. The new NPN leader even attempted to transplant part of the UPN platform (free education) into his new party and based his NPN candidacy for the governorship on a frank promise to ensure a fair share of the national cake for 'his' people. Though unable to defeat incumbent Governor Michael Ajasin, he did succeed, by whatever means, in ending the almost monolithic UPN vote in his State (see Table 5.6). These defections to the NPN were augmented by those of Alhaji Shitta Bey (member, Lagos State Senate), Oladosun Oshinwo (speaker of the Lagos House), Chief Soji Odunjo (commissioner in Ogun State), Alhaji Habeeb Akeem (chairman of one of the Lagos State parastatals) and many others.

To the East, the NPN also followed a strategy of winning over prominent individuals: Dr Michael Okpara (former Eastern Region Premier), Dr B. U. Nzeribe (1979 GNPP vice-presidential candidate), Chief Phillip Umeadi (the UPN's vice-presidential aspirant in 1979), Senator Nathaniel Anah (former NPP official), Chief S. G. Ikoku (from the PRP, as already discussed). Perhaps the party's most important addition, in this context, was 'Emeka' Ojukwu, the former Biafran leader, who had been officially 'pardoned' by the President in mid-1982, returned to Nigeria buoyed up by a massive publicity campaign, received numerous honours (including the title of the Ikemba of Nnewi in his home town), and declared for the NPN. The party's 'Eastern strategy' was reinforced by the selection of two prominent personages for the governorships of Imo and Anambra States, Chief Collins Obih and Chief Chris Onoh, as well as the presence of Dr Alex Ekwueme as incumbent Vice-President and Dr K. O. Mbadiwe, the presidential adviser on national affairs.

Nevertheless, the NPN's big-man, patronage-based strategy came up against certain limitations, particularly in this period of increasing austerity. Ignored, short-changed or minority factions or individuals frequently moved, or were moved, towards opposition parties. The indeterminate nature of the rotation principle of the party's zoning policy (described above) produced an important defector, Chief M. K. O. Abiola (the wealthy industrialist and press baron), when it was decided that the presidency, which he coveted, would not rotate if the incumbent sought re-election. The primaries and gubernatorial nominations produced a series of conflicts within the NPN – analogous to those of the UPN in Oyo and Ondo – in Cross River and Kwara States.

In Cross River State, where the NPN had scored two-thirds of the popular vote in

1979 and which thus constituted an important element of the NPN's 'national character', incumbent Governor Clement Isong was denied a second attempt at the governorship as a result of his defeat in the, allegedly rigged, party primaries. His successor, Senator Donald Etiebet, had been supported by the party's 'Lagos wing' headed by Senate President Joseph Wayas who apparently held Isong responsible for the defection of Jacob Esuene, a former military governor (1968–75) and wealthy brewer, who subsequently became the UPN gubernatorial candidate. Isong was also in disfavour in Lagos for his public criticisms of the President. No doubt the NPN's apprehensions at the growth of the UPN in Cross River were well grounded, since the old AG had enjoyed substantial support there during the First Republic. These fears were exacerbated as Isong and his 'Home Front' – which comprised the State's commissioners, party officials and 38 of the party's 54 House members – went over to the UPN.

Similarly, in Kwara State, the renomination of Governor Adamu Attah triggered a long-standing quarrel between the incumbent Governor and an intra-party opposition headed by Olusola Saraki, NPN Senate leader, with the latter vowing to withdraw all support from the former, perhaps even placing it at the disposal of a rival party. In a State where the NPN had won by a margin of only some 13,800 votes out of a combined UPN–NPN total of 362,643, the Senator's support was crucial; and when it was withdrawn a UPN victory was the outcome. Other than personality differences and power rivalries, it is difficult to ascertain any substantial causes of the split.

Niger State, more than most States, mirrored the problems of Nigerian politics where ethnicity intersects with chop. The smallest (in terms of population), poorest, and one of the most multi-ethnic of the 19 States, Niger had elected a Hausi–Fulani Governor, Awwal Ibrahim, in 1979, in a State dominated by the Nupe and Gwari peoples with their historical rivalries. With Nupe leaders pressing for more political-administrative offices and the Gwari for increased amenities and projects, and both resentful at perceived Hausa–Fulani domination, the two groups defected in large numbers to the NPP – sufficient to give the latter one Senate seat and two House of Representatives seats, thus breaking the NPN monopoly in the State, but not enough to unseat the Governor or eliminate the presidential majority (though both saw their winning margins substantially reduced).

The fragmentation of the PRP, already described, produced a number of relevant developments in Kaduna and Kano States. Aminu Kano's death at the outset of the election campaign initially appeared to minimise prospects for an already divided party that had relied substantially on its leader's personal appeal and charisma. In Kaduna, where a PRP Governor had constantly been opposed by an NPN-dominated House (see next chapter), this in fact turned out to be the case. Alhaji Lawal Kaita, the NPN gubernatorial candidate, who had been defeated by the impeached Abdulkadir Balarabe Musa in 1979, rightly saw an opportunity to capitalise on the intra-PRP divisions. But Balarabe Musa's belated return to the official PRP enhanced the chances of the party's gubernatorial candidate, Alhaji Musa Musawa. The contest was further complicated by a strong bid by the NPP – backed now by the Imoudu-Rimi PRP remnants, including then Governor Alhaji Musa Rimi – for the governorship. In the event the NPN victory was clear but qualified, as Tables 5.5–5.8 show.

But in Kano State a genuine and intensive competition developed between the official PRP with Senator Sabo Bakin Zuwo as its gubernatorial candidate, the NPP (Rimi-Imoudu PRP) whose candidate was, of course, Abubakar Rimi, and the NPN under the leadership of Alhaji Aminu Bashir Wali. The close and crucial campaign was thus characterised by a former governor running with the support of a different party, a candidate chosen by the official rump of the former governing party, and an NPN aspirant backed by all the influence of the federal ruling party. The result, the election of Sabo Bakin Zuwo, could be seen as a 'victory' by all three contenders: the PRP because it retained State control despite its internal split and its leader's death; the NPN because it improved its share of the vote (notably in the presidential elections where, in 1979, the Kano vote had failed to provide Shagari with the necessary 25%, thus giving rise to the 'twelve and two-thirds controversy' described in the next chapter) and because it could count on the shrunken PRP as a reliable ally; and the NPP because it had broadened its ethnic mix and made substantial inroads into the North.

This general pattern of defections, decampings and realignments was replicated practically everywhere in the federation. In Bendel State, for instance, Governor Ambrose Alli's UPN was undermined by a series of decampings, mainly to the NPN, which, under former Military Governor Samuel Ogbemudia, was able to offer prospects for positions and rewards after the anticipated victory. The NPN strategy was clearly successful. Even the multi-ethnic equilibrium put together by Solomon Lar, NPP Governor of Plateau State, was challenged, but not defeated, by a formidable NPN coalition of 'big men' headed by John Jato Kadiya, a former federal minister in charge of the Federal Capital Development Authority. Both UPN and NPP actively recruited anti-NPN support in Rivers State in particular among dissident minorities – thus giving rise to questions about the workability of a possible post-election PPA; but this strategy did not manage to overthrow Governor Melford Okilo and his coalition of minorities. In Benue, considerable intra-party friction within the NPN, including a stop-Aku (Aper Aku, the NPN Governor) movement led by J. Akure, a Tiv businessman, was unable to halt the Governor's renomination and subsequent victory. However, the NPP campaign headed by Paul Unongo did divert some sectors of the Tiv vote and attract support from among the ethnic minorities suspicious of Tiv intentions.

And finally, the GNPP, whose earlier disintegration has already been outlined, was removed from its two loci of power in the North East, Borno and Gongola States. The Borno contest turned into a three-way struggle between NPN, UPN and GNPP. But in Gongola, the former GNPP Governor Abubakar Barde decided to run on the NPP platform. His regime, particularly characterised by corruption and inefficiency, was challenged by Alhaji Bamanga Tukur of the NPN and the Reverend Wilson Sabiya of the UPN.

Assessment of party rule in the Second Republic

The preceding analysis of individual and group realignments within and among the parties elucidates a central characteristic of the Second Republic's party system, namely, that party loyalties and alliances could be shed, exchanged or renounced practically at will. By election time, party lines were so blurred, issues so confused and the actual electoral machinery so discredited that *no reliable analysis of the election results is possible*, despite the several election studies published since August 1983. At best, certain salient trends can be noted (see Tables 5.5–5.8) and, in combination with one's more or less subjective impressions and fragments of information, integrated into a generalised analysis of the changed power constellations from August 1983 until the military *putsch* of 31 December 1983.

Of these trends, the most extraordinary was the massive, unforeseen 'victory' of the NPN which escalated through all five elections. From Shagari's almost half of the national presidential vote (more than the combined votes for Zik and Awo) to

Table 5.5 *Results of the 1983 Presidential election*

State	Votes Cast	Shagari NPN	Awolowo UPN	Azikiwe NPP	Waziri GNPP	Yussuf PRP	Braithwaite NAP
Anambra	1,158,283	385,297 *33.36*	23,859 *2.06*	669,348 *57.79*	36,165 *3.12*	16,103 *1.39*	27,511 *2.38*
Bauchi	1,782,122	1,507,144 *84.57*	98,974 *5.55*	55,258 *3.66*	37,203 *2.09*	54,554 *3.05*	18,979 *1.07*
Bendel	1,099,851	452,776 *41.17*	566,035 *51.45*	53,305 *4.35*	11,723 *1.05*	7,359 *0.67*	8,653 *0.79*
Benue	652,795	384,045 *58.83*	79,690 *12.21*	152,209 *23.31*	19,897 *3.05*	6,381 *0.98*	10,573 *1.62*
Bornu	718,043	348,974 *48.6*	120,138 *16.73*	26,792 *3.76*	179,265 *24.96*	26,996 *3.76*	15,698 *2.19*
Cross River	1,295,710	696,592 *54.00*	505,922 *39.43*	46,418 *3.61*	15,582 *1.29*	8,229 *0.54*	10,967 *0.85*
Gongola	735,648	282,820 *38.44*	160,720 *21.85*	148,055 *20.13*	25,530 *3.47*	81,205 *11.04*	37,318 *5.07*
Imo	1,588,975	398,453 *25.07*	22,649 *1.43*	1,054,436 *66.99*	52,354 *3.29*	19,370 *1.16*	32,694 *2.06*
Kaduna	2,137,398	1,266,894 *59.28*	225,878 *10.57*	225,919 *10.58*	80,862 *3.08*	300,476 *14.02*	37,369 *1.75*
Kano	1,193,050	383,998 *32.19*	48,494 *4.06*	274,102 *22.98*	35,252 *2.95*	436,997 *36.63*	14,207 *1.19*
Kwara	608,422	299,654 *49.25*	275,134 *45.22*	16,215 *2.66*	7,670 *1.26*	3,693 *0.61*	6,056 *1.00*
Lagos	1,640,381	125,165 *7.59*	1,367,807 *83.39*	119,455 *7.28*	11,748 *0.72*	6,570 *0.04*	8,636 *0.05*
Niger	430,731	274,085 *63.17*	15,772 *3.66*	112,971 *25.23*	12,994 *3.01*	8,736 *2.03*	8,182 *1.90*
Ogun	1,261,061	43,821 *3.47*	1,198,033 *95.00*	5,022 *0.04*	6,874 *0.55*	4,449 *0.35*	2,862 *0.23*
Ondo	1,829,343	355,217 *20.03*	1,412,539 *77.25*	20,340 *1.11*	11,629 *0.63*	7,052 *0.39*	10,566 *0.58*
Oyo	2,351,000	885,125 *37.55*	1,396,225 *59.39*	34,852 *1.48*	15,732 *0.57*	9,174 *0.39*	9,891 *0.42*
Plateau	652,302	292,606 *44.86*	38,210 *5.86*	280,803 *43.05*	18,612 *2.85*	11,581 *1.77*	10,490 *1.61*
Rivers	1,357,715	921,654 *67.88*	251,825 *18.55*	151,558 *11.15*	12,981 *0.95*	4,626 *0.34*	15,051 *1.11*
Sokoto	2,837,786	2,605,935 *91.83*	75,428 *2.66*	63,238 *2.23*	46,752 *1.65*	24,280 *0.85*	22,152 *0.78*
Abuja	135,351	127,372	1,102	4,156	1,103	641	977
Total	25,454,166	12,047,648	7,885,434	3,534,633	640,128	1,037,481	308,842

Figures in italics are a percentage of total votes cast in each State.

Table 5.6 Initial results of the 1983 Gubernatorial elections

State	Votes Cast	GNPP	NAP	NPN	NPP	PRP	UPN
Anambra	1,869,192	Okafor 22,863 / 1.22	Onyeme-lukwe 21,866 / 1.16	ONOH 901,390 / 48.22	Nwobodo 887,221 / 47.46	Nwankwo 14,515 / 0.77	Mba 21,337 / 1.14
Bauchi	2,365,419	Nuhu 18,709 / 0.79	Mohamud 15,830 / 0.67	TATARI-ALI 2,104,493 / 89.63	Doma 42,434 / 1.81	Umaru 45,204 / 1.93	Ahmed 138,749 / 5.1
Bendel	2,248,097	Onogun 9,176 / 0.50	Udi 7,880 / 0.40	OGBE-MUDIA 1,443,164 / 56.70	Ewhare-kuko 20,867 / 1.13	Obasee 6,406 / 0.28	Alli 760,604 / 40.81
Benue	942,567	Adum 12,623 / 1.55	Gajir 7,894 / 0.95	AKU 497,355 / 52.33	Unongo 392,882 / 41.68	Agan 4,692 / 0.65	Surma 27,121 / 2.88
Bornu	1,094,459	Abba-Gana 266,142 / 24.32	Bello 15,386 / 1.41	JARMA 616,170 / 56.30	Othman 24,922 / 2.28	Razaq 29,763 / 2.72	Goni 142,076 / 12.98
Cross River	2,541,413	Effiong 10,633 / 0.42	Utuk 8,913 / 0.35	ETIEBET 1,549,758 / 60.98	Okon 35,329 / 1.39	Akpan 8,040 / 0.32	Esuene 928,740 / 36.54
Gongola	1,071,768	Bagula 21,143 / 1.97	Elkanah 9,247 / 0.86	TUKUR 500,207 / 46.67	Barde 181,474 / 16.93	Gombi 12,234 / 1.14	Sabiya 347,463 / 32.42
Imo	1,674,272	Emelike 17,817 / 1.06	Mwosu 15,484 / 0.92	Obih 662,787 / 39.59	MBAK-WE 952,886 / 56.91	Onuoha 8,496 / 0.51	Eke-anyanwu 16,802 / 1.00
Kaduna	3,255,194	Nuhu 71,401 / 2.19	Danladi 33,118 / 1.02	KAITA 2,114,069 / 64.96	Yusuf 420,526 / 12.92	Musawa 480,169 / 14.75	Jumare 135,911 / 4.18
Kano	1,682,766	Adamu 17,378 / 1.14		Wali 423,811 / 24.39	Rimi 501,122 / 28.51	BAKIN-ZUWO 715,523 / 43.27	Shanono 24,932 / 1.53

State	Total	Candidate	Votes (%)	Candidate	Votes (%)	Candidate	Votes (%)	Candidate	Votes (%)	Candidate	Votes (%)	Candidate	Votes (%)
Kwara	872,039	Otun	5,784 (0.62)	Salami	4,621 (0.49)	Ata	339,495 (42.66)	Jimoh	10,307 (1.10)			ADEBAYO	511,832 (54.65)
Lagos	1,759,434	Owo-yemi	7,562 (0.43)	Ayanwale	5,187 (0.30)	Hakeem	81,720 (4.64)	Edu	57,723 (3.28)	Adelaja	6,288 (0.36)	JAKANDE	1,600,954 (90.36)
Niger	656,572	Gurdi	9,020 (1.37)	Lawal	6,663 (1.02)	IBRAHIM	425,330 (64.78)	Bada koshi	203,193 (30.95)	Sheshe	7,358 (1.12)	Ibrahim	5,008 (0.76)
Ogun	1,357,378	Ade-yemi	5,530 (0.41)	Ilori	2,794 (0.21)	Ocunjo	59,526 (4.38)	Solarim	5,159 (0.38)	Sore-mekun	3,810 (0.28)	Onabanjo	1,280,559 (9.434)
Ondo	2,356,146	Omo-shile	11,720 (0.5)	Omoboye	13,840 (0.59)	OMO-BORIOWO*	1,288,981 (54.70)	Ijasin	18,766 (0.80)	Onuwake	7,454 (0.32)	Ajasin	1,015,385 (43.09)
Oyo	2,840,200	Layonu	9,551 (0.34)	Ojo	5,938 (0.21)	OLUN-LOYO	1,650,531 (58.00)	Balogun	42,216 (1.49)	Dawodu	6,800 (0.24)	Ige	1,125,164 (39.06)
Plateau	896,347	Da-Fom	11,279 (1.26)	Kutok	8,052 (0.80)	Kediya	432,546 (48.26)	LAR	434,845 (48.51)			Gomwalk	9,625 (1.07)
Rivers	2,337,451	War-mate	18,877 (0.81)	Sodianye	5,290 (0.22)	OKILO	1,886,261 (30.70)	Giadom	259,002 (11.08)	Koi-Briggs	11,619 (0.58)	Akene	156,402 (6.69)
Sokoto	3,459,586	Maccido	26,158 (0.76)	Kamba	16,630 (0.48)	NADAMA	3,320,573 (95.98)	Gari	32,425 (0.94)	Musa	21,846 (0.63)	Bayero	41,954 (1.21)
Total	35,280,300		573,366		204,633		20,298,167		4,523,299		1,390,217		8,290,618

Table 5.7   *1983 Senate election results*

States	GNPP	NAP	NPN	NPP	PRP	UPN
Anambra			1	4		
Bauchi			5			
Bendel			5			
Benue			5			
Borno			5			
Cross River			5			
Gongola			5			
Imo			1	4		
Kaduna			5			
Kano					5	
Kwara*	1		1			2
Lagos						5
Niger			4	1		
Ogun						5
Ondo						
Oyo						
Plateau			2	3		
Rivers			5			
Sokoto			5			
Abuja			1			
Total	1		55	12	5	12

*Election postponed in Assa/Ilorin Senatorial District.
Elections put off indefinitely in Ondo and Oyo States.

Table 5.8   *1983 House of Representatives election results*

State	NPN	UPN	NPP	PRP	Total Constituencies
Anambra	15		14		29
Bauchi	20				20
Bendel	18	2			20
Benue	15		4		19
Borno	24				24
Cross River	26	2			28
Gongola	21				21
Imo	10		20		30
Kaduna	33				33
Kano	3		2	41	46
Kwara	9	5			14
Lagos		12			12
Niger	8		2		10
Ogun		12			12
Ondo		No Election			22
Oyo		No Election			42
Plateau	10		6		16
Rivers	14				14
Sokoto	37				37
Abuja	1				1
Total	264	33	48	41	450

constitution-amending majorities in both the Senate and House of Representatives, and 13 State governorships (reduced by court decision to 12 following proven charges of rigging in Ondo), the National Party was able to advance from its 1979 plurality to a clearly hegemonic position.

The election results point to a Darwinian survival of the strongest (the NPN in particular, but also the NPP and UPN) and elimination of the weakest (neither GNPP nor PRP gained more than a fraction of the presidential vote; only the PRP managed to retain one governorship and that with a reduced margin; the sole new Party, NAP, scored consistently under 1%). If these results could have been achieved through fair, honest elections – and been perceived as such – they *might have been* a basis for the evolution of a two- or three-party system. With the minor parties disintegrating and their leaders absorbed by the larger parties, and given the new strength of the governing NPN, the UPN and NPP would have been under considerable pressure to overcome personal differences between their leaders and form a single anti-NPN party.

Table 5.9 *Party control of states*

Party	Number of States	1979 %	Name of States	Number of States	1983 %	Name of States
NPN	7	36.8	Bauchi, Benue, Cross River, Kwara, Niger, Rivers, Sokoto	13	68.4	Anambra, Bauchi, Bendel, Benue, Borno, Cross River, Gongola, Kaduna, Niger, Ondo, Oyo, Rivers, Sokoto
UPN	5	26.3	Bendel, Lagos, Ogun, Ondo, Oyo	3	15.8	Kwara, Lagos, Ogun
NPP	3	15.8	Anambra, Imo, Plateau	2	10.5	Imo, Plateau
GNPP	2	10.5	Borno, Gongola	–	–	–
PRP	2	10.5	Kano, Kaduna	1	5.25	Kano
NAP	–	–	–	–	–	–
Total	19	100.00		19	100.00	

But even within the context of barely mitigated fraud, rigging and patronage – which will be discussed below – was it not reasonable to expect the emergence of a one-party-dominant or even one-party state? India, Kenya and Ivory Coast, to name a few, were obvious precedents for such a development. An adequate explanation of the failure of the Nigerian political system to evolve into a more consolidated form of elite domination will have to await future data and analysis. But it is possible to give some of the more useful, and frequently overlapping, explanations for the collapse of the party system in the Second Republic and its replacement by yet another military government. For analytical purposes, I have adduced eight partial explanations: the first three relate to 'given' factors inherited, as it were, by the Second Republic; the next four focus in particular on the interests and behaviour of the political class itself; an eighth factor, namely intra-military dynamics, will be examined in chapter 8.

Table 5.10 *Party consolidation during the Second Republic: the House of Representatives*

State	Total Number of Seats		No. of Seats Won by 2 Dominant Parties		No. of Seats Won by 2 Dominant Parties		% of Seats Won by 2 Parties	
	1979	1983	1979	Total	1983	Total	1979	1983
Anambra	29	29	NPN/NPP 3 + 26	29	NPN/NPP 15 + 14	29	100	100
Bauchi	20	20	NPN/GNPP 18 + 1	19	NPN 20	20	95	100
Bendel	20	20	UPN/NPN 12 + 6	18	NPN/UPN 18 + 2	20	90	100
Benue	19	19	NPN/NPP 18 + 1	19	NPN/NPP 15 + 4	19	100	100
Borno	24	24	GNPP/NPN 22 + 2	24	NPN 24	24	100	100
Cross River	28	28	GNPP/NPN 4 + 22	26	UPN/NPN 2 + 26	28	92.8	100
Gongola	21	21	GNPP/UPN 8 + 7	15	NPN 21	21	71.4	100
Imo	30	30	NPN/NPP 2 + 28	30	NPN/NPP 10 + 20	30	100	100
Kaduna	33	33	NPN/PRP 19 + 10	29	NPN 33	33	87.8	100
Kano	45	46	NPN/PRP 7 + 39	46	NPN/PRP 3 + 41	44	100	95.7
Kwara	14	14	UPN/NPN 5 + 8	13	NPN/UPN 9 + 5	14	92.8	100
Lagos	12	12	UPN 12	12	UPN 12	12	100	100
Niger	10	10	NPN 10	10	NPN/NPP 8 + 2	10	100	100
Ogun	12	12	UPN 12	12	UPN 12	12	100	100
Ondo	22	22	UPN 22	22	No Election		100	—
Oyo	42	42	UPN/NPN 38 + 4	42	No Election		100	—
Plateau	16	16	NPN/NPP 3 + 13	16	NPN/NPP 3 + 13	16	100	100
Rivers	14	14	NPN/NPP 10 + 4	14	NPN 14	14	100	100
Sokoto	37	37	GNPP/NPN 6 + 31	37	NPN 37	37	100	100
Abuja	—	1			NPN 1	1	1	100
Total	449	450		433		384		

(i) The *'structural' argument*. It is still possible, though increasingly difficult, to find proponents of the thesis that the party system, and with it the Second Republic, was inadequately structured. Tighter rules about party financing, more careful administration of the 'licensing' process or of FEDECO, or stricter enforcement of the regulations respecting the legislature or executive, the argument goes, could have averted the collapse. While there is much in this critique, as the preceding discussion of the operation of FEDECO as well as the next chapter on structural pathologies show, this view largely mistakes symptom for cause. It has been argued, at the outset of this chapter, that the party system was in fact exceptionally well designed technically, but deficient in terms of content. The carefully layered governmental structure ensured a share of state power to the various national, State and local party elites; and this, in contrast to the First Republic, turned politics from a winner-takes-all struggle into a widely perceived positive-sum game. If a structural deficiency was at work here, one might argue, it was that the central government, with its powers and sources of revenues, clearly dominated the State governments, which in turn overpowered local governments (see chapters 7 and 9). But the principle of federal supremacy was essential to the realisation of the 'modernisation', 'nation-building' paradigm at the root of elite consensus in the Second Republic. In this scheme of things, 'national unity' provides the broadest possible basis for elite accumulation, while 'ethnicity' (or regional population power) positions the accumulating class in rank order of access.[36] At the centre, therefore, party government was necessarily more 'representative' and 'democratic' on account of the permanent need for broad-based coalition building and balancing of interests. But at the State level, the 'one-party sub-states' pursued an accumulation process that was anything but democratic; yet even at this level, the formally liberal-democratic structures allowed for the 'safety valve' of electoral competition and minority representation in those multi-ethnic States (Bendel, Gongola, Kwara, Niger) where interests could not be consolidated in other ways. This overall process might be termed the *special Nigerian version of pluralism*. To repeat, therefore: the deficiencies in the party system of the Second Republic must be sought in its *content*, not its structure.

(ii) The *ethno-demographic argument* takes existing ethnic group numbers and relative strengths and makes them the basis of political life. However, like colonial and subsequent Eurocentric interpretations of 'tribalism' (as presented in chapter 1), this view neglects the links between class and ethnicity. Nevertheless, the peculiar ethnic mix of Nigeria probably precludes a one-party or even one-party-dominant system based on a single ethnic group, since no party based on one ethnic group can be in a position to impose itself on the country. Indeed, the existence of a multiplicity of ethnic groups is, if anything, conducive to the further development of democracy in the sense that the bargaining, compromise, relatively balanced composition of federal bodies (civil service, parastatals) and, even, tolerance that Nigerian federalism necessitates compel at least some representativeness. This is equally true of military and civilian regimes. Certainly, as has been demonstrated, most of the political parties were unable to extend their mass appeal beyond a single ethnic group (UPN, NPP, PRP in particular). But this was a challenge as well as a limitation, and where 'chop' rather than ethnicity became a party's primary strategic concern (NPN), the other parties came under relentless pressure to adapt similarly (PPA, PPP) or go under. This is not to suggest that the NPN somehow transformed itself into a supra-ethnic party, however. Rather, it was most successful in adapting to the almost Adam Smithian conception of ethnicity in the Second Republic according to which each ethnic formation, pursuing its own ethnically defined interests, in the aggregate moves toward equilibrium, if not harmony (thus realising a kind of theory of 'unintended consequences'). Subject to the rules of the game ('federal character') the respective elites could enact and reproduce ethnicity at local and, especially, State levels. But broader-based combinations and coalitions of ethnic units would have to be formed in order to attain power at the federal level. Thus, the NPN (and tendentially the PPA/PPP) was not so much a supra-ethnic party as a series of alliances and unions based on access to 'chop' – and chop was most lavish at the national level. The demographic-ethnicity argument is therefore quite inadequate in itself to explain the fundamental problems of the party system.

(iii) According to the *level-of-development thesis*, Nigeria simply lacked the economic, social and cultural preconditions to sustain political parties. An insufficiently developed political culture, a low level of literacy and awareness, and economic underdevelopment precluded the successful operation of a party system. Here again, this argument, following modernisation theory, assumes a unilateral evolution toward the forms and processes of Western liberal democracy. But it must be recalled from the preceding two chapters that Nigerian democracy was designed by and for elite formation and domination. The 1979 Constitution set up the parties as the major repositories of state power with control over the entire state bureaucracy, as well as labour, business and agriculture. In other words, the system did not provide for any form of countervailing mass power, not even in the form of a plebiscite. Nor did it allow for the democratisation of state or private institutions (workers' management, for instance) or any measures to transform the political culture (literacy/training programmes, etc.). On the contrary, democracy stopped at the level of elections of the political class to the elite-controlled party offices; beyond these, demobilisation and depoliticisation were the norms. While level of development therefore figured in the undermining of the party system (for example, the stupendous costs of the elections and of maintaining the thousands of elected officials and their appointees), it does not explain the failure to mobilise and democratise the population for self-rule.

(iv) The *excessively-rigged elections explanation*. As a direct, triggering phenomenon, electoral fraud was certainly an important factor in bringing down the party system. Indeed, the manifest inaccuracies of the election returns, the huge costs of conducting them (more than N300 m. – over 10% of federal recurrent revenues) and the scale of deaths, injuries and property damage collectively represent the military's major pretext for the 1983 New Year *coup* (see chapter 8). Ballot-rigging in and of itself was not the central issue, however. Various practices aimed at 'confirming' dominant trends – ballot-box-stuffing, phantom voters, exchange of ballot boxes between polling booth and counting centre, manipulation of final returns, etc. – had, for historical reasons, become a normal and indeed in some measure functional aspect of Nigerian 'democracy' – functional because these techniques generally worked to consolidate the locally or regionally dominant party, thus 'regulating' subsequent competition for scarce resources. The practice of universal rigging could be postulated as a theory of balanced-vote inflation: so long as all sides rigged in approximately the same proportions, the end result could be considered fair, if not correct. The 1979 election results were largely perceived in this light. If any one party's gains should be disproportional, however, the equation collapses. As the 1983 returns trickled in after 6 August each bringing greater and greater 'victories' for the NPN, the remaining party elites saw their chances for access to patronage, clientelism and state office greatly diminish. At this point, protests, violence, lawsuits and hence a process of *delegitimation* set in. As Okey Opara in the *National Concord* of 15 August 1983, commenting on Shagari's 91.83% of the Sokoto vote, laconically put it: 'these things just aren't so'. If the parties had been unable hitherto to mobilise the population for national goals, the elections certainly did, though hardly in a manner conducive to the ends envisaged by the political class. Cynicism and frustration beset the Nigerian public in a variety of ways:[37]

> the students who were given 10 or 20 registration cards and a wad of cash to hop all over town voting for a certain party; the soldier who insisted on stopping a wailing funeral party, only to find a coffin full of stuffed ballot boxes; the party men who found they could buy and thumbprint a booklet of 50 ballots right at the polling station; the young man who saw his brother accept thousands of naira to change the result of a senatorial election; the businessman who stumbled on a beehive of ballot thumbprinting in the home of a top government official on election eve – all of these people know that the 1983 elections were extensively and imaginatively rigged . . .

> Those without direct evidence had only to examine the reported figures to know something was seriously amiss. Nigerians know that on a day when the turnout was manifestly light the governor of Sokoto, Shagari's home state, could not have scored 700,000 more votes than the president himself the previous week. They know that in a free and fair election the NPN could not win 110 of the 126 state assembly seats in Oyo, where it won nine in 1979. They know that the NPN's total sweep of legislative seats in Borno, Bauchi, and Kaduna does not reflect the realities of opposition party strength in these states. They know that many of the figures are incredible.

(v) The course of the 1983 elections in many respects merely manifests a more fundamental explanation of the causes of the collapse of the party system: the *behaviour of the political elite*. The central tendency of the elections, namely the immoderate, unmitigated use of state power for the achievement of particular gains, appears most suggestive in this context. Once in office, as the next chapter will demonstrate, the legislators' first concern was not with 'development', not with the manifold crises that required urgent attention, not even with realising the party programmes on the basis of which they had been elected, but with their personal emoluments. Analogous to the elections, the problem of the political elite's behaviour in the Second Republic was not that it promoted malfeasance, corruption and waste – every post-independence political/administrative class has done these things – but that *this time the scale and scope of the state class' plundering was exceptionally widespread and blatant*. The novelist Kole Omotoso has nicely expressed this tendency in terms of a well-known Nigerian metaphor:[38]

> Those who ruled the country from 1914 to 1960 saw it as an enterprise which must yield profit, some huge cake from which they nibble without end. Those who came in 1960 saw Nigeria the same way. Except that it was a cake they would like to gobble for as long as possible. The army intervened and brought others to come and gobble the national cake. Then others still within the army, came and said 'mba o'. They even tried to change the vocabulary. Instead of national cake, they spoke of national mortar to build a new nation. Having set things up with a new set of rules they retired long before they were tired! Those of the 'long caps' came and what did they do? Gobble the cake? No way. They found the flour, the water, the flavours, the icing, the colouring and even the oven to bake the cake; all these they ate up completely.

This dysfunctional immoderation leads back to the point made earlier about the excessive power accruing to the parties in the absence of effective countervailing power in society and economy. Since this was so, *party exigencies came before all else*. Because elected officials were effectively beholden to their party, rather than the electorate, whose consent could be bought, coerced or rigged by the dominant party in any case, and since only party position ensured access to state largesse, the principle of 'democratic responsibility' became responsibility towards the 'big men' of the party. The 'national interest' was converted into party interests. Political appointments, more than ever before, were therefore based on patronage, expediency and clientelism; merit, qualifications and competence were only incidental. Thus political appointments at all levels resulted in a massive entry of hacks, drones and mediocrities into the public service. When the party is effectively equated with government (and vice versa), then the elaborate machinery of checks and balances is almost wholly circumvented. The party's aggregation and articulation functions degenerate into a system of intra-elite brokerage wherein political outputs are simply commodified. Contrary to the intent of Section 201 of the 1979 Constitution, which enjoined associations other than political parties from contributing to the coffers of a party/individual, the situation came to resemble that of the First Republic. The *National Concord* editorial of 15 August, written shortly after the 1983 presidential election, stated:

> Governments give contracts to individuals and companies and get funds for parties in return; individuals and companies give funds to parties and get contracts from the governments that control such parties in return, a kind of you-rub-my-back-I-rub-your-back arrangement. This arrangement increases the tempo of corruption in government.

(vi) The *emergence of a 'new' political-tycoon class*. The *Concord* editorial also alludes to a special political type, the 'freelance celebrity' ('this synthetic product of a warped electoral machinery') as a major donor to the political parties in the Second Republic. It is not that the middleman, nor the general intertwining of the political/administrative class with business and foreign elites in a relationship of mutual reciprocity, were qualitatively new phenomena in Nigeria. Previous chapters have dealt in detail with this relationship and its evolution. Quantitatively, however, the level, intensity and pervasiveness of corruption attributable to the political class increased so substantially and rapidly as to justify speaking of the transformation of 'quantity into quality'. Paul Beckett rightly posits the evolution of a 'stratum of plutocrats of enormous and unprecedented wealth – wealth sufficient to last for generations, and to make the holders completely independent of the public sector merocratic system'[39]. This 'tycoon class' had in some measure elevated itself beyond the older public service sector which was correspondingly weakened in relation to it. Indeed, the emergent political-business class more and more eclipsed the old technocratically-minded state elite (including the military elite) and its related professional, technological stratum of doctors, lawyers, academics, journalists, etc. – that is, precisely those groups who had most supported recivilianisation and who were most dependent on liberal democracy to provide the 'modern' infrastructures (light, power, law and order, medical services, roads, etc.) as well as occupational mobility based on 'performance' and 'merit'. But as unchecked accumulation and the politicisation of everyday life frustrated this initially democratically minded technocratic-administrative elite, their legitimating support for the Second Republic was progressively withdrawn – except inasmuch as they were able to establish clientelist connections with members of the political-business elite – especially and most perceptibly following the 1983 elections.

This relative autonomy of the new plutocratic stratum extended to its immunity from (and contempt towards) what more and more aptly could be termed the masses, namely, 'the vast majority of Nigerians' who had 'remained in a condition of a permanent austerity'.[40] Locked into a mainly self-created process of unmitigated accumulation, immune from countervailing pressures from both adjacent and lower strata and unconstrained by ideological or moral scruples, the tycoon class set off a whole series of self-enriching but ultimately dysfunctional developments. Where previously elite accumulation had necessitated some redistribution by way of 'trickle-down' effects, the new tycoons appropriated and exported huge quantities of the national wealth (thirty leading Nigerians were said to have had about N5 billion stored away abroad, a sum roughly equal to the total foreign debt at the time of the military *coup*[41]). Contract padding and middleman commissions soared from the once standard '10%' to 50 and 60%, and often much more. Scandals involving the Ministry of External Affairs, the Abuja Development Authority (whose records were destroyed by an unexplained fire at the federal communications building in Lagos), the Nigerian National Supply Company, and the legislators negotiating a contract renewal with a Swiss import-monitoring company were complemented by charges that 'ghost workers' were draining N50 m. per month from federal payrolls. Chinua Achebe, citing certain reports, in fact concluded that up to 60% of the national wealth was consumed by corruption.[42] It is important to stress that this plutocratic-tycoon stratum was almost exclusively a product of the party system. Very seldom in the process of elite-formation in Africa has the correspondence between the political class and the exploiting/accumulating class been so immediate and so complete. Revelations following the 1983/4 *coup* (see chapter 8) have not only confirmed this correspondence but also revealed its astounding magnitude.

(vii) The *loss of a sense of purpose, of any unifying national-developmental ethos*. That the parties failed to formulate alternative programmes and ideologies has been shown above. As essentially a series of ethnically and/or chop based groupings of the political elite, it has been argued, the parties' central 'purpose' was to gain a maximal share of power within the framework set by the consolidating elite groups and, through it, access to accumulation. Since, however, the parties were necessarily the main purveyors of political values and policies, their sterility and incapacity were superimposed on society as a whole. Their practices of violence, coercion, corruption, electoral fraud, suppression and intellectual bankruptcy became the leitmotifs for the other strata as well. As early as 1981, Claude Ake lamented that 'our pursuit of development has been a journey without maps, our priorities have been misplaced and our efforts ambivalent and perfunctory'.[43] Three years later, Paul Beckett wrote of a crisis beyond the economic crisis, namely, 'a deeper crisis, inherently moral' not merely of national ideology, but also 'of personal, social and political values':[44]

Unlike the crisis of unity of the 1960s which threatened the existence of Nigeria as a political unit, the crisis of the early 1980s threatened not so much the country's existence as its positive quality and promise. This moral crisis, in other words, tended to call into question all that is positive in a country which, just a decade ago, seemed characterized mainly by hope, promise and improvement in individual lives.

(viii) *Intra-military dynamics*. Although this complex issue will be examined in chapter 8, it is worth noting that in the survival-of-the-fittest contest that the Second Republic had become, the sole organised counter-force to the hegemonic political-business ruling class – apart from the latent power of the still unorganised and not yet conscious masses – was the military. Yet as a faction of the elite class, which, moreover, had a strong vested interest in the survival and successful operation of the liberal-democratic machinery that it had, after all, created, the military was unable to bring itself to strike until the existing problems of the Second Republic had practically run their course. Three important factors stand out – others, as just stated, are dealt with later – as crucial to the military's decision to end party politics. (a) The fact that the political-business elite's behaviour had become so rapacious and unchecked as to threaten the tenuous intra-elite balance and so to delegitimise the system of elite domination as a whole. (b) The re-emergent intra-elite struggles precipitated by the surreal nature of the system of institutionalised plunder by the dominant party elite, practices which progressively alienated, for instance, the local industrialists, the technical-professional middle classes, and most notably the growing capitalist-farmer stratum that, including such former top military leaders as Olusegun Obasanjo and Shehu Yar'Adua, was well connected to an increasingly impatient military establishment. And (c) pressure from the intra-military caste of junior officers and NCOs, who, like the general population, had grown disaffected and alienated from the civilian government; if not contained and mollified, such pressures pointed to a Rawlings- or Doe-type of rank-and-file insurrection and the end of elite rule.

This chapter has argued and attempted to demonstrate that the political party system lay at the core of the deficiencies and dysfunctions of the Second Republic, and that elite behaviour was the defining characteristic of that party system. Nevertheless, the actual operation of the structures and institutions of Nigerian liberal democracy, though in large measure explicable in terms of parties, must also be examined on their own terms, again mainly as a function of elite behaviour. This is the subject of the following chapter.

Notes

1. William Graf, 'Nigeria: Rough-Hewn Democracy', *The Globe & Mail*, 10 September 1983.
2. For a further discussion of these notions, see chapter 6, introductory section.
3. *Daily Times*, 28 December 1978.
4. *Daily Times*, 18 January 1979.
5. *The Punch*, 2 April 1979.
6. On this, see the encounter between E. C. N. Chima and Sinatra Ojo, 'New Wine in Old Bottles? A Debate', in William Graf, *Elections 1979: The Nigerian Citizen's Guide to Parties, Politics, Leaders and Issues*, Lagos, 1979, pp. 69–74.
7. S. E. Oyovbaire, 'Democratization of the Political Process – The Sword of Damocles', in S. E. Oyovbaire (ed.) *Democracy in Nigeria: Interpretative Essays*, Benin City, forthcoming, here quoted from manuscript, p. 284.
8. See the 1979 party programmes reproduced in Graf, *op. cit.*, pp. 75–115, and especially the 'Sampler of Party Promises, Assertions and Utterances', pp. 65–6.
9. *Africa*, No. 92, April 1979, p. 12. An interesting interpretation of this ideological homogeneity is provided by Jean Herskovitz, who writes (in *Foreign Affairs*, No. 29, Winter 1977/78) that 'the similarity of the political parties' programmes testified to the clarity of Nigeria's problems'.
10. For instance: Dudley, 1982; Diamond, 1981; Kirk-Greene and Rimmer, 1981, chapter 3; Oyediran, 1982; Ofonagoro, 1980.
11. Here see *New Times*, Vol. 2, No. 28 (July 1983), p. 3.
12. In the event, Shagari's 978 votes compared favourably with those of Maitama Sule (504), Adamu Ciroma (293), Sola Saraki (214), Joseph Tarka (104) and Iya Abubakar (92); the required majority was established by the voluntary withdrawal of the other candidates.
13. Which Joseph (1981, p. 87) has described as 'an amalgam of Marxism, Fabianism, Christian humanism with a strong dose of Hegelianism, and finally the Chief's own unique reflections on the problems of language, ethnicity and the federal state. It can further be noted that Awolowo's writings provide nearly all the major issues and even arguments put forward by the UPN'.
14. As explained to me in a series of discussions extending over several years, by Professor Omo Omoruyi, an MCA and early Club 19 supporter from Bendel State.
15. Omo Omoruyi, 'The Choice before the Igbos', *Sunday Times*, 17 July 1983.

16. About mid-way through the 1983 campaign, when an overwhelming 'victory' for the NPN could readily be foreseen, this interchangeability of party allegiance was humorously brought home to me in a palm-wine station in Benin City. I was among a group of politically involved Nigerians, most of whom had come over to the NPN in recent months. Someone invoked the by then familiar NPN slogan, 'One Nation! One Destiny!' To this, 'One Nation! One Chop!' was the quick response. 'One Nation! One Contract!' 'One Nation! One Percentage!' 'One Nation! One Dash!' The list of rejoinders was a long (and, on a hot day, most welcome) one.

17. On this, see Keith Panter-Brick, 'Scandal of FEDECO's Inaccuracies', *West Africa*, 9 March 1981, pp. 477–81.

18. See, e.g. Dudley, 1982; Diamond, 1981; Kirk-Greene and Rimmer, 1981; Oyediran, 1982; Ofanagoro, 1980; Panter-Brick, 'Nigeria: The 1979 Elections', *Africa Spectrum*, Vol. 14, No. 3 (1979); Amadu Kurfi, *The Nigerian General Elections 1959 and 1979*, Lagos, 1983.

19. Olatunde Ojo, 1981, p. 52. Dudley, 1982, p. 222 suggests a 'calculus of rationality' on the part of the minority groups, which he describes as follows: 'Whichever party wins the Presidential elections will control the ultimate political power in the federation. Given the population distribution between the different States, the party most likely to win the Presidential election will be the party which wins the greatest support in the 'northern' States, and if past experience is any guide, it is unlikely that either the UPN or the NPP – with their ethnic basis – stands a chance of winning such support. Of the other parties, the PRP's ideological commitment is more likely to restrict its electoral appeal than win its widespread support.'

20. All these issues are described and evaluated in the next two chapters.

21. Richard Joseph best describes the 'demonology' surrounding these two figures. He concludes with a summation of the 'ethnic trap' that therefore constrained the two parties: 'The clear lesson of the 1979 elections is that individuals who have become identified as the foremost champions of their people's interests – whether or not such an image has been intentionally sought – cannot expect to win power when the whole nation is considered a single constituency.' (1981b, p. 18).

22. Symptomatic of the difficulties involved here was the UPN's unwillingness, expressed at its December 1981 convention – and contrary to Awo's publicly stated intent – to support a merger of the opposition parties, preferring instead a loose, non-binding 'Grand Alliance' of 'progressive forces'. This of course avoided hard choices of leadership and co-ordinated strategy. See *West Africa*, 12–18 December, pp. 3027 and 3029–31.

23. See his 'Shagari's First Two Years', *Africa Report*, January/February 1982, p. 7.

24. 'Split from the Word Go', *West Africa*, 25 January 1982.

25. 'Factions of the GNPP', *West Africa*, 2 August 1982.

26. Quoted in 'Strategic Split in the PRP', *West Africa*, 18 January 1982.

27. *West Africa*, 12 December 1983, p. 2874.

28. For details see *National Concord*, 26 February 1983.

29. On this, see *West Africa*, 7 March 1983, p. 629.

30. *National Concord*, 26 February 1983.

31. *West Africa*, 7 June 1982, p. 1552; see also *New African*, May 1983, pp. 17–19.

32. See *West Africa*, 1 February 1982, p. 335, and 7 November 1983, p. 2592. Wole Soyinka, in refusing to participate in a government-sponsored seminar on the Ethical Revolution, sent a telegram to the organisers (reproduced in *Daily Sketch*, 11 April 1983) calling the Revolution itself 'bullshit offloaded on a long-suffering nation by over-surfeited hypocrites' and the seminar 'a distraction cynically engineered to cover up three and a half years of naked plunder unmatched in scale and insolence anywhere in the world'.

33. For examples and details, see Diamond, 1982, p. 652–5.

34. Regrettably I am unable, for obvious reasons, to cite my sources of, and direct experiences with, these developments. But even today, anyone who was involved in any way in political life in the Second Republic is able to recall the value of party nominations in the parties represented in his or her State.

35. *New Times*, Vol. 2, No. 28 (July 1983), p. 67. In the discussion that follows I have relied on the Nigerian press, as well as my own observations.

36. On this, see Eme Ekekwe, 'The State, National Development and the Present Systemic Crisis', paper presented to the Nigerian Political Science Association 10th annual conference, Nsukka, 1–4 June 1983, mimeo., pp. 8–9.
37. Larry Diamond, 'A Tarnished Victory for the NPN?', *Africa Report*, November/December 1983, p. 22.
38. *Sunday Concord*, 22 January 1984, p. 5.
39. Paul A. Beckett, 'Perspectives on Elections in Nigeria', paper presented to African Studies Association, Los Angeles, 28 October 1984, mimeo., p. 12.
40. Okwudiba Nnoli, 'The 1983 Elections: Voting for Austerity', presidential address to NPSA convention, Nsukka, 1–4 June 1983, mimeo., p. 13.
41. Beckett, *op. cit.*, p. 12, quoting Western press accounts.
42. Achebe, *op. cit.*, p. 40.
43. Claude Ake, presidential address to NPSA, Kano, May 1981, reproduced in *West Africa*, 25 May 1981, p. 1162.
44. Beckett, *op. cit.*, p. 11.

6

Structures and (Mal)Functions of Nigerian Democracy

Consolidation and legitimation

Inasmuch as the 1979 Constitution was the first autochtonous charter of government in Nigeria's history and aspired to replace the authoritarian bases of military rule, it was a *relatively progressive* document. One example of this was the search for national integration through a more rationalised political structure. The process of constitution-making itself, as has been seen, was designed to ensure that much of the population (the urban educated elements in particular) would identify with the new charter and feel that they were active participants in the formation of the Second Republic, and this despite the elitist character of the formulation process.

In its declared determination to achieve 'unity' and 'stability', the constitution (for example, in its preamble) proclaimed the principles of constitutionalism, limited government, separation of powers, popular sovereignty, free elections, etc. as universally binding. It further enshrined a number of explicit provisions which amounted to a mandate for active state involvement in promoting national integration. This was the express intent of the departing Military Government which was bent on[1]

> consciously using certain institutions such as the Armed Forces, the Federal Civil Service Commission and Federal Courts as vehicles to stress and promote the indivisible unity of the nation rather than the competitive aspect of Federalism.

Under the heading of 'Political Objectives' the constitution (Art. 15) declared the nation's motto to be 'unity and faith, peace and progress'. From this it established the principle of national integration as a goal to be realised, negatively, by prohibiting 'discrimination on the grounds of place of origin, sex, religion, status, ethnic or linguistic association or ties', and positively by:

(i) providing adequate facilities for encouraging free mobility of people, goods and services throughout the federation;

(ii) securing full residence rights for every citizen in all parts of the federation;

(iii) encouraging intermarriage among persons from different places of origin, or of different religions, or belonging to different ethnic or linguistic groups;

(iv) promoting or encouraging the formation of associations that cut across ethnic, linguistic, religious or other sectional barriers; and

(v) fostering a feeling of belonging and of involvement among the various peoples of the federation, to the end that loyalty to the nation should override sectional loyalties.

Further articles ensured that the composition of the federal government and its various agencies should reflect the 'federal character of Nigeria and the need to promote national unity' (Art. 14(3)). In other words, none of these bodies was to be predominantly staffed by members of certain ethnic, sectional or regional groups to the exclusion of others. The constitution-makers specified what they meant by the federal character of Nigeria:

> the distinctive desire of the peoples of Nigeria to promote national unity, foster national loyalty and give every citizen of Nigeria a sense of belonging to the nation notwithstanding the diversities of ethnic origin, culture, language or religion which may exist and which it is their desire to nourish and harness to the enrichment of the Federal Republic of Nigeria.

Thus, according to Art. 135(2), the President was enjoined to choose his Cabinet so as to ensure the appointment of at least one minister from each of the 19 States, who was an indigene of that State. Indeed, the President himself was elected, not merely by a simple majority of the population, but by a majority which included at least one-quarter of the votes cast in each of at least two-thirds of all the States (see Arts. 125, 126). And the civil service and other national agencies were required to promote this federal character in their recruitments and appointments. Similarly, the political parties had to be national rather than ethnic or regional (Arts. 202, 203), and this was defined by provisions requiring them, among other things, to be open to citizens from all groups and sectors, to operate in several geographic areas, to forego symbols and slogans of an ethno-nationalist nature, to elect a leadership from most of the States, etc.

And finally, the presidency itself was intended to foster national unity. The CDC argued that an executive president, separately elected by a national constituency and combining real and formal authority in one person, would be most appropriate to Nigerian conditions, because his enhanced powers would facilitate development, national integration and stability – all primary goals of the 'modernising' elites and all contributing to a formally conceived national identity. The presidency also had an important symbolic value. The Westminster model was rejected not only as unsuited to contemporary Nigerian needs but as a symbol of the colonial past. Against this, the new executive structure was seen as both 'modern' and 'indigenous'. The CDC sub-committee on the executive and legislature foresaw the future chief executive as performing and being seen to perform the following roles: 'symbol of national unity, honour and prestige'; 'a national figure – a political leader in his own right'; and 'an able executive – someone who can give leadership and a sense of direction to the country'. (CDC Report, II:67).

Separated and divided powers

The nineteen-State formula, initiated during the first series of military governments and constitutionally entrenched, was an improvement over the former regional arrangements because it made all the units approximately equal in size, and no single unit was able to dominate the federal government. At the same time, the greater number of national sub-units was intended better to preserve the special culture, social systems and political style of the many peoples of the nation. In the words of the Irikife Report 'such new political entities were necessary in the interest of fostering greater participatory democracy which ultimately is the bedrock of political stability'.[2] In comparison with previous federalisms, the powers of the central government were increased considerably. The list of exclusively federal powers had grown since the fall of the First Republic, under both civilian and military governments, and many of the previously concurrent powers have been accorded to the centre. The 1979 Constitution's Second Schedule confirmed these trends, and the operation of military government since 1983 has further reinforced them. Yet, even the highly centralised federalism of the Second Republic did attempt to ensure the protection of minority rights and aspirations so that when the interests of minority groups, especially political ones, were ignored or violated (as they often were), the victims at least had formal recourse to the courts for possible redress.

Thus, the centralist tendencies of the military government, as discussed in chapter 3, were firmly entrenched in the 1979 Constitution (Smith, Brian, 1981:372–3). Nevertheless, the relentless centralism of the military era was mitigated by the multi-party system which in 1979 gave no one party a majority in the National Assembly, by the States' independent – though carefully circumscribed – powers, and by the fact that State politicians, unlike military-bureaucratic officials, were directly responsible to their constituencies. Thus 12 State governments challenged and successfully reduced the federal government's share of federally collected revenues in the legislative deliberations leading to the promulgation of the relevant bills. Further indications of the States' growing countervailing powers under the civilian regime were described by Brian Smith (*ibid.*:367):

> Anambra State, for example, has questioned federal execution of its housing policy. Pressure for State police forces has been resisted by President Shagari on the grounds that some States are already claiming too much autonomy and that 'if you allow them to have a police force of their own there is a danger of secession of which we already had a bitter experience'. Governors belonging to the United Party of Nigeria, the People's Redemption Party, and the Great Nigerian People's Party have questioned the jurisdiction of the federal government in the control of land use. State governors have fought against the attempt to replace them on the National Economic Council by 'economic experts'. The Okigbo Commission on revenue allocation, furthermore, recommended a number of transfers of functions to the States.

The overall tendency, then, was toward a continuation of the centralised federalism which had evolved between 1966 and 1979, modified, however, by a certain degree of State autonomy and controlled within a more or less functional constitutional order. In strictly structural terms, these arrangements were no doubt suited to the peculiar Nigerian situation. Smith in any case concludes that (*ibid.*:378):

> it may well prove that a highly centralized arrangement is the most suitable one for a federation which did not have its origins in separate political units voluntarily seeking political union, but was a political development from an amalgam of unitary colonial structures for purposes of effective colonial domination.

Irrespective of the nature of the current regime, federalism represents a concession to the extreme diversity of the country and attempts in a formal way to realise the organising principle which both the colonial administration and its immediate legacy precluded: that of 'unity in diversity' through equilibrium. There are sound economic and political reasons for wanting to preserve One Nigeria: national defence, competitiveness in the world market, maintenance of a large domestic market, prestige, cultural affinities, sheer convenience and rapid development are some of them. But substantial ethnic, cultural, regional, religious, developmental and especially, intra-elite differences cannot be ignored. Hence constitutional federalism attempted to account for both centripetal and centrifugal forces with the notion of unity in diversity: unity represents the ideal, long-term goal, diversity expresses current reality; the idea of unity in fact promotes a feeling of (future) one-ness, while the guarantee of diversity makes popular acceptance of differences more palatable. Or, expressed in terms of elite consolidation and ruling-class interests, unity provides a dominant, central 'trough' for the most successful, while diversity ensures a multiplicity of secondary, sub-national 'troughs' as a kind of consolation for loss of access to the larger sinecures, patronage appointments, travel opportunities, status enhancements and the like.

Like the American constitution, the Nigerian constitution divided political power among the 'rule-making', 'rule-implementing' and 'rule-adjudicating' branches. The principle of *checks and balances*, though nowhere spelled out as such, was implicit in this division of powers according to their ostensible functions in government. Thus the National Assembly's primary task was to legislate; its legislation could be vetoed by the President – witness President Shagari's refusal in November 1979 to accept the high salaries awarded by the National Assembly to all members of the legislature and executive – or declared unconstitutional by the Supreme Court. The President's powers could be limited by National Assembly laws, especially by means of restricting the funds available to him or by vetoing his ministerial appointments, as happened when the National Assembly refused to confirm a full half of the candidates nominated for Shagari's first cabinet (most of whom were, however, subsequently approved). As a last resort the National Assembly could impeach the President – an action which was not initiated at the federal level, but for which there was a precedent in the June 1981 impeachment of Governor Balarabe Musa of Kaduna State. The judicature for its part was influenced by the President's power to appoint judges to high courts; and the constitution accorded it no power whatever to initiate legislation, merely to adjudicate existing laws. Its decisions on constitutional interpretation were occasionally crucial, for instance its October 1979 verdict that President Shagari had in fact been duly elected in twelve and two-thirds of the 19 States.

The general effect of the system of checks and balances was supposed to be the creation of a broad need for intra-governmental co-ordination. Even while such a system caused 'friction and delay', it promoted 'compromise and consultation' in the workings of government and thus – ideally – was to bring about a greater degree of active co-operation and identification between the component parts of the political system. Of course, it was not possible to confine the functions of lawmaking, law-execution and law-interpretation to these neat compartments, and not only did the executive manage to usurp many powers assigned to the other arms of government, but party power politics often overrode formal constitutional provisions. These developments will be discussed presently.

The National Assembly

The bicameral federal legislature in the Second Republic, composed of a *House of Representatives* of 450 members and a *Senate* of 96, was structured as the highest representative body of the liberal-democratic order and was the agency through which 'popular sovereignty' was transmitted. As such it was supposed to articulate the 'will of the people', and its legislation was passed 'in the name of the people'. Such legislation, though limited somewhat by constitutional provisions and presidential veto powers, potentially embraced almost all facets of national life. In particular, the National Assembly was invested with wide powers with respect to the control of the public purse, and it was these powers and the perquisites linked to them that made the acquisition of assembly seats an intensive pursuit of the state-centred political elite. Section 55 of the constitution provided, *inter alia*, that only the National Assembly should have the powers of fiscal appropriation from the Consolidated Revenue Fund or any other public fund, and of imposing or increasing any tax, duty or fee. A special Joint Finance Committee of the two houses was established by the constitution to deal with financial questions.

The basis of *popular representation* in the National Assembly was both numerical and geographical. For elections to the House of Representatives, the nation was divided into electoral districts subject to the constraint that no one constituency's boundaries might lie within more than one State. Dividing the number of registered voters nation-wide (in 1979, 47.7 million) by the number of seats to be filled in the House (450), on average every 100,000 or so voters were represented by one deputy.

For elections to the Senate, on the other hand, representation was by geographical unit. Each of the 19 States, regardless of population, was sub-divided into five approximately equal territorial constituencies, each of which returned one Senator. The reason for instituting this principle of geographical representation and establishing a second chamber related to the same complex of forces and interests that produced federalism and the federal character of Nigeria. The constitution-makers apparently felt that a unicameral legislature based solely on representation by population would produce a parliament heavily dominated by the more populous States, which had important ramifications for the North–South equilibrium. To illustrate, if the National Assembly had been unicameral and consisted of a House chosen according to representation by population, then the Northern States together would have returned 238 members while the Southern States would have elected only 209.[3] Unless handled carefully, imbalances of this nature would have been a possible source of conflict. That this could be so, was borne out in the Sharia Appeals Court controversy referred to in chapter 4.

The single-member or first-past-the-post constituency system promoted certain tendencies highly valued by the framers of the constitution and the social classes to which they belonged. It routinely 'weeded out' the many fundamental opposition parties, special-interest and single-issue movements and organisations with limited popular appeal: such groups could not achieve a majority within more than a very few constituencies. Not surprisingly, such electoral systems are associated with high-consensus, two-party systems (as in Great Britain or the USA) or single-party-dominant systems (as in India or as Nigeria might have become after August 1983), since minority and radical parties tend to merge with, or be swallowed by, larger conglomerate parties in order to achieve at least a diluted form of representation.

The overall effect of seating only the winning candidates from each constituency in the national (or State) parliaments was to produce legislatures in which only the established dominant social interests were represented, while minority, reformist or radical interests were simply eclipsed as *the legislature over time became a virtual mirror of the status quo*. Businessmen in particular, as well as lawyers and other professionals, large-scale farmers and upper-level civil servants, tended to predominate.

Comprehensive, systematic data about the socio-economic antecedents of legislators are still lacking. But even at a relatively impressionistic level it is evident that the National Assembly consisted overwhelmingly of individuals from the upper social classes. One partial study (Aliyu, A. Y., 1980) – a non-random sample and limited to 7 of the 19 States – pertaining to the origins of State representatives is suggestive of these tendencies. From it, one may infer that by far the greatest percentage of State legislators came from business, the civil service[4] and the teaching profession – by no means mutually exclusive categories – and that many more were chiefs or aristocrats.[5] On the other hand, farmers, the numerically largest occupational category in the States investigated, were clearly under-represented, while trade unionists and manual labourers were not represented at all. Surprisingly, lawyers and other professionals were not strongly represented, at least not in the population sample analysed here.

Table 6.1   *Percentage distribution of social and occupational backgrounds of House of Assembly members*

State	Farmer	Civil Servant	Teacher	Lawyer	Business	Chief/ Aristocrat	Clergy Relig. Leader
Bauchi	25	18.8	15.6	—	37.5	—	3.1
Benue	17.2	17.2	31.0	—	31.0	24.7	—
Borno	18.7	31.2	6.2	—	43.8	—	—
Cross River	5.5	14.5	14.5	3.6	54.5	30.5	3.6
Imo	4.4	13.3	8.9	13.3	57.8	13.3	—
Kano	31.5	—	3.5	—	63.15	1.5	1.5
Kwara	—	59.1	13.6	9.1	18.2	22.7	4.5

Source: Aliyu, A. Y., 1980.

Table 6.2   *Percentage distribution of annual income of House of Assembly members*

State	Less than N5,000	N5–9,999	N10–19,999	N20,000 and above	No Response
Bauchi	46.9	34.4	12.5	6.2	—
Benue	10.4	51.7	20.7	17.2	—
Borno	31.2	37.5	18.7	12.5	—
Cross River	12.7	30.9	45.4	7.4	3.6
Imo	—	22.2	62.2	15.6	—
Kano	17.5	57.9	14.0	1.5	8.7
Kwara	9.1	59.1	27.3	4.5	—

Source: As for Table 6.1.

In any case, as Table 6.2 suggests, State legislators' incomes were uniformly high, well above the average national per capita income of a few hundred naira. In view of the high cost of getting nominated, to say nothing of getting elected and, once elected, of the need to devote considerable time to legislative affairs, it is not surprising that few low-income persons sat in State assemblies and the National Assembly.

Structurally, the National Assembly did have the authority and capacity to play a central role in the government of the Second Republic. But its record in the first legislative period indicates that it by no means enacted this role with complete success. Many of its initial problems were of a technical or logistical nature. For instance, the absence of a code for the conduct of parliamentary business forced the legislature to resort to the 1963 Standing Orders – procedures derived from and conceived for a parliamentary-executive system rather than for the needs of the presidential system.

Lack of facilities such as office space, qualified technical and clerical personnel (including especially legal draughtsmen), and library and research support, together with lack of translation capacities in the four working languages, also seriously impaired the Assembly's work. For if the legislature – and particularly the committee system – was to fulfill its role in the system of checks and balances and pass effective laws, it needed this whole range of supports; otherwise it would have to rely upon the executive branch or interested lobbies or outsiders to furnish the information and expertise.

In addition to these material problems, the legislators' inexperience – not surprising, after thirteen and a half years of military rule – limited the effectiveness of the Assembly's performance. As early as 60 days after the opening session, the *Daily Times* of 4 December 1979 complained that the lawmakers had spent all their time passing motions, but had no substantial legislation to show for their efforts. The complaint was not without foundation: at the end of the first year of civilian rule the House of Representatives had in fact passed 264 motions but enacted a mere 22 bills; the Senate's ratio was 106:20. By the conclusion of the first electoral period, the *National Concord* of 28 July 1983 was referring to the National Assembly as being among the world's least productive legislatures and accusing the legislators of a lack of commitment and understanding.

Observers of the National Assembly, and particularly of the House of Representatives, consistently spoke of the 'pandemonium' typical of the proceedings, of discouraging 'absenteeism' and 'chronic lateness' on the part of members. They also found a widespread 'lack of understanding of the issues and even of the rules' which did not, however, prevent members voting on each and every item of legislation, thus giving rise to the impression 'either that some members are told how to vote beforehand or that it does not matter to them how they vote'. Either way, 'the conclusion can be drawn that the vote does not depend on the debate of issues nor conviction about them'.[6]

Allegations of obstructionism and self-aggrandisement were also made. The first charge stemmed mainly from the Senate's refusal to confirm the President's ministerial nominees and from the National Assembly's reluctance to pass the first budget for almost four months, though here again an informed decision was difficult without the fuller information which would have been provided by more adequate back-up facilities. The second charge, however, was more plausible in view of the Assembly's apparent obsession with its own emoluments and welfare as well as its role in elite formation. Shortly after election, it proceeded to vote itself a pay package that would have made Nigerian lawmakers among the world's most highly paid. If enacted, the relevant legislation would have cost taxpayers some N46,859,830 annually.[7] The magnitude of the legislators' claims was well brought out in a *New Nigerian* report which is worth reproducing at some length here. In addition to salaries ranging from N22,000 to N16,000, the Senators and Representatives sought the following:[8]

> Every member of the House of Representatives is to be provided with a CVU car and an official driver.
>
> Moreover, any member who wishes to obtain a car loan from his bank will have the loan guaranteed by the National Assembly.
>
> These are some of the resolutions passed by the House of Representatives . . .
>
> Other recommendations of the committee . . . include the provision of alternative accommodation in the completed Federal Government flats at Victoria Island because of the inadequacy and distance of the Badagry Road members' quarters.
>
> The Victoria Island flats should be provided with colour television sets, air-conditioners, telephones, boys quarters and uninterrupted water and electricity supply while adequate uniformed policemen should be on security duty for 24 hours.
>
> On feeding, the house resolved that regular food should be provided for members who wish to eat in the restaurants while kitchen facilities should be provided for members who would prefer to prepare their own food.
>
> Arrangements would also be made with manufacturers of essential commodities like beer and soft drinks to supply members at control prices, while it is envisaged that monthly social parties would be arranged for members by the house committee.

Other recommendations adopted by the house include the setting up of a disciplinary committee within the quarters to serve as arbiter in the case of family disputes.

While all members of the house should be issued with diplomatic passports as soon as possible, they would also be entitled to sponsored local and overseas working trips during the recess periods.

A residential library should be provided to accommodate the speeches and lectures of eminent scholars anywhere in the world which is related to the work of the house and members should be encouraged to attend and present papers at seminars and conferences relating to their various committees within and outside the country.

Other benefits to be enjoyed by the members include secretarial offices and staff in their constituencies and federal capital, shopping centres and other recreational facilities such as swimming pools, squash courts, billiards, other indoor games as well as the use of the VIP lounge at domestic and international airports in the country.

On health, they resolved that while a well equipped clinic is to be made available at the members' residential quarters and the services to be for 24 hours, all medical bills for members and their families within the country would be settled by the National Assembly.

Furthermore, members would be entitled to overseas medical treatment at the expense of the National Assembly.

In the event of the death of a member, apart from the National Assembly buying the coffin and conveying the body and the family to the member's home, a sum of money to be determined by the Joint Select Committee on Remuneration would be paid to the accredited next of kin.

They also resolved that women's hairdressing salons and a men's barber shop are to be provided within their shopping centre while musical equipment including amplifiers, record players and loudspeakers should be installed to cover their bar, restaurant and cafeteria.

On furniture, the house approved a stay of execution on the furniture being supplied presently to the flats at Victoria Island because of its low quality. Members demanded similar furniture to those at the Badagry Road flats and the carpeting of the rooms and steps should be made wall-to-wall.

The legislators are also to enjoy a 50 percent discount on all their laundry services.

Small wonder then, that Stanley Macebuh wrote about the 'Imperial Senate',[9] or that Tunde Adeniran (1982:2768) deplored the 'cheapening' of the legislature and the 'venal atmosphere' created by the Senate, not on account of the aggrandisement of its powers, but because of its flagrant self-preoccupation. So unreasonable were the demands thought to be that the National Economic Council (made up of the 19 State Governors, the Governor of the Central Bank and the Vice President) as well as the President himself felt called upon to intervene with a plea for greater moderation. Small wonder, too, that the National Assembly's actions produced considerable popular cynicism and are still cited in analyses of the reasons for the 1983 *coup*.

Doubts about the Assembly's competence were increased when the police had to be called in early 1981 to prevent violence between the members, in this case between rival factions of the People's Redemption Party. On that occasion an honourable member produced a gun and dagger in the House of Representatives and vowed to kill anyone who approached him. The House was also the scene, in April 1982, of a tug-of-war for the Mace which resulted in the shattering of that symbol of authority. Apparently the Speaker, Chief Edwin Ume-Ezeoke, perceived a plot against him and adjourned the House. His exit was blocked by perhaps a hundred members, at which point the Mace fell. After the Speaker's 'escape', during which both he and the Sergeant-at-Arms were said to have been manhandled, the rump of the Assembly passed a motion of no-confidence divesting him of his position. Violent incidents occurred in several State legislatures as well. The *New Nigerian* of 24 June 1983, in an editorial condemning out-breaks on the floors of the Ondo, Oyo, Kano, Kwara and Kaduna State Houses, wrote:

In less than three years of the return to civil rule, our legislators at the national and state assemblies have exceeded themselves in virtually everything objectionable. Apart from their pugilism, their truancy is legendary. Their presiding officers have cried themselves hoarse over this, threatening, in several cases, to open attendance registers. Generally, they have not shown that maturity and commitment to the social well-being of this country expected of them. Whatever does not gratify their selfish interests is unimportant. The heavy backlog of bills, pending in the various houses is a sad reminder of the leadership qualities of our law makers.

The presidency

Sooner or later any serious discussion of Nigerian politics under the Second Republic turns to the role of the President. Indeed, it can be plausibly asserted that more has been written about the executive presidency than about all the other institutions established by the 1979 Constitution and nullified by the 31 December 1983 *coup.*

The President (together with the Vice-President) was the sole Nigerian politician to be elected by a *national constituency.* He thus had to extend his appeal beyond any limited ethnic, linguistic, religious or regional base in order to be perceived as a 'national' figure. Indeed, the constitution provided that not merely a simple majority (or plurality) of all the votes was required for election, but in addition that the winning candidate must receive not less than one-quarter of the votes cast in each of at least two-thirds of all the States. If a first election failed to produce a winning candidate according to these criteria, a second or 'run-off' election was to be held within seven days, pitting only two candidates against each other: (a) 'the candidate who scored the highest number of votes' in the first election, and (b) 'one among the remaining candidates who had a majority of votes in the highest number of States, so however that where there is more than one candidate with a majority of votes in the highest number of States, the candidate among them with the highest total of votes cast at the election shall be the candidate for the election'. If after the second election neither candidate had both a majority of total votes cast and at least one-quarter of the votes in at least twelve and two-thirds of the States, a third run-off between the two contenders was to be arranged within one week and the candidate with a simple majority of votes was to be declared President.[10]

The second requirement raised problems, for what actually constituted 'not less than one-quarter of the votes cast in each of at least two-thirds of all the States in the federation' was open to various interpretations. The problem was posed in concrete terms when it turned out that in the 1979 elections Alhaji Shehu Shagari, in addition to the greatest number of votes of any of the five candidates (plurality), had won at least a quarter of the votes in 12 States but only about 20% in a thirteenth, Kano State. Following a protracted controversy, FEDECO stated its decision to apply 'the ordinary meaning' of twelve and two-thirds of the States of the federation (Section 34A, subsection 1(c) ii of the *Electoral Decree*):[11]

> In the circumstances, the candidate who scores at least one-quarter of the votes cast in 12 States and one-quarter of two-thirds, that is, at least one-sixth of the votes cast in the 13th State satisfies the requirement of the subsection.

The decision was subsequently vindicated by the Supreme Court following a suit brought by Chief Awolowo.

Once elected, the President's political role expectations changed somewhat: the post-election image of a national, quasi-paternal and almost 'non-political' leader was intended to be an important aspect of *system-integration* and *legitimation.* President

Shagari, in an interview with a panel of journalists just over six months after assuming office, conveyed his changed self-image, in these words:[12]

> The whole concept of our constitution is to try and weld the various peoples of Nigeria into a united family, and that is what we have set ourselves to do, to remove all barriers between sections and groups in the country and that has been my pre-occupation as a first executive president, the first elected leader, who looks at the country as a whole as his constituency. This is a new innovation which must succeed. We need a leader who regards himself as belonging to every part of Nigeria and that is what I am. The whole country is my constituency and I would like to regard every part of Nigeria as my home . . .
>
> My task is to unite and if I am in a position of president, I would like to feel as if I don't belong to any party. As long as I am here I belong to all Nigerians and I have equal interests in every part, every section.

At the same time, the office of president was endowed with substantial powers which, according to the Constitution, 'shall extend to the execution and maintenance of this Constitution, all laws made by the National Assembly and to all matters with respect to which the National Assembly has for the time being power to make laws'. This was a very broad mandate indeed and it is not at all surprising that most of the apprehensions about a potentially all-powerful President were expressed in relation to this *executive function* and the powers associated with it. For the presidency in effect combined into a single authority the 'powers of the cabinet, the head of government and the individual ministers with the symbolic authority of the head of state in the First Republic' (Nwabueze, 1982b:84).

Under civilian government, the executive branch of government was much larger and more all-pervasive than is commonly supposed – and thus by far the richest source of patronage and clientelism. At the federal level it included, in addition to the President and Vice President, all the Ministers of the federal government (Cabinet), a whole series of special advisory councils and committees, the President's special advisers, experts, etc., the entire civil service, and the agencies of defence and law enforcement, *viz* the armed forces and the Nigeria police. Of all these hundreds of thousands of members of the state bureaucracy, only the President and Vice-President were chosen by election. All other executive officials were appointed and hence not directly subject to popular confirmation. It was the President as chief executive who was entrusted with the command and control of this massive bureaucratic apparatus *on behalf of* the population. Not to have staffed these offices with capable persons (Shagari's first government was notoriously replete with party drones, hacks and hangers-on; his second was somewhat less so) and not to have exercised control over this vast apparatus (corruption, patronage and inefficiency were rife) amounted to a betrayal of this crucial mandate.

The President's powers of *appointment* included the selection of all the Ministers of the government, subject to confirmation by the Senate and the constitutional provision that at least one member be appointed from each of the 19 States (in the second Cabinet in fact two members were selected from each State). These Ministers had no formal independent source of power, but were exclusively responsible to the President, who could transfer or dismiss them at will. The President's appointed personal or special advisers were also entirely responsible to him. These powers of appointment also covered the federal judicature, the top posts in the civil service, all ambassadors, high commissioners and other leading diplomats, and most members of the federal executive bodies set up by the constitution. Here again, these appointments were subject to Senate confirmation and were supposed to reflect the federal character of the country.

However, this, in itself positive, goal of consciously promoting the nation's 'federal character' – otherwise expressed as 'the need to promote a sense of belonging and loyalty among all the peoples of the Federation' – was bound to come into conflict with the imperatives of party politics (see chapter 5). Quota nominations for positions in the Cabinet, civil service and State governments produced massive-scale 'appointments reflecting only the membership of the party or alliances of parties which control the government',[13] a situation that necessarily excluded talented or competent individuals whose partisan credentials were more ambiguous. For this reason, the 'federal character' of presidential appointments was only too often transformed into the federal character of corruption.

Similarly, the executive and legislative powers overlapped to some extent. Since the legislature as a law-making body subject to intra-party compromise was normally able to frame legislation only in the most general terms, the executive, with its large and comparatively well-equipped administrative machinery, constantly found ways of carrying out the letter of the law while completely circumventing its spirit. This possibility was of course more relevant during the period of the first legislature when the President's party did not enjoy a majority in the National Assembly; after August 1983 the problem was submerged under a massive NPN majority.

The President's relative ascendancy over the legislature may be illustrated by examples of the national budget and national economic planning. It was up to the President to prepare the annual budget which he then laid before the National Assembly. After due deliberation, the approved or amended budget was then returned to him for execution. Similarly, the President caused National Development Plans and programmes to be prepared on a long-term basis. Again, subject to the legislature's approval, he subsequently executed these plans. In the absence of a united, determined and tenacious National Assembly, therefore, the chief executive was closely involved in establishing the short- and long-term socio-economic priorities of the nation and would then be the chief instrument of their implementation. No number of formal checks and controls could contain the chain of patronage, mismanagement and corruption that pervaded this massive executive apparatus.

The constitution-makers had clearly recognised the dangers inherent in investing the President with excessive executive powers. A number of members of the CDC had argued that[14]

> a president with such wide powers and armed with the organized forces of the state could easily become a dictator, and could dismiss the Legislature which, as an institution, has no organized force under its control and no machinery for preventing usurpation of power by the executive. The stage is then set for personal rule by the President. The great tragedy of personal rule is its inhibiting effect on personal liberty. Every challenge to any act of government might be viewed as a challenge to the State and to the entire political system. Even vigorous party politicking becomes a threat to the state.

Certain developments during Shagari's first term of office demonstrated that the CDC's reservations were not unfounded. When, for instance, the UPN-affiliated *Nigerian Tribune* of 28 July 1981 published allegations that the President had bribed opposition legislators with cars and cash (Mercedes-Benz plus N50,000) to support certain government bills, the chief executive deployed the state's coercive powers in retaliation. The *Tribune's* offices were searched by some 100 policemen and its editor and editor-in-chief (and later the editor of the *Sunday Tribune* as well) were held in custody while their offices and homes were searched. Despite threats, however, no legal action was taken and the case was eventually dropped – not least, one assumes, as a result of a counter-offensive by a large number of UPN supporters who in September occupied the Lagos offices of the (then) NPN-inclined *National Concord*. Other national newspapers, such as the *Daily Sketch* and *Daily Standard*, were also the object of draconian executive measures.[15] Another important precedent was set when, in the train of the 1981/2 oil-glut crisis, the President succeeded in getting the National Assembly to pass an enabling bill[16] which endowed him with a broad range of economic 'emergency powers' such as the right to impose higher tariffs and duties, to ban or restrict the importation of many goods, to increase prices of certain goods, and to set greater penalties for violations of the new provisions – powers which were then all too readily misused for state-sponsored hoarding, profiteering and suppression of dissent.

The single executive was also supposed to be able to act decisively and to project the 'rugged' image, foreseen for him by the CDC subcommittee, of 'strength, unity, single mindedness and clear locus of responsibility' and of the 'able executive – someone who can give leadership and a sense of direction to the country'.[17] The President, as the centre of a political system otherwise fragmented by federalism and the separation of powers, had sufficient power and authority to co-ordinate the work of the legislature, civil service, armed forces public bodies and commissioners, and ministers of the government, and to harness all these endeavours in the service of national goals (however and by whomever they might have been set). This suggests the crucial role intended for the presidency in the process of 'national development' and elite consolidation. That 'development' and 'modernisation' – along the capitalist road, to be sure – remained primary goals of the Nigerian polity, was affirmed by the CDC:

> The paramount need of Nigeria is for development. We want to be able to develop our economy, to modernize and integrate our society, to secure and promote stability in the community and to safeguard civil liberty.

The presidency, as the symbol and focus of national loyalties, was intended to play a key role in the process of integration.

> In the absence of firmly established political institutions, a strong executive presidency takes on added importance in the task of national integration. It could provide the basis for the synthesis of positive divergent forces in the country, until viable institutions which reflect the organization and structuring of national ideals could be firmly established. (King, 1977:267)

Hence the President was not merely the symbol of a yet-to-be-achieved national unity, he was seen as an active agent of it. This is important, because it points anew to the perceived importance of a strong and decisive chief executive in the further evolution of a cohesive, state-centred elite. Nigeria's Second Republic lacked too many of the socio-economic preconditions of the Western liberal democracies after which it was structurally patterned; if the Nigerian President occupied much the same *de jure* role as his American counterpart, his *de facto* powers were very differently structured. For, on the one hand, he was expected to induce a bloated state apparatus to effect 'development' and hence socio-economic change, while at the same time state actions – irrespective of which elite group holds state power at the moment – were and are restricted by the country's dependence on the world market system and its position in the international division of labour. In terms of domestic politics, however, there are in Nigeria, unlike in more thoroughly industrialised societies, fewer organised 'countervailing powers', such as a broad middle class, a militant working class or a developed 'civil consciousness', which set limits on what government ought and ought not to do, or for that matter articulate interest groups outside the elite patronage network (which of course includes the military) to compete for society's resources. Certain authoritarian popular political values, resting on charisma, tradition and mystique, also contributed to investing the executive with a certain 'legitimacy'. Similarly, the state must play a much greater role in society and economy – in industrial development, finance, education, planning, resource allocation, popular mobilisation and technology transfer, to name a few. For all these reasons, the Nigerian executive President was (and the head of the AFRC now is) a much more visible, dominant and powerful *intra-societal* figure than his Western equivalents. But at the same time the presidency was hampered and diverted by even more powerful external pressures and domestic problems which are analysed in chapter 11.

Problems of legislative–executive relations

The presidential system's peculiar structural intent therefore was to attempt simultaneously (a) *to accommodate* the *diversity* of sectional, ethnic and even class differences, as well as the inter-party and intra-elite struggles which these produced, within the lawmaking branch where the elected representatives of the various groupings enacted the processes of 'interest aggregation and articulation', and (b) *to ensure continuity*, uniformity and hence stability of policy execution by the 'national' and independently elected figure of the President and the institutions of the state bureaucracy which he headed. Unlike the parliamentary-executive system of the First Republic, the presidential-executive system was thus not dependent on volatile and shifting majorities, but permitted the President to carry on even in the absence of continuous parliamentary support. True, the checks and balances inhibited executive (as well as legislative) power, but a number of transitional and temporary measures were built into the system to ensure that the executive (as well as the legislature) was never completely immobilised. Thus when the President was initially unable to secure Senate confirmation of his 18 ministerial candidates, government was run in the interim by appointed civil servants under the direction of the President. Thus, too, a Consolidated Revenue Fund was established from which the President could draw – as in the case of the 1980 supplementary appropriation bill – monies for up to six months (at a level not exceeding the previous year's expenditures) in the event of the National Assembly delaying passage of his annual budget.

The presidential system thus structurally vitiated the immediacy and directly confrontational quality of past legislative–executive relations. No simple vote of no-confidence could bring down a government of the Second Republic. As the history of the first legislative period in both the federation and the States revealed, the frantic rush to form party alliances and ensure legislative majorities was largely a futile undertaking, at least insofar as legislative–executive relations were concerned. For a party's relative strength in the legislature did not *directly* determine its political influence in government. This did not mean, however, that the presidential system ended all opposition, as President Shagari appeared to believe:[18]

> The beauty of it is that in this system there is no organised official opposition, and it will take some time before the legislature realises that there is no organised opposition. There are some groups who regard themselves as opposition parties or as members of the opposition. I don't regard anyone as opposition because there is no opposition, that we are all working towards the same goal and that no party in the legislature could regard itself as an alternative. They are just a part of government.

Legislative majorities *were* still required to confirm executive appointments, pass legislation (notably that introduced by the executive) and in general to sustain the administration of the state. No chief executive could govern for long without majority legislative support, as might be attested to by Governor Musa of Kaduna State whose State House of

Assembly impeached him, and by Governor Ambrose Alli of Bendel State whose appointments, bills and appropriations were consistently delayed by a recalcitrant House. What did change, in contrast to the First Republic, was the relative significance of the legislative majority coalition and the directness of its influence on the executive.

However, the very same constitutional principles which were intended to lend the Nigerian polity its resilience and accommodative quality – federalism, checks and balances, liberal rights – were also at work to produce a series of problems which were never resolved in theory or praxis. The separate elections by popular vote of the House of Representatives and the Senate on the one hand and the President on the other – to say nothing of State Houses of Assembly and Governors – in effect diluted the principle of popular sovereignty. Rather than a single 'popular will', which a parliamentary system is said to produce, a whole series of overlapping 'popular wills' was created. Government was in this sense divided against itself. This was, of course, the intent of the framers of the constitution who were concerned with preventing any 'tyranny of the majority' by a given party or party coalition at any particular moment, and with ensuring 'continuity' and 'stability' as just discussed. But in a 'new' government, in particular, where mechanisms of conciliation and patterns of adjustment and compensation were not firmly established, these overlapping and interdependent, popularly elected institutions tended to advance their respective claims in an antagonistic manner.

In theory, for example, the National Assembly was the highest embodiment of the principle of popular sovereignty. Professor Nwabueze, basing his opinion on a number of precedents drawn from British jurisprudence, appeared to support this theory when he argued that the legislature was the prior instance (1982c:1–2):

> Without legislative authorization . . . neither the President nor a State Governor nor any other executive functionary can act against a Nigerian. Nor can they give to themselves the necessary legislative authorization. A law made by the legislature, the National Assembly or a State House of Assembly, can of course authorize an executive functionary to fill in details by means of regulations . . . The relation is that between a superior and subordinate or inferior authority.

In a parliamentary system, with its fusion of legislature and executive, of course, the point is self-evident. But ambiguity arose in the presidential system when the President was elected directly by the people, implicitly with a mandate to execute on 'their' – rather than the legislature's – behalf. In the case of disputes, then, the two separate representatives of 'the popular will' were pitted against each other and frequently resorted to outright trials of strength to determine who would prevail.

In analysing sources of friction between these two arms of government, it is useful to bear in mind that, following upon, and succeeded by, a military government which centred on executive authority, the presidential system needed some time to 'run in' properly. Much of what has been attributed to 'conflict' or 'antagonism' between the executive and legislature – where it could not be traced to struggles for access to state largesse – turned out to be merely the result of inadequate experience or preparation. The Senate's refusal to confirm the President's ministerial nominees, for instance, was rooted less in hostility than in the President's failure to supply it with adequate information about the candidates' backgrounds, to inform it which Cabinet posts they were to be allotted, or to consult with it prior to presenting the list.

This and a number of other examples indicate that both legislature and executive had abundant reasons to develop their relationship into one of productive but non-intransigent dialogue and debate, since at bottom they upheld the same constellation of class interests. Within the context of legislative–executive relations, of course, this example was also indicative of a minor, though important, shift in power from the presidency to the National Assembly. The important intervening variable here, however, was the evolution of the party system, as discussed in the previous chapter. In order to overcome the chronic friction and delays inherent in the separation of powers (as well as the division of powers or federalism), the development of a mega-party was an obvious solution. Once in power, a ruling party was in a position to deploy the state's resources and powers – selective appointments, apportioning of benefits, favouring of States or regions, and manipulation of the electoral machinery – to ensure itself a majority in all the elected and appointed institutions of the Second Republic. This was precisely the NPN's 'accomplishment' by 1983, with results to be described in chapter 8.

To sum up, the picture painted here of the 1979–83 Nigerian constitutional order yields a highly differentiated impression. It was, first, a charter based upon and reflecting its historical context. It went beyond the structural limitations and deficiencies of its predecessor 'received' constitutions and the unpredictable decrees and edicts issued by the military government, to formulate a document for contemporary Nigerian conditions. As such, it acquired a considerable symbolic and unifying significance and proclaimed the polity's capacity to 'learn from experience'. Second, it did reflect a wide range of popular interests and desires. The end of military rule, the fact of having one's own national constitution, the provisions for unity and oneness, the strictures against corruption coupled with the principle of public accountability, the emphasis on pluralism and minority safeguards, the declared intent to implement socio-economic rights – all these represented goals shared in all probability by the great majority of the politically aware population. The cynicism engendered by the parties' conscious subversion of Nigerian constitutionalism ought not to prevent one from recalling the mass enthusiasm and (guarded) hopes which went into the formation of the Second Republic.

On the other hand, third, the demilitarised constitutional order was essentially a rationalisation of existing power relationships, a kind of balance-sheet of the socio-economic *status quo*. It was therefore not a charter which addressed the *fundamental* problems of Nigeria's political economy – economic disarticulation, dependency, inequality of distribution, etc. – nor which took account of the pressures toward basic changes. Fourth, what it did attempt to do was to provide an arena for the enactment of intra-elite struggles while simultaneously ensuring that communal and/or class struggles could be diverted or diffused before welling up into a challenge to the social hegemony of the ruling groups. In the light of Nigeria's past political decay, caused in large measure by intra-elite conflict, this was intended as an important function of the 1979 constitutional order. Two crucial questions remained unanswered, however.

(i) Since the foundation of the intra-elite coalitions, which momentarily held together disparate and to some extent antagonistic factions of the ruling classes, was premised on the capacity of the system continuously to 'deliver' substantial benefits to all groups (and hence depended, above all else, on constant economic 'growth', not necessarily coupled with 'development'), was the political order sufficiently resilient to adapt to possible economic fluctuations and shifting strengths within the elite coalition? Barely four years after the system's inauguration, in fact, economic recession coupled with growing pressure on the military from within led to the New Year's *coup* of 1983/4. These developments are analysed in chapter 8.

(ii) And, in the longer term, if the liberal-democratic political order – or for that matter, any political order – was made by and for an essentially state-bourgeois class, could it then withstand the stresses and strains which were bound to develop as more and more Nigerians emerged from 'traditional' society into the industrial-urban or agrarian cash-crop economy, and as their growing needs for social benefits, education and job security were translated into demands which must eventually be taken into account? For at the same time as they are integrated into the capitalist economy, the 'masses' tend to become more aware, articulate and insistent on the realisation of these demands. The very factors which enable them to serve capitalism – literacy, mobility, training – are also at work, in the long run, to transform them into a direct challenge to the dominant elitist order. Growing politicisation, in other words, helps to undermine the passive consensus on the basis of which the elite has hitherto been able to rule. By 'passive consensus' is meant that aggregate of unarticulated interests of the great majority of the population in any developing society – the illiterate, impoverished inhabitants of remote villages, the atomised and largely ignored masses at the periphery of urban complexes, the *de facto* disenfranchised and deprived of the 'modernising' society – who remain objects (rather than subjects) of whatever the current ruling system. As successive social classes – the growing urban proletariat, the perhaps 70–80% of the population loosely termed 'peasant' – crystallise, achieve an awareness of their class interests, and press for the realisation of their newly articulated demands, latent antagonisms are caused to come to the fore. Thus the political system, whether military or civilian-led, has been and will continue to be placed under considerable pressure to adapt or transform itself. In 1979 it may well have been that an over-whelming majority of the political ruling factions were able to agree upon a liberal-democratic political structure which sustained 'their' socio-economic order. But this order, like its current military 'corrective' variant, was far from a popular dynamic order enabling the Nigerian polity to cope with the imminent demands and challenges with which it was and will be confronted as the passive consensus becomes unravelled in coming decades.

Notes

1. Speech delivered by Chief of Staff Brigadier Shehu Musa Yar'Adua on 22 September 1978, reprinted in *New Nigerian*, 24 September 1978.
2. Federal Ministry of Information, *Federal Military Government Views on the Report of the Panel on Creation of States*, Lagos 1976, p. 13.
3. Based on 1979 constituencies in the Federal House of Representatives. The 'missing' representatives were of course the seats set aside in the 450-member House for the Federal Capital Territory, and actually elected in 1983.
4. The percentage of civil servants elected would certainly have been much higher had not the Military Government decreed that all public employees give at least four months' notice of termination prior to contesting an election.
5. It is worth noting, however, that this again is an instance of the continuing historical decline of traditional rulers' pre-eminence, particularly in the North. During the First Republic, in addition to a separate federal House of Chiefs, aristocrats were strongly represented in the lower houses. In Dr Aliyu's words: 'As a careful study has shown, 82% of the Northern House of Assembly in 1959 belonged to the traditional aristocracy, a percentage which rose to 85.3% in the membership of the Assembly in 1961–65.' The subsequent decline in this class's representation 'may be explained largely in terms of their loss of control over the police, judiciary and prisons since 1966, and the impact of local government reforms and

partially in terms of their identification with political parties which lost the elections in their States'. See also chapter 9.

6. *West Africa*, 19 April 1982, p. 1050; similar observations can be found in virtually every account of the National Assembly between 1979 and 1983.
7. *New Nigerian*, 7 June 1980.
8. *New Nigerian*, 17 November 1979 (corrected somewhat).
9. A term used in several of his *Daily Times* features in 1979 and 1980.
10. 1979 Constitution, Section 126 (1)–(5). The history of these provisions is quite significant in terms of the composition of the President's 'national' constituency and may therefore be briefly recapitulated here. The heterogeneous economic, political, sectional, cultural and ethnic diversity of Nigeria as well as the experiences of the First Republic demonstrated clearly that not two, but several, political formations would surely emerge on the reciviliani-sation of the political system. In a situation in which a number of candidates – in 1979, five, in 1983, six – compete for the top political office, it is extremely unlikely that any one candi-date could achieve both a plurality of all votes cast and a full one-quarter of the votes cast in at least two-thirds of the States. Anticipating such a situation, the CDC, in its draft constitution, provided for a run-off election between 'the candidate who secured the highest [number of] votes at the first election and that one among the remaining candidates who has a majority of votes in the largest number of States' (*CDC Report*, Vol. I, p. 44). If this second run-off elec-tion failed to produce a candidate with the required popular majority and territorial spread, only then was the presidential election to be placed in the hands of the 21 legislatures of the nation: both Houses of the National Assembly, together with all the State Assemblies, would choose the President by simple majority. Moreover, the CDC's deliberations on the mechanics of electing the President were conducted between 18 October 1975 and 3 February 1976, a period in which Nigeria still consisted of 12 States and hence posed no problems with respect to the 'two-thirds rule'. Following the creation of seven new States on 3 February 1976, the CDC either did not think to adjust the rule, or assumed that the necessary changes would be made by the Constituent Assembly (as pointed out in *Daily Times*, 20 August 1979). But the CA did not deal with the relevant provisions. At the same time, the provisions for a run-off election were somehow omitted from the 'clean copy' of the constitution – presumably as a result of a CA decision – which for a time seemed to imply with virtual cer-tainty that the President would be chosen by this electoral college of federal and State legisla-tures. The 'clean copy' was then submitted to, and accepted by, the Supreme Military Council, while FEDECO and other federal agencies vitally concerned with its provisions raised no objections. Remarkably, although the final version of the constitution was published and widely disseminated by the end of 1978, the 'missing' provisions for a run-off election were only 'discovered' by the press, the broadcasting media, the political parties and the concerned public at the beginning of March 1979, when a public controversy broke out. A member of the then-dissolved CA, Dr J. O. J. Okezie then petitioned the Supreme Court to reinstate the second popular election, since the CA had never abolished it (*Daily Times*, 15 May 1979). His suit was, however, rejected on the grounds that it was not addressed to the responsible institution: the Military Government (who for its part had merely ratified the CA's submission). Eventually, the departing Military Government, in a last-minute consti-tutional amendment, abolished the electoral college and anchored the final provisions in the constitution (see *Sunday Times*, 30 September 1979). Where, one might ask, were the 'guardians of the public interest' when the constitution was first published? Why did it take so long for an awareness of the omission to surface? The *Daily Times* (20 August 1979) had an answer to these questions: 'In a word, the entire nation, led by our founding father, simply goofed'. The 2/3 rule, however, was not intercepted, and did find its way into the electoral laws and the constitution, where it remained. Not until mid-way through the 1979 elections did it become apparent that no presidential candidate was likely to gain sufficient support to meet several requirements, by which time of course it was too late to amend the rules.
11. Quoted in *Daily Times*, 18 August 1979.
12. Quoted in *New Nigerian*, 29 May 1980.

13. S. E. Oyovbaire, 'Structural Change and Political Processes in Nigeria', *African Affairs*, Vol. 82, No. 326 (1983), p. 19.
14. *CDC Report*, Vol. I, p. xxx.
15. *West Africa*, 10 August 1981, p. 1845.
16. Federal Republic of Nigeria, *Economic Stabilisation Temporary Provisions Act 1982*, Lagos 1982. Admittedly the decree applied only for an initial 12-month period, but was subsequently renewed.
17. *Op. cit.* p. xxxi.
18. Quoted in: *New Nigerian*, 29 May 1980.

7

The States in the Federation

Sub-state government in Nigeria

It is a truism of Nigerian politics that the country's continuing existence as a nation-state hinges on its capacity to evolve and maintain an adequate system of federalism. This imperative is reflected in the country's recurrent national goals, usually defined – by the respective elites – as unity, stability and development.[1] From colonial unitarism to the centrifugal regionalism of the First Republic, from the centralism developed under the military government from Ironsi to Obasanjo to the modified 19-State federalism inherited by the Second Republic, up to the renewed military centripetalism of the Buhari Government and the minor adaptations since the Babangida *coup, the issue of federalism dominates politics in the Nigerian postcolonial state.*

The search for structural equilibrium persists because of the permanent fragmentation that inheres in post-independence political life: A strong centralism is necessary – at least in the absence of a unifying set of goals or ideology – to impose coherence on the mass of regional, local, class and sectoral interests which, without central direction, would threaten the coherence of the state itself. The unmitigated regionalism of the First Republic stands as one unacceptable pole of decentralised federalism. But the obverse, and equally unacceptable, pole is represented by the brief unitary government attempted by the Ironsi regime. The massive opposition it generated clearly demonstrated the absolute need for an adequate number and balance of sub-national and sub-State units to account for the cultural, socio-economic, linguistic, and political diversity of interests within the Nigerian population. The twelve, then nineteen State 'solutions', the 'federal character of Nigeria', the 'representative bureaucracy' and the multi-ethnic composition of civilian and military governments alike are unambiguous evidence of the need to account for this structural imperative.

The kinds of issues raised here may be addressed, in the first instance, in terms of conventional theories of 'social engineering' or 'pluralism'. For the structuring of sub-federal and sub-State government is in no way based on an attempt to produce fundamental socio-economic transformation, but rather represents a series of pragmatic structural innovations, implemented from above – not unlike colonial structural policy – and aimed at adapting and channelling the existing social and economic forces into a more efficient, more 'legitimate', 'modernising' political system, namely 'from destructive imbalance to a sustainable competitive balance' (Panter-Brick, 1980:117). In this view, the dysfunctions and contradictions of the developing society are largely a matter of trial-and-error efforts at 'nation-building' or 'institution-building' to produce the factoral combination which will ultimately result in 'unity', 'stability' and 'development'.

Both military and civilian governments have been constrained to make allowance – the former *de facto*, the latter *de jure* – for the regional, ethnic and other potentially destabilising pulls of the Nigerian state. While both the Buhari and Babangida regimes have resurrected the command-federalist system practised by the first series of military governments, the Second Republic represented a sustained and systematic attempt at finding an equilibrium among, and constitutional channels for, the country's diversity (defined primarily as a diversity of elite interests). Any political structure which aspires to be more than a temporary 'corrective' will have to come to terms with, and institutionalise, the manifold interests, goals and problems of sub-national aspirations.

The overall structure of State government from 1979 to 1983 may be usefully conceptualised in terms of its correspondence with the structures of the federal government. The application of the principle of checks and balances will be illustrated here with reference to the State House of Assembly and the State executive.[2] (The judiciary will be dealt with, as part of the state bureaucracy, in chapter 10.)

The two central agencies of State government subject to popular control were the legislature and the executive. (i) The State legislature, unlike the National Assembly, was unicameral. Election of State legislators was by population, with the number of constituencies for each State determined by trebling the total number of seats which the State had in the federal House of Representatives. (ii) The State executive was headed by the Governor, who operated like the President in the federal system, his central task being the execution of legislation passed by the House. The Governor was the only elected State officer whose constituency was State-wide. To be elected he had to receive the highest number of votes cast, a majority which included not less than one-quarter of the votes cast in at least two-thirds of all the State's local government areas. Thus some State Governors managed to come to power on the strength of support from a single ethnic group, namely, those in the ethnically relatively homogeneous States such as Oyo, Sokoto or Anambra. In the more heterogeneous States such as Bendel, Lagos or Cross River, on the other hand, the successful candidate had to assemble a broader spectrum of groups.

The Commissioners of Government of the State were the equivalent of the Federal Council of Ministers. The Governnor could appoint and define the responsibilities of all such State ministers, subject to ratification by the House of Assembly. Through this body, the Governor enjoyed control over the State civil service and had the capacity to command and control the entire executive arm of State government. These powers naturally included the power of appointment and dismissal. Here the Constitution enjoined the Governor, in exercising such powers, to have 'regard to the diversity of the people within the State and the need to promote national unity' (compare the President's mandate to appoint at least one Minister of the Government from each State).

Like the federal government, the actual operation of the State governments indicated substantial gaps between constitutional theory and political reality, caused in part by general unfamiliarity with the new governing structures, in part by certain individual and institutional deficiencies and in part by socio-economic contradictions which underlay the political system. A central dependent variable of State performance was the relative strengths of the political parties in the State Houses of Assembly, since this directly affected the relationship between the executive and legislature. Thus in those States in which one party both dominated the House of Assembly and produced the Governor – Anambra, Imo, Kano, Lagos, Oyo, Ogun or Ondo – the executive tended to dominate the law-making process in addition to its constitutional implementation role. This tendency, of course, undermined the principle of checks and balances, particularly when the legislature was controlled by the party machine and/or executive patronage. Indeed, many of these States became *virtual one-party States* in which the legislature's primary function was to legitimate the executive's policies and actions, not unlike the one-party Regions of the First Republic – mitigated, however, by the existence of the new structural arrangements which precluded the direct conversion of intra-State hegemony into national political power.

On the other hand, where the Governor's party controlled less than two-thirds of the members of the House (i.e. where the two-thirds majority needed to override a gubernatorial veto was lacking) patterns of co-operation and conflict did evolve. In Kwara State, for instance, during the first electoral period, the NPN Governor was forced to deal with a legislature composed of NPN 59%, UPN 35.7% and GNPP 4.8%. And in Gongola State a House made up of GNPP 35.7%, UPN 28.6%, NPN 23.8%, NPP 6.3%, PRP 1.6% had to collaborate with a GNPP Governor. Particularly in such multi-party States, therefore, the executive–legislature relationship showed signs of evolving in terms of trials of strength and of conflict and compromise.

As a general pattern, conflict developed when the State chief executive – perhaps recalling the military period when State Governors enjoyed legislative *and* executive powers – usurped or was perceived as usurping legislative rights, for instance with respect to ministerial appointments, changes in the educational or welfare system, State revenues and expenditures, and the like. In Bauchi, for instance, the Governor unilaterally repealed an existing edict concerning the wearing of motorcycle crash helmets. In Imo State the Governor dissolved a number of statutory boards and the Alvan Ikoku College council, while in Oyo the chief executive attempted to repeal an edict on pools betting. In Kano, Governor Rimi amended the tax law without consulting the House. And in Lagos State, Governor Jakande 'more or less unilaterally passed into law his party's policy of free education at all levels'.[3]

The legislature then reacted (or over-reacted) to assert its powers and re-define precedents for future action. In Bendel State, for example, the House of Assembly twice rejected Governor Alli's executive appointments and later challenged his suspension of local governments and statutory boards across the State. Or in Borno State the House rejected as excessive a bill fixing the Governor's salary at N20,000.[4] When political differences became too acute, the Houses did not hesitate to resort to the instrument of impeachment to rid themselves of an undesirable governor. In mid-1982, the Rivers State House of Assembly unsuccessfully moved to impeach Governor Melford Okilo and his deputy, Dr Frank Eke: numerous similar incidents could be related. By the time of the Rivers attempt, impeachment proceedings had been threatened in four States, actual impeachment had been instigated in three further States, and one Governor (in Kaduna) had been removed from office. Indeed, the impeachment weapon, symptomatic of the confrontational style of Nigerian politics, extended into intra-legislative relations as well. The Ondo House of Assembly's Speaker and Deputy Speaker were voted out of office in June 1981 for embezzlement. In October their counterparts in the Lagos House were suspended by their party, the UPN, for 'anti-party activity'. And in Sokoto a vote of no-confidence removed the House Speaker there.

The 'successful' impeachment in Kaduna State is worth considering further. The 1979 State elections produced a PRP Governor, Alhaji Balarabe Musa, but an NPN-dominated House of Assembly: of 99 seats, 64 were won by the NPN, 16 by the PRP, 10 by the GNPP, 6 by the NPP and 3 by the UPN. As the only example of its kind among the 19 States, Kaduna State was widely thought to be a 'test case' for the possible future of relations between the two branches of government. Unlike the federal President, however, the new Governor was unable or unwilling to establish a legislative coalition, preferring instead to attempt to govern alone.

In his first policy statement, Alhaji Balarabe announced the abrogation of the emirate and traditional councils together with the repeal of community and cattle taxes –

measures which not only appeared to challenge the House's law-making prerogative but also struck directly at the conservative power base of the NPN. This perceived threat from 'the left' was further enhanced by the Governor's membership of the informal caucus of quasi-oppositional 'progressive governors' as well as his affinity to the 'radical' group within the PRP, as the party began to disintegrate into a left and right wing during 1980/81. The House of Assembly retaliated by consistently blocking the Governor's Cabinet and civil service appointments, whereupon the Governor proceeded to install these officials without legislative confirmation. A prolonged, highly publicised dispute[5] ensued in an environment of growing intransigence and hostility. Ultimately, the House brought impeachment proceedings against the Governor which, in conformity with constitutional procedure, resulted in the latter's removal on 22 June 1981. Alhaji Balarabe's application to the Kaduna Court of Appeal was rejected on the grounds that impeachment proceedings were a political process not subject to judicial review.[6]

The episode posed fundamental questions about Nigerian liberal democracy. On the one hand, the legislative branch's law-making function was defended and asserted, even though that defensive action was based less on constitutional considerations than on party-political strength. But on the other hand, yet another instance of obstructionism and conflict helped to undermine the stability and legitimacy of the system of checks and balances which assumed co-operation and relatively harmonious operation of the two arms of government. And, as even a cursory reading of the impeachment document[7] reveals, nothing like 'gross misconduct' in office in the sense of malfeasance, corruption or exploitation of position for personal gain – the only pretext, apart from death or incapacitating illness, under which impeachment was said to be permissible – was involved. Rather what the Kaduna State Assembly in fact did was to pass a vote of no-confidence in the governor.

Finally, the *actual* behaviour of individual State legislators, executives and administrators inevitably had a profound influence on the performance and legitimacy of the political system. And here again, most of the circumstances already established for the federal government seem to have applied to the States as well. Although systematic studies of individual actions are lacking, a generalised impression based on media accounts and ongoing military probes reveals a picture of nepotism in government services, ethnocentric behaviour, considerable use of coercion and intimidation (particularly in the 'one-party' States), continuous conflict in a variety of forms, and, above all, an open uncompromising drive for self-aggrandisement punctuated by endemic corruption. 'Many of the ministers and commissioners in the Nigerian governments', wrote Dele Giwa with understatement in the *Sunday Concord* of 25 October 1981, 'have become rich men that they weren't two years ago'. As an example he cited the 1981 burial, at public expense, of the father of Bendel State Governor Professor Ambrose Alli. The N471,525 'state' funeral featured the following:

> Nearly 50,000 naira was spent on beer; 54,000 naira was given to chairmen of local governments – a purely political give-away; 40,000 naira for construction work; more than 15,000 naira was spent on liquor and about 5,000 on soft drinks; sundry work, whatever that means, cost more than 15,000 naira; and one Mr J. J. Odigie spent almost 7,000 naira for his accommodation.
>
> Two dancing groups were given 550 naira respectively. And the most ridiculous item on the expenditure break-down was the 500 naira handed to rain doctors, and the unfortunate tax payers of that state had to cough up the money.

Politics of federalism

The ultimate locus of power in Nigerian government, military or civilian, is the federal government, and this was codified, during the Second Republic, by the constitution's allocation of an exclusive list of broad 'enumerated' powers to the federal government with relatively few 'residual' powers for the State governments. Both tiers of government were entitled to legislate on the relatively small list of 'concurrent' matters, though many of the twelve items on this list were also contained in the exclusive federal list (job safety and welfare measures, for instance), and could thus be pre-empted by the central government. Federal powers were further enhanced by Section 59(a) of the constitution, which authorised the federal government to promote and enforce the fundamental objectives and directive principles anchored in Chapter II, and by Item 67 of the exclusive legislative list, (the 'implied powers' provision) which empowered the federal government to enact legislation on 'any matter incidental or supplementary to any matter mentioned elsewhere in this list'.

Furthermore the sub-division of the nation into 19 component States was intended not as a form of dual sovereignty, but as a system of co-operative federalism which presupposed a complementary, co-operative relationship between the States and the central government. Merely to pose the federalist norm in this way, given the realities of Nigerian political life, is to recall the wide gap which developed between constitutional theory and the conflicts, divergences of interest and the like that were actually present. Such incidents as the unilateral decision to close the Igbeti marble plant (owned jointly by private investors and the Oyo government) taken by State Governor Bola Ige, on the grounds that his government should have exclusive control of mines and minerals in the State; or Governor Michael Ajasin's decision to explore for oil in Ondo State despite the fact that oil prospecting was legally a federal monopoly, are evidence of the existence of substantial antagonisms between the States and the federation which were rooted in economic interests, political party conflicts, policy differences, and the like.

There were more. During 1980, the UPN-governed States of Oyo, Ondo, Ogun, Bendel and Lagos, contrary to a federal ban reaching back to the Military Government, legalised and encouraged gambling and pools promotions. Although after a time lag the federal government retaliated with a series of raids on gambling houses, according to *West Africa* of 5 January 1981:

> nothing could deter the UPN states, which seemed poised on a collision course with the Federal Government. Gambling has therefore been legalized in these states, but there are reports that the revenue has not been spectacular, as pools promoters and proprietors of the gambling houses, conscious of the fact that the states have no police backing, have refused to pay the usally lucrative gambling taxes.

In another UPN-governed State, Lagos, Governor Lateef Jakande in 1980 unilaterally proclaimed the introduction of free universal primary education, while at the same time abolishing all private schools in the State. Similar developments subsequently occurred in all UPN States. These measures were coupled with an announcement that children from States not providing free primary education would not be allowed to attend the Lagos schools. The potential federal-State confrontation contained in the Governor's actions – for example, their implicit restrictions on constitutionally guaranteed rights to freedom of movement and their clear discrimination against Nigerian citizens on the basis of place of origin[8] – was only relieved when a number of groups and individuals, rather than the federal government, challenged them in the courts. And in Oyo State a low-cost public housing project in Ibadan undertaken by the federal government was ordered to be demolished by the State government; Anambra State then replicated this anti-social measure by confiscating construction equipment belonging to contractors engaged by the federal government to build a badly needed access road in that State.[9]

Indeed, during the Second Republic, the consistent and determined opposition of the UPN-controlled States in particular, including even the Governors' refusal to display the President's portrait in public places, gave rise to rumours and suspicions of a UPN 'secessionist plot'.[10] Such, largely NPN-instigated, conspiracy theories quickly receded, however, as the UPN moved increasingly into the role of crystalliser of the anti-NPN forces (Nine and Twelve Progressive Governors; see chapter 6) and began to view itself as the nucleus of an alliance to wrest power from, and then replace, the dominant party.

The constellation of interests and issues at stake here became clear over the attempt to appoint Presidential Liaison Officers (PLOs) to represent federal policies in each of the 19 States. Taken without consulting the State governments affected, the measure was actively resisted by the nine Governors of the UPN, PRP and GNPP-controlled States and at first tacitly supported by the three NPP Governors. Compelling arguments were enunciated on both sides, the President claiming that he needed his 'own' agents in the States to oversee the execution of federal projects and to provide ongoing 'inputs' into national development planning, and the oppositional Governors arguing that they alone had been elected by their constituents to deal with State concerns. Although *prima facie* these arguments contain considerable merit, the fundamental issue here, as in so many power conflicts between the States and the federation, was control and disposition over the large State and federal resources, and the opportunities for self-aggrandisement and patronage which they entailed. Whether the federal government, through its PLO, or a State Governor representing a non-NPN State government, was in a position to influence the flow of federal funds, was obviously a crucial power-political matter. As *New African* of April 1980 aptly put it:

> As federal agents the governors have the advantage of dishing out contracts to their supporters. The new state PLOs would do the same for NPN supporters. Already reliable NPN sources in Lagos are claiming that a staunch NPN supporter in NPP-controlled Plateau has won a N6 m. Federal contract. Both sides have their eyes fixed on patronage, political influence and future elections. The suggestion that PLOs would be in competition with the governors is only a minor issue in the controversy over their appointment by the President.

Thus, federal-State conflicts were firmly embedded in partisan political disputes over access to resources and patronage. No mere textbook cases of 'federalism in action' or 'unity in diversity', these conflicts expressed vital interests and goals which helped to make up the destabilising dynamics of the Nigerian political system.

An important early manifestation of these tendencies was the controversy surrounding control over the Nigeria Police in the States. When, as just described, the UPN governors found themselves unable to enforce gambling tax regulations, they began to explore ways of establishing State police forces – contrary to constitutional provisions which made law enforcement an exclusively federal jurisdiction. Initial trials of strength were generally resolved in favour of the federal government, occasionally in rather dramatic fashion, as during a visit by Shagari to Bendel State in December 1980, reported in *West Africa*, 5 January 1981:

> Governor Alli had given orders banning meetings and processions during the period. On arrival at Benin Airport, President Shagari instructed the Police Commissioner to let the crowd (cordoned off by the police on Governor Alli's orders) come forward and meet their

president. An embarrassed Governor Alli watched as the police threw open the barricades to drummers and dance groups who surged in hundreds to meet the president. It was the first and most significant win for the president.

Although the article concluded that this incident settled the 'police debate', the underlying reasons for the non-NPN governors' attempts to check and counter federal police power during the Second Republic became more and more evident as the NPN increasingly instrumentalised the 'national' institutions of government. Incidents mounted of non-co-operation and conflict between State governors and police commissioners, notably in Kano, Kaduna and Anambra States; and by the 1983 election campaign, as the following chapter will show, the Nigeria Police was, with considerable reason, perceived in many States as a mere executive arm of the NPN.

The crucial issues: revenue-sharing and state-creation

Within the underdeveloped neo-colonial state, economic power, and with it all the attendant opportunities for political, economic and social development, as well as for patronage, perquisites and state power, is a function of revenues. In any federal system, but most particularly one in which fiscal relations between the centre and the component units are not consensually regulated, the relative share of federal and sub-federal governments in total revenues is therefore bound to be a central and contentious feature of political life. State-federal relations in the Second Republic were essentially determined by the restructured federal system implemented by the military government and controlled by the political parties. This system, which developed in the context of the oil boom of the 1970s, in a sense also unified the national economy inasmuch as all the States' individual dependencies on their own products – groundnuts, cotton, cocoa, palm oil, etc. – were replaced by a common dependence on oil revenues.

This dependence has been consciously fostered by the central government, first, by the political and administrative erosion of most independent regional powers, and second, by federal revenue distribution via the Distributable Pool Account which provided and provides some 70% of State revenues, half allocated to the States on the basis of population, the other half as an equal lump-sum payment to every State (thus also generating a strong incentive toward State formation, as discussed below). In addition, the federal government exclusively collected personal and corporate taxes, customs and excise duties, export duties, etc.; and it, and it alone, was constitutionally empowered to borrow money abroad. Altogether, about 90% of State incomes were (and are) dispensed by the federal government. Thus, while all the States have enjoyed an approximately tenfold increase in revenues (and corresponding expenditures) during the past fifteen years or so, this rise has been at the expense of increasing State dependence on the federal government – a natural state of affairs under centralist military rule, but an important tension-producing factor under a federalist civilian government.

The combination of multi-party politics and the operation of federalism in the 1979–83 era produced several important departures from the relentless fiscal centralism of military rule. On the one hand, State governments (and the dominant economic groups within them) were in many respects transformed into 'super-lobbies', each vying with the others for federal priority in the execution of public works or welfare projects, in securing funds and/or benefits, in arranging credits or loans from abroad, and in gaining the federal ear for new projects or plans. The relative dependence and subservience of these 'pressure groups' clearly contributed to the continued supremacy of the federal government as mediator and broker among these scattered interests. This has been described, in terms of party politics, in chapter 6.

The relative weakness of the States can further be attributed to their administrative incapacity, which in turn derives from a chronic lack of trained personnel. This situation gives the federal government a 'controlling interest' in practically every area of economic policy, including those policies which the States are intended to carry out, ranging from military expenditures to agriculture (where the central government built an ambitious 'Green Revolution' into its development plan), and from infrastructural improvements to investment priorities. But, as Brian Smith points out (1981:367):

> it is in the social services that the federal government has made most inroads into areas hitherto dominated by the regions. The education programme initiated by the military has been adopted by the Shagari government requiring expenditure of 2,265 million naira in 1980 or 27 per cent of federal recurrent expenditure. Again the programme is largely administered by the states with substantial discretionary federal grants. The federal government has also become involved in housing as a result of the National Party of Nigeria's campaign promises. The 1980 budget allocated 45.8 million naira for the recurrent expenditure of a new Ministry of Housing and Environment and earmarked some 500 million naira for the construction of 2,000 housing units in each state of the federation in 1980–81. The Federal Mortgage Bank is to make loans more readily available and a new town is planned for the outskirts of Lagos. Central policy-making and execution are expanding in precisely those areas which dominate state budgets, such as education, which accounted for 42 percent of Oyo state's 1980 budget and 48 percent of Rivers', for example.

On the other hand, the fact that the States were constitutionally guaranteed a fixed share of federal revenues, as well as the constellation of political party representation in the States and federation (12 out of 19 States were governed by non-NPN parties in the first electoral period, and each State was represented by five Senators and a proportionate number of members of the National Assembly), meant that the States were no mere passive recipients of federal largesse. On the contrary, they were able strongly to influence the process of fiscal allocations. Developments surrounding the 1981 Revenue Allocation Act well illustrate the point.[11] Following, but slightly adapting, the Okigbo Commission Report on Revenue Allocation, the President proposed a corresponding bill to the National Assembly which would have apportioned federal revenues as follows: federal government 53%, State governments 30%, Local Government Councils 10%, special fund and others 7% (the latter consisting of 2.5% Federal Capital Territory, 2% for special problems of the mineral-producing areas, 1% ecological problems, 1.5% revenue equalisation fund). Next, the House of Representatives modified the bill to arrive at the formula: federal government 50%, State governments 40%, LGCs 10%. Some months later, the Senate produced its rather more complex formula: federal government 58.8%, State governments 31.5%, LGCs 10% (including funds for the FCT, ecology and derivation).

The ultimate compromise formula, following considerable negotiations, was worked out by the Joint Finance Committee made up of 24 members of the two houses of the National Assembly. Its decision to support the Senate's formula – which actually increased the federal share – was rejected by the 12 non-NPN State Governors. Both before and after the JFC's decision, most of the States presented their alternative formulas, ranging from UPN ratios strongly favouring the States (for example, Ondo, Oyo, Ogun and Bendel proposed 30:50:10) through less drastic though still State-weighted GNPP and NPP proposals (Gongola 40:40:10, Anambra and Plateau 50:40:10), to the NPN-State proposals nearer to the President's original bill. In the event, the Supreme Court, in response to a suit brought by the 12 oppositional Governors,[12] on 2 October 1981 rejected the bill on the grounds that it had not been enacted by the entire National Assembly as constitutionally required. The importance of this States' 'victory' was, of course, largely symbolic, since the rejection of the revised bill meant that revenue allocation temporarily reverted to the ratio established by the centralist Military Government: federal government 75%, State governments 22%, LGCs 3%.

The crisis was resolved in January 1982 with the Allocation of Revenue Act which in all essential respects was identical to the 1981 bill invalidated by the Supreme Court. Most significantly, the post-1983 military governments have not attempted to reverse the revenue allocation formula established in 1982, despite the strong centripetal tendencies which are inherent in Nigerian military regimes. Initially, they merely left the Allocation of Revenue Act intact, then expressly confirmed its validity in the 1985 budget speech (since entrenched in Decree No. 36). The formula thus remains: federal government 55%, State government 32.5%, local governments 10%, disaster relief fund 1% and fund for development of mineral-producing areas 1.5%. Unlike previous military governments, therefore, the Buhari and Babangida regimes have recognised the need to extend the 'federal character' principle into the crucial area of fiscal distribution.

Furthermore, it should be recalled that the States, like the local governments, have a crucial role to play in the country's neo-colonial capitalist development plans. Under the Second Republic, the States' trade-off for accepting greater dependence on the centre was the guaranteed provision of massively increased revenue amounts. The new opportunities for large-scale spending and fostering of their own development projects had important social and political implications. The process of elite consolidation which temporarily achieved the establishment of a liberal-democratic structure at the federal level (and which necessitated a corresponding 'rationalisation' of traditional rule at the local government level) rested upon a parallel and mutually complementary process at the State level. The economic factors in State elite-formation are described by Brian Smith (1981:367–8):

> The states are playing a vital role for the development of capitalist enterprise on behalf of local business interests in providing capital, sometimes in combination with foreign investors (as in Plateau's ceramics industry, Lagos' scrap metal and international hotel, and Anambra's motor manufacturing company). Credit schemes, investment in infrastructure, partnerships between the state governments and foreign or indigenous business concerns, public ownership and the provision of land are the main ways in which the state governments are currently promoting a diverse range of economic activities including prestige property developments and manufacturing industry such as ceramics, pharmaceuticals, motor cars, steel, scrap metal, soft drinks, sugar refining, brewing, wood pulping, salt, rubber and bricks. Those sectors of society within the states with a vested interest in maintaining a supply of contracts, loans, grants and jobs in state owned companies and corporations will be keen to maintain a distribution of powers within the federation which permits such intervention.

This analysis of the interests and classes who have a stake in revenue-sharing helps to explain what became perhaps the most prominent and volatile issue in the 1979–83 legislative period and into the 1983 electoral campaign: the problem of the creation of more States.

Although the Military Government, having created seven additional States in 1976, appeared to regard the issue as settled, demands for still more sub-federal units were by no means stilled. By the 1979 electoral campaign, all five 'licensed' parties had incorporated such proposals into their platforms and campaign promises. Throughout the period of the Second Republic, and most particularly during the recession after 1981, the frequency and intensity of these demands perceptibly grew. Apparently large, popular and well-funded 'movements' arose in virtually every State, each with its own headquarters, list of prominent supporters (including supporters in the high councils of the existing parties), and its constant publicity, advertisements, demonstrations, etc. As a result, the federal government was 'now presented with organised political and popular pressure on a scale that no other issue has aroused since the return to civilian rule'.[13]

'Moreover, proposals for new State creation burgeoned from the handful under discussion in 1979 (see Panter-Brick, 1980:124–5) to the dozen or so mooted in 1980–81,[14] and to the 38 proposals received by the Presidential Committee on the Creation of States in late 1981 (see Kraus, 1982:110). This committee, constituted in March 1981, chaired by Vice-President Alex Ekwueme and made up of representatives of the five political parties, the federal executive and the National Assembly, presented its findings to the President in April 1982. Although its specific recommendations were not made public, their import may be inferred from the subsequent recommendations of (a) the report of the December 1982 House of Representatives Committee on States Creation, which proposed 21 new States,[15] 11 from the former Northern Region and 5 each from the former Eastern and Western Regions, and (b) the corresponding January 1983 Senate Committee which came out in favour of 26 new States for a total of 45.

Meanwhile, a joint conference committee of the National Assembly was entrusted with the regulation of procedural questions. Its Creation of States and Boundary Adjustments Bill 1982 clarified some of the relevant constitutional complexities, and provided, *inter alia*, for a referendum to ensure that the populations in the areas affected really wanted the new States, for FEDECO management of the related procedures, and for the preparation of a New States Creation Bill to give legal sanction to the proposed changes.[16] That these constitutional provisions needed clarification was apparent from the following synopsis of the required procedure laid down in Section 8, which of course reflects the departing military's intention to inhibit any further proliferation of States (commentary in Joye and Igweike, 1982:99–108).

> At least two-thirds of the members representing the areas requesting the creation of a new State, in each of the Senate, House of Representatives, State House of Assembly and affected Local Government Councils, had to submit a corresponding request to the National Assembly.
> At least two-thirds of the people living in the area of the proposed new State had to approve a referendum on the creation of that State.
> A simple majority of all the States of the federation and their Houses of Assembly would have to support the results of the referendum.
> And finally, a two-thirds majority of both the Senate and House of Representatives would have to approve the proposal.
> Changes in the boundaries of existing States were similarly difficult and subject to the approval of all the peoples concerned.

Before any new State could be created or an éxisting one modified, therefore, the agreement of both those included in the new unit and those from whom that unit was derived, had first to be obtained, plus the assent of the representatives of the entire country. Admittedly, the same results could have been produced by means of constitutional amendment to the existing procedure for State creation. However, according to Section 9(2) of the constitution such legislation would have required not only a four-fifths majority of both houses in the National Assembly – and not merely the two-thirds majority needed for 'normal' constitutional amendments – but also a corresponding affirmative resolution by two-thirds of all State Houses of Assembly. Thus, State creation required a high degree of consensus among the peoples, regions, elites and parties, which, given the heterogeneous and fragmented nature of the Nigerian demand structure, was highly unlikely to be achieved – unless and until new State proposals were integrated into a comprehensive 'package' which accounted for all the groups and interests involved, pulled them all into equilibrium, and held out the prospect of some advantage or *quid-pro-quo* to all concerned. The search for such a package[17] became the major endeavour of political life in the final months of the Second Republic's first term of office. After the 1983 elections, of course, State creation would have been much easier, but then subject to fears that the arrangements could be manipulated by and for the dominant NPN.

All these considerations demonstrate anew the centrality of the States issue in Nigerian politics. More complex, however, is any explanation of the persistence, volatility and salience of the issue. Such an explanation would have to account in particular for the supra-class, supra-ethnic and supra-regional mass support for the creation of more States. Although any comprehensive theory of State creation will have to await both the passage of time and the accumulation of more empirical data, one may, with a view to the reports of the 1976 Panel on the Creation of New States (Federal Ministry of Information, 1976) and the 1982/3 Presidential, House of Assembly and Senate committees on State creation,[18] suggest some of the principal justifications which have been advanced for increasing the number of sub-federal units. Despite their number and variety, they can be classed under three broad categories:

Cultural pluralism. This category takes in the notions of 'cultural considerations', 'ethnic traditions', 'self-determination' and the like, which constitute the chief argument in favour of new States found in most of the partisan literature. This rationale recognises the persistence of heterogeneity across religious, linguistic, historical, regional, ethnic, economic and even kinship axes, and attempts therefore to justify a system of federalism which allows each cultural bloc a sphere of relatively autonomous operation and development within which to pursue its unique personal identity. As long ago as 1966, Chief Awolowo first formulated this motivation for the creation of more States, when he argued that such a measure 'would enable each linguistic group not only to develop its peculiar culture and institutions but also to move forward without being unnecessarily pushed or annoyingly slowed down by others'.[19]

Political balance or, in the 1983 Senate Committee's term, 'administrative convenience'. If the principle of cultural pluralism is successfully structured, then 'national unity' will be enhanced, negatively, by removing potential arenas of ethnic, religious or other conflict. On the other hand, however, the reduction of States to a plethora of ethnic-group enclaves would also eliminate the need for ethnic group co-existence and co-operation and hence to some extent undermine the civilian politicians' and military leaders' maxim of the federal character of Nigeria; it would also impede regional collaboration and fragment the country into an almost pre-colonial state of ethnic inwardness. Needless to add, federal supremacy would be virtually absolute.

Positively, a larger number of smaller States would be more dependent on the central government for administrative guidance and co-ordination. As Keith Panter-Brick (1980:124) has suggested with reference to the 19-State system, 'a federation of nineteen States, most of which have access to the prime source of revenue only through the maintenance of the federation, may have a structural stability of its own, despite its plural nature'. The number and variety of possible inter-State coalitions, and the quantity of overlapping relationships among them would be increased, thus creating, in terms of pluralist theory, 'a fluid pattern of crosscutting associations of groups based on mutual interests and salience of demands' (Odetola, 1978b:183).

Further, the projected new and more homogeneous States, by bringing government 'closer to the people', might, it was thought, increase their sense of identification and,

Table 7.1 *Senate committee recommendations for the creation of new States (January 1983)*

Present	Planned	Capital
1. Anambra	1. Anambra	Enugu
	2. New Anambra	Onitsha
	3. Ebonyi	Abakaliki
2. Bauchi	4. Bauchi	Bauchi
	5. Gombe	Gombe
	6. Katagum	Azare
3. Bendel	7. Bendel	Benin City
	8. Anioma	Asaba
		Ogwashiukwu or Agbor
	9. Delta	Ughelli
4. Benue	10. Benue	Makurdi
	11. Okura	Ayangba
5. Borno	12. Borno	Maiduguri
	13. Gujba	Bade
	14. Kukawa	Giadem
6. Cross River	15. Cross River	undecided
	16. New Cross River	Calabar or Ikom
7. Gongola	17. Gongola	Yola
	18. Taraba	Gakum
8. Imo	19. Imo	Owerri
	20. Aba	Aba
9. Kaduna	21. Kaduna	Kaduna
	22. Katsina	Katsina
10. Kano	23. Kano	Kano
	24. Jigawa	Kachako
	25. Lautai	Hadeija
	26. Chari	Bambatta
	27. New Kano	undecided
11. Kwara	28. Kwara	Ilorin
	29. Kogi	Lokoja
12. Lagos	30. Lagos	Ikeja
13. Niger	31. Niger	Minna
14. Ogun	32. Ogun	Abeokuta
	33. Ijebu	undecided
15. Ondo	34. Ondo	Akuro
	35. New Ondo	Ondo
16. Oyo	36. Oyo	Ibadan
	37. New Oyo	Oyo
	38. Oshun	Oshogbo
17. Plateau	39. Plateau	Jos
	40. Nassarawa	Lafia
18. Rivers	41. Rivers	undecided
	42. Port Harcourt	Port Harcourt
19. Sokoto	43. Sokoto	Sokoto
	44. Zamfara	Gusau
	45. Kebbi	Kebbi
Totals 19	45	

Source: West Africa, 10 January 1983, p. 111.

like local government, better mobilise the population for (government-defined) development goals. In this connection, State creation might accelerate political as well as economic and social development 'by establishing smaller constituencies which can be penetrated more effectively from the point of view of communication. More direct contact between developmental leaders and citizens can enable the national government to communicate its goals and policies more effectively' (King, 1976–7:167).

The creation of more States would contribute to political balance in a number of more literal senses as well. If properly effected, it should maintain an equilibrium between North (at present with ten States) and South (nine), a situation which the President's special advisor considered necessary for national stability.[20] Presumably, a similar equilibrium between East and West and minority and majority ethnic group areas[21] would be desirable for the same reasons.

Economic development. The 1976 Panel rightly concluded that 'the basic motivation in the demand for more States is rapid economic development. All other reasons adduced by State agitators were in the view of the Panel to a large extent mere rationalizations to achieve the basic purpose of development' (Federal Ministry of Information, 1976:10). And the *sine qua non* of development, in the Nigerian context, is revenues. The 80–90% of State revenues which the federal government supplies is, as has been demonstrated, mainly apportioned from the Distributable Pool Account in such a way that approximately half is divided among the States equally and half relative to population, formulas employed consistently by military and civilian federal governments alike. It is the sums which are distributed equally that produce such strong incentives for the formation of new States. For if a given area is divided into two or more States, the whole area will receive a greater total share of federal revenue, and 'this, as well as the prestige, the contracts, the employment and (at least in theory) the stimulus to development that would follow, is a very attractive proposition to those areas which feel they have been neglected by their States' administrations'.[22] Also attractive was the prospect of a new State capital as a focus of development and source of new opportunities (Joye and Igweike, 1982:100):

> State capitals are usually thriving centres of political and economic activity. Their establishment can be expected to result in more government jobs to fill executive, legislative and judicial positions in the new government, and to provide the supporting staff of administrative and clerical workers. A new capital may mean improved public works like water, electricity and local roads, and new public facilities like hotels and restaurants to cater to the government employees and business people drawn to the new capital. A new State government is likely to mean more government scholarships for local students.

These economic motives were interlinked with political ones. Here again, the potential rewards of new Statehood were substantial. In addition to the Governor and Ministers, there would be a new State bureaucracy, a multiplicity of advisory bodies, parastatals (or the chance to create them), a judicial system, and so forth at the State level. Under constitutional governments, the catalogue of benefits would also include a State legislature with its manifold possibilities of patronage, as well as delegates to federal legislative houses. Of course, isolated voices were raised during the Second Republic against this virtually unchecked process of State-proliferation, arguing that as an unproductive and revenue-consuming exercise, it could not be sustained by the economy. At some point, it was argued, State creation becomes counter-productive (Nwabueze, 1982c: 29–30):

It is believed that that point has now been reached. The creation of more states *now*, while it might serve political interests, would operate as a drag on development by stretching the resources of the country to a point where meaningful application of them for development becomes frustrated, and by diverting resources needed for development to the payment and maintenance of an unduly proliferated apparatus of state government. The country's resources, as they are at present, cannot take such an increased financial burden of new governmental structures. The Technical Committee on Revenue Allocation has observed that 'the increased size of government budgets in both capital and recurrent expenditures was largely the result of the creation of seven additional states in 1976, accounting for 99 percent increase in those budgets in 1977–8. The lesson of this should be clear in handling demands for additional creation of States.' It would be reckless not to heed this lesson.

One major aspect of 'corrective' military government is its relative immunity from direct popular pressures which might prove dysfunctional to the 'stability' of the political system and the elite rule which it ensconces. Whereas the civilian regime would almost certainly have produced as many as 45 States – a development in which both the political elites and the masses had strong material and subjective interests – and that in a period of economic crisis,[23] the military's reluctance to proceed with such system-threatening measures – indeed its interest in an administratively simple, small number of States – and its ability to hold quasi-separatist mass enthusiasm in check point again to its crucial role in, as it were, saving the system from itself.

Certainly, the political-economic forces pressing for more States, properly integrated into a revised structure of federalism, might stand a chance of contributing to more 'even development', as all the panels and commissions cited above argue (though without specifying the criteria and goals of this 'even development'). And even development is surely one precondition for political balance and cultural pluralism. But in addition to the three more or less official motives of State-creation just discussed, a fourth, implicit, one must be added: *economic self-aggrandisement*. Just like the federal system, State governments were ruled mainly by self-interested elites who sought the power, wealth, patronage and clientele networks which for one reason or another they had not been able to develop in the federal system or elsewhere. This tendency is far less blatant, but no less real, under military government. Thus, as Gavin Williams reminds us (1976:46), pressures for the creation of more States are:

> aimed at regulating political competition by ensuring to the bourgeoisie of each State an arena in which it is protected from outside competition, and by increasing the number of contenders so as to produce an equilibrium of diverse alliances at the centre rather than the domination of a single region and party.

In other words, the 'rationality' of elite rule in Nigeria requires that there be ample opportunity for members of these classes to enter the system in positions of greater or lesser prestige and power from which they too can further their means of self-enrichment. This is one reason why

> the most ardent advocates of new States or regions have always been aspirants to high positions in the political, administrative, professional and business fields who have failed to attain positions of prominence at the national, regional or State levels, and who hope to attain such heights in smaller constitutional entities. They rationalise their inordinate ambitions by pleading reasons of national unity. (Nnoli, 1981:161)

The issue of State creation, affecting as it does both the immediate concerns of the population for material well-being and the sensitive areas of their self-esteem, identity and aspirations, here presents itself as an optimal ideological means of further entrenching elite rule. Indeed, sub-national politics more generally, as this chapter has attempted to demonstrate, had much less to do with fostering initiatives from below – though these could and did develop – than with entrenching a now much more 'national' and 'rational' elite hegemony from above. Essentially, federalism under the Second Republic was designed to encourage subordination of the masses to the leadership of the elite, while at the same time promoting links and a mutuality of interests between and among the elites in the leading positions of the federal system and sub-systems.

Notes

1. These, at least, are the terms in which national goals are generally put. As Eddie Madunugu rightly suggests, such aims as 'national unity' and 'stability' are defined mainly by the Nigerian elites. He reformulates the problem, in political economy terms, as: '. . . how can the ruling class of Nigeria unite its various economic, ethnic and religious factions so as to achieve a permanent and stable social hegemony over the entire country', *Problems of Socialism: The Nigerian Challenge*, London, 1982, p. 10.
2. Descriptions of their structures and functions are contained in, e.g. Graf, 1979; Joye and Igweike, 1982, and Nwabueze, 1982b.
3. *Daily Times*, 'Opinion', 10 October 1979.
4. On this development, see 'MPs Reject Pay for a Governor', *Daily Times*, 31 October 1979.
5. Reproduced, in pamphlet form, as *Why They Fear our Forces of Democracy and Social Progress*, and excerpted in *West Africa*, 6 July 1981, pp. 1519 22.
6. *National Concord*, 30 June 1981; *New Nigerian*, 30 June 1981.
7. Reproduced in *West Africa*, 6 July 1981, pp. 1523–6.
8. Which the constitution (Section 39(1)) of course expressly forbade.
9. These two examples are cited in Nwabueze, 1985: chapter 5.
10. See *New African*, April 1980, pp. 61ff.
11. On what follows, see, e.g., *West Africa*, 12 October 1981, pp. 2369–70; *New African*, January 1982, p. 69; *Africa News*, 26 October 1981, pp. 2–3.
12. The Governors' grounds for the suit, and a clear statement of their other grievances against the Federal Government, are contained in their joint statement, reproduced in *West Africa*, 23 February 1981, p. 357.
13. *West Africa*, 21 September 1981, p. 2161.
14. See *West Africa*, 21 September 1981, pp. 2161–2.
15. The proposed entities included: New Anambra and Ebonyi States from Anambra State; Gombe and Katagum from Bauchi State; Anioma and Delta from Bendel State; New Cross River from Cross River State; Taraba from Gongola State; Abia from Imo State; Katsina from Kaduna State; New Ondo from Ondo State; New Oyo and Oshun from Oyo State; Port Harcourt from Rivers State; Zamfara from Sokoto State; Jigawa, Lautai and Chari from Kano State; Gujba from Borno State; Nassarawa/Middle Belt from Plateau State; and Kogi from Benue State. See *Africa News*, 14 February 1983, pp. 4–5.
16. Cf. *West Africa*, 13 September 1982, p. 2380; *Africa News*, 14 February 1983, p. 5.
17. On the protracted procedures for new State creation devised and partly carried out during the Second Republic, see Dean. E. McHenry Jr. 'Disaggregating Governmental Units: A Comparison of the Demands for More States and More Local Government Areas in Nigeria', paper presented to ASA, Los Angeles, 25–28 October 1984, mimeo. pp. 11–13.
18. As reported in *West Africa*, 12 April 1982, p. 1025; and 10 January 1983, p. 111. On all this, see further *CDC Report*, Vol. I, pp. xxvii–xxix.
19. Quoted in *Africa News*, 14 February 1983, p. 5.

20. *New Nigerian*, 1 August 1980.
21. A case for the latter is made by Prof. Peter Ekeh, 'Criteria for Creating More States', *New Nigerian*, 7 February 1980. Further see 'Recipe for Creation of New States in Nigeria', *New Nigerian*, 15 March 1980, which argues for consideration of political party interests as well.
22. *West Africa*, 21 September 1981, p. 2161.
23. Here it is sufficient to recall the bitter irony of a situation in which, even as plans for at least doubling the number of States were being formulated by the various elites in the legislatures and executives, existing State administrations were close to breakdown due to non-payment of teachers' and civil servants' salaries, lack of skilled personnel, infrastructure deficiencies, chronic supply shortages, rising corruption and much else.

The Military Returns

Chronicle of the Buhari coup

Nigerians awoke on the morning of 31 December 1983 to learn that the Second Republic had been replaced, during the night, by a new Federal Military Government, the fourth since Independence. Initially, the *coup* appeared to be confined to the capital city. Brigadier Sanni Abacha, delivering the 8.30 a.m. announcement on Lagos radio, proclaimed the military's mission as discharging its 'national role as promoter and protector of the national interest' in doing away with an 'inept and corrupt leadership' that had precipitated the 'grave economic predicament' of the past four years. Meanwhile, in most States of the federation, the military presence was either very muted or, ostensibly, non-existent. Few roadblocks, manoeuvres or struggles were evident, and there was virtually no violence. Many State radio stations continued regular programmes without so much as a mention of the *coup*.

As the day progressed, however, the full scope of the action became more evident. Two afternoon broadcasts announced the 'voluntary retirement' of all the service chiefs – thus producing speculation about a new 'majors' *coup*' paralleling that of January 1966 – and requested brigade commanders to take charge of their State governments pending the appointment of military governors. At 10.30 p.m. Brigadier Abacha announced, on Lagos television, that the new head of state would be Major General Muhammed Buhari, GOC of the First Mechanised Division of the Nigerian Army stationed in Kaduna, former Governor of Bornu State under Murtala Muhammed, former chairman of the NNPC, and one of the top soldiers who had decided to remain in the service after recivilianisation in 1979.

On New Year's Day, Buhari, by now evidently in control, provided a rationale for the *coup* and a broad framework for public policies under the new military government. The military's main reasons for intervening, he stated, were to arrest economic decline and moral corruption:[1]

> The corrupt, inept and insensitive leadership in the last four years has been the source of immorality and impropriety in our society, since what happens in any society is largely a reflection of the leadership of that society.

As this quotation suggests, the military leaders' diagnosis of the deficiencies of the Second Republic was based on certain *symptoms* – mismanagement of the economy, corruption, 'indiscipline', wrong policies – rather than on any underlying socio-economic analysis; this point will be taken up later.

Invoking a continuity between the brief, but still widely popular, Murtala Mohammed regime and the new military leadership – and thus incidentally acquiring some measure of instant legitimacy – Buhari outlined the structure and organisation of his 'successor' military government: with its 19-member Supreme Military Council (SMC), a Federal Executive Council (FEC) and a National Council of States (NCS), it would be a structural replica of the Mohammed/Obasanjo regime.[2] In contrast to the bloated civilian executive, with its forty or more ministries, there would now be only 18 federal ministries. The proliferation of local government councils would also be cut back from nearly one thousand to the 301 originally created by the 1976 local government reform (see chapter 9). The judiciary and the civil service would be left intact.

Policy-making would follow from the rationale for military intervention. The economy in particular would receive a 'new impetus and better sense of direction', beginning with short-term measures to alleviate hunger (no mere rhetorical flourish!) and to pay salary arrears owed by various State governments to their employees. In the long term, significantly, the country would repay its international financial obligations and maintain its standing in the international capitalist economy. Of course, 'corrupt officials and their agents would be brought to book'. And all treaties and diplomatic relations entered into by the previous government would be honoured.

Proceeding with measured deliberation – too deliberately for many sectors of public opinion as well as important elements within the military itself, and thus consistently goaded on from 'below' – the SMC almost daily announced new measures to restore (their concepts of) probity and efficiency to political life: banning of all political associations and politicians, compulsory retirements of 17 federal permanent secretaries (and subsequent appointment of 33 new ones), a further 34 retirements of senior police officials and 13 naval officers, corresponding retirements of State officials, probes of the Federal Capital Development Authority and the Nigerian National Petroleum Company, dismissal or retirement of some 3,000 federal civil servants at all levels, substantial personnel reductions in Nigerian overseas missions and information offices, pruning of political and other non-essential public employees at all three levels of government, re-examination of all major government contracts with both foreign and domestic private firms, reduction in travel allowances (but not in *Hajj* allowances), restrictions on numbers of businessmen and students permitted to travel abroad, revocation of wrongly obtained oil licences, and so on.

Even before the new political machinery was in place, groups of soldiers began an impromptu campaign of forcing markets and shops to bring down prices and make available scarce commodities that in many cases had been hoarded. The same strategy underlay the subsequent systematic policy of 'war against indiscipline' and 'leadership by example', beginning with a series of army raids on warehouses where hoarded goods were stored and selling off the goods at low prices or often giving them away. Many of the stockpilers, it turned out, had occupied high offices in the deposed civilian government.[3]

Individual military governors proved to be most zealous and ingenious in these matters (though the local actions owed much to the lack of central direction or a co-ordination plan for dealing with the more or less correctly diagnosed ills of the previous regime). Lieut.-Colonel David Mark, Governor of Niger State under Buhari, posed as an ordinary patient in a hospital and, after experiencing inadequate and discourteous care, dismissed the staff members responsible. Commodore Otiko, then Governor of Ondo State, had 35 employees of the state broadcasting station who arrived late for work caned. The same Governor, following a precedent set in Ogun State, also introduced taxes on merrymaking 'ranging from N25 to N100, plus N200 where the celebrants close a street'. Plateau State Governor, naval Captain Samuel Atukum, sold off all Mercedes-Benz and Peugot 505 official cars and replaced them with less pretentious Peugot 504s; at the same time he banned after-hours use of all government cars.

Public servants in the federal capital who appeared late for work were made to cut the ministries' grass at the weekend. In Ogun State, 63 civil servants unable to recite the national anthem and pledge were suspended indefinitely by Governor Oladipo Diya. For their shoddy organisation of a public event in Cross River State, the Commissioner of Information and the committee responsible for Children's Day Celebrations were docked one month's pay. And in Lagos a couple were refused the solemnisation of their marriage because they were unable to recite the national pledge or anthem.[4]

A list of the politicians investigated and detained, numbering literally hundreds, perhaps over a thousand, reads like a proverbial Who's Who in the Second Republic. By early April 1984, the SMC announced final plans for a special military panel to try an initial 175 politicians and businessmen (out of the 700 or so investigated) for various 'economic crimes'. In a process extending over the entire life-span of the Buhari government and well into the Babangida period, trials and convictions of members of the political-tycoon class brought out the massive scale of public looting and corruption under civilian rule. The revelations attending the trials underline the surreal nature of the system of institutionalised plunder that had evolved under the Second Republic. But in some ways the official announcement, on the first anniversary of the *coup*, of the release of 2,511 persons from detention (including 144 political detainees) was even more suggestive. Almost all those released had to repay sums ranging from thousands to hundreds of thousands of naira to the government as well as meeting various other conditions. Despite the at times agonisingly slow pace of the government investigations, General Buhari was able to announce, in his 1984 Independence Day Speech, that the special investigation panels and the tribunal on the recovery of public property had so far recovered some N112,119,482 and £688,185, as well as N348,644,840 from FEDECO and N48,073,077 from the National Assembly.[5] A *National Concord* editorial of 2 February 1984 calculated that the federal government had lost more than N2.1 bn to 'embezzlers, ghost staff and other categories of fraudulent workers' under the Shagari regime. Nigerians, the newspaper concluded, had 'lost the ability of being shocked'.

The regular announcements not merely of the economic crimes committed by the ruling class of the Second Republic, but also and especially – as the statistics cited above imply – of the sheer scope and scale of state plunder no doubt enhanced the Buhari government's 'corrective' legitimacy more than any combination of campaigns against indiscipline, Independence Day exhortations and 'leadership by example'. Virtually the entire Nigerian banking system, including the Central Bank and responsible government officials, have since been deeply implicated. For instance, the Johnson Matthey Bank (JMB) affair has revealed the extensive collusion of Nigerian officials, British banks and Asian merchants in defrauding Nigeria of billions of naira.[6] Over-invoicing, forgery of inspection certificates relating to phantom goods, short-shipments, and circumvented international banking regulations were among the means by which this was accomplished. Naturally, the well-known traffic in liquid naira was part of this syndrome, so that when Buhari effected a rapid currency changeover a few months after assuming power, billions of naira held abroad (particularly in Britain) were made worthless – a most effective move against the speculator-comprador class within and without. As part of the same strategy, the government also stopped payments for letters of credit issued during the Second Republic and demanded that all overseas claims be supported by proper invoices, bills of lading and certificates of delivery in Nigeria.

State agencies were also instrumentalised beyond what was considered acceptable in Nigeria. The subsequent Nigerian National Supply Company (NNSC) scandals[7] well illustrate this tendency. Once in power, the NPN ensured the appointment of its own brokers to all important positions in the company. Up to one-fourth of all incoming rice shipments were allocated to these political directors who then sold the rice, at a mark-up of 300%, to market women at the company's gates. When in response to popular pressure the company appointed marketing officers to allocate the rice direct to the public, the officials simply sold most of the rice to their own agents, who then re-sold it at an even higher mark-up. Sugar too, as a result of conspiracies and over-invoicing, was sold at excessive prices. Prices for these two staple commodities were inflated by well over 1,000%, thus making their consumption impossible for most of the population – and all this at a time of increased austerity and at the height of Shagari's 'ethical revolution'. The presidential task force on rice, headed by Dikko, was created to overcome the resultant shortages and price inflation!

In view of these revelations, and those described in chapter 5, one can only note S. G. Ikoku's observations on arriving with other members of the political-business class at Kiri-Kiri prison, Lagos, in January 1984 (Ikoku, 1985:17):

> As we stepped into the courtyard of the block, we were greeted with vociferous shouts and hand clappings. It was a grandstand ovation from armed robbers to 'fellow robbers'. For among the loud-throated shouts could be heard clearly 'welcome, oh fellow armed robbers'.

For all its more or less well conceived measures and pronouncements, the Buhari regime did not manage to formulate a consistent strategy, much less a coherent programme. Its basic approach might best be termed indignant (albeit measured) activism. Nevertheless, the contours of a general programme can be inferred from what it did, said it would do, and left undone.

For instance, the principal executive decrees it promulgated reveal a number of patterns. The Constitution Suspension and Modification Decree of 1984, like the similarly entitled document of January 1966, established the legal groundwork for military rule. But it did not abolish the entire 1979 Constitution, most notably the civil rights provisions, the legal system, the territorial and local government structures and the 'Fundamental Objectives and Directives of State Policy'; it merely did away with all political offices in the executive and legislative branches, both federal and State. A special decree, the Political Parties (Dissolution and Prohibition) Decree 1984, liquidated the parties and related organisations and all their assets.

The post-Shagari military's concern with economic probity was reflected in the Exchange Control (Anti-sabotage) Decree 1984, which prescribed severe penalties for violators of exchange-control laws, and in the Banking (Freezing of Accounts) Decree 1984, which permitted the head of the Federal Military Government to freeze bank holdings and investigate the financial affairs of persons suspected of having been involved in a variety of offences, including bribery and malfeasance. These powers were rounded off by the Recovery of Public Property (Special Military Tribunals) Decree 1984, which authorised the head of the FMG to constitute tribunals to investigate the assets of any (former) officer suspected of illegal dealings or improper self-enrichment. This law was a particularly severe one. Not only were those tried by the tribunals considered in effect to be guilty until proved innocent and any appeal precluded, but sentences (also set by the tribunal) were predetermined and draconian: conviction automatically carried a minimum sentence of 21 years, except where amounts totalling not less than one million naira were involved, in which case a mandatory 'life imprisonment' (not less than 25 years) sentence was imposed. In the Nigerian context, these penalties may or may not be deemed appropriate for such major offenders as Dikko and Akinloye who directly contributed to the hunger and privation suffered by a large sector of the population, or other ex-politicians – such as the wanted Professor Sunday Essang, former Minister of Works, Emmanuel Osamor, former Minister of Police Affairs, or Dr Wahab Dosunmu, former Minister of Housing and Environment – whose alleged looting and misconduct affected the well-being of millions. But as formulated, the decree was applied in blanket fashion to virtually anyone who had had dubious dealings with the civilian government, since according to *West Africa* of 9 April 1984:

> It cover[ed] every person who may have made money through a public officer abusing his office – and that could include the petty contractor who got that little contract from the chief clerk in the ministry of this and that, to supply paper or milk, or even the 'businessman' who got a loan from the bank manager without 'adequate' security, because he paid back a percentage to the manager.

Also in this context, one might mention the Robbery and Firearms (Special Provisions) Decree 1984 which established special tribunals to try and sentence armed robbery and firearms cases, as well as the State Security (Detention of Persons) Decree 1984, which enabled the Chief of Staff, Supreme Headquarters to detain for up to three months (renewable) persons suspected of jeopardising state security or contributing to economic adversity. To these were added, in the course of time, the far-reaching Special Tribunal (Miscellaneous Offences Decree) to be discussed below, the Counterfeit Currency (Special Provisions) Decree, and the Civil Service Commission and Public Offenders Decrees which constituted the administrative basis for the civil service purges also to be discussed later.

Despite its willingness to leave the catalogue of liberal rights intact, the Buhari government, like its predecessors, was prepared to modify or restrict specific rights or sets of rights when this was deemed essential to the execution of its mission. The 'economic decrees' just described represented a qualification of the right to private property (or right to life, in the case of the armed robbery decree). And the Public Officers (Protection Against False Accusations) Decree 1984 allowed the FMG to close down any medium, whether print or electronic, that, in its view, made 'any false statement or [spread] any rumour calculated to bring public officers to ridicule or disrepute' and to jail its personnel. As in the case of other related decrees, the onus of proof was on the accused.

To sum up, then, the Buhari government's 'programme' was one of probity, efficiency, proper management and law and order. Part of this programme was the exemplary punishment of public officials who did not conform to these norms. This is all evident from the aims and objectives of the FMG as outlined by General Buhari at his first press conference following the seizure of power.[8] As in the case of previous military governments, this was not a programme of social change or self-centred development, much less a proposal for revolutionary transformation. The Buhari government, like its predecessors, was bent on preserving – by making more honest, efficient and predictable – the existing socio-economic order even while 'rotating' the political elites that presided over it. This observation will be expanded and analysed in the three sections that follow.

Logic of military intervention

Officially and self-evidently the military's reasons for intervening in political life were the moral deficiencies of the political class and the latter's inability to govern the country in such a way as to ensure 'unity', 'stability' and 'development' (as defined in terms of the interests of the elite stratum as a whole). More specifically, the rigging, fraud and corruption of the August/September elections, as well as the economic reverses caused by the global economic crisis after 1980, were constantly cited as pretexts.

Certainly as a general contextual explanation these factors provide a collective justification for the military intervention. The degeneration of the political class as a whole, irrespective of party or position, into what amounted to a gang of plunderers (and thus their apparent willingness to commit a form of immoderate 'class suicide'), the decline of the essentially mono-mineral and import-dependent national economy as a consequence of falling oil revenues, the severe hardships faced by the mass of the population, the frauds and violence produced by the election campaign, the mounting debts of public and private corporations, the unpaid salaries in the public sector (especially in non-NPN states), the chronic shortages of food, industrial inputs and basic consumer goods, the decline of all public services from health to education, the flagrant corruption throughout the state sector and the widespread privation – all these have been well documented and need not be reiterated here.

Yet these factors only constitute an (incomplete) explanation of *why* the military chose to strike; they do not reveal the logic of the *timing* and *substance* of the *coup*. For as I wrote literally on the heels of the event: 'If the military struck in direct response to either of these causes – economic crisis or ballot rigging – it ought logically to have made its move two years ago or last summer.'[9] Two central reasons seemed to militate against military intervention *at that time*.

(i) The liberal-democratic structures had by no means collapsed; or as *The Times* of 2 January 1984 (rather optimistically) put it, 'democracy might have been faltering, but it was not dead'.[10] For one, the elections had in fact been brought off with what seemed comparatively little violence, especially in view of the drastic, practically unchecked NPN 'gains'. Even though the ground rules of 'balanced vote inflation' (as described in chapter 5) had been substantially violated and the NPN, with the help of state patronage and the support of a disproportionate number of 'heavyweights', appeared to have exceeded the limits of mutual acceptability, there was a general, if cynical, acceptance (resignation?) that the party had been the front-runner in any case. Moreover, the NPN hegemony furthered the already evident trend away from exclusively ethno-centric politics and in the direction of supra-regional, supra-ethnic coalitions based on access to state resources and offices. Had a Zik-Awo coalition come about, in fact, the tendency toward a two-party 'chop'-centred system might have been reinforced.[11] In some cases, the most blatantly fraudulent electoral results had been overturned by the judiciary (some 60% of the election results were said to have been challenged in the courts), and 'make-up' elections had been held in some of the most disputed States and constituencies. The second Shagari regime had also begun to take more consistent measures to deal with the economic crisis and indeed had submitted a potent-sounding budget to the National Assembly only a few days before the *coup* – which the two succeeding military governments have since attempted to carry out with few modifications.

(ii) The military's corporate interests were well looked after under the Second Republic. The liberal-democratic structure was the soldiers' creation in the first place. And many former military personnel were politically involved in the Second Republic. Among the most prominent were former Biafran leader Odumegwu Ojukwu and the former military Governor of Bendel State, Samuel Ogbemudia. Third, all the top military-political leaders, including former head of state General Olusegun Obasanjo, retired from active service at or before the coming of civilian government – not least to enjoy the material benefits they had accumulated in office. The post-1979 Nigerian officer corps was therefore staffed mainly by younger individuals who had had little or no part in previous military governments (though an important group of long-serving officers had chosen to remain in the services and in fact largely constitute the core officials of both the Buhari and Babangida governments). Fourth, it was thought that bigger salaries, more generous benefits, new barracks and the latest in imported military hardware, all reflecting huge peace-time military budgets, had ensured the military's loyalty to the civilian regime.

Why, then, did the military strike in December 1983? Though a completely accurate account may never emerge, a number of quite plausible hypotheses present themselves.

One of these is almost self-evident: the *coup's* timing was a simple matter of seizing an opportunity. With much of the civil service, as well as the legislature and executive not 'on seat' during the Christmas–New Year holiday – including the President himself who had gone to Abuja – gaining control of strategic points and political institutions was easier. But, logistically, preparations would have had to be thorough and made well in advance. For the roughly 150,000-strong armed forces, dispersed throughout the country, to seize power over a nation of 100 million, a good deal of careful planning would have been required.[12] Unlike the January 1966 *coup*, when a demoralised and discredited First Republic was toppled by five majors and a force of less than 10,000, the December 1983 *putsch* must have involved the entire military establishment, since even one or two *resisting* recalcitrant divisions could have forestalled, or at least inhibited, the *coup*, and since nation-wide co-ordination would have been necessary to its success.[13] In fact, *West Africa* of 9 January 1984 reports army sources as suggesting that the *coup* plan was evolved up to four months before the event and its execution postponed twice. As Army Chief of Staff under Buhari, Major-General Ibrahim Babangida stated that originally the overthrow was planned for July 1983, just prior to the elections, but then postponed to await their results.[14] Retired General Theophilus Danjuma believes that a junior officers' *coup* had been planned for early 1983, but was postponed when word of it got out.[15] *Africa Confidential* of 4 January 1984 quotes Nigerian Intelligence reports to the effect that half a dozen *coup* plots developed in the first nine months of 1983.

A further hypothesis concerns long-standing policy differences between military leaders and the chief executive during the Second Republic. The military was known to have been irritated at Shagari's handling of the Nigerian forces in the Chadian civil war in 1981/2. The commander of the Nigerian peacekeeping force had proposed the more effective use of his troops, but Shagari had demurred. The military's perspective was expressed by Babangida, who said that the civilian leaders consistently failed to take the army's advice: 'Look at a simple thing like the whole damn policy concerning Chad. It was dictated to them by some people outside the country. We would provide the expert advice but nobody would listen.'[16] Furthermore, the military leaders were unhappy at the President's decision in 1982 to invite Ojukwu to return, with all state honours, from exile in Ivory Coast. Many officers, especially those of Northern origin, considered him a tribalist, traitor or war criminal.

The notorious 'Jaguar deal' has also been offered as a 'last-straw' explanation for the military's decision. According to reports first published in *The Observer*, when army and navy officers learned of a £22m. kickback to top NPN officials attendant upon a £300m. contract for 18 Jaguar ground attack fighters concluded between the Federal Republic of Nigeria and British Aerospace, they finally determined to proceed with the *coup*.[17]

In any case, the apparently illogical timing of the *coup* was no doubt an important factor in its success. Not only did the delay give the population time to see that an NPN greatly increased in size and power was unable to deal effectively with the 'contextual' problems of economic crisis and corruption throughout the political class, it also insulated the military against accusations of partisanship, for, according to *West Africa* of 30 January 1984:

> had the coup come before or during the election, there would have been a stronger inter-
> pretation to see it as an anti-NPN move, and it would certainly have been welcomed by the
> losers in the elections as such, and maybe even have led to a corresponding backlash within the
> army. A coup after five months had to be a much more considered affair, a measure taken
> against all the political class.

Not until several weeks afterwards did an explanation begin to emerge that satis-factorily reconciled the dual nature of the contradiction between the apparently random and arbitrary nature of the *coup*'s execution and the existence of long-term, nation-wide planning. As first suggested by Richard Synge, in *The Sunday Times* of 8 January 1984, the *coup* was in fact a pre-emptive move by the military leaders to forestall an impending – and presumably more drastic – *coup* led by junior officers and supported by the ranks. The point was then taken up by the Western and Nigerian press[18] and, though nowhere fully documented, has entered into the realm of accepted truth.

There is much in this hypothesis. Junior officers in the Nigerian forces are known to be more radically oriented and more amenable to direct action than their seniors; the 1966 'majors' *coup*' was a first signal of this. The post-*coup* spontaneous actions by groups of soldiers from the ranks to force down market prices showed their common-ality of interests with ordinary Nigerians. Significantly, the military leadership was able to contain such actions only with difficulty. There is also the 'demonstration effect' of the Rawlings and Doe rebellions in Ghana and Liberia which may point the way to a qualitatively new form of rank-and-file military *coup* in Africa. And finally, after the *coup* there was a deliberate and comprehensive re-deployment of junior officers in an apparent attempt to dissipate potential opposition to the military leaders. More than 100 officers were said to have been reposted within a twelve-hour period – 'thus setting a new Nigerian army record'.[19] Nevertheless, strong rumours persist that at least one junior-ranks *coup* was attempted during the Buhari regime's first hundred days, and that another foiled plot resulted in the execution of 42 officers and men just prior to Independence Day 1984.[20]

Class interests and elite hegemony

The notion of a pre-emptive *coup* directs our analysis towards a *class interpretation of military intervention*. To recall some of the points made in chapters 3 and 4: The military officer caste, in terms of education, wealth, life-style and fundamental outlook, must be 'located' principally as part of the elite class, as distinct from the urban and rural 'masses', or indeed the military rank-and-file, and this leads to a permanent *inter-class struggle* in the military itself as well as the larger society of which it is a part. However, the manifold and complex contradictions within the elite class lead to various forms of *intra-class conflict* at the top. The sub-class of politicians and allied business groups, who happen to be of an older generation, are in general more locally and ethnically based and operate as a political class. The bureaucratic-technocratic-military sub-class, who happen to be younger on average, derive their power positions from membership in institutions – civil service, military, universities – which are based on an ethos of rationality, impersonality and universality (i.e. are more 'national'), yet subject to many of the same ethno-sectional loyalties and alliances as the other factions of the elite class. Both have in common their dependence on the state as a source of realisation of their corporate interests and/or self-enrichment. In the light of the existence of an essentially non-productive state elite, then, a system of regulated distribution of offices and power is required to prevent intra-class conflict from developing as, say, during the First Republic when regional and sectional rivalries threatened elite rule as a whole, or as under protracted military government when resurgent, influential comprador fractions of the bourgeoisie are unable to contribute to and profit from 'modernisation' and 'development' processes determined by a narrowly based elite fraction.

It is evident that the tycoon class of the Second Republic had engaged in looting, corruption, repression and the conspicuous flaunting of its rapidly acquired wealth to an *unacceptable, dysfunctional degree*. Chapter 5 has described the emergence of a practically uninhibited political-business plutocracy at the expense of other factions of the elite. Left unchecked, the predatory activities of this class would shortly have produced such systemically unsupportable manifestations as a proliferation of new States up to a total of 45 (just as it had created more than three times the 1976 number of Local Government Areas), the world's largest cabinet (which in 1983 already rivalled that of the state-socialist countries of Eastern Europe) and the world's best-remunerated legislators. In a revealing article on 'The High Cost of Democracy', *West Africa* of 6 February 1984 estimates the total cost of the 1983 elections alone to have been more than N2 bn. To this it adds the expenses of maintaining the executive branch which tested the limits of the patronage system with its hundreds of 'ministers, advisers, presidential assistants, board members, official and unofficial hangers-on'. The 1983 budget for the National Assembly totalled almost N160 m., that for the presidency about N382m. FEDECO's expenditures alone between 1979 and 1983 have been estimated at N694.7 m.[21] All these developments were of course at work, *mutatis mutandis*, in the States as well. The *West Africa* article observes that 'politics became the country's leading industry'. It is said that oil revenues between 1979 and 1983 approximated some N1 bn more than realised between 1960 and 1979 – and still the country was more than N20 bn in debt at the time of the Buhari coup![22]

The strategy of maintaining elite equilibrium through liberal-democratic structures was in some measure successful so long as the economy was expanding. But with recession, it was clear that more pay-offs to more groups and interests had to be made than the economy could support. The austerity measures repeatedly invoked by the executive were simply unenforceable since too many obligations had to be met.

In the situation of a shrinking economy, a high degree of *executive autonomy* is needed to implement measures to maintain the economy as a whole and elite hegemony within it. This was the task originally foreseen for the executive presidency, but the President, in the Second Republic, was secured only against pressure from 'below', not against the *claims of powerful inner-party forces*, whose financial contributions and continuous active support had to be purchased by offices, contracts, patronage and special benefits. Thus the President was beholden to particularist interests and the civilian regime was, in a very real sense, incapable of 'saving' itself in a situation of negative growth.

For this reason, the officer class intervenes with the *objective* mandate of preserving the dominant socio-economic order with its class interests and elite hegemony. *Subjectively*, of course, the mandate is expressed in terms of morality, efficiency, redemption and the like. It is this combination of objective and subjective motives that furnishes the military's *raison d'être* and 'iron will' to 'get the country working again'.

It is also this combination of factors that produces its self-image as a 'corrective', a mere guest in power with the specific task of restoring order, rationality and stability. This it does in accordance with its concept of 'patriotism' and 'the national interest'. The paradox of the current military regime (and every military regime since independence) is that it derives much of its popularity and legitimacy from this very self-proclaimed 'corrective' mission; yet with the passage of time the popular conscious- ness grows impatient with the ossification, corruption and lack of measurable change which the military – as merely one faction of the elite – is incapable of transforming, once its limited corrective aims have been asserted.

In this context, it is worth reiterating the point, developed in chapters 3 and 4, that the military is subject to the same social contradictions, ethnic imperatives and parti- cularist motives as the larger society. While the military elite is more capable, as a rule, of suppressing or administering away centrifugal intra-elite differences as well as con- taining pressure from below, it also lacks the sensitivity and self-adjustment processes to maintain a long-term balancing and co-ordination of group and class interests. Morris Janowitz has put this phenomenon into a comparative perspective:[23]

> Those organizational and professional qualities which make it possible for the military of a new nation to accumulate political power, and even to take over political power are the same as those which limit its ability to rule effectively.

Beyond this essentially functional role, however, the military elite, like other factions of the Nigerian elite, is constrained and guided by its specific, corporate and factional interests. Terisa Turner and Arnold Baker, in a challenging, original study,[24] posit factional elite interests as the central motive for the renewed military intervention. To follow their argument for a moment, the recivilianising military elite of the late 1970s cohered around capitalist agriculture. The Land Use Decree (see chapter 9), the Green Revolution and the handover of power to an NPN that guaranteed priority to these capitalist farmers – who included Obasanjo, Yar'Adua *et al.* – represented conscious attempts to secure pre-eminence for this class of 'gentlemen farmers' or the 'new feudal oligarchy'. As evidence of systematic state preference for the capitalist farmer faction, Turner and Baker cite the massive loans made to them by the Agricultural Develop- ment Bank under the direction of the World Bank and the Shagari government's exemption of Obasanjo and Buhari (who had been Commissioner for Petroleum during the period in question) from investigation during the official probe into the allegedly 'missing' N2.8 bn from the NNPC accounts.

Yet with the return of civilian government in 1979, the new feudal class necessarily reverted to a subordinate position, since in the rentier state, the comprador-middleman stratum of 'traders, contractors, smugglers, commission-takers, currency dealers, and their accountants, lawyers, front men and hangers-on run Nigeria' mainly in league with international capital.[25] When this political-tycoon faction dominates the state, then 'the logic of commerce prevails over that of production'.[26] Capitalist agriculture, together with local import-substituting industries and national capital, is threatened by the dysfunctional effects of unchecked competition: decay of infrastructures, lack of planning or even co-ordination, preference for luxury imports rather than inputs for local production, export of capital combined with domestic inflation, etc. In terms of the specific interests of the gentlemen farmers, their operations were impeded by government importation of foodstuffs which could be made available far more cheaply than local produce and by:[27]

> the chaos caused by commercial capitalism. For instance, fertilizers which were to be available for the 1984 crop season did not arrive on time because the procedure for approving import licences [had] become so politicized that, even though none of Nigeria's foreign exchange was immediately involved due to World Bank financing, the import approvals were not forthcoming.

The NPN, increasingly dominated by the political-business plutocracy, was no longer able to represent the interests, and hence to rely on the support, of the non-comprador factions of the elite, notably the new feudal oligarchy. Given an identity of interests between the latter and the narrow military elite – which Turner and Baker assume rather than demonstrate – then the motive for military intervention is self-evident.

Whether or not one accepts all its nuances, Turner and Baker's argument underlines the tenuous quality of intra-elite arrangements and points anew to intra-elite conflict as an explanation of military intervention. In particular, it enhances the argument advanced earlier that the specific factional interests of the military elite can be identified and related to its ostensibly 'corrective' mission. Predictably, for example, the Buhari faction – amidst massive retrenchments and 'national sacrifices' – undertook a far-reaching promotion exercise throughout all three service branches,[28] and the first post-Shagari military government was well on its way to becoming one of the world's most top-heavy military organisations. That 'defence' spending would not be cut, was reaffirmed by military leaders on several occasions. Major-General Babangida, speaking at a Gold Medal Public Affairs lecture in Lagos, invoked Nigeria's international responsibilities and unnamed threats to national security to rationalise continued high defence outlays,[29] including ample provisions for increasing salaries and perquisites.

Lacking any system-transforming mission, the military government finds it expedient (and legitimacy-producing) to leave not only the civil service essentially intact, but also the judiciary, the management of parastatals and indeed traditional rulership as well. In this way a functional alliance enters into and reinforces broader corporate-class interests.[30] Subject to purges of the worst offenders, the public service provides administrative–technocratic continuity, and the existence of an essentially independent judiciary serves as a legitimator of military rule.

Admittedly the relationship between the military elite and the upper levels of the state bureaucracy had first to be adjusted and rationalised. The layer of unambiguously political appointees had to be stripped away since it was too discredited to contribute to the military's corrective mission. At the top levels, this process was relatively easy, since these state bureaucrats were generally indictable for the same economic crimes as their politician-patrons, while at the middle levels far-ranging 'retrenchment' exercises could be executed. By October 1984 the total number of public employees purged or retrenched was estimated at between 150,000 and 200,000.[31] The undifferentiated, arbitrary nature of the adjustment process inevitably deprived the civil service of many competent, honest individuals, affected corporate morale and initially reduced the services' efficiency and innovativeness, just as happened in the earlier purges. But the exercise both enhanced the military's corrective image and ensured a compliant, subservient state bureaucracy – at least until the 'repoliticisation' of the civil service over time produced a new, active stratum allied to and profiting from the military government.

The maintenance of a (relatively) free press is also desirable here, again subject to restrictions, since the media remain one of the few channels for the rulers to gain some insight into what the ruled are thinking (and vice-versa). In any event, given its overwhelming initial popularity, the military can well 'afford' to allow the press a considerable latitude; as time passes, repressive measures tend to increase. Thus as early as mid-1984 the Public Officers (Protection Against False Publication) Tribunal found two *Guardian* journalists, Tunde Thompson and Nduka Irabor, guilty of disclosing 'classified' information and sentenced them to one year in prison. (From the reverse perspective, the press, under military government, also practises extensive self-censorship, though this is not to overlook the crucial role played by a minority of journalists such as Thompson and Irabor, in maintaining a critical public awareness.)

The traditional rulers, if won over to the new military regime, are also important factors of legitimation and source of feedback about popular demands. Even more than its predecessors, the Buhari regime attempted to court and enlist the emirs, obas and chiefs.[32]

Even within itself the military government, like all other military governments before it, is constrained to reproduce the 'federal character of Nigeria'. No doubt the post-January 1966 violence invoked by perceived attempts to impose first Igbo, then Northern, hegemony on the military, and the civil war that ensued, were a compelling reminder that the army leadership must be seen to reflect the ethno-regional make-up of the society that it aspires to 'correct'. What initially appeared as 'Northern domination' at the top of the new junta – since a clear majority of the SMC *were* Northerners – was somewhat mitigated by the presence of Tunde Idiagbon, a Yoruba, as a key member of the inner ruling triumvirate with Buhari and Babangida, by the presence of three Igbo and three Yoruba members of the SMC, and by the appointment, so far as possible, of military State Governors who were indigenes of the States under their command. Similarly, the Federal Executive Council included several prominent civilians (Professor Tam David-West, Dr Mahmud Tukur, Dr Ibrahim Gambari, Dr Bukar Shaib) from the outset.

Transnational dimensions

Thus, contrary to the popular image of the military as an independently powerful, 'modernising' avant-garde, the Buhari faction (and indeed the Babangida faction after it) was subject to certain well-defined domestic constraints. Far from being an apolitical national force, the military was and is allied to indigenous class interests, particularly the new feudal class and the emergent national bourgeoisie to whom it looks for a measure of increased productivity and the success of import-substitution strategies, an alliance which, as has been demonstrated, was clearly reflected in priority loans and imports to business and agri-business. Yet at the same time, the FMG took over intact and implemented virtually *all* the measures proposed by Shagari's 1981 Stabilisation Act as well as the budget proposals set down by him just two days before the *coup*. Among the first decisive acts of the Buhari regime were the repayment of the first $50 m. instalment of a $1.9 bn loan from a consortium of European banks, and intensive negotiations with the International Monetary Fund for a refinancing of debts. One year after the *coup*, Major-General Buhari was able to state with pride, in his budget speech, that his government had honoured all medium- and long-term debt obligations. The currency withdrawal exercise may be seen as linked to this priority. Buhari also assured international oil brokers and fellow OPEC members that Nigeria would maintain fixed price levels and adhere to existing production quotas; this was said to reflect the government's desire to retain the confidence of its foreign trading partners in the Nigerian economy.[33]

How can one account for these apparent contradictions, between the military as corrective and its pursuit of particularist interests, between domestic activism and accession to international constraints, between nationalism (especially economic nationalism) and an essentially unchanged Nigerian position in the world capitalist economy?

One important and much invoked explanation is the existence of the important inherited 'givens' of a transnationalised, dependent economy, namely, massive debt-servicing costs (which at the time of the Babangida *coup*, took up 44% of export earnings[34]) and an unstable international oil market. Even though the civilians may have siphoned off and exported funds sufficient to pay the total foreign debt, as is often claimed, and may have squandered much of what did remain in the country, any governing elite in Nigeria is in large measure subject to the constraints of an international economic system in which it plays a peripheral, or at best semi-peripheral, role. The transnational imperatives at work here can be illustrated with reference to Nigeria's position vis-à-vis OPEC and the IMF.

Concerning OPEC, the large population base and heavy export-import dependence of the Nigerian economy makes it one of the most vulnerable units in what amounts to an international oil oligarchy. The interests of the transnational oil companies in maintaining high, stable and regulated oil prices outweigh consumers' interests in cheaper petrol and petroleum products. The threat posed to these interests by a comprador-dominated, gangster-capitalist Second Republic amounted to nothing less than the spectre of the collapse of the international oil system. Particularly in the period after the 1983 elections, Nigeria was known to have been unofficially increasing its oil sales beyond its agreed OPEC quota and to have responded unilaterally to a cut in North Sea oil prices. In addition, perhaps as much as 20% of Nigerian oil output was being smuggled or otherwise disposed of outside the purview of the state.[35] Prior to the *coup*, an increasingly powerful lobby of middlemen, traders and compradors proposed that Nigeria should withdraw from OPEC, increase oil sales unilaterally and in this way generate sufficient foreign exchange to finance imports.[36]

By the same token, the Nigerian state, under comprador hegemony, was a growing threat to the stability of the international financial system. Not only was the country overextended in its obligations to international banks and lending institutions, thus making repayment irregular and uncertain in a period of declining oil production; it was unable even to establish how much was owed, and to whom. Under civilian government, it was increasingly impossible to impose the kinds of restraints proclaimed in Shagari's 1983 budget – reduced borrowing, austerity, import cutbacks, currency devaluation, etc. – that might have restored fiscal stability, ensured prompt repayment of outstanding debts and hence reassured the international banking community. Here again, the rapacious, dysfunctional effects of unchecked interest pursuit by the political-business plutocracy caused a substantial intra-elite conflict surrounding the application of state policies.

Seen from this perspective, the objective function of the 1983 *coup* was to rescue the neo-colonial capitalist order and the overall system of elite rule. To accomplish this, both the political-business class and the representative liberal-democratic structures had to be overturned, even as the position of Nigeria in the world capitalist economy had to be restored. To be sure, the Buhari faction did retain some measure of relative autonomy inasmuch as it was able to renegotiate a 250,000 b/d increase in Nigeria's oil production quota within OPEC as well as to forestall compliance with the most severe conditions demanded by the IMF for granting a further loan. But the limits of this autonomy were evident in the fundamental policy measures that the regime was constrained to take. Its economic adjustment programme in many ways conformed to and even surpassed IMF expectations, for instance in the prompt repayment or refinancing of short- and medium-term debts, the emphasis on increasing foreign-exchange revenues, the rationing of certain commodities, the import restrictions, the raising of interest rates, the cutbacks in public spending, etc. Yet a formal agreement between the IMF and the Buhari regime foundered on the issues of trade liberalisation (potentially economically disastrous in a mono-mineral, import-dependent economy), cuts in state subsidies to the petroleum industry (which would have eroded the tenuous degree of self-sufficiency achieved in this key industry) and currency devaluation (which would have forced up the cost of inputs for local industry and reduced luxury consumption by the elites). The Buhari regime therefore attempted, on the strength of increasing foreign-exchange revenues and a slowly improving macro-economy, to go it alone without the IMF. A kind of *ersatz* devaluation was achieved in April and May 1984 with the replacement of the old naira with new notes – a measure, as noted earlier, aimed also at the comprador/trader faction, including its smuggler and counterfeiter elements, who in many cases had stores of illegal money at home or abroad. After a year in office the Buhari government had increased federally collected revenue by 14% (although this was substantially reduced by greater debt-servicing costs), doubled the country's foreign reserves, reduced the overall budget deficit from N6.2 bn to N3.3 bn, decreased imports by 11.4%, increased exports by 25.3% and honoured all medium- and long-term debts.[37]

Austerity without development

However, the double bind that locked the Buhari regime into the international financial system also undermined its 'corrective' mission and deprived it of much of its popular support. Without the roughly $3 bn IMF loan needed to bridge the balance-of-payments gap while switching from imported to locally produced inputs, neither indigenous manufacturing nor agricultural industries were able to reorient production to conform to the changed priorities.

Thus capitalist agriculture – the Buhari government's top priority in 'development' strategy – was unable, in the face of tightened credit and import restrictions, to import the necessary fertiliser, agricultural machinery and spare parts. And upon the successful development of agro-industry depended the success of any strategy of self-sufficient import-substitution.[38] For these reasons, local industry, unable to secure sufficient inputs either at home or abroad (and hitherto it was dependent on imports for some 70% of these inputs) was forced to operate at between 30 and 40% of capacity. By 1985, manufacturers, who had had to cope with a drastically reduced N2.8 bn allocation for raw material imports during the previous year, were forced to get by with N1.7 bn – a 40% drop. And capital spending in all public sector areas, excluding agriculture, remained at roughly half the 1983 level.[39] The gaps and shortages created by the flagging production of these two vital sectors were in part filled by traders, middlemen and smugglers whose activities drove prices up well beyond the record levels reached during the heyday of the Second Republic. Massive government-sponsored projects (the $5 bn steel programme, the $2.4 bn petrochemical plant and the planned $7 bn natural gas liquification project) would also depend on productivity in these sectors. Significantly, during the Buhari period major profits were registered only in the banking and brewing sectors.

In this situation, the 'corrective' regime had little option but to attempt to resolve its multiple problems by imposing a comprehensive austerity programme. But austerity in a dependent economy merely increases the proportion of surplus exported abroad. To make up the shortfall, the Buhari government, like all similarly beset Nigerian governments before it, formulated a programme of cutbacks in social services, retrenchments, wage freezes and later rollbacks, imposition of taxes, etc., the burden of which fell primarily on the broad mass of the population. Thus, to select a few examples at random, the number of teaching hospitals was reduced and user fees introduced for medical and other social services; student tuition and boarding fees were doubled; new taxes were levied in the form of sales taxes, poll taxes,[40] wage levies, school levies, cattle taxes, etc. (which, however, were not matched by increased personal taxation of the rich); as many as 3 million private sector employees lost their jobs as did hundreds of thousands in the public sector, while those who remained were subject to salary reductions and erosion of benefits; infrastructures from water to roads and electricity deteriorated; policies were formulated (but not executed) to make parastatals stand on their own; local governments and their services were deprived of revenues; and inflation and corruption could scarcely be contained. This list could be extended much further.

Perhaps most indicative, under a regime whose declared priority was food self-sufficiency, was a rise of 1,000% and more – and this on top of the huge price increases under Shagari – for basic foodstuffs such as rice, vegetable oil, beans, sugar, salt and milk. A bag of gari, for instance, went from N60 to N145, a few ounces of table salt from 20k to N1.10, a bottle of palm oil from N1.5 to N4, a 2.5 kg. yam from N1.50 to N5 or a dozen eggs from N5.50 to N9.50, and a 50k tin of milk to N1.20. The general inflation rate had risen from 25% in 1983 to about 40% by the end of 1984.[41]

By early to mid-1985, therefore, the Buhari regime was largely isolated from its initial basis of mass legitimation – the productive local industrialists, the capitalist agricultural sector, the more radical, activist groups in the military, important sectors in the technocratic civil service, and probably a majority of the population who had initially welcomed it. Caught between the millstones of domestic distress and the exigencies of the international capitalist system, it lost the initial reservoir of mass support and popular enthusiasm accruing to it as the 'deliverer' of the people from the deprivations of the Second Republic and the harbinger of discipline, efficiency and probity. Not unlike the Gowon regime a decade before, it descended perceptibly into a state of torpor and a splendid isolation. Lacking Gowon's brokerage and balancing skills, however, Buhari and his enforcer Tunde Idiagbon resorted mainly to command and repression to sustain their increasingly unpopular policies. The malaise of the Buhari regime translated into a *series of inter-linked crises*.

Leadership crisis. A government constrained to exact sacrifices at home and to appease powerful creditors abroad may attempt to resolve or at least suspend the contradiction by means of charisma, mass mobilisation or other forms of personalist rule. The success of this solution presupposes that there is a point from which to be led and a destination to be reached. But in view of the grossly class-divided nature of the society and the particularist bases of elite rule – military or civilian – it was practically impossible to generate dynamic, goal-oriented leadership out of the repressive context largely created by the Buhari regime's policies and omissions. To follow S. E. Oyovbaire's analogy, leadership in Nigeria has been a scarce, essential commodity that, unlike other goods, can neither be imported nor hoarded:[42]

> It is therefore not surprising that between 1981 and 1983 when Messrs. Umaru Dikko and Adamu Ciroma divided between themselves the chairmanship of many task forces on importation of essential commodities, there was no task force to import leadership. And when recently the military regime began to discover hoarded essential commodities by NPN stalwarts, the regime has not been able to discover hoarded leadership. And this was a period when every Nigerian knew, with the exception of the decadent elements in the defunct NPN, that Nigeria had never had it so bad in the history of this scarce commodity in this country.

Professor Oyovbaire also expressed reservations about the influence of traditional rulers on the new regime, the reinstatement of officials who were 'uncomfortably close to the displaced Shagari regime' and various other State appointments.

A regime forced to rely so extensively on established forces – as indeed all military governments in Nigeria have been so far – is of course susceptible to a rapid loss of its corrective *raison de'être*. When this happens, immobilisation, corruption and opposition are the results. Opposition under the military government, especially following the Rawlings and Doe examples, develops, *inter alia*, within the ruling structures themselves, among the majors and captains who may thus represent the sole possibility of social change in this situation, at least in the short term. A counter-*coup* is therefore on the political agenda at any time, particularly if a comparatively large sector of the lower and middle-range bureaucrats, intellectuals, smaller business groups and independent professions becomes disaffected.

Ideology crisis. A non-revolutionary government bent on streamlining and regulating the *status quo* will not evolve a coherent mobilising ideology. Instead, it will establish bodies such as the National Council on Information and Culture to launch national campaigns aimed at achieving: 'unity, stability and national security, war against indiscipline, war against economic sabotage, ostentatious living, corruption and public disorderliness (establishment of queuing culture among Nigerians)',[43] as well as 'law and order',[44] patriotism and nationalism. The Council, in order to propagate these values, established National Consciousness and Enlightenment Committees (NACEC). At the same time, the National Council of State launched its War Against Indiscipline (WAI) to 'correct the ills of government'.[45]

What these exhortations and campaigns have in common is that they represented initiatives from the top down. Much like Shagari's 'ethical revolution' and its vehicle, the Ministry of National Guidance, they reflected goals and aspirations formulated by the governing class for society at large. The WAI promoters were quite explicit about this:[46]

> The Council agreed that the programme should meaningfully begin with the leadership in various segments of the society and be extended down to the grassroots, to also include its introduction in the mosques and churches, family units and schools. The Council finally approved that the programme should be launched by the Military governors in all the states of the federation and be vigorously pursued as an on-going policy of the Federal Military Administration.

And Group Captain Omeruah, speaking in support of WAI, declared that 'if the leadership could change for the better, the followership would also change'[47]. So long as the questions were not addressed: Discipline for what? Stability for whom? Unity of what?, ideology, like leadership, remained a 'scarce commodity' under Buhari's military government, just as it had been under the civilians.

Mobilisation crisis. While the peasantry was essentially ignored in the regime's efforts to promote capitalist agriculture, labour was regarded as a potentially disruptive, undisciplined factor. The government decreed 'industrial peace', meaning that, in Buhari's words, 'frivolous industrial actions, particularly strikes and lock-outs would not be tolerated'. As a substitute for organised struggle, he proposed 'a real wage policy' based upon increasing workers' purchasing power. Thus:[48]

> If your money wage can buy 10 loaves of bread and we manage to reduce the price of bread so that the same money wage can buy 20 loaves of the same size of bread as before, your real wage has doubled.

In this way, the demands of labour were equated with those of the other 'pressure groups' – by implication as 'excessive' and 'immoderate' as, for instance, those of the political-tycoon class – and therefore needing to be subjected to the same restraints, discipline and 're-education'. On the strength of this equation, of course, the maintenance of the *status quo* is ideologically justified.

Authority crisis. The general urge for discipline and order under military rule is worth pursuing further. For one thing, it reflects the pragmatic, activist ethos that predominates at the upper levels of the military hierarchy. Beyond the emphasis on punctuality, efficiency and obedience described earlier, there emerged a preoccupation with toughness, institutionalised violence and enforced conformity. The reintroduction of public execution of armed robbers, in the Nigerian context, can be argued as functional both in terms of public security (since the entirely inadequate police force is unlikely to recapture escaped or corruptly released robbers) and legitimacy production (the measure is undoubtedly supported by a huge majority of the population). But to extend the punishment to harsh and brutal treatment in the prisons and to the return of those convicted to their home villages for public execution cannot be justified by the same criteria. The Special Tribunal (Miscellaneous Offences) Decree, stipulated the death penalty by firing squad for a whole range of (mainly economic) offences such as trafficking in hallucinatory drugs, setting fire to public buildings or property, 'sabotage' of oil pipelines or the electricity system, illegal import or export of oil and oil products, counterfeiting, and destruction of public property. On the subject of these and other 'judicial murders' (as former. Chief Justice Sir Adetokunbo Ademola has termed them), the then Justice Minister and Attorney General, Chike Offodile, asserted that, if any punishment more severe than death existed, the federal government would be prepared to implement it.[49]

The relentless application of this decree did on occasion manage to shake a society which had in large measure lost the ability to be shocked. It was applied retroactively, for instance to execute three youths convicted in April 1984 for smuggling cocaine, and with a severity disproportionate to the crimes committed, as in the case of the death sentences handed down to the 'cocaine women' who, as widows, mothers of large families, and in some cases pregnant, were generally thought not to merit the death penalty.[50]

In fact, the anti-woman campaign that emerged from the 'cocaine women' issue in early 1985 reveals much about the increasingly authoritarian ethos of the military leadership (as well as the by then abject state of subservence of the Nigerian press and other mass media). The fact of drugs being smuggled in women's 'private parts' was played up and widely styled as an 'abuse of womanhood' and a 'violation of women's sacred trust'. Somehow this was akin to prostitution in which, like forgery, armed robbery, industrial sabotage and many other crimes, more and more women were involved. Lacking discipline and 'traditional virtues', women were said to be turning to immodest attire, rebellious behaviour in the home and child neglect on an unprecedented scale. In a society where traditional patriarchy by and large continues to prevail in the household sphere, the main onus, in a period of austerity, to reduce expenditures and sustain the family falls upon the women who are therefore the main targets of any campaign aimed at re-establishing 'discipline'. In a perceptive article, Iya Agan wrote:[51]

> poverty, malnutrition and hard labour – the realities of life for millions of women – may constitute more serious violations of the female body than a few grammes of cocaine hidden in their 'private parts'. Instead, the suggestion has been that criminality among women is increasing and this is taken as a measure of the social problems the country is facing.

The Miscellaneous Offences decree was also invoked to impose 21-year sentences on those caught cheating in examinations or a 10-year jail term on a 17-year old youth convicted of tampering with a NEPA electric meter attached to a private home in Lagos. To judge by the latter case, the theft of a few hundred hours' worth of electricity was identical in culpability to the embezzlement of a million naira from public funds (after reduction of the offender's sentence by the SMC). And this says nothing about preferential treatment while in prison. A medical student from Sokoto, Bello Dikko Tambawal, was arrested solely on account of his middle name! Even prominent but non-conformist public figures such as the Afro-beat musician Fela Anikulapo-Kuti (who had been in disfavour with past military and civilian regimes as well) were disciplined in this way: despite public protests, he was sentenced in June 1984 to a ten-year jail term by the Port Harcourt anti-sabotage tribunal. 'Buhari', *West Africa* of 30 September 1985 wrote, 'who came in promising greater accountability, soon declared himself unaccountable'. The transformation from WAI to WAE – War Against Everybody – was complete.

Unless and until social-psychological studies are carried out on the disciplinarian, revanchist, conformist syndromes that underlie these punitive acts[52] one can only speculate about the motives of the ruling military stratum under Buhari. But in terms of class analysis, it is evident, following Nnoli's argument about the pre-1979 military government, that this fixation on dedication and discipline takes the existing neo-colonial capitalist order as given, 'while the only crucial explanatory variable in the development of praxis is the degree of ritualistic conformity to the prevailing normative system superimposed by the country's ruling class' (1981:55).

Legitimacy crisis. In Nigeria, decades of misrule and government turnover have established a general ethos of tolerance (or resignation?), not only of corruption and permissiveness on the part of the elites, but also of authoritarian government policies and the sacrifices they impose. At the same time, however, this generalised tolerance has certain, generally perceived – but admittedly scientifically not demonstrable – limits. When the ruling classes of the Second Republic passed beyond these limits in their looting of the public treasury, they clearly violated this special Nigerian version of the social contract. By the same token, as the Buhari–Idiagbon faction resorted increasingly to violence, it fell into a deep crisis of legitimacy which ultimately called for drastic 'corrective' measures.

The regime had managed to alienate practically every sector of society by the end of its first year in office. The rising opposition, which took the form of strikes, protests and stoppages, was met with a corresponding increase in the size and scope of the security apparatus. The Nigerian Security Organisation (NSO) under Alhaji Lawal Rafindadi, a Shagari appointee, not only extended its activities into more and more spheres of political life; it became practically unaccountable to any agency but the head of state and an instrument for the enhancement of the personal power of Rafindadi himself who was made a member of the SMC. Arbitrary arrest, torture and indeterminate detention were widely practised, and this systemic brutality – which Nigeria had hitherto largely been spared under military rule – entailed 'breaking suspects' skulls during interrogation, beating them to a pulp to extract information, starving and denying them toilet facilities'.[53]

Yet the universality of social discipline, upon which much of the regime's legitimacy depended, was undermined by a number of widely known and resented exceptions. At the height of the currency changeover, for instance, 53 suitcases, belonging to the Emir of Gwandu and ambassador D. A. Waziri, who were returning from Saudi Arabia, were not inspected by airport customs but simply cleared through.[54] Alhaji Abubakar Alhaji, permanent secretary to the Finance Minister, was robbed of £17,000 in his Vienna hotel room – on the face of it sufficient grounds for indictment under Decree No. 7 (operating a foreign bank account). But not only was the delinquent official not brought to trial then, but the recommendation by the Niger State tribunal that he be dismissed and banned from holding public office for 10 years was also ignored; and instead, he was promoted to the Ministry of National Planning to oversee the country's Fifth Development Plan. Fraud continued to be alleged with respect to the issuance of import licences, and indeed, fraud which was said increasingly to discriminate against Southern businessmen.[55] Such tendencies renewed fears of growing 'Northernisation' in public bodies from the SMC downward, and the Nigerian vocabulary was enriched by such terms as 'military wing of the NPN', 'Bida Mafia' and 'Suleija Mafia'. Meanwhile questions lingered about Buhari's continued suppression of the report submitted by a commission of inquiry into the workings of the NNPC during the Second Republic. Initiated by Shagari, it was alleged to be critical of Buhari's role in the scandal as the then head of the NNPC.

Correcting the corrective

Despite the massive opposition generated by the Buhari regime among broad sectors of society as well as factions of the elite, it was not public opinion *per se*, nor any alliance of alienated professional groups, class alignments, business groups, poor peasants or impoverished workers that actually implemented the subsequent 'corrective of the corrective'. It is only when a sufficiently cohesive faction *within* the military forms and – no doubt influenced by and/or sympathetic towards this 'public opinion' – determines that existing governing arrangements must be revised, that a regime turnover is effected. Of course the decision to do so will hinge on the insurgent faction's estimates of its prospects for establishing both mass legitimacy and a workable intra-elite alliance. The former was practically ensured by Buhari's isolation and unpopularity, while the latter was rather more complex.

Like the larger society, the military elite was increasingly alienated from the Buhari–Idiagbon ruling clique. The activities of the National Security Organisation extended into the military itself, where Babangida and other top officials were placed under surveillance.[56] They were directed mainly at the more purely 'military' faction in the ruling group, of which Babangida was Chief of Staff, and reflected a growing fissure between it and the 'politico' faction headed by Buhari and Idiagbon. In particular, rivalries and differences developed between Idiagbon as Buhari's second-in-command and Babangida, with a popular following in the army, who resented the lay-off of some 30,000 soldiers and the dismissal of certain popular officers (such as Babangida's confidant and head of the Military Intelligence Agency, Aliyu Mohammed), and who advocated an increase in defence spending.[57]

The anti-Buhari forces within the military were strengthened by verbal interventions on the part of former military rulers. Retired Maj.-General James Oluleye called for the repeal of Decree No. 4 which 'inhibit[ed] the development of knowledge'.[58] Former Chief of State, Olusegun Obasanjo, broke his long silence to deny the Buhari regime's claim to be an offshoot of the 1975–9 military government.[59] And in his well-publicised Ibadan speech just three weeks before the Babangida *coup*, he delivered a cautiously formulated attack suggesting that the Buhari government had neglected 'federal-character' representation in public agencies, had succumbed to indiscipline, had grown unresponsive and ought not to have levied school fees.[60] It was subsequently learned that he also wrote a personal letter to Buhari's Minister of Commerce and Industry, Mahmud Turkur, in which he opposed the regime's practice of countertrading as a drain on the national economy.[61] More will be said about the countertrade problem in a moment.

The 27 August 1985 *coup* that replaced Buhari's SMC with Babangida's AFRC

(Armed Forces Ruling Council) was therefore long expected though initially it met with little enthusiasm. With Buhari in his home town of Daura in Kaduna State celebrating Eid el Kabir, and Idiagbon making a pilgrimage to Saudi Arabia, the *putsch* appeared to have been a consensual, non-violent operation (though a few bodies were said to have been seen near army headquarters in Ikeja).

No less constrained than his predecessor Babangida was nevertheless able to establish a distinct *style* and *image* more appropriate to the integrating and aggregating functions that Buhari had been incapable of performing. An indigene of ethnically heterogeneous Minna in Niger State with an Igbo wife, Babangida projected a more conciliatory, affable image than the austere and aloof Buhari or the shrill and uncompromising Idiagbon.

As essentially a successor regime, the 'new' government was even more solidly rooted in the military establishment than its predecessors. All the service chiefs were reappointed to their old positions, with Commodore Ebitu Ukiwe elevated to the important post of Chief of General Staff (the former Chief of Staff, Supreme Headquarters) vacated by Babangida. The supreme policy-making body, the AFRC, was for the first time made up entirely of military men, a bare majority of whom were still of Northern origin. All but five members of the dissolved SMC were appointed to the AFRC; it admitted some younger officers at the rank of lieutenant-colonel, and its ethno-regional and religious balance and intra-service representation were more adequate.

The executive, now styled National Council of Ministers rather than Federal Executive Council, reflected Babangida's attempt to achieve a balance between military and civilian leaders, between the regions, and between a variety of interests. Of the 22 ministers whose appointments were announced two weeks after the *coup*, only six were carry-overs from Buhari's 18-man executive; ten of the new appointees were civilians, twelve military officers. The cabinet included several astute political appointments clearly intended to regain the legitimacy lost through the alienation of certain interests by the Buhari regime. Prince Bola Ajibola, the new Justice Minister, was president of the Nigerian Bar Association and an opponent of those decrees that permitted detention without trial as well as of military tribunals generally. Former director of the Nigerian Institute of International Affairs, Professor Bolaji Akinyemi, was made Minister of External Affairs; he had had a hand in the formulation of Murtala Mohammed's activist foreign policy and had been critical of the Shagari government's lower profile. The Minister of Agriculture, Water Resources and Rural Development, retired General Alani Akinrinade (the former Chief of Defence Staff), had become a leading gentleman farmer on his estates near Ile-Ife and as such a prominent spokesman for both capitalist agriculture and the military's corporate interests. Dr Olukoye Ransome-Kuti, the Minister of Health, was not only a well-known paediatrician but also the elder brother of Dr Beko Ransome-Kuti, vice-president of the Nigerian Medical Association which Buhari had banned, and of Fela, the imprisoned musician. The appointment of Jibril Aminu, formerly Vice-Chancellor of the University of Maiduguri, as Minister of Education was no doubt intended to restore links with the academic community. Very significant was the nomination of Dr Kalu Idika Kalu, formerly a World Bank official and strong supporter of the IMF loan, as Minister of Finance. And Professor Tam David-West, a holdover from the Buhari FEC, who had opportunely switched from a pro- to anti-countertrade position, was retained as Minister of Energy and Petroleum.

The National Council of States was similarly constituted, with 13 new State governors appointed and the rest redeployed, with three majors among them (including the self-proclaimed socialist Abubakar Umar, Governor of Kaduna), and with the governors assigned to jurisdictions other than their state of origin. Twelve were from the army, four from the air force, two from the navy and one from the police.

The Babangida regime was able to ensure substantial 'instant legitimacy' simply by proclaiming itself the restorer of "natural justice' and the agent of national reconciliation[62] and by abolishing the most unpopular policies enacted by Buhari. Thus, in rapid succession the government repealed Decree No. 4 and released the imprisoned journalists, opened the cells of the NSO and exposed its workings to public view, and released 87 political prisoners who had been detained, without trial, since the fall of the Second Republic. Among the latter – who might still be indicted – were some well-known members of the political-tycoon class, such as ex-governors Michael Ajasin, Lateef Jakande, Balarabe Musa, Bamanga Turkur, Mohammed Goni and Clement Isong, as well as ex-ministers Ademola Thomas (Internal Affairs), Ismael Igbani (Agriculture), Ibrahim Tahir (Communications), Ahmed Musa (Housing), Ibrahim Gusau (Industry), Ishaya Audu (External Affairs), Ali Baba (Internal Affairs) and Garba Wushishi (Information). Later, in early 1986, the bans on the NMA and the National Association of Nigerian Students were also lifted.

The emergence of Babangida as the military 'President' of Nigeria is thus indicative of the intra-military factional adjustments required in the post-Buhari period. With his power base directly in the army (rather than in the more overtly 'politicised' faction of the military), this 'soldier's soldier' has been both a central figure in every *coup* since 1975, including his key role in averting the 1976 Dimka–Bisalla attempt, and known to enjoy a special rapport with the junior officers and lower ranks in the armed forces. If the 27 August *coup*, like the Buhari one, did in fact represent a pre-emptive *putsch* – and rumours of both grassroots and ethnically grounded *coup* plots had shadowed Buhari's entire 'term' in office, though only the BBC suggested this as a motive for Babangida's action – then Babangida was the logical figure to forestall a more drastic, radical move from below or a divisive, 'tribal' strike from an ethnic faction, either of which would have threatened the nationally organised, transnationally dependent foundations of elite hegemony. The Babangida regime represents, in the first instance, a *reconsolidation of the military's corporate interests and factions*; and this constitutes a central factor in any explanation of the elite factional alliances that enjoy intra-societal hegemony on the strength of this retrenched military rule.

Factional shifts within the elite stratum

Whom and what, then – beyond the military itself – does the Babangida government 'represent'? Or, more specifically, which group interests and goals does it uphold and further? And which are neglected or suppressed?

Three interrelated and, in some measure, contradictory layers of interests may be cited whose goals and means of achieving them are linked to those of the Babangida-led military elite.

Elite rule as a whole, as demonstrated above, was jeopardised by the dysfunctions of a military government which initially intervened to defend those interests against the chaos inflicted by the political-tycoon class. The Buhari regime was neither able to overcome the economic crisis it inherited, nor to manage it adequately, thus producing a systemic legitimacy crisis. Practically every social sector and elite faction was therefore disaffected. True, Buhari had managed at least to *contain* the economic crisis, but the basic dilemma, which his authoritarianism could not address, at least not without further fragmenting the various elite factions, was how to effect economic change without forfeiting elite and mass backing. Babangida, with his consolidated military base (and hence somewhat enhanced degree of relative autonomy) and his conciliatory image, has been able to implement policies which, on careful scrutiny, are very similar to those proposed by Buhari.

Thus the pivotal issue of whether or not to accept the IMF loan and all its conditionalities – which Babangida initially seemed to favour[63] – was 'democratically' thrown open to wide public discussion which, like the 1975–8 constitution-making exercise, created the semblance of popular participation. Under its four-month cover, the government was able, gradually and less painfully, to meet, *de facto*, most of the contested IMF conditionalities: devaluation of the naira (which in fact Buhari had begun to do), a start in privatisation of parastatals (which Buhari had merely proclaimed his intention of doing especially in the agriculture, brewery and hotel branches), 50% reduction in their subsidies and commercialisation of their operations, withdrawal of petroleum subsidies, and general reductions in government expenditure.

A key element in this package was 'wage discipline', and here again the differences in style, if not substance, of the two military regimes are striking. Where Buhari did not venture to reduce the military's expenditures but instead concentrated on the more vulnerable civil service, Babangida began his wage rollback strategy with the military itself. Within a reduced overall military budget,[64] the armed forces' pay was cut by 2.5% for recruits and corporals and 20% for the ranks of brigadier and above. With that measure implemented, public servants' pay reductions could be carried out with comparative ease,[65] and this in turn exerted a strong downward pressure on wages and salaries in the private sector. 'Shared' sacrifices and the exhortations that accompanied them were in any case sufficiently convincing to induce the Nigerian Labour Congress to abandon its threats to call a general strike if the cuts were implemented.

These moves were shrewdly consolidated and integrated into a rudimentary ideological rationale in Babangida's Independence Day speech of 1985. Proclaiming a 15-month economic emergency, he advocated 'a vigorous search for a New Political Order' and declared his administration's fundamental objectives to be 'economic reconstruction, social justice and self-reliance'.[66] The speech also referred to 'hard choices', 'great difficulties' and 'sacrifices' – prophecies which were borne out by the 1986 budget which, in addition to confirming the policies just listed, imposed a special levy to pay for 'free' primary education (but also eliminated school fees), reduced defence spending by 19.4%, levied a 30% surcharge on all imports (thus further *de facto* devaluing the naira by the same percentage), and implemented a one-time levy of 5–15% of all companies' after-tax profits. At the same time, the debt-servicing problem was deferred by Babangida's declaration that foreign loan payments would be limited to 30% of export receipts.

Thus Babangida's policies were fundamentally identical to those proposed by Shagari and partially attempted by Buhari. But, implemented more equitably and palatably, they more effectively perform the 'corrective' function of military-led elite rule.

(That alternative economic resuscitation measures are at least conceivable, has been marvellously suggested by Lawson Omokhodion. Substantial cuts could be made in military spending, he argues, since it is both unproductive and contains a relatively high foreign exchange component. This in itself would produce annual savings of hundreds of millions of naira. Then suspending construction work at Abuja would free some N250 m. per year. A ban on Muslim and Christian pilgrimages would save N40 m. annually [since both are heavily government subsidised]. Projecting data from a study by the Nigerian Institute of Social and Economic Research, he estimates that Nigerians have, over the past decade, salted away N10 bn in foreign bank accounts: a return of even one-quarter of that amount would end all discussion about an IMF loan.[67] In fact, former Finance Commissioner, Maj.-General James Oluleye has related how the Buhari government did ask the British government to help recover monies stolen by the political-tycoon class and deposited in British banks. But when Prime Minister Thatcher threatened to have published the names of *all* Nigerians holding accounts in the UK, this 'marked the death of the request'.[68] It would be extremely difficult to locate a more pointed illustration of what binds the various elite factions under the aegis of the military government!).

A second group of key supporters and beneficiaries of the Babangida faction are the technocratic and 'national' elements of the *civil servants*, the *gentlemen farmers* engaged in agrobusiness, local and foreign *transnational corporate interests* (especially oil and banking), and the more productive *'national' bourgeoisies* – in short, the same basic alliance that opposed the political-tycoon class dominating the Second Republic and that resisted any Nigerian go-it-alone strategy within OPEC. For this group, *the IMF loan* was the potentially divisive issue. Comprador civil servants (whose spokesman was Kalu I. Kalu), gentlemen farmers dependent on foreign capital, technical inputs and international markets, and the transnational interests stood to gain in the short term from the injection of fresh capital and in the long term from the social-disciplinary effects of implementing the conditionalities (wage freezes, absence of price control, convertibility of currencies, etc.). On the other hand, the IMF package would have undermined local import-substituting manufacture by raising the costs of imports (and industry depends on foreign suppliers for 70%–80% of its inputs) and – with trade liberalisation – by making Nigerian products uncompetitive and destroying the country's embryonic national bourgeoisie. The rising inflation triggered by higher import prices, the abolition of import licensing and the rise in petrol prices would have sharpened the economic crisis to an unacceptable extent and rapidly delegitimated the regime in popular opinion.

The issue of *privatising the parastatals* further complicates these factional cleavages. As explained in chapter 4, state ownership of certain sectors of the economy is one of the pillars of Nigerian state capitalism, and strong vested interests in the state bureaucracy itself as well as in dependent (and mainly unproductive) industries have resisted proposals for privatisation. Yet with a total state investment of some N34 bn (made up of a basic equity investment of N11.43 bn plus a variety of loans, subventions and grants[69]), parastatals present themselves as a relatively quick source of revenues which could be used to promote agrobusiness or import-substituting industries, while shares could be sold to the several factions of the bourgeoisie already benefitting from the indigenisation programme. Babangida, in his 1986 budget speech, announced his government's pending disengagement from direct ownership of the parastatals.

It is the special accomplishment of the Babangida leadership to have recognised, and at least temporarily articulated, all these potential conflicts among the Nigerian elite. Its circumvention of the IMF issue, its commitment to OPEC solidarity, and its ostensibly equitable austerity programme in a period of crisis have accounted for most of the vital interests of the current elite coalition. Crucial social infrastructural sectors, such as health, education and law and order, have been partly attended to. Raw materials, machinery and equipment have been allocated to manufacturers, thus producing a mini-boom in that sector.[70] Programmes proclaiming the goals of food self-sufficiency and rural development, industrial self-sufficiency and self-sustaining development, purposeful sacrifice and international creditworthiness, export-promotion and economic diversification, commercialisation of the state sector and investment promotion, address the common interests of most of these elite factions.

A third dimension of intra-elite support for the Babangida government is its success in restoring a *North-South equilibrium* among the factions of the bourgeoisie. It is not necessary to subscribe to a conspiratorial theory of an all-powerful 'Kaduna Mafia' to recognise the emergence, through the Mohammed/Obasanjo, Shagari and Buhari inter-regnums, of a powerful, relatively cohesive group of Northern-based but nationally operative interests. First coined in 1978 by a Nigerian journalist at the Constituent Assembly, Mvendaga Jibo, the term has since gained popular currency. An informal group of well-connected individuals, it is said to comprise a technocratically and 'modernisation'-oriented coalition of 'northern intelligentsia, top economic and political managers of local power, gentlemen farmers, businessmen, as well as ex-military and police commanders'[71] – by no means mutually exclusive categories. The actual personalities and their influence within the group vary from account to account, but General Shehu Yar 'Adua, Obasanjo's Chief of Staff, Supreme Head-quarters, and now a wealthy gentleman farmer, is consistently styled as a key figure. It was he who directly attended to the Mafia's interests during the recivilianising exercise (and who allegedly ensured the construction of the Kaduna refinery and the establish-ment of Abuja as the new capital[72]), and who has since been its link with the military. During the Second Republic the group was apparently, initially, well represented in the NPN; in the executive its agent was Adamu Chiroma, Shagari's Minister of Agriculture, who via the 'Green Revolution' upheld the interests of its gentlemen-farmer grouping. Nevertheless, Mafia members were unable to predominate within the growing tycoon class that the NPN produced and were cut off from the really lucrative opportunities for plunder by rival Northern factions, as personified by Dikko. Increasingly threatened by economic mismanagement and frustrated at their waning influence within the party, the theory goes, the Kaduna Mafia engineered the Buhari *coup*.[73]

On the face of it, the theory seems to be well supported by the composition and basic policies of the Buhari regime. Thirteen of the 19 members of his SMC were well-connected Northern Muslims, and an increased Northern component was installed in the diplomatic service, parastatal managements, the Central Bank and other state agencies. Three figures in particular stand out in the Buhari administration.[74] Mamman Daura, Buhari's cousin, former editor of the *New Nigerian* and a wealthy (mainly import-substituting) businessman, was said to be the architect of Buhari's economic plans. Mahmud Turkur, former Vice-Chancellor of Bayero University, was appointed Minister of Commerce and Industry. Said to be the Mafia's counterpart to Dikko under Shagari, he skewed the issuance of import licences toward Mafia interests, thus beginning the recreation of a Kaduna-centred tycoon faction. A third figure, Leme Jibil, an independently wealthy owner of companies and factories, was less well-known but nevertheless influential within the inner circles of the Buhari administration. He was apparently the main force behind Buhari's countertrade policies.

Countertrade, begun in December 1984, represented a final *ad hoc* attempt by the Buhari government to escape from its economic immobilism by obtaining the techno-logy, spare parts and raw materials essential to domestic economic recovery while circumventing the need for an IMF loan and not too blatantly violating OPEC rules. To do this, it concluded arrangements to barter Nigerian oil for the desired inputs. Deals were made with Brazil, France and Austria, and others were pending, at the time of the Babangida *coup*, with Italy, France, Canada, Romania and the Soviet Union. Although the total amount involved in the deals consummated, some N2 bn, was relatively small in terms of Nigeria's overall oil production, countertrade had important effects on intra-elite factionalism.

Countertrade between raw materials producers and manufacturers, in conformity with general patterns of 'unequal exchange', resulted in Nigeria 'paying' for the foreign products at above-market prices.[75] This of course even further devalued Nigerian oil. In such deals goods are seldom purchased at the cheapest available price. Brazilian sugar, for instance, which was part of the exchange, was priced well above world market levels.[76] Nigerian businessmen claimed that Brazilian exporters were inflating the value of their products by up to one-third and that the oil to be delivered to France would be discounted by at least 10% in the spot market.[77] Indeed, the Aboyade Committee appointed by Babangida to investigate the 1984 and 1985 countertrade agreements uncovered evidence of extensive invoice inflation, absence of price and inspection controls, and effective undermining of oil prices. It specifically indicted Idiagbon (who used his position to force the signing of the deals), Turkur (who approved the often dubious import licences) and Buhari for his government's 'indecent haste in signing the contracts'.[78] Again, the global price of Nigerian oil was effectively undermined. These measures, in a situation of falling oil prices (to which they significantly contributed), further threatened Nigeria's position within OPEC and hence, more generally, within the world capitalist system. Long-standing customers complained bitterly about the 'discounts' accruing to the country's new countertrade partners. They demanded corresponding countertrade arrangements or lower prices for themselves, and backed these demands with a refusal to lift oil from Nigerian fields, with the result that production dropped from 1.6 m. b/d in June 1985 to about 800,000 b/d by the time of the *coup*.[79] Nigerian countertrade therefore invoked OPEC's condemnation – though it has been practised at times by virtually all OPEC states, especially the other 'high absorbers' like Indonesia – as a covert means of discounting oil prices and an overt device for exceeding production quotas.[80]

For these reasons, the interrelated issues of the allocation of *import licences, countertrade* and *Northern predominance* are absolutely central to any explanation of the motives for the Babangida *coup*. Contrary to their popular 'rational' and 'technocratic' image as the champions of a disciplined, 'national' capitalism for the Nigerian state, the various elements of the Northern-based bourgeoisie popularly termed the Kaduna Mafia were clearly moving toward a systemically dysfunctional, particularistic and short-sighted form of state plunder. They were in the process of transforming themselves into a new tycoon class, albeit, unlike their counterparts in the Second Republic, inhibited by a shrinking economy and a firmer military presence. The Babangida *coup* could thus be justified as a countermeasure against this nationally divisive, unproductive and profiteering coterie of middlemen and fixers whose wealth derived from sales of import licences as well as 'percentages' of countertrade deals. Nevertheless, the Babangida faction is hardly representative of a reassertive 'South' against a monolithic 'North'. Again, its special accomplishment, in terms of the ethnic composition of the elite stratum, is its restoration of the rough contours of the 'federal character'. It thus *rationalises* and to a considerable extent *consolidates the North–South balance of elite interests*.

A fragile equilibrium

However, the new image of openness and fairness, the far-reaching exercise in nomenclature – which in many ways was merely a substitute for progressive change – and the raft of new appointments could not eliminate the complex of pressing economic–structural problems and potential class conflict to which the *coup* was essentially a reaction. Even a relatively open, relatively representative corporatist military governing elite remains vulnerable to counter *coups*, (i) from 'below', that is, from the younger generation of more 'radical' junior officers who, despite the token appointments just mentioned, are mainly excluded from a share of power (and indeed have been kept geographically dispersed), perhaps backed by an increasingly restive 'Lumpenmilitariat' in the ranks, or (ii) from a rival, sectorally and/or ethnically based faction within the ruling officer caste itself.

This second possibility was well demonstrated by the forestalled counter-*coup* of 17 December 1985, just four months into the Babangida interregnum. Despite initial rumours that the attempt was staged to restore the Buhari–Idiagbon faction and with it the lost power of the Kaduna Mafia, it appears to have been the isolated act of a group of mainly lieutenant-colonels and group captains, led – and largely financed – by Maj.-General Mamman Vatsa, a childhood friend and service mate of Babangida, and Minister of the Federal Capital Territory under both Buhari and Babangida. So far, no convincing explanation of the plotters' motives has been advanced. Certainly the pretexts given by their leaders – as selectively interpreted by spokespersons for the Babangida regime – were very tenuous: Babangida's rejection of the IMF loan, salary cuts for the military, the involvement of middle-level military officers in public office, the retention of certain compromised officers by the new regime, and Babangida's 'liberal' stand on human rights.

If any ideological pattern can be discerned here (and assuming the reasons given to be an adequate account), it is a rather 'reactionary' and elitist one. Such motives, formulated and acted upon at a time when Babangida's popularity was at its zenith, stood almost no chance of realisation. Moreover, as Dare Babarinsa wrote, 'for a man from Niger State to succeed another man from Niger State', in the ethnically charged Nigerian power context, 'is almost a sacrilege'.[82] The Vatsa plot was therefore widely perceived as not only futile but also as regressive in intent. It has been compared to the February 1976 Dimka–Bisalla conspiracy, which had no real basis among the masses or among a significant number of elite factions, and which probably represented nothing more than the self-interest of the plotters themselves. In this context, Ray Ekpu has recalled the 'course-mate syndrome' in the Nigerian army, namely, 'the view that all course-mates must march upwards in a row in the same manner that they march at parades'.[83] Under exceptional conditions such as those surrounding military intervention, however, corporate solidarity is shaken as individual members outpace their cohorts and the predictability of career progress is eliminated. This is compounded by rivalries for the 'political' offices where opportunities for self-enrichment are far greater, offices which comparatively few military leaders can aspire to (never more than 100 in any given military government, and often far fewer). The resultant intra-service and political-military conflicts are a partial explanation of the chronic instability of military governments.

There is an ever-present spectre of an unforeseen counter-*coup* which could negate the tenuous legitimacy of 'corrective' military rule. The 1976 *coup* attempt managed to assassinate Murtala Mohammed; the 1985 plot, pre-empted before it could be executed, revealed the instigators' (alleged) plans to bomb selected areas such as the President's residence, Dodan Barracks, strategic bridges and other military concentrations around Lagos, while a naval gunship was to bombard Lagos from the harbour[84] – plans which, if true and if realised, would have resulted in an incalculable number of casualties. The point about such conspiracies, however, is that they remain a constant threat to military regimes so long as important factions are not integrated and regime legitimacy is not consolidated. That this factor was perceived by the military elite is evidenced by the nationwide broadcast, following the execution of the convicted conspirators, by Maj.-General Domkat Bali, Defence Minister and chairman of the Joint Chiefs of Staff.

For him, the 'most serious effect of the abortive coup' was that it had shaken the '*esprit de corps*' and 'internal cohesion' of the military establishment. Another important consideration was the deterrent to foreign investment and hence the threat to economic recovery that it represented. The conspirators were sentenced on 25 February and ten of them shot on 5 March 1986.[85]

The fundamental contradiction in a military government resting on the legitimating pillars of an image of openness and human rights, on the one hand, and an activist, no-nonsense, 'corrective' ethos on the other was revealed in the post-conspiracy events. The execution of the main plotters indicated a preference for the latter, thus undermining the regime's human-rights claims. These claims were further called into question by the April 1986 massacre of students, a series of repressive measures against the trade unions, detention of university lecturers and intellectuals and the banning of student organisations. A similar dilemma emerged with respect to the treatment of the former politicians who had been held without trial throughout the course of the Buhari regime. Babangida's decision to release most of them displayed both 'compassion' and frustration with a public opinion that overwhelmingly sought retribution. The issue came to a climax when on 17 January 1986 the Uwaifo Panel investigating the politicians' crimes acquitted Shagari and Ekwueme of individual charges of corruption and malfeasance. While the formal, legalistic criteria used to arrive at the verdict may have been the only ones possible within the panel's judicial mandate, the acquittal produced an immediate public outcry and protest. This transformed the question of guilt or innocence into a basically moral issue of ultimate responsibility as well as one of political-symbolic implications, thus transferring the ultimate decision to the jurisdiction of the AFRC itself. Again, the supreme policy-making body, rent between its conflicting sources of legitimation, simply kept the ex-political leaders in custody, thus satisfying no one but gaining time and accumulating inertia.

When, similarly, Nigeria seemingly blundered into the Organisation of Islamic Conferences (OIC) as a full member – a process begun under Buhari – thus raising in an immediate and acute way the more or less dormant religious issue and with it Nigeria's status as a secular state, Babangida neither confirmed nor repudiated Nigeria's membership. Instead, he convened a Presidential select committee, in which Christians and Muslims were equally represented, to make recommendations. Not unexpectedly, the committee argued for the preservation of the country's secular status.[86] But here again large sectors of the population were left dissatisfied.

In a period of reconstruction and readjustment, the apparent paradox of a 'smiling general' and a tough-minded military government willing to listen to, and in some cases follow, public opinion may well help to prolong a ruling coalition of elite factions beset by a structural legitimacy problem. But in the longer term, Babangida may be compelled to develop consistent policies based on the concrete interests of the coalition his government represents. Then, in Adabayo Williams' words:[87]

> his strength may also be his profound weakness. He may be led to misconstruing his historical mission as that of placating aggrieved interest groups: a sop to sullen feudalists there, a smile at sulking industrialists here. Government then becomes a perpetual hostage of the manipulators of our differences.

These considerations no doubt figured in President Babangida's decision, announced on 13 January 1986 (and echoing Mohammed's 1976 pledge) that his government would not 'stay a day longer than is absolutely necessary' and would therefore recivilianise by 1 October 1990.[88] As an initial measure towards this end, he appointed a 17-member 'Political Bureau' to 'kick-off, as it were, the national debate on a viable future political ethos and structure for our dear country', and to present his administration with a range of political options. Although the Bureau did contain a more 'progressive' component than the CDC's Fifty Wise Men – for example, Edwin Madunagu of *The Guardian*; S. E. Oyovbaire, a prominent political scientist from the University of Benin; Ibrahim Halilu and Pascal Bafyan of the NLC – and more social scientists and intellectuals than lawyers and 'heavyweights', it is also evident that the current exercise, like its predecessor, the 1977 Constitution Drafting Committee, is conceived of as an elite affair, official calls for participation and involvement notwithstanding. Not only did this first recivilianising body consist mainly of prominent academics and officials, its very terms of reference ensured that the Political Bureau tapped and utilised the collective wisdom of 'experienced and seasoned statesmen, administrators and industrialists'.

The promise of 'imminent' recivilianisation, and all the public discussion and deliberation that will enter into it, will no doubt prolong the current military government's legitimacy as it has for past military regimes. And the interval may allow an elite stratum for the moment forced on to the defensive, to realign and reconsolidate its longer-term interests – provided of course that falling oil revenues and multiple internal contradictions do not overtake this factional realignment. But in the absence of real and abiding socio-economic reforms as well as substantial changes in the structure and mode of elite domination, the system remains crisis-prone and hence unstable.

Notes

1. From the text of Buhari's speech, reproduced in *West Africa*, 9 January 1984, pp. 56–7.
2. However, as Peter Enahoro wrote (*Africa Now*, January 1984): 'This is not like 1966 when a prolonged breakdown of law and order eventually provoked a mutiny among middle-ranking officers; nor is it like 1975 when the Gowon regime brought woe upon itself. This time we are faced by men who have operated the strings of power before and who have now returned purposefully to place themselves at centre stage. It looks like a long stay.'
3. In one of the most notorious revelations, 'a huge, four-bay warehouse was found packed to the rafters with 100-lb. bags of presidential task force rice', estimated at 'one million bags, enough to feed the whole state for weeks' (*Manchester Guardian Weekly*, 15 January 1984). The former President's brother-in-law and erstwhile transport Minister, Dr Umaru Dikko, has been linked by considerable and compelling evidence to this and many similar incidents. Dikko, safely in exile in London after fleeing the country a few days following the *coup*, attributed the military's actions to a plot masterminded by the 'Kaduna Mafia' whose most prominent member was former Chief of Staff, Maj.-Gen. Shehu Yar'Adua. He defended the huge amounts of public and private funds diverted to the NPN during the Second Republic, with these words: 'A politician's first aim is to obtain votes, and that is what I was concerned with. Besides, whatever money a politician makes goes back to the people because he wants their votes.' (*The Observer*, 22 January 1984). Small wonder that the Nigerian media dubbed him 'the country's most-wanted man', and that the new rulers of Nigeria were prepared to arrange a complicated plot to kidnap and return this former politician who was said to have stolen more than £1 bn from the country; see D. Pallister and Ad'obe Obe, 'Why Dikko is Nigeria's Most Wanted Man', *Manchester Guardian Weekly*, 15 July 1984.
4. The incidents related in this paragraph have been chosen at random from Nigerian press reports in the two years following the *coup*, particularly the first few months. Literally hundreds more could be cited.
5. See *West Africa*, 8 October 1984, p. 2053.

6. See especially *Newswatch*, cover story, 13 January 1986.
7. Reported at length in *Newswatch*, cover story, 27 January 1986.
8. Reported in Reuters and UPI dispatches, 5–9 January 1984.
9. *Globe and Mail*, (Toronto) 7 January 1984.
10. The *Financial Times* (3 January 1984) also argued that 'on the face of it, the takeover could scarcely have been less predictable'.
11. For a directly opposed interpretation, however, see Wole Soyinka, 'Electoral Fraud in Nigeria and the Western Press', *South African Outlook*, January 1984, pp. 7–9.
12. The *Manchester Guardian Weekly* would disagree; in an editorial of 29 January 1984 it wrote that 'the smoothness of the military takeover is deceptive; its efficiency may owe more to previous experience and the correct anticipation of popular assent than to a well-prepared plan by the generals to solve the nation's ills.'
13. Western and Nigerian media accounts agree – apart from suggestive comments in *Africa Now*, January 1984 – that the sole intra-military resistance to the *coup* occurred during the attempted arrest of Shagari at Abuja and that Brigadier Bako was shot while attempting to negotiate the President's surrender. Some reports suggest a pitched battle between the presidential guard and the arresting troops resulting in 'several hundred' casualities. In any event, Shagari apparently fled from Abuja, made his way to Nassarawa, thence to Makurdi where he surrendered on learning that the new SMC head was Buhari whom the President trusted. (See *West Africa*, 23 January 1984, p. 185.)
14. As reported by *West Africa*, 30 January 1984, p. 195.
15. *Ibid.*
16. From an interview in *Nigerian Gaurdian*, quoted in *Africa Confidential*, Vol. 25, No. 1 (4 January 1984).
17. As reported by *West Africa*, 26 March 1984, p. 691.
18. See, e.g., *The Times*, 7 January 1984 and 18 April 1984; *Christian Science Monitor*, 27 January 1984; *Manchester Guardian Weekly*, 29 January 1984. Babangida, in an interview with *Agence France Presse*, however, denied the possibility of a *coup* or counter-*coup* by junior officers, stating that there was 'a very good cohesion in the officer corps' (as reported in *West Africa*, 30 January 1984, p. 243).
19. *The Times*, 18 January 1984.
20. See, respectively, *The Times*, 18 April 1984 and *The Observer*, 18 November 1984.
21. *Newswatch*, 2 December 1985, p. 27.
22. These figures do not even hint at the N1 bn said to have been spent to 'buy' the 1983 elections (see chapter 5).
23. Morris Janowitz, *Military Institutions and Coercion in the Developing Nations*, Chicago, 1977, p. 77.
24. Terisa Turner and Arnold Baker, 'Soldiers and Oil: The 1983 Coup in Nigeria', McGill University, Centre for Developing Area Studies Discussion Paper No. 28 (October 1984).
25. *Ibid.*, p. 7.
26. *Ibid.*, p. 16.
27. *Ibid.*, p. 15.
28. *West Africa*, 19 November 1984, p. 2356; according to *New African* (March 1985, p. 61), promotions during the preceding six months included 500 junior officers, 90 senior officers and nine brigadiers advancing to major-general.
29. *West Africa*, 11 March 1985, p. 489.
30. Indeed, for Franz Nuschler, Klaus Ziemler, *et al.* (*Politische Herrschaft in Schwarzafrika: Geschichte und Gegenwart*, Munich, 1980, p. 40), the functional aspects of the military-civilian alliance far outweigh common class interests or value preferences.
31. *West Africa*, 4 February 1985, p. 215.
32. For details, see *Africa Now*, March 1984, pp. 65–6.
33. *Africa*, April 1984, p. 40.
34. However, when interest on promissory notes issued to creditors during the last year of the Shagari regime is added, the debt-service ratio for 1984 was roughly 50%; see *New African*, March 1985, p. 55. When the military assumed power, the country's combined short-,

medium- and long-term debts were N7.625 bn; if short-term trade arrears are added, the total was N11.1 bn; internal debts were at N21.991 bn; see Shehu Othman, 'Classes, Crises and Coup: The Demise of Shagari's Regime', *African Affairs*, Vol. 83, No. 333 (1984), p. 452.

35. As reported widely in the Nigerian press since the *coup*. Terisa Turner ('Oil Syndicate is Smashed in Nigeria Probe', *African News*, 19 March 1984, p. 3) estimates a total loss of $16.7 m during the Shagari period. The importance attached by the Buhari government to this 'oil leakage' was reflected in the imposition of the death penalty for those convicted of smuggling or otherwise illegally dealing in oil. See also next section.

36. Turner and Baker, 'Soldiers and Oil', p. 12. Indeed, as they suggest, the House of Representatives in December 1983 voted to withdraw from OPEC unless a higher Nigerian quota could be negotiated – a move which apparently caught the executive members concerned with petroleum entirely unawares.

37. *West Africa*, 7 January 1985, p. 4.

38. In any case the import-substitution strategy is a dubious one, since the Nigerian manufacturing base is extremely narrow: four basic consumer industries (cigarettes/brewing, cotton and textiles, soaps, detergents and vegetable oils) constitute more than 60% of the country's manufacturing output.

39. *New African*, March 1985, p. 55.

40. The poll or community tax is a particularly invidious tax. A lump-sum levy on every adult male resident of a given area whose income is below N600, it is perceived as a tax on the poor.

41. As related by *New African*, March 1985, p. 56; *West Africa*, 27 August 1984, p. 1713 and 19 November 1984, p. 2314; *Newswatch*, 9 September 1985, p. 33.

42. S. E. Oyovbaire, 'Leadership in Nigeria: The Living Legacy of the Late General Murtala Mohammed', ASUU Guest of the Month Lecture, University of Benin, 13 February 1984, mimeo, p. 1.

43. Federal Government of Nigeria, *News Review* (Nigerian High Commission, Ottawa), 31 March 1984, p. 4 (henceforth: FGN:NR).

44. *Ibid.*, 31 January 1984, p. 6.

45. *Ibid.*, 31 March 1984, p. 3.

46. *Ibid.*, p. 5.

47. From a prepared speech to delegates' conference of the Nigeria Labour Council, March 1984, quoted in *West Africa*, 12 March 1984, p. 582.

48. *News Review*, 31 April 1984.

49. Quoted in *West Africa*, 22 April 1985, p. 805.

50. For an analysis of the social backgrounds and circumstances of the 'cocaine women', and for an account of the many appeals against these sentences, see *West Africa*, 10 June 1985, pp. 1166–7.

51. Iya Agan, 'Hard Times for Nigerian Women', *AfricAsia*, No. 16 (April) 1985, p. 8.

52. Syndromes no doubt shared by certain sectors of the population. The United States branch of the Bendel Students' Union, for example, would have convicted ex-politicians executed and their bodies publicly mutilated, while the families of escaped but wanted politicians would be arrested and kept as hostages; see *Nigerian Tribune*, 14 January 1984.

53. *Concord Weekly*, 12 September 1985.

54. It has been alleged that the officer who saw the clearance through, Major Jokolo, was the Emir's son and Buhari's ADC, see *New African*, October 1985, p. 12.

55. See *Newswatch*, 9 September 1985, p. 15; see also the discussion below.

56. *Concord Weekly*, 12 September 1985.

57. Babangida's technocratic propensities and belief in military-led development are well known. Indeed, according to Susanne Cronje, he sees himself as a Nigerian Atataturk with a vision of a Brazilian-type 'Arms City' within the framework of which 'defence and national planning are mutually inclusive and development generating' (*New Statesman*, 6 September 1985).

58. Quoted in *West Africa*, 19 August 1985, p. 1724.

59. *Newswatch*, 9 September 1985, p. 13.

60. Text of Obasanjo's speech, 'Which Way Forward?', reproduced in *West Africa*, 19 August 1985, pp. 1694–5.

61. *Newswatch*, 9 September 1985, p. 13.
62. *Newswatch*, 9 September, 1985, pp. 18–19.
63. As indicated, for instance, by his appointment of Kalu Idika Kalu, a former World Bank official and strong proponent of the IMF loan, as Minister of Finance.
64. Thus reversing somewhat a tendency toward increasing military budgets, which had evolved along the following lines: 1977/78:N1.027 bn; 1979/80:N1.222 bn; 1981:N/A; 1982:N953.4 m; 1983:N1.185 bn; 1984:928.24 m; 1985:N975.64 m; 1986:N907 m; see *Newswatch*, 13 January 1986, p. 26.
65. For details of the military and civil service reductions, see *West Africa*, 18 November 1985, p. 2407 and 11 November 1985, p. 2390.
66. Quoted in *West Africa*, 7 October 1985, p. 2076; subsequently codified as The National Economic Emergency Powers Decree No. 22.
67. Lawson Omokhodion, 'Surviving Without IMF', in *Newswatch*, 14 October 1985, p. 18.
68. Quoted in *West Africa*, 23 September 1985, p. 1988.
69. *Newswatch*, 13 January 1986, p. 26.
70. See *Newswatch*, 2 September 1985, p. 25.
71. *West Africa*, 30 September 1985, p. 2035; further see Othman, 'Classes, Crises and Coup' *op. cit.*
72. According to Eme Ekekwe, 'The State, National Development and the Present Systemic Crisis', paper presented to Nigerian Political Science Association annual conference, 4 June 1983.
73. In fact, Dikko, from exile, specifically named Yar 'Adua as the planner of Buhari's *coup*.
74. On these, see Dan Agbese in *Newswatch*, 9 September 1985, p. 28.
75. *Afric Asia*, No. 22 (October 1985), p. 9.
76. *West Africa*, 5 August 1985, p. 1594.
77. *Africa Economic Digest*, 29 June 1985, p. 32.
78. *Newswatch*, 3 March 1986.
79. Terisa Turner, 'Experiences of Research on Oil in Africa: The Energy and Social Development Research Group, University of Port Harcourt, Nigeria', paper presented to annual meeting of ASA, New Orleans, 23–26 November 1985, mimeo., p. 16.
80. *Africa Economic Digest*, 29 June 1985, p. 31.
81. See *International Herald Tribune*, 21 22 December 1985.
82. *Newswatch*, 10 March 1986.
83. *Newswatch*, 17 February 1986.
84. *Newswatch*, 6 January 1986.
85. In addition to Vatsa, those executed included: Squadron Leader Asen Ahura, a pilot with the presidential fleet; Squadron Leader Martin Luther, also with the presidential fleet; Lt. Col. Chris Oche of army intelligence; Lt. Col. Musa Bitiyong, director of logistics at army headquarters, Lagos; Lt. Col. Mike Iyorshe of the Jaji Staff College; Maj. Daniel Bamidele also at the Jaji College; Wing Commander Ben Ekele, commander of the Air Strike Group at Makurdi; Wing Commander Adamu Sakaba, commandant of the Makurdi air force base; and Commander Andrew Ogwiji, commanding officer of the NNS Olokun at Apapa. Five further officers were jailed for varying terms. And Brigadier Malami Nassarawa was to be retried. See *Newswatch*, 17 March 1986.
86. *West Africa*, 17 February 1986, p. 380.
87. *Newswatch*, 17 February 1986.
88. *News Review*, 23 January 1986, p. 5.

9

The 'Grassroots' State: Local and Traditional Politics

In chapter 7, Nigerian federalism was depicted as a permanent and indispensable mechanism to integrate and mediate a series of conflicts and contradictions arising from the country's peculiar constellation of class, ethnic, economic and social forces. The relationship between federal and State governments, particularly under the Second Republic, was analysed in terms of the accommodation of diversity versus the need for centralism as the precondition for economic growth, generally defined in terms of 'modernisation' and 'development'. Right at the centre of this tension between centripetal and centrifugal forces, and hence profoundly moved by them, are situated the local and traditional forms of government. Within a generation, local government has evolved from its multi-tiered neo-colonial diversity to single-tier uniformity, to virtually unchecked proliferation and back again to controlled and strictly delimited organisational units. Yet paradoxically, the greater the extent of standardisation, the larger has been the relative autonomy of these sub-federal governments. A similar paradox underlies the rapidly changing role of traditional rulers. For even as their powers have eroded, or been eroded, their actual authority and affective strength have been enhanced, so that the institution is, in some ways, now more entrenched than at any time since the First Republic. How do these forms of 'grassroots' political organisations interrelate to each other, and how do they collectively intermesh with, and react to, the successive forms of federalism?

The special role of local government

Historically, local government in Nigeria has evolved extremely diverse, and to a large extent, developmentally dysfunctional structures. The differential impacts of colonialism, the varying needs and structures of pre-colonial societies, and the effects of indirect rule, all contributed to a bewildering variety of local governments in the semi-autonomous Regions of the post-independence period (see Mackintosh, 1966:208). Despite occasional 'reforms' or reshuffling, central–local power relationships basically retained their colonially-imposed organisational forms until 1976, with the few changes occurring less on account of constitutional amendments than as a reflection of real power shifts (1966, 1975, etc.).[1]

Thus – and again parallel to the overall socio-economic development of the country – in local government, too, a distinct Northern and Southern pattern emerged. In the

North, with its traditionally large and centralised emirates and its geographical area four times greater than that of the South (despite an only marginally larger population), successive local government reorganisations (for example, the Native Authority Law of 1954) merely modified the colonial multi-tier Native Authority System which revolved around the emir. In this way, the emirs were able to retain intact their control over their historical territories, thus essentially preserving pre-colonial relationships and largely preventing the intrusion (or 'penetration') of a greater central presence. The South, on the other hand, with its denser population and smaller geographical area, tended to model its local government systems on British practice. Within the South, moreover, Eastern and Western variants emerged. The far more fragmented East – which in 1948 had contained 217 Native 'Authorities, in contrast to the 13 in all of Sokoto, Katsina, Kano and Zaria (whose combined population was larger than that of the entire East) – tended towards stronger central authority, and in the train of the civil war established something like the French Integrated Prefectorial System. In the West, which most resembled the British local government system, there was a gradual evolution away from the pre-1966 two- or three-tier system, towards a single-level arrangement integrating, in places, the council manager system adapted from the United States.[2]

Under the military regime, particularly after 1970, the need for reform became increasingly apparent. In addition to the chronic problems of corruption, inadequately trained staff and financial constraints, the Military Government created a state administered predominantly from the centre. The twelve, later nineteen, States, deprived now of many of their independent powers, increasingly encroached upon the constitutionally unprotected local governments' jurisdictions. From the other side, the influx of oil revenues rendered State and central governments less dependent on taxes and other revenues raised at the local level, thus weakening the interest-based linkages between the lower and upper tiers. Yet in terms of the central government's development strategy, it was essential that local government remain comparatively viable and independent, (a) because a central presence in the local areas would enable the FMG to monitor and adapt programmes whose success depended on local co-operation and mobilisation, and (b) because the military's centrist federalism presupposed the maintenance of a strong dependency of the sub-national units (States) on the central government, a relationship which could best operate if the local governments were accorded sufficient independent powers to enable them to function as a 'check' against excessive State power.

Thus, a far-reaching structural reform became desirable. The reasons for the change, as Oyediran and Gboyega suggest, related to the regional problems which it was expected to overcome. In the North, 'the need was to modernize the system by emphasizing popular participation and control and thereby diffusing the power of the emirs and traditional rulers', while in the South, 'the need was to revitalise and consolidate the local government system which had become the object of contempt'.[3]

The post-1976 reorganisation addressed these needs by implementing a uniform, structured reform: it replaced the multiplicity of local government levels and subsystems with a nationwide organisation which clearly and without exception made local government the third tier of the political system. Authority was located in a primarily secular, democratically elected body – the first LGCs (Local Government Councils) varying in membership size from ten to thirty individuals, were composed of at least 75% of elected members and no more than 25% appointees of the Military Governors[4] – rather than invested in religious and/or traditional figures. With due regard to the Udoji Report's injunction to take account of ethnic groupings, population, geographical conditions and the people's customs and traditions, local government areas were delineated so as to encompass populations of between 150,000 and 800,000, thus breaking up, incidentally, some of the larger Northern emirates, with effects on these traditional authorities to be discussed presently. LGCs were by regulation supposed to be elected for a three-year term and were enjoined to establish at least two committees, one for finance and general purposes, and one for education.

The LGCs' relative, but carefully delimited, autonomy within the new federalism was to begin with some measure of fiscal independence from their respective States. The reform provided that local government grants would be paid by the federal government while the State governments were also supposed to allocate 10% of their revenues to the LGCs. However, the local governments' powers of revenue raising were hardly increased beyond property, licensing and community taxes. Their functions were at the same time expanded beyond the traditional areas of vital statistics registration, health, education (nursery, primary and adult), and public works programmes into a number of services previously provided by the State: the upper level of rural health services, agricultural extension work and animal care, social and community development, libraries, and the co-operative movement. Both fiscal and political autonomy were formally guaranteed, first by decree, then by the constitution. One residual area of State control did remain in the form of staffing policy. All local government personnel from GL04 level upwards were appointed by the State Local Government Service Commission, a procedure which, given the informal patronage links prevalent in the State bureaucracy, in fact represented an important avenue of State influence over LGCs. The 'trade-off', however, was the establishment of a unified local Government Service Board, a kind of central personnel agency which provided staff from a national pool: local government officials were now graded parallel to, and received emoluments comparable with, State and federal civil servants, a measure intended to alleviate LGCs' chronic inability to attract qualified and competent personnel.

The actual implementation of the new local government system must also be considered, not as an isolated set of reforms, but as an integral part of the military's recivilianisation programme. Since political parties were still proscribed at the time of the first LGC elections in December 1976, local councillors generally were compelled to contest elections on the basis of 'apolitical' appeals rather than on partisan issues or party programmes. This, coupled with the decision to make the elections largely indirect – local government areas were allowed to opt either for direct elections or indirect ones arranged by the State governments: only ten chose the former,[5] to say nothing of the co-optation of up to 25% of the council members, as just mentioned – ensured that already prominent and usually wealthy and/or respected individuals were chosen with a mandate to uphold local socio-economic conditions, particularly since many traditional rulers, themselves banned from contesting the elections, openly campaigned on behalf of favoured candidates.[6] In other words, 'depoliticisation' of the elections and their relative removal from direct, popular participation produced (or rather reproduced) at the local government level the patterns of elite formation which characterised the State and federal tiers of government as well (but one in which traditional rulers played a diminished role; see next section).

Local government as a nodal point of elite formation is worth examining further. With its greater (and federally guaranteed) revenues – ten to twenty times larger than during the pre-civil war period[7] – and its increased relative autonomy, post-1976 local government initially held a new allure for aspiring members of the elite, particularly (a) those who would be unable to secure a niche in the federal or State bureaucracies or elected organs, and (b) those who, sensing the new opportunities to build a political reputation, to forge clientele networks and to accumulate wealth, regarded local government as a proverbial springboard into political offices at higher levels which would become available with imminent recivilianisation. The massive re-entry of these incipient elites into local government in large measure undermined the purpose of the LGC reforms, namely, to encourage popular awareness and enlightenment at the 'grassroots' level, through, for example, a better distribution of resources and literacy/training campaigns. Elite rule for purposes of self-enrichment, however, presupposes the maintenance of peasant subservience and limited popular participation.

These basically political problems were compounded by serious organisational and administrative shortcomings: faulty voter registration, shifting and nebulously defined qualifications required of voters and candidates, inadequate publicity, and lack of official guidelines for the whole process. (Concerning the latter, the Local Government Edict and the Electoral Regulations were not officially approved and published until January 1977, well after the elections had taken place (B. C. Smith, 1982:1)). Not surprisingly, therefore, voter turnout was extremely low (24.96%), a large number of candidates (39%) were returned unopposed, and this initial testing of the prospects of democratic participation could not be termed a total success. Nevertheless, the Local Government Council, with its controlled decentralisation of political powers, was firmly embedded in the structure of the Nigerian state. Elections were more or less successfully held in December 1976, and the 301 local governments began work in 1977.

Thus Nigerian local government was not only constitutionally anchored as a third, democratically elected tier of government, but its establishment, structure, composition, finance and functions were (and remain) clearly defined by law. In fact, since the publication of the 1976 *Guidelines for Local Government Reform* by the Murtala Mohammed government, the proclaimed organisational principles of sub-State government have been representativeness, participation, devolution and autonomy. Why did the Nigerian military rulers set out to reverse the otherwise universal African – including pre-1976 Nigerian – trend towards local government decay, a trend about which Paul Collins (1980:206) has argued that 'the use of local government for "development" purposes has mainly been confined to the collection of taxes on behalf of the central government? And why, more importantly, have these formal prescriptions, as well as the aspirations which they represented, foundered during the past decade as a result of (a) massive corruption and poor execution at the local level, (b) intervention by State governments including dismissal of elected counsellors, dissolution of LGCs and their replacement by politically determined appointees, and creation of new LGAs, (c) systematic deprivation of funds and entitlements, and (d) failure of federal governments to enforce State obligations to local governments?

Answers to these questions are in some measure facilitated by a large and growing body of literature which analyses local government reform in Nigeria variously as an attempt at extending democratic participation, as an assault on traditional rulers' powers and privileges, as the realisation of a logical and long-overdue reform, as a device to combat 'administrative constipation', or as a practical and integral measure of the new federalism. These partial theses, together with the material presented here, may be compressed into two central analytical categories relating to the concrete, corporate interests of the country's ruling classes: (i) the imperative to maintain continuous systemic development within the 'modernising', institution-building paradigm, already alluded to, which is essential to the survival of the Nigerian elites and (ii) the realities of material and class constraints which continuously thwart this imperative and produce a series of related structural-political crises.

(i) *Systemic development*. It is generally agreed that local governments can play an important role in the development (however defined) of Third World countries. Correctly organised and motivated, they can act as focal points of local initiative towards economic and social development and as agencies for the implementation of national or regional programmes and policies, particularly national development plans.[8] Concerning the latter, local government's part may be crucial: providing staffs and organisations for project administration, furnishing the central authorities with information about local needs and conditions, and actually realising and maintaining the development programmes (Nwomonoh, 1978:252ff.)

Local government, moreover, is the tier of government 'closest' to the population and as such potentially involves more people and better corresponds with local needs, loyalties and interests. As a member of the Constituent Assembly, Alhaji M. A. Rimini, subsequently Governor of Kano State, argued for an enhanced role for local government:[9]

> Local Government is the most important government of our land. The Local Government is the nearest and most immediate government to the man. The man in my village does not care about who the President is. He does not even care about who the Governor of Kano State is. He cares only about those who are Councillors and Chairmen of his Local Government.

From the state's point of view, therefore, local government may make important contributions in the areas of political socialisation and legitimation. Since in Nigeria, as throughout Africa, the great majority live and produce literally 'at the grassroots' in rural areas, and since any realistic strategy of development must start from the rationalization of agriculture and the transformation of rural society, it is essential that government 'penetrate' into these as yet largely 'unmobilised' sectors. For this purpose, local government, if properly geared towards, and responsive to, local norms and attitudes, is obviously better placed than the central authorities – including 'development administrators' – to facilitate system maintenance and 'development'. It may perform an important educational function in preparing people to act within the regional or national political system. At the local level people must deliberate and vote on directly relevant and hence more comprehensible issues. Elected councillors tend to be more accessible and responsible than other elected representatives or appointed officials. Experience gained as a voter, candidate or representative at the local level may be a preparation for comparable political action at other levels. The ethos of democratic participation thus established might well be an important factor in basis-mobilisation for socio-economic development. If so, the result could be more balanced growth at the local level and hence greater self-reliance which reduces dependence on external expertise and funding.

These kinds of developments are no doubt what the formulators of the *Guidelines* envisaged when they described the aims and functions of local government as:

1. To make appropriate services and development activities responsive to local wishes and initiatives by devolving or delegating them to local representative bodies.
2. To facilitate the exercise of democratic self-government close to the local levels of our society and to encourage initiative and leadership potential.
3. To mobilize human and material resources through the involvement of members of the public in their local development.
4. To provide a two-way channel of communication between local communities and government.

(ii) *The realities of material and class constraints*. Even the most superficial counterposing of this theoretical role of local government in systemic development – together with the *Guidelines* as its codified formulation, which has been termed 'one of the most significant political changes ever introduced in the history of Nigeria' (Aliyu, 1978/9:131) – against the reality of local politics in Nigeria reveals a massive gap between theory and praxis. This gap may be attributed mainly to a lack of material enablements and to the persistence of class conflict from above.

At the most fundamental level, given the chronic national shortage of trained manpower, it has been practically impossible to recruit and train qualified local government personnel, and this at the same time as experienced people have left local government service for better opportunities in other sectors of the economy. Despite constitutional guarantees, revenues from State and federal governments have not materialised in sufficient quantities, particularly after the 1981/2 recession precipitated by falling oil sales. The lack of funding has reduced local government's ability to deliver the services and facilities expected of it, which in turn has alienated many citizens from their 'grassroots' government. Elections were not held at all in the Second Republic,[10] so that the principle of LGC autonomy was gravely undermined. In addition to corruption and nepotism, the working of local government has been hampered by the fact that the system was created 'from above' and not preceded by any systematic consultations with the groups and institutions most affected by it. As a result, as Aliyu has put it (1978/9:141), the new system 'has facilitated the emergence, at local (in particular, but also) State and national levels, of a new leadership group that is ignorant not only of the operation of government but of their role in it'.

In a sense, Professor Aliyu's assessment is rather charitable in that it assumes that the post-1976 LGC officials were concerned about their role in the new political structures. No doubt, some were. But, as just suggested, it is evident that available opportunities for plundering the system were not so grossly neglected. For instance, the Chanchaga LGC in Niger State, within days of the 1976 elections, placed an order for bottles of aspirins costing N9.50 rather than the standard 50k. In Sokoto State, a judicial inquiry probing the dealings of Kaura Namoda local government learned that government councillors had begun registering themselves as LGC-appointed contractors immediately after their swearing-in ceremony. Hundreds of similar incidents could be cited from across the federation.

Moreover, the class composition of the LGCs – though again analysed at a more or less impressionistic level, since there is still a dearth of empirical studies – mirrors the dominant class structure in large measure. As Sorkaa suggests, the ostensibly non-political councils after 1976 represented, more than anything else, the local Chambers of Commerce: contractors, large-scale traders and artisans, and other members of the local bourgeoisie. Since wealth had now become at least as important a criterion as birth for election following the formal exclusion of traditional rulers, mainly the local 'big men' – with 'big' defined as some combination of financial backing and traditional-ruler support – could realistically aspire to office. Once the election was won, these groups not only sought to recoup their campaign expenses – a fluid category that included bribes, gifts and other inducements – but to use their new powers to turn a substantial profit as well. Thus the LGCs' priorities have been anything but mass welfare and popular participation. Despite their initial promise, local governments, especially during the heyday of the Second Republic, more and more 'serve primarily as conduit pipes for transferring resources to the emergent local elites that have supplanted the oligarchies' (Gana, 1982:9).

Many of these problems were recognised by an important National Conference on Local Government Reforms held in Zaria in 1979. Its recommendations included more independent financing and greater overall autonomy for local governments, increased political education for the population, better conditions of service for local government personnel, and the like.[12] Three years later another Conference on the Evolution of Local Government in West Africa at Ile-Ife produced an almost identical set of pre-scriptions, though it emphasised more strongly the need for greater democratic partici-pation at this 'grassroots' level.[13] Both conferences, as well as virtually the entire post-1976 literature on Nigerian local government, stress the crucial importance of the changing role of traditional rulers to the success or otherwise, of local government – an issue to which we now turn.

The 'rationalisation' of traditional rule

Within the overall context of elite domination, alternating military–civilian forms of government and the capitalist development imperative, the situation of Nigeria's tradi-tional rulers is both ambiguous and well into a process of transformation.

On the one hand, the continuity of traditional rule, with its deeply imbedded 'indig-enous' links and affective relationships to the people – despite compromises and changes effected by colonialism and since – invests it with a certain stability and legitimacy not yet enjoyed by the comparatively recent 'modern' political system. For this reason, successive post-independence regimes have been at pains to establish some form of *modus vivendi* with the traditional rulers, attempting in this way to enhance their own popular acceptance. Osagie and Wey (1977:17–18) allude to this phenomenon when they suggest that:

> there is a high probability of the transplanted model succumbing during any national crisis without any important segment of society feeling any profound sense of loss. On the other hand, there has been remarkable stability in the traditional political subsector because Afri-cans have generally respected the 'rules of the game' as handed over to them by their ancestors, and because traditional leadership is part and parcel of an overall culture, as opposed to the modern political model at the national level which is nothing but the remnant of colonialism. This fact explains why a coup against the Oba of Benin, the Sultan of Sokoto, the Alafin of Oyo or the Ashantihene is inconceivable and in fact sacriligious.

But, on the other hand, traditional rule, seen again in the context of a strategy of 'nation-building', 'institution-building' or some variety of the Eurocentric 'stages of growth' model, is positively dysfunctional. Traditional social systems are thought to impede the growth of a 'national' political system and economy, to prevent popular awareness from transcending the horizon of family, kinship group or tribe, and thus to retard the evolution of more literate, more aware, more skilled and more deployable 'citizens' – the human material needed to sustain and nurture this 'modernising' devel-opment strategy.

Here, it is worth inserting the qualification that the task facing the Nigerian political economy is not simply to overcome conflicts between a series of entrenched, archaic and localised traditional classes and 'a new middle class of Africans who had assumed leadership of the nationalist movement (vowing) to liquidate the institution of tradi-tional rulers' (Offiong, 1982:1), as is frequently assumed. Rather – as Markovitz (1977:chs IV–VI) has shown for Africa as a whole – there is in fact a high degree of correspondence between so-called 'traditional' and 'modern' elites. The former, and their kin, were best placed to capitalise on the opportunities afforded by colonialism. Many did so, thus linking traditional affective loyalties to 'modern' (capitalist) accumulation, and have become the main agents of capital formation and system development. Many, however, did not, preferring to co-exist alongside the 'modern' economy. And those of humbler origins who have since entered the elite class have by and large done so with the support and collaboration of the traditional groups – so much so that having attained wealth and/or position in the 'modern' sectors they too seek honours, chieftancies and the like bestowed by the traditional leaders.

Nevertheless, the point about the basic incompatibility between 'traditional' elites, *performing qua traditional rulers*, and 'new' elites (including those whose leadership role is legitimitated by 'traditional' antecedents) *attempting to create a 'modern' economy, society and political system* is essentially a valid one. The former tend to retain a large portion of relatively scarce resources, especially land (or to prevent them from being generated, as in the case of mechanisation or cash-cropping), while the latter are interested in deploying those resources for a process of 'development' and/or specula-tion of which they are the main beneficiaries. These conflicting interests and goals produce quite divergent concepts of social organisation and political structure. The fundamental axis of cleavage runs, here again, through the elite class itself, and must be seen as primarily a *functional* conflict.

So far, the main directions of this struggle are evident: the 'modernising' elite, backed by the power of the state, has steadily managed, partly by co-optation, partly by coercion, and partly by structural reforms, to erode the formal powers and influence of the strictly 'traditional' rulers. The process began at the 'national' political level, developed inwards to the sub-national units, and has, with the 1976 reforms, broken into the local sphere as well.[14]

Thus, the First Republic's Senate, as well as the Regions' Houses of Chiefs – whose functions in the respective national and sub-national political systems were, of course, by no means identical – were constituted entirely of traditional rulers, thus repre-senting a recognition of the special role that this class was supposed to play in political life. However, the members of these upper houses were entirely appointed and hence already in some measure subordinate to the leading elected office-holders. As token *ex officio* members, rather than equal voting members (as had been the case for senior traditional rulers under the Lyttelton Constitution), they lost considerable influence in these bodies which henceforth were controlled by the popularly elected members. Regional institutions were also established by the Independence Constitution: in the West and East, so-called Minority Councils were established to advise the Governor on local issues of welfare, development and discrimination, while in the North a Council of Chiefs, chaired by the Northern Region Premier, dealt exclusively with traditional affairs such as recognition, deposition and approval of chiefs.

Whenever traditional rulers failed to support, or otherwise came into conflict with, the powerful regional politicians during the First Republic, fines, exile, de-stoolment or persecution often resulted, particularly in the factionalised Western Region. Throughout the Regions (and again, not unlike under colonial rule)

> politicians deposed traditional rulers at will: merged kingdoms and sacked rulers; created chiefdoms where none existed before or even appointed chiefs without chiefdoms; and discov-ered new groups of villages (like Dr. Michael Okpara, former Premier of the defunct Eastern Region who discovered new villages in Ibeno area in 1961) and appointed chiefs for such places. (Offiong, 1982:7)

Yet conversely (and paradoxically) the aspiring political leaders were forced to con-cede the traditional rulers' key role in securing mass support for their ethnically-grounded parties. Traditional constituencies thus became the initial and most reliable sources of the 'new' elite's mass support. Before and after independence, therefore, the political leaders courted the traditional rulers with all the inducements which the new system could provide: seats in the upper houses, political appointments (in particular ministries without portfolio) with their corresponding salaries and benefits, and much more. At the same time, the traditional rulers, increasingly deprived by the 'modernising' political system of their status, were compelled to look elsewhere for an institutional basis of security and prestige, without which their ability to provide for their 'constituency', and hence their traditional popular support, would be jeopardised. Inevitably, they turned to the political parties who for reasons of legitimation were interested in gaining the emirs', chiefs' and obas' support. The specific relationship between party and traditional rulership naturally varied from Region to Region, but Reed's (1982) conclusions about the West are indicative of more general patterns in the South at least:

> From the perspective of the party, traditional rulers were seen as an asset which the Action Group could not afford to overlook. Awolowo's assessment of the situation was that traditional rulers had an 'incalculable sentimental value for the masses in Western and Northern Nigeria' and that practical politics demanded that they be used to support the Action Group. This the party attempted at both the regional level, where the power of recognition lay with the governor, as well as at the local level. Here traditional rulers were members of the Local Council which recorded the lines of succession while it also paid the salaries of the traditional rulers. If a given traditional ruler did not cooperate, the Action Group was not adversely disposed to reducing or eliminating his salary or rewriting the succession which could result in his losing his recognition. Thus, traditional rulers were heavily motivated to support the Action Group. The Action Group utilised this resulting support among the traditional rulers in order to dominate Local Councils which appeared to be leaning towards the NCNC. A number of traditional rulers did not hesitate to load Councils with partisan members.

In these ways, traditional rule, albeit distorted, dependent and otherwise transformed, was also further entrenched.

The first military government (1966–79), in line with its 'corrective' mandate to 'rationalise' the political–economic system, progressively reduced the scope of traditional rule even further in the direction of ceremonial tasks and legitimation of the 'modern' order: yet it too was unable to impinge on the 'hard core' of the traditional rulers' relative autonomy. Indeed, the latter's powers actually increased somewhat, at least initially, for reasons analogous to the civil service's expansion of powers at the same time. For the military, having banned 'political' activities, for a time were able to use the chiefs and emirs as administrative-transmission links between them and the people, and at the same time gain some measure of 'feedback' respecting popular needs and resentments to guide the governing process. But, institutionally, the military provided very little scope for traditional leaders beyond the local level. The upper houses were abolished along with the Westminster Model, and comparatively few patronage and/or token positions were available after January 1966. Less responsive to popular sentiments and by training and outlook very much identified with the 'modernising' elite, military government is generally willing, and more able than civilian government, to undertake the structural rationalisation of traditional rule.

These reflections bring this excursus back to its starting point: the local government reforms since 1976. Given the already-mentioned development strategy which views local government as a central instrument in national development planning and as a primary socialiser of mass attitudes and behaviour, the relationship between the reforms and the transformation of traditional rule becomes evident. The reforms aim at converting local government bodies into democratically elected councils – a clear assault on the affective bases of traditional rule. The goals here are related to the desire to inject greater efficiency, responsiveness and, not least, consonance with State and federal government policies into the local tier of government. In this way, in the longer term, overall regime legitimacy is likely to be enhanced as, in Ralph Miliband's words (written for quite a different context) local government position gives 'status, prestige, honour and influence to people who otherwise had very little or none of it'.[16] This in turn facilitates a certain spirit of collaboration, co-operation and ultimately co-optation among the elites at the three tiers of government, in contrast to the always latent and frequently manifest antagonism between 'traditional' and 'modern' elites.

These conclusions border on speculation, however, since the military's 1976 reform by no means represented an all-out offensive against traditional rulership. Indeed, the *Guidelines* (having irrevocably transformed the traditional rulers' position) specified that:

> Nothing in these reforms could be construed to mean an attempt at reducing or abolishing the traditional functions of our Emirs, Obas and Chiefs. On the contrary, the reforms recognise the crucial nature of the position of the traditional authorities and care has been taken to preserve the organic unity of our traditional institutions and societies.

These assurances notwithstanding, it would appear on balance that all promises relating to the continuation of traditional rule, and the corresponding concessions contained in the reform, reflect the ongoing need to establish a functional, non-antagonistic but provisional relationship between the new LGCs and these traditional authorities. This has been partly accomplished by the creation of emirate and traditional councils headed by an emir or paramount chief and appointed by the State Governors 'after appropriate consultation within the area'. According to the *Guidelines*, these councils may be constituted in one of five rather complex ways, which need not be described here. What is important, however, is that although the traditional councils' independent financial base has been reduced and all formal governing powers removed from them, they do retain such key functions as advising LGCs on a wide range of matters, participating in tax assessment and collection, pronouncing on traditional chieftancy and religious issues, and attending to a wide range of representative tasks.

Dynamics of politics at the basis

The preceding sections have dealt with the organisation, functions (and dysfunctions), and class interests of local and traditional government more or less as if they were self-contained political sub-systems. Although these are important areas of inquiry whose operations bear directly on the working of the larger Nigerian political system, military or civilian, they do not account for the factors of *process* and *interaction* among and between the various levels of government. In this section, therefore, the specific interrelations will be analysed with a view to determining the direction and intensity of the power shifts and political dynamics which shape and condition politics at the 'grassroots'. The relations of particular interest here are those between (i) State government and local government, and (ii) State authority and traditional authority. However, it should be noted that the interrelationship between traditional rule and local government constantly enters into and mediates these two sets of dynamic interactions.

(i) *Relations between State government and local government.* Because of their central role in development strategy and their potential influence in party politics and resource allocation, the local governments were bound to become the object of partisan politics after the transition to civilian rule. Anticipating precisely such developments, the departing military government endowed local government with a broad range of apparently autonomous powers and ensured that they were constitutionally anchored and safeguarded. More than that, the territory of the federation was and remains in fact defined in terms of the 19 States, which were delineated, in the 1979 Constitution's

First Schedule, by the LGAs which they comprised (or, more precisely, which comprised them). From this, the predominant line of judicial opinion inferred, at least in the first months of the Second Republic (and again since the return of military rule), that no State government was legally competent to alter local government boundaries, since any such act would amount to a unilateral revision of the constitution. Thus, when Governor Ambrose Alli in February 1980 attempted to dissolve a number of LGCs in Bendel State, and to replace them with caretaker committees, Chief Justice Victor Ovie-Whisky declared the Governor's actions unconstitutional.[17] Not only ought the Governor to have conducted official enquiries before dissolving the LGCs, the Justice found, but his appointment of caretaker councils to replace them violated the principles of representativeness and democracy which lay at the base of the local government structure. Subsequently, in his capacity as head of FEDECO, Mr Ovie-Whiskey pronounced that no newly created LGAs could be recognised for election purposes unless they were first created by an amendment to the constitution.[18]

Yet barely a few months after the Justice's first pronouncement, Vice-President Alex Ekwueme was lamenting some State governors' propensity to dissolve the popularly elected LGCs and replace them with 'political party activists and officials'.[19] The Vice-President's observations were borne out by similar developments during the next few years: in Anambra State 23 LGCs were dissolved and the seats of all its elected and appointed members declared vacant, while 54 new LGAs were created and 'sole administrators' appointed to run them. In Gongola, 17 local government management committees were dissolved and 40 new areas created. The Ibadan municipal council was broken up. Kwara created 24, Borno 30 new local governments. Similar developments then occurred in Lagos and Cross River States as well, and spread into virtually all the remaining States (see Table 9.1).

Table 9.1   *Proliferation of local government areas, October 1979 — December 1981*

	No. of LGCs October 1979	New LGCs	Total 1981	Percentage Increase
Anambra	23	41	54	134.8
Bauchi	16	27	43	168.8
Bendel	19	41	60	215.8
Benue	13	10	34	101.5
Borno	18	34	52	188.9
Cross River	17	30	47	176.5
Gongola	17	40	57	235.3
Imo	31	29	50	138.1
Kaduna	14	40	54	285.7
Kano	20	9	29	45.0
Kwara	12	12	24	100.0
Lagos	8	15	23	187.5
Niger	9	9	18	100.0
Ogun	10	20	30	200.0
Ondo	17	2	19	11.0
Oyo	24	30	54	125.0
Plateau	14	7	21	50.0
Rivers	10	—	10	—
Sokoto	19	13	32	68.4
	301	409	710	135.9

Source: Adapted from Egwurube, 1982:4

Quite clearly, State governments' actions in arbitrarily reorganising, removing and interfering with local governments were contrary to the spirit of the *Guidelines* and the constitution. The continued failure to carry out local government elections and the proliferation of local governments to as many as one thousand by December 1983 did in some measure 'make nonsense of the constitutional provisions',[20] which foresaw forms of constructive co-operation between these levels of government. In early 1983, *West Africa* of 10 January concluded that Nigerian local government was in 'disarray', pointing to the fact that 'now there is not a single local government council . . . which can be said to conform to the constitution's requirement that each state shall ensure the existence of a system of local government by democratically elected local government councils'. It is most significant that the post-Shagari military government', as one of its first decisive acts, restored the number of LGCs to the original 301.

With the general heightening of confrontational politics after 1980, and in particular with the polarisation of political power between the NPN-dominated centre and the twelve States controlled by opposition parties, the right of disposition over local government became the object of a structural power struggle. Although the constitution was silent on which government had the power to create and alter local governments, and on which procedures were to be applied in doing so, the dominant legal and political interpretation gradually came to agree that the States had such power. This was inferred from several sources. Section 7(1) of the constitution both guaranteed the existence of a local government system and empowered the State government to ensure the LGCs' existence 'under a law which provides for the establishment, structure, composition, finance and functions of such councils'. These provisions were taken to mean that all important aspects of local government fell under the legislative purview of State governments. But at the same time – by implication – they were supposed to shield the LGCs from direct and arbitrary intervention on the part of the State executive, as in the Bendel State case just cited. From a different perspective, Item 31 of the exclusive legislative list specifically removed from the National Assembly's powers the right to create or modify local governments. This was only marginally qualified by Item 11 of the concurrent legislative list which enabled the National Assembly to legislate on voter registration and procedures regulating elections to LGCs.[21] Similarly, the areas named in the constitution were not expressly defined as local government areas (some could in fact be taken to refer to cities), nor were the boundaries of these areas constitutionally specified (see Nwabueze, 1982b:60–1).

These considerations relating to the constitutional dimensions of State-local government relations illustrate a peculiar contradiction of Nigerian federalism. *On the one hand*, the 'nationalised' elites,[22] whether led by politicians engaged in partisan struggles or by soldiers acting as a 'corrective', had and have no vital interest in establishing a local government system which, by entrenching local autonomy and providing institutional foci for resistance to State and national development plans, patronage networks and political control, impedes their development strategy. Again, this would be dysfunctional. Rather, the superordinate governments' interest in local government lies in rationalising, not transforming, it. The resultant pattern of interactions is geared to ensuring that the local governments operate more efficiently and rationally as *instruments* of central and, in particular, State policies, but entirely within the policy frameworks and political interests of the ruling party, party coalition or military government. The fundamental problem which develops in the process of the 'homogenisation' of intra-State politics, however, is that 'grassroots democracy', which is supposed to facilitate and sustain local initiatives, is in fact undermined by being made the object of partisan politics or military policy.

On the other hand, the respective strategies and goals underlying military and civilian instrumentalisation of local government have very differentiated effects on the latter. Within a constitutional framework of a formal separation and division of powers, 'rationalisation' for the political elite means the establishment of more or less secure networks of patronage and clienteles, a process which is best furthered if intra-State political control is consolidated vis-à-vis the central government and over the local governments themselves. Thus the more the State government elites are able to roll back the federal presence in 'their' States (especially where State elites represent a different political party from that dominant at the centre), while preventing the tendentially autonomous local governments from establishing countervailing patronage networks, the more they are able to consolidate their own positions. Here again, it is evident that the unmitigated pursuit of elite interests through state institutions was in fact incompatible with the democratic purposes for which those structures were (theoretically) designed. The new powers and revenues accorded to local governments after 1976 attracted not only the local commercial capitalists (as discussed above) but also the State political class who sensed both possibilities for further self-aggrandisement and a means of enhancing their sources of political support. The State-centred political class, consciously and right from the outset, set out to subordinate local government to itself – in violation of both the spirit and the letter of the *Guidelines* and the 1979 Constitution. Elected LGC members were dismissed arbitrarily and the councils were often dissolved long before the expiration of their terms. In their place, State officials appointed caretaker councils and 'management committees' staffed by party members and reliable political allies whose central concern was to advance their party's and their own interests and who remained beholden to the State governor and his party. Furthermore, the State administrative apparatus permeated local government operations and hence impinged on their autonomy:[23]

> State governments minutely scrutinised and altered local government budgets. The secretaries of the new authorities, most of them administrative officers seconded from the States, were loyal to their State rather than their local government superiors, and acted as colonial District Officers or French Prefects rather than as servants of autonomous bodies. States even held up – as they are still alleged to do – federal allocations to the local governments.

The States' failure to organise LGC elections scheduled in 1980 – indeed, not a single local government election was held during the Second Republic[24] or since – amounted to an outright denial of democracy. (Admittedly, State electoral commissioners did finally agree, in late 1983, to hold nation-wide local government elections on 21 January 1984, but these were again deferred following the New Year *coup*.)

But under a centralist, command-oriented military government, the more 'classical' local government functions of development and mobilisation gain in relative importance, mainly because the shunting aside of the political class makes local government one of the few remaining agencies – along with the civil service and traditional rulers – through which the military elite is able to perceive popular needs and moods and to transmit commands. The military's longer-term interests in 'feedback', execution and stability are served by the presence of a relatively greater autonomy of local government – thus, as S. E. Oyovbaire suggests, in a way refuting the conventional interpretation that federalism 'is basically incompatible with authoritarianism or military rule'.[25] In the Nigerian context at least, grassroots federalism has so far fared better under military government, perhaps in part confirming that a secure, more or less legitimate central authority is a prerequisite to effective decentralisation at the base.

At the very core of State-local government relations is the issue of finance. No federal or State government – the literature is uncharacteristically unanimous on this – has ever delivered local government allocations in the prescribed or agreed amounts. If military governments have tended to be equally parsimonious, civilian governments have inclined to be more arbitrary and/or explicitly political in determining amounts and timing. Both have pre-empted some of local governments' traditional sources of revenue, but both have also provided new forms of allocations contingent on LGCs' utility to other levels of government.

This suggests yet another contradiction in the Nigerian local government system. On the one hand, the regular provision of sufficient and predictable revenues to local governments stands to alleviate their chronic problems of underfunding and short-term planning perspectives. For these reasons the 1976 reform was followed by the cancellation of all local governments' outstanding debts and the provision of a start-up grant of N100 m., 75% of which was distributed according to population and 25% shared equally. State governments were supposed to match this federal grant, but for various reasons did not. The 1979 Constitution, in Section 149, specified that LGCs were entitled to receive a fixed share of national revenues, an entitlement which was eventually quantified by the 1981 Allocation of Revenue Act at 10%. The formula for distributing the local government allocation was 50% divided equally among all LGAs, 40% according to population, and 10% by land area. Again, State governments were to contribute a fixed general grant to the local governments via the State-Local Government Joint Account.

On the other hand, the resulting de-emphasis on locally generated revenues and growing dependence on superordinate governments reduce local initiative and increase dependency. Where these developments coincide with central-State political confrontation – as was the case after 1979 – local government becomes a virtual client of the partisan State government. Given the class composition of the LGCs and the circumstances of their coming to power, their first concern was for self-aggrandisement. Following the promulgation of the 1981 Revenue Act, the Nigerian Association of Local Governments put forward proposals for massive increases in councillors' emoluments and lavish benefits,[26] entirely in the spirit of similar initiatives taken by the federal and State legislators two years earlier. State governments were in many cases (notably Bendel State) quite prepared to accord huge pay increases to the LGC officials, particularly since these could be made from the anticipated federal grant.

Conversely, however, State governments did away with several key traditional sources of local government revenue. Lagos State government, for instance, undertook property rating taxation, while the State governments of Kaduna and Kano abolished *haraji* and *jangali* taxes, as well as the PAYE system, for political reasons. Local government accordingly became more and more dependent on statutory grants. Although post-reform statistics are incomplete – and entirely lacking for the Second Republic – a study of six States for the period 1976–9 hints at the size of this dependence. Whereas prior to the reform the majority of local government revenue had been internally generated, the corresponding post-1976 shares of locally raised funds in the total budget were: Bendel 23.5%, Kwara 19.8%, Lagos 28.7%, Ogun 14.8%, Ondo 13.4%, Oyo 10.7%.[27]

Thus, the record of local government during the Second Republic paralleled that of the federal and State governments; it was one of waste, growing dependency and missed opportunities. The increased revenues from the federal account – albeit never in the promised amounts, and almost always without the State contribution – were therefore not used for democratisation and development, but squandered on higher material costs resulting from the excessive fragmentation of local government units, higher administrative expenditures for larger salaries and bureaucratic proliferation, clientelism and corruption resulting from political appointments (which also intensified the problem of skilled personnel), and, in many States, greater expenditures resulting from State policies that encumbered the local governments with new tasks (for instance, Universal Primary Education in the LOOOB States).

Since the 1983 *coup*, the military's policy with respect to local government financing has moved back toward fixed-percentage grants from federal revenues, a policy which, of course, functions best in an expanding economy. The Buhari government, owing its tenuous legitimacy in the first place to its claim to be able to restore economic efficiency and rationality in a situation of diminishing revenues and to manage austerity, ·reduced – or in many cases did not even assign – revenues due to local governments via the States.[28] Nevertheless, a 'Committee on the Review of Local Government Administration in Nigeria', whose white paper was submitted shortly before the Babangida *coup* of 27 August 1985, recommended *inter alia* that the 10% of the Federal Revenue Account accruing to local governments be paid promptly and in full through the State-Local Government Local Account. Recognising that it is 'unrealistic' to expect State governments to pay 10% of their *total* revenues to local governments, the report's authors proposed that 10% of *internally generated* State revenues be paid to the LGCs.[29] State governments were also to pay the salaries of primary school teachers, thus removing an item that has accounted for up to 60% of local government expenditures. And finally, certain local revenue sources were reintroduced: *jangali* taxes, poll or flat rate taxes, community taxes, tenement rates, entertainment taxes, radio and television fees, and the like.

The Buhari government began, and the Babangida regime continues, to implement these reforms. Though hampered by a drastically diminished 'national cake' from which to allocate local government revenues as well as by the dubious administrative capacity of local government to undertake these increased tasks, the reforms do attempt to combine the stability and long-range planning perspective of a guaranteed allocation with the self-sufficiency-inducing incentives of relative local autonomy and revenue generation. Nevertheless, such measures, implemented from above and not preceded by legitimating local elections, do not appear in themselves capable of establishing a viable system of grassroots democracy in Nigeria.

(ii) *Relations between State authority and traditional authorities*. Until the 1978 Land Use Decree, as anchored intact in the 1979 Constitution (Section 274(5)(d)) and reaffirmed by post-1983 military governments, the functions of traditional rulers included the determination of customary law and practice with respect to rights of land tenure and land use. But that Decree removed all aspects of land ownership, control and management from the competence of the traditional rulers and councils, and vested all lands within each State – save only lands already under the control of the federal government and its agencies – in the then Military Governor of the respective State. The principle has survived subsequent changes in government form. The governor's mandate is to administer such land 'for the use and common benefit of all Nigerians'.[30]

While all land is thus vested in and subject to overall disposition by the State governor, its *control* and *management* are statutorily allocated: (a) in the case of non-urban land, to the local governments, and (b) in the case of urban land, to the State governor. The two agencies are to consult with, respectively, a Land Allocation Advisory Committee and a State Land Use Allocation Committee. In a sense, private land ownership in perpetuity has been eliminated (in so far as it existed as an 'overlay' upon traditionally communal forms of land holding), since the highest interest which an individual can hold or acquire in a piece of land is now a so-called 'right of occupancy' which may be granted for a fixed or indeterminate period – in other words, is revocable. Land so held may not be sold, leased, mortgaged or otherwise alienated without the governor's consent. The decree also provides for differential limitations on the size of individuals' landholdings as at the date of commencement of the decree (29 March 1978), as follows: where the land was developed, no limit; where the land was undeveloped and located in an urban area, half a hectare; and where the land was undeveloped and in a non-urban area, 500 hectares if for agricultural purposes or 5,000 hectares if for grazing purposes.

While the Land Use Decree has thus in a sense suspended *dysfunctional* private land ownership and made the right of occupancy conditional on the more or less productive utilisation of the property (insofar as these regulations are enforced at all), it has also done away with (or at least failed to make provision for) the preservation of former customary rights or native customs (also considered dysfunctional) with respect to the use and occupation of land. The 1978 decree contains nothing comparable to Section 50 of the old Land Tenure Law which empowered the local chiefs and native courts to control lands held under customary rights of occupancy and to mediate in disputes. The former law, intended to operate as an intervening layer or buffer between the people and the government, was apparently seen as perpetuating traditional rulers' powers and impeding the deployment of land for 'modern' economic development.

Here again, then, the overriding goal of development, within the framework of the dependent capitalist economy, provides the conceptual key to an understanding of the land 'reform' measures and the diminution of the traditional rulers' powers as a component part of them. This may be inferred, for example, from the then Lt.-General Obasanjo's national broadcast on the report of the Land Use Panel which, underlining the goal of 'fast economic and social transformation', asserted that 'lack of immediate availability of land for use when required by all concerned had become a major obstacle to economic development and national progress'.[31] This is, of course, essentially a correct assessment inasmuch as communal land ownership generally – but not always; consider the case of cocoa farming – constitutes an obstacle to the cultivation of plantation and cash crops and the development of capital- and technology-intensive forms of agriculture:

> The present land tenure system in the southern States makes it impossible for enterprising farmers to mobilise their labour and capital resources as freely as they would want to (because) first, the sale of land is rare thereby confining a farmer and his future generations to his family land; and second, the partible system of farmland inheritance leads to fragmentation of farm holdings. . . . In particular, these conditions have adversely affected treecrop cultivation which normally requires large acreage. People frown on the use of the family land for growing perennial crops which would mean a diminution of land available for food production. (Akinbode, 1978:20)

For Dr Akinbode and others committed to this development strategy, the basic problem of agricultural development is thus the 'inefficient allocation and utilization of our natural resources, especially land', so that the Land Use Decree is to be welcomed as 'a rational allocative mechanism for land'. From this point of view, the landlords, traditional rulers and family or kinship heads are objectively an obstacle to development and, therefore, 'in the interest of society as a whole' must be prepared to 'sacrifice their particular interests'.

The converse impediment to productive capitalist development is the group of land speculators, profiteers and the like, whose activities Lt.-General Obasanjo saw as generating gross inequality and a disincentive to development. This helps to explain the decree's limitations on property size. These latter provisions, however, are extensively mitigated by the fact that the decree is silent on the size of developed land owned prior to 29 March 1978, that no upward limit on developed land holdings is set, that compensation rates are extremely generous, and that individual occupancy up to the fixed limits is simultaneously possible in any number of States.[32]

Thus the 1978 land 'reform', whatever the intentions of its framers, has effectively 'reformed' (or rationalised) only the communal land-tenure system. To have achieved all its stated objectives, it would have had to (a) couple land reform with agricultural reform, which was attempted, belatedly and somewhat illogically, with the 'Green Revolution' launched in the first legislative period of the Second Republic, and then only from above, and (b) ensure effective land redistribution as a precondition for small- and medium-holding capitalist agriculture; this too, though provided for in the decree, has not been implemented. For these and other reasons the *Daily Times* of 11 May called the decree anything but a socialist law, arguing that it was a

> clear licence for the bourgeois politicians, bureaucrats, businessmen, estate agents, lawyers etc. anxious to build up private wealth rapidly to utilize bourgeois land laws, the judicial system and the capitalist market mechanism to intensify the break-up of communal lands.

Some empirical evidence for this assertion has been furnished by Peter Koehn. Though confined to land-use applications in Kano and Bauchi States during the last years of the Obasanjo military government, and though by no means drawn from a comprehensive or 'scientific' sample, Koehn's findings correlate convincingly, on an impressionistic level, with more or less well-known nationwide trends. He demonstrates that, in the two States concerned, the provisions of the land tenure laws and decree were systematically used by the 'process gatekeepers' to enrich the wealthy and well-connected and to prevent those without wealth and influence even from gaining access to the land-allocation process. In particular, those employed in State and, to a lesser extent, federal bureaucracies were most successful in their applications, followed by private Nigerian businessmen (self-employed and traders) and representatives of transnational firms. By contrast, 'poor rural and urban residents were effectively barred from all types of statutory rights of occupancy' mainly by restricting access and selectively controlling entry to the State land-allocation process (1983:467–8, 481). Scarcely any traditional rulers are to be found in Koehn's group of successful applicants.

It was in the logic of the 1979–83 (formally) liberal–democratic system, with its partisan politics, multiplicity of parties and at times intense political competition, that it should have further undermined the essentially 'apolitical' role which traditional rulers are supposed to play. Indeed, traditional rulers, who were prevented by the 1976 LGC reform from running for local office, were *ipso facto* excluded from participation in the Constitution Drafting Committee and Constituent Assembly and hence from the constitution-making process itself.[33] Analogous to their situation in the First Republic, the emirs and chiefs were increasingly pressed to become directly involved in politics in less institutionalised ways: if their involvement was on behalf, or at least in the interests, of the dominant political groups and/or their policies, then the traditional rulers generally managed to enhance their own position, wealth and influence in the recivilianised system – though paradoxically usually at the cost of eroding the 'traditional' aspects of their rulership. Conversely, non-collaboration with the political class in many cases resulted in direct persecution, using all the means of the 'modern' state, of the recalcitrant traditional ruler – at times abolishing or gravely weakening the emirate or cheftancy, but at others reinforcing and renewing it.

It has been argued that the central, and for the time being, immutable 'political' quality of traditional rule is its continuous legitimacy, which in turn derives from its closeness to the people and its identity with their collective memories and aspirations. Particularly in the rural areas, the traditional ruler's influence is often crucial to the successful implementation of State or federal mobilisation or development measures, and

> no occasion supports this contention better than the period of a national campaign. The rural health worker needs the co-operation of the village and hamlet heads to reach his targets. They have so far not declined to give. If governors know this, and there is no reason to suggest they don't, they will not be accusing them for lack of co-operation.[34]

But in the Second Republic the traditional rulers' influence was not limited to the implementation of policies and programmes formulated by the 'political' leaders; it extended into the politicians' bases of mass popular support. This was especially so, since none of the five political parties 'licensed' in 1978, nor the sixth admitted in 1983, aspired to transform the post-colonial socio-economic situation. For these reasons politicians in the Second Republic by and large assiduously courted traditional rulers. The proffered inducements – which were rarely rejected – included pensions, 'favour-able' settlements of chieftancy disputes, patronage appointments for the ruler or his kin, ongoing consultations respecting new policies or allocations, etc. Indeed, during the last election campaign of the Second Republic, President Shagari committed his government to a comprehensive constitutional amendment to enhance the position of the traditional rulers.[35]

In return, the traditional rulers were expected to render a whole series of legitimating services to the politicians, ranging from public endorsement of a candidate or party and public appearances on behalf of the politicians, to the conferment of honorary titles upon them. The pressure for involvement in politics also emanated from 'below': from traditional rulers' 'subjects' who, frequently distrusting or misunderstanding the state bureaucracy and the elected politicians, pressed them to intervene directly on their behalf. Thus emirs and obas

> were asked to lead delegations to Governors, the President of the Senate and the Speakers of the Houses to ask for their separate local government area or the siting of a local government headquarters in a particular village or town, for the creation of a separate State, the location of a particular industry or government project in their area, etc. (Offiong, 1982:9)

The basic anomaly in this situation is that this substantial *de facto* political power accruing to the traditional rulers has not been institutionally anchored or otherwise guaranteed. It has already been demonstrated that their structural positions in federal, State and, since 1976, local governments have been abolished. Like the 1976 Traditional Rulers' Edict, the 1979 Constitution scarcely recognised their political existence, apart from allowing them to be members of mere advisory bodies such as the Federal Council of State and the State Council of Chiefs.

Moreover, most traditional rulers are paid according to civil service scales, thus bringing them in close proximity to the state bureaucracy and increasing their depend-ence (a) under civilian government, on the 'modern' legislatures (which fix their salaries and employment conditions) and executives (which implement them), and (b) under military government, on the State Governors who perform both functions. In this context, Mohammed Haruna rightly referred to a process of 'keeping traditional rulers in political harness with fat salaries, fringe benefits and undefensible perrequisites', which he documented with the example of Benue State where[36]

. . . the chairman of the Council of Chiefs in the state now earns 21,000 Naira annually, a salary far ahead of that of the country's Chief Justice. First class and second class chiefs earn 17,500 and 12,000 Naira respectively and third class chiefs earn 8,700 Naira.

Under civilian rule in particular, the state was able to create a variety of lucrative positions and sinecures for 'co-operative' traditional rulers: as *ex-officio* members of local councils (notably in Kaduna), as chairmen of public boards and commissions, and as honorary office-holders such as university chancellors. Frequently, too, village heads were elevated to first, second- or third-class chiefs; chieftancies or emirates were created where none had previously existed; and new 'palaces' (= residences) were built, with government funds, for the new or promoted rulers.

The cumulative effect of all these measures and omissions has been to reinforce the tendencies under discussion. Making traditional rulers in fact into public servants prevented them, both constitutionally and in accordance with the 1977 Electoral Decree, from contesting public office. In theory – that is, following from the 1979 Constitution, Section 173(4) which provided that appointees as State Commissioners must be qualified for election as members of the State House of Assembly, in combination with Section 10(f) which barred public servants from becoming commissioners – traditional rulers also were not permitted to serve as members of State or federal executive bodies. The point was reinforced by the Electoral Decree, section 73(1), which simply precluded emirs, obas, obis or paramount chiefs from running for elected office. However, traditional rulers were here and there appointed to State executive positions, on the tenuous grounds that they could not in fact be considered as civil servants, but rather occupied a 'special position' in the constitutional order. An important precedent was established when in October 1979 Governor Bola Ige of Oyo State named the Ataoja of Oshogbo as commissioner without portfolio and another oba as special adviser to the governor. The Oba of Benin was appointed a special adviser to the Bendel State government. Though the appointments held, the traditional rulers concerned became identified with the respective Governors' party, the UPN. With their official neutrality thus compromised, they stood to become political targets should a different party gain State power – or for that matter, should the governors be succeeded by others from the same party. For similar reasons, over-'politicised' traditional rulers are of little use to a 'corrective' and ostensibly 'non-political' military regime.

But, as already suggested, a refusal to be drawn into partisan politics could also result in severe persecution of traditional rulership. Within weeks of recivilianisation the Borno State government transferred to the local governments the traditional rulers' power to appoint village and district heads. In Anambra State, the Governor removed the Obi of Onitsha from the Council of State, while in Imo State eight traditional rulers were deposed and replaced. One of the replacements, as a non-indigene, was not even qualified for appointment. In Oyo and Ogun States there were many incidents of executive confrontation with traditional rulers, threats and counter-threats, cases of wrongful de-stooling and the like. Again in Imo State, the House of Assembly in 1981 passed a chieftancy law abolishing the title 'His Royal Highness' as a form of addressing traditional rulers. And even in Kano State, Governor Alhaji Abubakar Rimi, though not exactly 'waging a jihad' (Offiong, 1982:7) against the Emir of Kano, did attempt to undermine the ruler's position by appointing a number of first-class chiefs over his opposition, an act which, in the wider context of the confrontation between PRP populism and the NPN alliance with the Islamic aristocracy, helped to set off religious rioting in July 1981.

As these events suggest, the treatment of traditional rulers was at least partly dependent on political party policies and leaders since 'as the constitutional channels for the participation of traditional rulers (decreased), the opportunities for participation in the parties increased' (Reed, 1982:38). The NPN, as the party which best mirrored the *status quo*, not surprisingly was most supportive of traditional rule. Its 1979 and 1983 manifestoes spoke of the importance of the institution as an instrument of stability and law and order, and pledged to secure the rulers' participation in governance (and to remunerate them accordingly). The PRP by contrast was committed to the eventual abolition of the institution: Governor Rimi's dispute with the Emir of Kano typified the party's attitude. The GNPP, though without a clearly defined policy on the subject, reacted strongly to what it perceived as the traditional rulers' support of the NPN. In (GNPP-controlled) Borno State, for instance, the deposition of a traditional ruler set off riots in June 1980 in which fourteen NPN supporters were killed. The NPP was also quite vindictive towards non-co-operative chiefs, as the Anambra and Imo State incidents demonstrate. Much the same may be said of the UPN which, on the one hand, consistently rewarded friendly obas, obis and chiefs with, among other things, government positions and pensions, but, on the other hand, threatened or actually acted against traditional rulers who failed to support it, most particularly those suspected of backing the NPN.

With the return of military government, however, the traditional rulers' position, like that of local government, has largely reverted to the *status quo ante*. Relatively insulated now from partisan political manoeuvring, they have *de facto* – as before – moved partly into the role of 'people's representatives', communicating local needs and wants to the military leaders or bureaucratic officials. In the 'apolitical' and conciliatory ethos which the current military regime aspires to establish, the visible support of the traditional rulers is an essential legitimacy-producing factor. Even more than their predecessors, therefore, both the Buhari and Babangida regimes have taken steps to win over and enlist the emirs, obas and chiefs.[37] But at the same time there have been no indications of any substantial rollback of their 'rationalised' status and no restoration of their institutionalised rights and privileges.

It would appear, then, that – assuming the continuation of elite rule at all three tiers – the objective socio-economic and cultural bases and functions of traditional rule have been irrevocably undermined. This, of course, is precisely what the 'modernising' political elite have claimed for decades. However, the neo-colonial capitalist development strategy is unable, at this stage, to overcome the economic disarticulation and dependency and gain the mass support which would be the precondition for eliminating the continuing popular appeal of traditional rule and to obtain for itself the identities and loyalties now vested in the obas, emirs and chiefs. Hence the *subjective* need for traditional rule is likely to persist for some time to come, particularly for the duration of military government, albeit succumbing more and more to the immense 'rationalising' pressures discussed here. Such projections are of course contingent upon the survival of elite rule and the constellation of interests which it represents.

'Grassroots' politics, in the Nigerian context, is hardly the appropriate metaphor for actual power-political relationships operating at the political base. Local and traditional governing institutions have been and are being more and more instrumentalised, (a) by the superordinate tiers which continue to arrogate their functions and powers, mainly in the interests (b) of the 'modernising' elites who, as *politicians*, politicise them and incorporate them into patronage and clientele networks, and, as *soldiers*, subsume them into chains of command and the production of legitimacy. Either way, local government loses its autonomy and links with the local population, and traditional rule loses its independence and authenticity. Popular participation, involvement and democratisation are at best secondary or tertiary goals.

Yet as central and State governments succeed each other without effectively 'penetrating' the population, local and particularly traditional rule is constantly renewed as the major source of continuity and order bridging periodic crises and breakdowns. The formal structures of federalism and the legal provisions respecting the composition and functions of traditional authority – as Philip Mawhood reminds us with his case study of developments in the Kano emirate[38] – by no means define the real influence of 'grassroots' authority in society:

> In a system where all modern positions of authority are available to patronage or popular election, the chiefs may even stand higher relatively than they did; traditional legitimacy is one of the few permanent assets that a political actor can possess.

The point applies in particular to local government, where, as has been demonstrated, traditional rule continues to exert a crucial, if not dominant – though *de facto* – influence. The operation of local government, and especially the performance of its 'developmental' tasks – whether these are defined from above or below – would be unthinkable without the co-operation of traditional authorities and the popular mobilisation that they may promote or inhibit. At the same time, traditional rulers have a vital stake in the viability of local government inasmuch as it provides them with links to the 'modern' political system, a means of realising their interests and goals, and hence represents a large part of their *raison d'être*. Some effective combination of local and traditional rule, perhaps in the form of an institutionalised interest association, therefore suggests itself as a possible means of consolidating 'grassroots' interests. The opportunity to do so is probably greatest under a relatively legitimate military government in its early stages since, as has been seen, a wider scope of relative political and fiscal autonomy prevails, and the 'corrective' military regime must rely on traditional authorities to bolster its own legitimacy. Moreover, it depends in part on local government when it initiates the inevitable[39] recivilianisation exercise, an exercise currently pledged for 1990.

Unless and until solidarity develops at the 'grassroots', however, the paradox of Nigerian basis government will remain: the more these institutions are instrumentalised and deformed, the more they persist. The paradox, as already suggested, can be accounted for by the permanent contradiction of 'grassroots' government, namely, that even as it must foster mobilisation from below it has to serve elite interests above. Within the parameters of neo-colonial capitalism, the contradiction is expressed, for the time being, as a stalemate.

Notes

1. B. Harris, 'The Reorganisation of Local Government Under Military Rule in Nigeria 1966–74', in Collins, 1980, p. 213.
2. For accounts of these trends, see Ola, 1984, chapters 2–4; Harris, *op. cit.*, pp. 213ff.; Aliyu, 1978/9, pp. 131–5.
3. O. Oyediran and E. A. Gboyega, 'Local Government and Administration', in Oyediran, 1979, p. 169.
4. A. Abu, 'A Review of the Local Government Reforms', *New Nigerian*, 27 September 1979.
5. A. F. Gboyega and O. Oyediran, 'A View From Ibadan', in Panter-Brick, 1978, p. 266. Aliyu, 1978/9, p. 137, emphasises the prominence of rigging and bribery in this context.

6. A. Y. Aliyu, 'As Seen in Kaduna', in Panter-Brick, 1978, p. 277.

7. J. O. Egwurube, 'Local Government Under the Second Republic – Some Problems of Definition', paper presented at a National Conference on Problems of Political Stability and the Future of the Second Republic, Ahmadu Bello University, Zaria, 26–29 April 1982, mimeo., p. 8.

8. Cf. Ajibola and Oyejide, 1975, p. 123.

9. *Report of the Proceedings of the Constituent Assembly*, 994 (1977).

10. The LGCs' three-year terms ran out in 1979, but the scheduling of new elections depended on the preparation of a prescribed new voters' register by FEDECO – despite the existence of the 1979 federal register – which in turn depended on a National Assembly bill to authorise the exercise. For various reasons, however, the National Assembly failed to enact the bill.

11. Both examples cited in Sorkaa, forthcoming.

12. Consensus and recommendations reproduced in *New Nigerian*, 21 May 1979.

13. As reported in *West Africa*, 29 March 1982, pp. 842–3.

14. For a historical account of the traditional rulers' position under colonialism, see especially Crowder and Ikime, 1970.

15. On this, see Reed, 1982, p. 20.

16. Ralph Miliband, *Capitalist Democracy in Britain*, London, 1982, p. 137.

17. *New Nigerian*, 29 February 1980.

18. *West Africa*, 12 April 1982, p. 1025.

19. *New Nigerian*, 31 May 1980.

20. *West Africa*, 1 November 1982, p. 2825.

21. Reliable guides through this legal morass are: S. Ade Oladusu, 'Who Creates Local Governments: States or Federal Government?', *New Nigerian*, 8 February 1980 and Joye and Igweike, 1982, p. 95–8.

22. I define and discuss this concept in my *Political Economy, Political Class and Political System in Recivilianised Nigeria*, Working Paper No. 47, Boston University, African Studies Centre, 1981.

23. *West Africa*, 10 January 1983, p. 80.

24. Lagos State alone sought to hold LGC elections early in 1980, but failed to do so partly because of the lack of an adequate voters' register and partly due to a court verdict which restrained the State from conducting separate elections (*Daily Times*, 27 June 1983).

25. S. E. Oyovbaire, *Federalism in Nigeria: A Study in the Development of the Nigerian State*, London and Basingstoke, 1985, p. xv.

26. For details and amounts, see A. Gboyega, 'Local Government Reform in Nigeria', in P. Mahwood (ed.), *Local Government in the Third World*, Chichester etc., 1983, p. 239. This paragraph, and the one following, rely heavily on his arguments.

27. L. Adamolekun, O. Osemwota, D. Olowu, *Report on the Performance of Local Governments in Bendel, Kwara, Lagos, Ogun, Ondo and Oyo States*, December 1980.

28. See *West Africa*, 30 July 1984, p. 1523.

29. As reported in *West Africa*, 26 August 1985, p. 1750.

30. Land Use Decree, Part I – General. Considered solely at this general level, the Decree can readily be (mis)interpreted as an intended 'socialist measure, as a charter for the common man, a charter of egalitarianism and of social justice', Ben O. Nwabueze, 'Governmental Powers in Relation to Economic Affairs and the Economy under the New Constitution', lecture delivered to the Nigerian Institute of International Affairs, 14 February 1979, reproduced in booklet form by NIIA, 1979, p. 26. That this is by no means the case, will be demonstrated below.

31. Lt.-General Olusegun Obasanjo, 'Broadcast to the Nation on the Report of the Land Use Panel', Lagos, Federal Ministry of Information, mimeo., n.d. (1978).

32. For a reliable interpretation of the related provisions, see Nkemnacho, 1978/9.

33. True, holders of 'non-paramount chieftancy titles and offices' were permitted to sit in the CDC and CA. But the binding decision on which positions were paramount was the province of the State Military Governor. Thus Reed, 1982:34 concludes that 'although minor chiefs were allowed to participate in the ratification of Nigeria's new constitution, majòr traditional

rulers were excluded. This specific exclusion of traditional rulers both from the selection process for a Constituent Assembly as well as from membership in the Assembly stands in direct contrast to earlier constitutional review processes.'

34. *New Nigerian*, editorial, 16 June 1980.
35. See *Daily Times*, 18 July 1983.
36. *New Nigerian*, 7 January 1983.
37. See *Africa*, April 1984, p. 10.
38. Philip Mawhood, 'The Place of Traditional Political Authority in African Pluralism', *Civilisations*, Vol. 33, No. 1 (1983), pp. 226 and 229.
39. I take it as axiomatic that any Nigerian 'corrective' – as opposed to revolutionary or even radical-military regime would sooner or later have to recivilianise. See my 'The Nigerian New Year's Coup of December 31, 1983: A Class Analysis', *Journal of Black Studies*, Vol. 16, No. 1 (September 1985).

10

The State Bureaucracy

Whether or not the Nigerian state bureaucracy is regarded as a manifestation of 'the overdeveloped postcolonial state',[1] or in terms of a 'state elite',[2] 'bureaucratic bourgeoisie',[3] etc., it is evident that it is collectively the largest, most cohesive and – together with the military – the best organised and most continuous 'modernising' institution in society. Particularly in chapters 3 and 4, as well as 6 and 7, it has been demonstrated that the bureaucrats are an essential, though largely unproductive, corporate interest group in civilian and military regimes alike.

Specificity and the Nigerian 'ecology'

Not by chance, most of the relatively few analyses of the specificity of the Nigerian bureaucracy start explicitly from the work of Fred W. Riggs – itself also rooted largely in American structural-functionalism and systems theory – which advocates an 'ecological approach' to the study of public administration.[4] According to this approach, the Nigerian bureaucracy, 'as a subsystem within the larger system, . . . exists in the social setting of Nigeria and hence is conditioned by history and tradition, as well as physical factors of geography, climate and resources, collectively known as the ecology of the bureaucracy'.[5]

Any argument based on context or 'ecology' or 'environment' must have at least two dimensions: a diachronic one and a synchronic one. This book so far has attempted to constitute a diachronic analysis of the historical and socio-economic evolution of Nigerian political life from the colonial period to the present. Here, therefore, let us merely recall some salient developments as they have affected, and continue to affect, the 'ecology' of the Nigerian state bureaucracy.

First, the administrative apparatus inherited by the Nigerian post-independence government was in all important respects *identical to the British bureaucratic-authoritarian system* which preceded it. Just prior to, and immediately following the British departure (1954–66: from the Gorsuch Commission Report to the first army *coup*), the civil service was thoroughly 'Nigerianised'. This process of transferring power to the 'successor elite' in the state bureaucracy thus produced several permanent structural deficiencies: (i) an administrative or 'intendant' class separated by training, education and wealth from most of the population; (ii) a dearth of qualified personnel at all levels; (iii) a network of patrons and clients, and hence a great potential for corruption; (iv) a stratified and ossified civil service structure not interested in popular needs and demands which, moreover, was cleft between seniors and juniors and rent by rivalries between the older 'generalists' and the emerging 'professional-technical cadres'; and (v) the nucleus of a self-interested state class attempting to transform the political power which their positions conferred into the economic power which it could 'buy'; this of course implied the exploitation of ethnicity and sectionalism to entrench one's political power.

Second, like politics, administration in the First Republic was highly *regionalised*. In the Regions – the chief recipients of capital surplus (for example, from the Marketing Boards) and the main arenas of ethnic politics – political power and with it economic power were concentrated (see chapter 3). As the unified colonial civil service was gradually phased out after 1954 and the independence government was prepared for centrifugal federalism, the most able and experienced civil servants joined the Regional bureaucracies. There, they were closely allied with the dominant political and economic elites and indeed in part merged with them. Furthermore, the bureaucracy, whose existence antedated that of the other political institutions and which therefore by and large attracted the best-qualified people, was *ipso facto* stronger and better organised than the remaining sub-systems such as the parties, executives and legislatures.

Third, the regionalisation of politics also necessitated some measure of trade-off of the principle of merit in favour of the *principle of representativeness*, for instance in the attempts to 'Northernize' the civil service of that less developed Region.[6] Where these attempts failed – producing *inter alia* an influx of Igbo civil servants into the North – the result was open ethnic hostility.

Since then, recruitment, promotion and development policies have had to be directed toward finding an ethnic-territorial balance – if need be, at the expense of 'merit' – in all federal public bodies from government agencies to parastatals. Chapter II of the 1979 Constitution attempted to entrench this principle of balanced representation, which both military and civilian governments have been constrained to adopt in practice. This peculiarly Nigerian variation of social engineering is especially important in the state bureaucracy. For the 'representative bureaucracy' is simultaneously a more overtly 'politicised' bureaucracy. Functionally, it has been shown to produce distorted career patterns, job frustration, insecurity, a propensity to corruption, weakening of corporate morale and firmer links between the administrative and political groupings of the state class. These dysfunctions, however, must be taken into account in the interests of elite consolidation and regime legitimacy, since 'the resultant elite-mass gap' can in this way be 'disguised by the dynamics of inter-ethnic competition which thus acquire autonomous importance'.[7] It has already been demonstrated that much the same may be said, *mutatis mutandis*, about all state agencies, elected or appointed, *de jure* or (as in the case of the military organisation) *de facto*.

Sam Egite Oyovbaire has been a particularly incisive critic of the 'representative bureaucracy' and the effects of applying the 'federal character' maxim. Where the principle is extended beyond expressly political positions such as spoils awarded by a president or governor (or for that matter, a military head of state or governor), he argues, 'it then becomes difficult to insist on competence and experience' in the civil service, parastatals, etc.[8] In a sense, therefore, the federal character principle absolutises ethnic/regional identities even while proclaiming them to be fused into a higher unity in diversity. As Oyovbaire writes elsewhere (1982b), the result is an administratively-legally perpetuated 'ethnic trap'. 'The Nigerian political process is constitutionally ordered to take strong account of sectional identities yet it is equally ordered to transcend them.' He substantiates the point with examples of quota admissions to Nigerian institutions of higher education, a scheme which he sees as having led to 'manipulation of personal identities in terms of states of origin', 'impersonation, dishonesty and corruption' as standard practices, 'communal violence and spoilt relations between sections of the federation', 'the diploma disease', and a 'progressive loss of legitimacy in the quality of education all over the country' (1982b:21–2).

Fourth, the public service has been thoroughly 'politicised' in a comparatively short time. The civil service's ascent to political power under the first series of military governments has already been discussed in detail (chapters 4 and 5). The salient developments in this period were the reassertion of federal supremacy within a modified centralism, together with a growth in the size and scope of the public service attendant upon burgeoning oil revenues, the expansion of state planning, the 'indigenisation' of large sectors of the economy, the growth in patronage networks, and the like. According to Akase Sorkaa's 'conservative estimate', federal and State government personnel increased from 72,000 in 1960 to well over one million by 1983, and the number of public enterprises went from 75 to 500.[9]

In 1972, the growing power of civil servants under General Gowon had led Adebayo Adedeji to assert that 'a new bourgeoisie is forming, a bourgeoisie that Karl Marx could hardly have foreseen – the bourgeoisie of the civil service'.[10] Murtala Mohammed's purges of well over 11,000 public servants in 1975 did weaken the power of the civil service and shake out some of its most corrupt elements – an essential pre-requisite for the return to civilian rule – but at the same time, the inquisition-like atmosphere in which they were conducted and the arbitrary nature of the dismissals lowered public service morale, inhibited its initiative and deprived it of qualified personnel.

A *fifth* factor determining the 'ecology' of Nigerian public administration is the all-pervasive corruption that characterises the system at every level. Despite an absence of quantitative comparative studies, scholars, corporate executives, traders, diplomats and tourists with international experience – including Nigerians – agree that the level of public-sector corruption is as great or greater than anywhere else in the world. Although, for the purposes of this study, it is sufficient merely to establish the presence of excessive corruption, one is inclined to agree with William Brownsberger in rejecting explanations relating to traditional systems of reciprocity, extended-family pressures, ethnicity, nepotism and the like, and in seeing Nigerian public service corruption mainly as *alienated corruption*:[11]

> simply an abuse of office unsoftened by traditional etiquette or love of family – the plain, selfish diversion of public goods to the highest bidder in violation of the western fiduciary norms that are not only embodied in Nigerian law but largely shared by traditional communities.

However that may be, excessive corruption – which repeatedly frustrates the Nigerian elite's proclaimed goals of modernisation, rationalisation, efficient management and development – is said to constitute the environment within which the civil service must operate. Indeed, this 'ecology' is employed as an apology for corporate omissions: how can one expect exceptional standards, the argument goes, from a public service embedded in the (corrupt) society of which it is a part?

Structural problems

The *synchronic* part of this analysis might best start from a description of the state bureaucracy in the Second Republic. The 1979 Constitution[12] recognised the importance of, and made numerous provisions for, the state bureaucracy. Those provisions suggest that an understanding of the Nigerian public service might be facilitated by a more detailed examination of the executive branch as the apex of the public service. Specific references to the categories developed by the 1979 Constitution are perhaps most illustrative here.

Government Ministers (= Cabinet) stand at the head of the executive branch. The relationship between the (elected) President and his (appointed) ministers during the Second Republic has been dealt with in chapter 6. The relevant point here is that, in contrast to the elected Cabinet Ministers of the First Republic, Ministers in the Second Republic were appointed by the President from outside the legislature, thus removing them from even that minimal popular control and ensuring that their primary loyalty would be directed toward the chief executive.

In contrast to military government, the ministerial system interposed an additional political 'layer' or 'buffer' between the top permanent secretaries and the chief executive. This was intended to establish a more functional division of labour within the public service than could be accomplished, for example, under military government where the top permanent civil servants (or non-responsible commissioners) were directly 'elevated' into the upper levels of political policy-making following the removal of the former intermediate stratum. The related problem of the responsibility and loyalty of the permanent secretaries – who under the military had evolved into 'super-permsecs' – was addressed by Section 157 of the constitution which empowered the President to appoint Secretaries to the Government, the Head of the Civil Service, Ambassadors and High Commissioners, and Permanent Secretaries, thus recognising the primarily political nature of these 'posts of confidence' and ensuring that they too would be allocated to party heavyweights, financial supporters and prominent regional/ local figures. This substantial metamorphosis in the top civil service's structure again reflected the thinking of the CDC who believed that such reforms had to

> recognise the special personal relationship which must exist between a minister and certain officials. If the minister is to have a productive working relationship with the Permanent Secretary there must be a feeling of personal understanding to a degree beyond official relationship in the oridinary sense of the term. This cannot be developed adequately if the permanent secretary is imposed by some outside body. It is therefore desirable that the appointment of permanent secretaries and similar posts of confidence . . . be made . . . by the President.

With the incorporation of these and related recommendations into law, therefore, the President's control over the nodal points of the executive arm was extensive. Subject only to the provisions concerning State confirmation and the inclusion of at least one minister from each State, and enjoined only to hold regular meetings with all the Ministers of Government (Section 136(2)), the President was entirely free to determine the number and duties of his ministers – only the post of Attorney-General was constitutionally prescribed – as well as the top secretaries and civil servants attached to the ministry. The principle also extended to the President's staff and advisers, as will be discussed presently.

Presidential control over the public service extended still further, however, and took in the appointment of the chairmen *and* members of the following bodies: the Council of State, the Federal Civil Service Commission, the Federal Electoral Commission, the Federal Judicial Service Commission, the National Defence Council, the National Economic Council, the National Population Commission, the National Security Council, and the Police Service Commission.

An interesting innovation in the civil service structure was the institution of the presidential adviser, who constitutionally (Section 139) was appointed 'at the pleasure of the President' and could be dismissed or given new assignments as he determined. Appointments of advisers were not subject to legislative veto and, once installed, their exclusive responsibility was to the President, not even mitigated by the headship of a portfolio or department which, in the case of the Ministers of the Government, could conceivably have produced a certain 'duality' of loyalties. In the extreme case, the adviser system could even further reduce the principle of executive responsibility and enhance the executive's power vis-à-vis the legislature, in a manner predicted by Bala Takaya:[13]

> These 'staff' posts will likely be sacred extensions of the Chief Executive himself; carrying his immunities and privileges not available to career bureaucrats. There are special assistants, special professional advisers, counsels, administration assistants (supplies), executive assistants (for relations with line ministries/agencies), press liaisons, economic advisers, political advisers and analysts, and so on . . .
>
> The ultimate result is the serious erosion of the delegated powers of the Cabinet Ministries and their diminution into second line executive over even the policy-making responsibilities of the Cabinet Departments. The ministries may end up receiving directives from the 'Aides' rather than from the Chief Executive himself. This is already taking place in the United States.

Ideological solutions

The preceding considerations demonstrate two facets of the tendency of the state bureaucracy to proliferate, in particular under the Second Republic. (a) The increased number of sub-federal units, from three to four Regions, then to 12 and then 19 States, has also increased the number of persons employed by the state/States as the total number of civil services has risen from four to 20, with constant demands, until December 1983, for the creation of still more States. To this must be added the personnel for the hundreds of local governments established or reorganised after the 1976 reform. (b) Recivilianisation produced a larger state apparatus by, first, reintroducing a whole new group of elected legislators, well over 2,000 in all, and, second, by creating an impetus toward executive aggrandisement which itself requires ever more personnel. Remilitarisation, on the other hand, has reduced the number of patronage-political appointments, but has not managed to roll back other sectors of the state bureaucracy beyond certain token retrenchments and retirements.

A fundamental problem of this enlarged bureaucracy is that its *raison d'être* has not grown and adapted apace. At the same time as public revenues have increased immensely in both absolute and relative terms – of the total investment of N82 bn foreseen by the Fourth National Development Plan 1980–85, the public sector's share was N70.5 bn,[14] although these projections of course fell far short of actual revenues – and government development plans for the total 'modernisation' of economy and society have been entrusted to the state bureaucracy for implementation, the entire bureaucratic apparatus remains enmeshed in the neo-colonial capitalist 'environment' with no clear 'mission' or will for radical changes. The wide range of pathologies already described, persists, and the public service remains as before inflexible, remote and resistant to initiatives from below. Paul Collins has summarised the situation as follows (1980:311):

> Apart from the inappropriateness of inherited techniques and procedures, common diagnoses of public service ineffectiveness have also included the following ailments. The first is low productivity, which is seen sometimes as the result of the pursuit of private business activities by public servants and sometimes as the result of resource-wasting rivalries between departments. It is also seen as the result of narrow bureaucratic perspectives that place the premium on controlling resource use, particularly public expenditure, rather than on the output or social and economic impact and benefits of expenditure. The second is poor policy-making and decision-making. The third is low executive or implementation capacity. The fourth and last is defective structures, usually over-centralization.

Neither the Gorsuch Commission (1954/5), which recommended destratification of the public service, nor the Adebo Salaries and Wages Review Commission (1971/2), which considered the problem of emoluments, nor the Udoji Public Service Review Commission (1974), which produced far-ranging organisational and remunerative changes – and was followed by the 1975 Mohammed purge – has been particularly effective in dealing with the problems of inefficiency, partiality and non-accountability to which Collins alludes. The weakness of all attempted reforms so far is that they focus on organisation, administration and 'management' of public service operations, rather than addressing the priorities and values of the political system, or opening that system to broader mass participation.

Some administrators, politicians and military officials in Nigeria have, during the past decade or so, attempted to supply the public service with this 'missing' political–ideological component. Drawing on the works of Riggs, Waldo, Fainsod and Weidner, among others, they have advanced the notion of 'development administration' as a panacea for what is described as Nigeria's 'bureaucratic pathologies'. Development administration begins with the goal of effecting change in the 'developing' society. In this it is said to differ from conventional 'administrative development' which aims merely at changing administrative procedures, that is, at improving the 'instrumental-ities of administration', so that development administration 'can thus be viewed as governmental administration for the purpose of promoting social and economic development in "transitional" societies' (Emezi, 1977:88, 90). What can be inferred from this is that: 'The role of development administration . . . as an agency and organization of government is to develop plan objectives and activate people and groups to perform in accordance with those objectives.' Or again, development administration is regarded as government activities that 'promote economic growth, improve human and organizational capabilities and promote equality in the distribution of opportunities, income and power, and which involve deliberate attempts at social and behavioural changes'.[15] Paul Collins also subscribes to the view

> that effective development administration requires a high level of creative assessment and innovation on the part of planners that envisages not simply the improvement of administrative performance but a restructuring of existing government machinery and administrative behaviour to make it more suited to sustain planned economic, social and cultural change (1980:3)

But in the context of Nigeria, and more generally of the South, this theory of development administration gives rise to a number of problems. In the *first* place, the goals and values for which development administration is being deployed are not at all clear. The 'reforms' apparently would be accomplished within the existing neo-colonial capitalist order and thus would reinforce elite hegemony, economic disarticulation, dependency, etc. – the same factors which precipitate *under*development in the first place. This is especially so, *second*, in view of the fact that the theory starts from the assumption that initiatives and other 'inputs' emanate from above: it is the (unmodified) civil service which is intended to set the goals, determine the means, then 'mobilise' and 'educate' the population on behalf of their realisation.

Third, development administration is essentially a Western model, developed under advanced capitalist conditions, which assumes an identity between development and 'modernisation' (= 'Westernisation'). A model of this kind has no room for the *specific* nature of Nigerian development with its external dependency, colonially and neo-colonially mediated class and economic structures and its skewed position as oil producer in the world economy. As Dwivedi and Nef rightly emphasise, the development administration paradigm[16] assumed that the 'problem,', whatever its nature, remained with the periphery. The 'solution' was always in the centre. In an extreme way, the prevalent attitude was not only that 'they' had the problem, but that they *were* the problem. Conversely, the West was postulated both to *have* and to *be* the solution. Traditional societies had to be saved, if not from the appeals of Communism, then at least from themselves. In this context it is not surprising to find a close association between military assistance on the one hand, and technical and economic development on the other.

Fourth, the huge and unwarranted assumption underpinning the theory is that not only could a public bureaucracy, which has hitherto acted merely as an administrative organisation – beset, moreover, by a wide range of 'pathologies' – somehow transform itself overnight, merely with an injection of 'development administration', into an energetic, disciplined and enlightened vanguard, but that this elitist institution would necessarily find a developmental élan to overcome the still-present 'environmental' problems. Again, to cite Dwivedi and Nef, the positive relationship between bureaucracy and development, which development administration assumes, is not only ahistorical[17]

> but also spurious from a structural viewpoint – bureaucracy could be as much a cause as a consequence of development. From a development point of view, a successful bureaucratization requires a number of social, economic, cultural and political conditions normally absent in most Third World nations. These include an expanding economic base, a tax base, professionally trained manpower, political legitimacy, cultural secularization, universalism, a relatively open society and a strong political superstructure capable of governing. The absence of these qualities, in turn presented another paradox: governing and managerial capacities were most scarce where they were most needed – in the underdeveloped regions.

This discussion underlines again a major theme of this book: that the *content* of development, as of politics, is prior to its *forms*. Without normatively fixed goals based on discernible values and premises, new regulations and procedures – which development administration amounts to – will remain mere alternative routes to the same destination: underdevelopment. For[18]

> in the context of neocolonialism, 'administrative reform' is perhaps the main ingredient to circumvent critical issues and frustrate large socio-economic reform. The same applies to planning. Proceduralism and technicalities take precedence over objectives, and planning becomes an aesthetic and rhetorical exercise, quite harmless to the status quo.

The judicature

Contrary to received notions about a separate branch of government, the judicature (the Nigerian version of 'judiciary') is related to and resembles the state bureaucracy. Like it, the judicature performs public functions and services – albeit more delineated in scope – enforces the laws in a special manner, and is an entirely appointed body organised according to the Weberian principles of 'rationality', 'hierarchy' and the 'division of labour'. Also analogous to the public service, the judicial branch's activities tend to encroach into the spheres of other branches: (a) of the legislature (or its military equivalent), inasmuch as precedent and other judge-made law, like rules and decisions of the bureaucracy, in fact amount to the determination of how laws are actually applied and implemented, and (b) of the civilian executive, because the courts are empowered to decide on the constitutionality of executive actions or omissions; under military government, the latter powers fall to the executive who, lacking the relevant expertise, frequently seek the judiciary's advice.

The administration of justice, however, differs in one important respect from the state bureaucracy, namely, that it is theoretically independent of any form of external influence, whether executive control from above – relativised but by no means abolished under military government – or democratic control from below. The centrality of the principle of independence in the Nigerian legal system is emphasised by Professor Nwabueze as follows (1982c:8):

> The essential character of a court in the constitutional sense is determined not so much by the legal qualification of its members or by the method of their appointment and dismissal, as by its independence and impartiality and the procedure for its proceedings and determinations. The procedure of a court of law is characterised by the following attributes: (i) absence of bias, i.e. a court of law is required to be free of bias or even an appearance of bias, which means in practical terms that a judge should be independent of the disputants in the case, and should have no interest of his own in the subject-matter of the dispute; (ii) openness, i.e. its proceedings must be in public, unless the interest of justice or other public interest dictates otherwise; (iii) presentation of their case by the parties of the dispute; (iv) the ascertainment of the facts in issue by means of evidence given on oath or affirmation; (v) the submission of argument on the facts and on the law by or on behalf of the parties; (vi) a binding decision which disposes of the whole matter by finding upon the facts and an application to the facts so found of the law as interpreted by the court.

Significantly, even when civilian political leaders contrive to convert the judicial apparatus to their own ends (for example, by persecuting political opponents, rigging election appeals, etc.), or military rulers create 'auxiliary' judicial bodies (military or administrative tribunals for specific matters such as armed robbery, malfeasance, smuggling, and the like), both are consistently at pains to preserve the appearance of judicial independence as a principle. The same applies to the issue of appointments and removals of leading members of the judiciary. Great care is invariably taken to designate persons 'of standing' as higher court judges, and dismissal or impeachment of leading members of the judicature is relatively rare, even under 'corrective' military rule. This suggests the *important legitimating function which the existence of a formally independent judiciary performs for the political system as a whole*. Without a reliable and generally accepted institution to accomplish the authoritative interpretation and adjudication of the (elite-defined) rules of social action, the popular acceptance of the political system as a whole would be threatened, a factor recognised by military and civilian rulers alike.

Whether or not the judicature is capable of performing this legitimacy function is at least partly determined by its structure. Even a cursory view of the overall organisation of the Nigerian legal system reveals three central traits:

(i) *Co-existence of laws with very heterogeneous sources.* A first basic distinction can be made between received English law and indigenous laws. The former, by definition imposed by colonial administration, was incorporated *in toto* into post-independence Nigerian law and, despite amendments, remains the core of Nigerian law, particularly at the upper levels of the criminal and civil law codes. Indigenous or customary law normally refers to surviving pre-colonial law codes (though strictly speaking, post-1960 Nigerian-made law ought to qualify as well), concessions to indigenous needs made by the policy of direct rule and perpetuated through the 'native courts' of the colonial period. As the concept implies, 'customary law' is founded on the traditions and customs accepted by the members of a community as binding among themselves. It is thus confined mainly to individual ethnic groups and is not standardised. Two classes of customary law are recognised: ethnic and Muslim law. Ethnic law is unwritten and normally interpreted by chiefs and elders. Muslim and Sharia law, on the other hand, is

written law based on the Koran, the practice of the Prophet and scholarly interpretations of these; it is thus religious law applicable only to persons of the Muslim faith
(and therefore, in a sense, 'received' law as well). Perhaps because it is closer to the
population and responsive to changing needs and attitudes (as well as to the fluctuating
interpretations of the elders), customary law in both its main variants appears more
dynamic, shifting and hence subject to more conflicts of interpretation than other forms
of law.[19]

(ii) *Federalisation of the legal system*. The legal system is subdivided into federal courts,
State courts, and a plethora of local, regional, and customary courts, corresponding to
the jurisdictions of the legislative and executive powers at the relevant political levels.

(iii) *Complexity*. From this complicated amalgam of indigenous and received law,
Sharia and ethnic courts, 19 State courts and several federal courts, a highly complex
structure emerges (though considerably simplified compared to previous arrangements). In this context it is significant to note that the 1979 Constitution only 'named'
federal and State courts – an implicit admission of the fact that the lower court system
is likely to be in continuous flux for some time to come.

Thus in structural terms the Nigerian legal system permits and to some extent
encourages a multiplicity of diverse and diffuse local and regional courts, adapted to
local values and customs, progressing toward increasing proximation at the State levels,
up to its federal apex which is entirely uniform. Of the six named courts, the judicial
powers of the federation are vested in the Supreme Court, Federal Court of Appeal and
Federal High Court, whereas the judicial powers of the respective States rest with the
State High Court, Sharia Appeal Court and Customary Appeal Court. Chapter VII of
the Constitution spelled out in detail the jurisdiction of each court and its relationship
to the other courts.

By way of conclusion, it is pertinent to ask how the judicature actually operates
within the political system. Unfortunately, the comparatively large corpus of works on
the structures and functions of the judiciary has not been matched by studies of its
actual operation and political significance. Nevertheless, it is possible to argue that on
the whole the administration of justice has been the most effective (or least ineffective?)
institution adapted by Nigeria from the colonial institutional legacy. Admittedly, the
courts' rulings on electoral disputes and legislature composition, for example, have
consistently supported the interests of the powerful groups and parties. Nowhere was
this tendency more blatant than in the several cases of 'political justice' arising during
the First Republic (see chapter 2), when the courts lent themselves to the condemnation
and incarceration of elected representatives for partisan political reasons (Awolowo,
Enahoro, Obi, etc.). In the case of Dr Chike Obi, who was convicted under the
surviving Draconian colonial sedition laws, Olu Onagoruwa has rightly suggested:[20]

> Clearly, the Supreme Court abdicated wholly the functions of scrutiny through vigorous
> judicial review conferred on it by the constitution and allowed the Federal Government to
> usurp from it the role of an arbiter between itself and the regions solemnly conferred on it by
> the constitution. The consequence of this abdication [*inter alia was that*] . . . it rendered the
> political and constitutional structure lopsided until it finally collapsed in 1966 after a series of
> legal and constitutional irregularities compounded by a succession of election riggings.

Under the two series of military governments, however, the courts struggled to maintain some independent scope for action, an effort facilitated by the military's 'corrective', as opposed to revolutionary or even reactionary, mission. For the military
made no sustained attempt to transform the basic structure of the legal system, prefer-

ring instead to leave the machinery in place, especially the courts and the human rights provisions, and merely to 'tinker' with it when necessary. True, the military did undermine the judicial system in a number of ways, for instance by dismissing or threatening to dismiss individual judges, by creating special tribunals (armed robbery, currency trafficking, petroleum sabotage) which removed important matters from the courts' jurisdiction, by making FMG decrees and edicts immune from judicial review (Decree No. 1/1966, Section 3(6)), by a 1972 decree making the Chief Justice appointable and removable by the head of the FMG and by quasi- and extra-legal measures (purges, tribunals) conducted in the wake of the 1976 attempted *coup*. All this notwithstanding, the courts were generally able to avoid direct conflict with the military and to entrench and extend many of their powers. In a number of instances they appeared as the upholder of the rule of law and of liberal rights as against the more arbitrary and unresponsive military government/civil service coalition.

Following recivilianisation and judicial reorganisation in accordance with the 1979 Constitution, the courts for a time seemed to have reasserted themselves and to have relatively quickly and smoothly assumed the role foreseen for them as the 'third branch' of government. For example, the Supreme Court was called upon to make its first highly political decision following the 1979 presidential election in which the Special Election Tribunal declared Shehu Shagari the winner in accordance with the 'twelve and two-thirds rule' described in chapter 7. The case, brought by runner-up Obafemi Awolowo, was clearly a crucial and precedent-setting one.[21]

Another important case, relating to the arrest and deportation of the majority leader of the Bornu State Assembly, Alhaji Shugaba Abdulrahman Darman, in 1980 suggested that the courts were moving into a 'corrective' role themselves in checking executive excesses. In January of that year, the (NPN) Federal Minister of the Interior, Alhaji Bello Maitama Yusuf, somehow determined that Alhaji Shugaba (GNPP) was not a Nigerian citizen and, hence, represented a security risk. In flagrant violation of due process, the unfortunate politician was pulled out of his bath in the early morning hours and deported to Chad. After a well-publicised series of legal moves and appeals, the Borno High Court in Maiduguri ruled that Alhaji Shugaba was in fact a Nigerian citizen and that his deportation was *ultra vires* since it violated his fundamental human rights. The court awarded damages of N350,000 to Alhaji Shugaba and assessed N10,000 as costs against the federal government (later reduced on appeal). The court's independence and its role in the system of checks and balances were thus affirmed.

With its 2 October 1981 invalidation of the 1981 Revenue Allocation Act, the Supreme Court demonstrated its crucial role in maintaining a formal equilibrium between the legislative and executive branches of government. Ruling that the Act had in fact been promulgated by the Joint Finance Committee composed of two dozen members of the two houses of the National Assembly, rather than by the National Assembly itself – which, as has been shown, had sole and non-transferable law-making powers for the federation – the Supreme Court ordered all public officials to forebear from disbursing funds among the States or government agencies according to the formulas contained in the Act. Oddly enough, the Court's verdict was celebrated by the four opposition parties, GNPP, UPN, PRP and NPP as a 'victory' even though its effect was to make the distribution ratio of federal revenues revert from the Act's proposed 58.5% federal government, 31.5% State governments, 10% local governments, 1% ecological problems, back to the pre-1979 centralist formula: 75% central government, 22% State governments, 3% local governments.[22] Presumably the opposition's delight derived from the defeat of *any* government bill, since the reduction in State incomes also affected revenues in the 12 States controlled by it. In any case, the federal judicature's power and independence were again confirmed.

On the other hand, judges at the State level and below were appointed – and intimidated, bought off and dismissed – by the respective State governments. Particularly in the 'one-party' States, a core of partisan, party-aligned officials was installed and could be counted on to uphold State executives' acts, to ignore certain violations of the law and, at election time, to rule in favour of the dominant party. In such situations, the judiciary was reduced to an extension of the State executive. One example may stand for many. When Mr Justice Sodeinde Sowemimo retired as Chief Justice of Nigeria in August 1985, he asserted that the Imo State judiciary remained mired 'in a mess' created by the corrupt and incompetent appointees left in office from the civilian era and that the military government 'must close its eyes and clear the bench'.[23]

With the return of 'corrective' military government, the growing assertiveness of the judicature appears to have been halted, but by no means reversed. True, the several special tribunals and pre-emptive decrees of the Buhari regime removed certain categories of offences – political corruption and malfeasance, armed robbery, etc. from the jurisdiction of the established judiciary. And the well-known semi-terrorist activities of the National Security Organisation described in chapter 9, certainly undermined the pretence that universal liberal rights were respected in Nigeria. But, like its predecessors, the Buhari regime could not dispense entirely with the legitimating role performed by the judiciary. Partly in reaction to the excesses committed under Buhari, Babangida has in fact proclaimed the rule of law to be a central feature of his 'correcting-the-corrective' government and begun to shake out the legal system in readiness for the promised return to civilian rule in 1992.

Regulating public officers' conduct

It is appropriate to conclude this chapter with a brief discussion of the 'official' attempts to prescribe norms of behaviour for the collectivity of public servants in Nigeria. The Code of Conduct, incorporated as the Fifth Schedule of the 1979 Constitution, represented an admission that corruption in its various forms remained an all-pervasive and undesirable trait of the state bureaucracy and the elected institutions, and expressed a widespread belief that public service probity was in fact a realisable goal. The meticulous and extensive Code, an important innovation for Nigeria – but not for Africa, since such codes were already in force in Zambia and Tanzania[24] – governed the acts and omissions of top civil servants and minor ministry clerks, of generals and rank-and-file soldiers, of the President, the Governors, Local Government Counsellors and everyone employed by them: in short, anyone who was in any way employed as a 'public officer'. So far as can be inferred from post-1983 military government decisions (and prosecutions!), the Code is still operative for all public servants.

Starting from the maxim that no public officer should put himself/herself into a position in which personal interest conflicts with official duties and responsibilities, the Code provides, among other things, that all public officers must regularly declare the extent of their properties, assets and liabilities as well as those of their spouses and unmarried children under 21 years. It expressly prohibits a broad range of behaviour, namely: (i) receipt of emoluments or salaries from any other public office or private business activity; (ii) maintenance of bank accounts abroad; (iii) after retirement from public service, acceptance of more than one paid public service post; in addition, certain retired public officers (President, Vice President, Governor, Deputy Governor, Chief Justice) may not be employed by a foreign enterprise; (iv) asking for or accepting favours for acts done or not done in the discharge of public duties; evidence of receipt of gifts or favours is in itself considered as a violation of this provision; (v) acceptance of loans or benefits from companies, contractors or businessmen; (vi) on the part of non-public servants, offering inducements to public officers aimed at affecting the officers' performance of their duties; and (vii) abusing in any way powers conferred by service position.

Like the Code itself, the institutions established for enforcing it were also extensive. A Code of Conduct Bureau, consisting of not less than nine members appointed by the chief executive, was supposed to receive, examine and *make public* the declarations of public servants' property, assets and liabilities mentioned above, and to refer relevant matters to the Code of Conduct Tribunal. The Tribunal amounted to an auxiliary arm of the judicature. Made up of a chairman and two other persons appointed by the chief executive in accordance with recommendations of the Federal Judicial Service Commission, it was designed to regulate, pronounce judgement on, and discipline public servants within the terms of the Code of Conduct. Its penal powers included dismissal, disqualification from (elected or appointed) public office, and confiscation of illegally acquired properties. Any appeal from the Tribunal's decisions was to be directed to the Federal Court of Appeal.

The significance of the Code of Conduct may be assessed from different perspectives. On the one hand, it appeared to impose upon civil servants standards and values which were not universally present in the 'environment' in which they operated. Such provisions as the ban on foreign bank accounts or on private business activities, for instance, were clearly resented by broad sectors among the ruling classes. This is undoubtedly why they were omitted from the Constituent Assembly's draft code and only inserted at the eleventh hour by the departing military rulers.[25] If the Code thus imposed 'impossibly high' standards on public officials, was there not a danger that, as happened in Zambia,[26] it might precipitate a mass exodus of qualified personnel into the private sector? However, this problem did not appear to have been seriously posed in Nigeria, and one may speculate that the advantages of public office as a primary institution of private accumulation still outweighed the difficulties of conforming to the Code, particularly since its provisions were not enforced during the Second Republic.

Another perspective sees the Code as too comprehensive and thus too unwieldy, with the result that it projected 'an image of petty bureaucratic tyranny prying into personal affairs, rather than the image it should have as an instrument of ordered freedom and welfare for all the people' (Dent, 1977). Proponents of this view would presumably have restricted the Code's application to upper-level public servants. Yet this course would undermine one of its important legitimising aspects – its universality. A substantial part of its appeal related to its unequivocal, if not entirely enforceable, assertion that *every* public official was bound to certain standards of behaviour and merited punishment for any departure from them. The Code, in other words, stood also as a statement of principles and aspirations, and as such ought not to have brooked any compromise.

In this connection, Oyelele Oyediran rightly suggested that the Code be regarded as integrally bound up with the Fundamental Objectives and Directive Principles of State Policy. Taken together, these constitutional sections provided an overview, he argued, of the 'environment within which the new leadership is expected to operate'.[27] That environment, of course, was that of formal liberal democracy including the prescription of an open, participatory political system in which all citizens conformed to the constitutional rules and norms. The universalisation of the Code to encompass *all* full-time public officials applied these democratic principles to the entire public service, thus aspiring to democratise the service itself and simultaneously set implicit standards for society as a whole. To be sure, this does not even touch on the issue of whether such *universal* principles can be effectively realised in a polity dominated by *particularist* (elite) interests, but this is a problem dealt with in other chapters.

What is evident is that the Code of Conduct did attempt to rationalise and codify desirable public-service behaviour *within* the parameters of the Nigerian liberal democratic state, so that the public could in theory demand certain standards from it, such as those enunciated by President Shagari:[28]

> appointments . . . based solely on merit, hard work, dedication to duty and in the spirit of the Nigerian constitution; . . . responsible leadership . . .; absolute loyalty to the government and the nation . . .; a sense of purpose and creativity . . .; discipline, productivity and [good] relations between the Public Service and the public . . .; and a total sense of commitment and involvement in the running of our affairs.

In any event, this outline of what the rules concerning public officers' conduct *ought to have* been, is, literally, entirely academic. Abstract codes of conduct, tribunals to enforce them and ombudsmen[29] to attend to the public interest, however meticulously defined and loudly proclaimed, proved utterly futile in the face of elite subversion of their letter and spirit. Indeed, the National Assembly repeatedly failed to pass the enabling legislation that would have made all this machinery operative. During the Second Republic, for instance, only the President and Vice-President ever made a public statement of their assets. All the other members of the myriad state bureaucracy chose to ignore these provisions – and with good reason, as the findings of the 1984 and 1985 military tribunals investigating corruption well demonstrate. Indeed, by October 1984, the total number of public officials purged and/or retrenched was estimated at between 150,000 and 200,000.[30] While most of these dismissals were no doubt justified, the effects of yet another corporate shake-up are certain to be increased insecurity, conservatism and lowered initiative. Predictably, therefore, renewed attempts will be made in coming years to immunise the public service from direct politicisation and to establish some form of security of tenure. And equally predictably, as chapter 8 has argued, the new military-civil service symbiosis will draw public officials back into the nexus of politicisation and corruption – a cycle that will hardly be broken unless and until the governing elite, military or civilian, ceases to operate within the neo-colonial capitalist political economy.

To sum up, it is evident once again that the 'modernisation' and (dependent) 'development' premises on which the state bureaucracy is founded, are inadequate and inappropriate except inasmuch as they serve to vindicate ideologically the maintenance of neo-colonial capitalism and elite hegemony within it. The formalised role differentiation based on the division of labour which is prevalent in advanced capitalist society, does not lend itself well to insertion into a relatively undifferentiated and weakly developed social structure with few countervailing powers. Where such a transposition is attempted, as in post-colonial Nigeria, the bureaucracy becomes an ensemble of elite interests and tasks with an almost irresistible tendency toward internal consolidation and isolation from the society supposedly being served. What is then 'served', as this chapter has sought to demonstrate, are the interests of the bureaucrats and their class allies. Thus the bureaucracy as an elitist interest group is detached from the political community of which it is a part. At the same time as it aggrandises and perpetuates its corporate interests, that is, becomes 'overdeveloped' and 'differentiated', it 'underdevelops' and 'de-differentiates' the really productive sectors of the political economy, notably agriculture, on whose surplus it thrives. But the 'rationalisation' and stimulation of precisely these sectors is a precondition for any broad and lasting process of development.

Of course it is not the state bureaucracy itself that underdevelops Nigeria. Rather, it is the political economy or 'ecology' as a whole and its agents in the state apparatus that sustain the process. With this statement, the limits of this chapter are set out. Here, the ethos of the state bureaucracy has been analysed *on its own terms*. While this approach elicits a number of important insights into the composition and operation of this bureaucratic elite, it does not account for the linkages and interdependences between the state bureaucracy and the broader state elite of which it is a part. Concerning the latter, its military-centred components have been examined in chapters 3, 4 and 8 and its civilian-centred sectors in chapters 2, 5, 6 and 7. One theoretical concept capable of bringing these diffuse partial arguments into a coherent analysis is the notion of *the Nigerian state* which is the subject of the final chapter.

Notes

1. Hamza Alavi, 'The State in Post-Colonial Societies: Pakistan and Bangladesh', *New Left Review*, No. 74, July/August 1972; for amplification see John S. Saul, 'The State in Post-Colonial Societies: Tanzania', *The Socialist Register 1974*, London 1974; for a critique see W. Ziemann and M. Lanzendörfer, 'The State in Peripheral Societies', *The Socialist Register 1977*, London, 1977.
2. Ralph Miliband, *Marxism and Politics*, London, 1977, esp. chapter 4.
3. Hartmut Elsenhans, *Abhängiger Kapitalismus oder bürokratische Entwicklungsesellschaft Versuch über den Staat in der Dritten Welt*, Frankfurt and New York, 1981, chapters 1, 5.
4. Here see Ikoiwak, 1980, p. iiff.
5. Andrew O. Oronsaye, 'Pathologies of the Bureaucracy' in W. D. Graf (ed.) *Towards a Political Economy of Nigeria: Critical Essays*, Benin City (forthcoming), here quoted from manuscript, p. 3.
6. See Ikoiwak, 1980, p. 121.
7. Alex Gboyega, 'The "Federal Character" or the Attempt to Create Representative Bureaucracies in Nigeria', *Revue Internationale des Sciences Administratives*, 1/1984, pp. 22–3.
8. Sam Egite Oyovbaire, 'Structural Change and Political Processes in Nigeria', *African Affairs*, January 1984.
9. See his 'The Quest for a Representative Bureaucracy in Nigeria and the Implications for National Development', paper presented to the conference of the Nigerian Political Science Association, Nsukka, 1–4 June 1983, mimeo., p. 7.
10. Adebayo Adedeji, quoting his own former address, 'Rise and Fall of the Civil Service' (Part I), *West Africa*, 30 March 1981, p. 687.
11. William N. Brownsberger, 'Development and Governmental Corruption – Materialism and Political Fragmentation in Nigeria', *Journal of Modern African Studies*, Vol. 21, No. 2, 1983, p. 225.
12. In Sections 135–48, 156–61, 173–92, 194–6, 197–200 as well as in the Third and Fifth Schedules.
13. Bala J. Takaya, 'Delegation of Authority in a Presidential System of Government' (Part 2), *New Nigerian*, 22 September 1979.
14. Cited by Adedeji, *op. cit.*, Part III, 13 April 1981, p. 804.
15. Milton J. Esman, 'Administrative Doctrine and Developmental Needs' in E. P. Morgan (ed.), *The Administration of Change in Africa: Essays in the Theory and Practice of Development Administration in Africa*, New York and London, 1974, pp. 3 ff.
16. O. P. Dwivedi and J. Nef, 'Crises and Continuities in Development Theory and Administration: First and Third World Perspectives', *Public Administration and Development*, Vol. 2,

1982, p. 62 (italics in original). Also see their 'Development Theory and Administration: A Fence Around an Empty Lot?', *Indian Journal of Public Administration*, Vol. XXVII, No. 1, January–March 1981, pp. 42–66; for a more general perspective see O. P. Dwivedi, W. D. Graf and J. Nef, 'Marxist Contributions to the Theory of the Administrative State', *Indian Journal of Political Science*, Vol. LXVI, No. 1 (January–March 1985), pp. 1–17.

17. Dwivedi and Nef, 'Crises and Continuities', *op. cit.*, p. 64.
18. Dwivedi and Nef, 'Development Theory', *op. cit.*, p. 24.
19. On this see the relevant passages in Obilade, 1979.
20. Dr Olu Onagoruwa, 'The Supreme Court in the Second Republic' (Part 2), *Sunday Times*, 16 September 1979.
21. Full text of the judgements of the tribunal and of the Supreme Court reproduced as special supplement to *New Nigerian*, 16 and 26 October 1979 respectively.
22. On this, and on the way in which the ratios were initially worked out, see Enukora Joe Okoli, 'Revenue Allocation Bill "a Nullity"', *West Africa* 12 October 1981, pp. 2369–70.
23. Quoted in *West Africa*, 26 August 1985, p. 1775.
24. In fact, Nigerian constitution-makers specifically drew from, and in a number of ways improved upon, the Zambian and Tanzanian codes. See *CDC Report*, Vol. II, pp. 40–41.
25. On the military's addition to the Code, as well as its other final constitutional amendments, see the text of General Obasanjo's relevant address to the nation, reproduced in *New Nigerian*, 22 September 1978; see also chapter 5 above.
26. A problem recognised by the CDC; see *CDC Report*, Vol. II, p. 41.
27. Oyelele Oyediran, 'Leadership in Nigeria's New Constitution', *Présence Africaine*, No. 115, 3rd Quarter 1980, p. 197.
28. Presidential address to the Secretary of the Government, the Head of Civil Service and the Permanent Secretaries at their swearing-in ceremony, mimeographed press release, n.d. [1979], pp. 1–2.
29. It is worth noting that the Nigerian equivalent to an ombudsman institution, the Public Complaints Commission (PCC) has also not performed well, for reasons entirely consonant with the 'ecology' argument presented here. Not only has it tended to operate in relative anonymity if not secrecy, but its work load has steadily declined as its selective handling of complaints has intensified. It has failed the social reform/moral crusader role foreseen for it on its establishment in 1975. See L. Adamolekun and E. L. Osunkunle, *Nigeria's Ombudsman System: Five Years of the Public Complaints Commission*, Ibadan, 1982.
30. *West Africa*, 2 February 1985, p. 215.

11

The Nigerian State and the State of Nigeria

Rentier state in the world market

The central characteristic and motive force of the Nigerian political economy through the 1970s and 1980s has been the discovery, development, exploitation and marketing of oil. In *qualitative* terms, the country's essentially neo-colonial capitalist mode and relations of production were not substantially modified by the rapid transition from the production of agricultural commodities (palm oil, rubber, tin, cereals, etc.) to petroleum as the main source of capital accumulation. Foreign trade was still oriented toward exports to the major metropolitan powers upon whom the economy continued to rely for the importation of technology- and capital-intensive manufactures and know-how. Nigeria's position in the international division of labour remained that of a peripheral, dependent producer of now a single strategically vital commodity (rather than a few) for the world market – producing, it is often said, what it does not consume and consuming what it does not produce.

Quantitatively, however, oil has dominated practically every sphere of Nigerian economic, social and political activity since the civil war; so much so that here, more than in most peripheral economies, one is justified in resurrecting the Marxian concept of the transformation of quantity into quality. In absolute terms, oil revenues have greatly inflated the overall size of state revenues (Table 11:1). Estimates by the Nigerian National Petroleum Corporation (NNPC) itself suggest that the country earned a total of N87 bn or US $101 bn in oil revenues between 1958 and 1983, with average annual revenues well over N7 bn. In relative terms, the impact of oil on the economy has been even more dramatic. As a share of all federally collected revenues, oil increased from about one-quarter to about four-fifths in the decade and a half starting in 1970 (see Table 11:1), and from about 5% of GDP at Independence to well over 50% in the mid-1980s.[1] And in the crucial area of foreign-exchange earnings, crude oil incomes

Table 11.1 *Revenues from exports and imports, 1970–83 (Nm.)*

	1970	1980	1983
Total exports	885.4	14,077.0	7,612.3
of which oil	510.0	13,523.0	7,337.4
Total imports	756.4	9,658.1	9,723.0
Balance of payments	+ 58.6	+ 2,402.2	– 244.8

Source: West Africa, 30 September 1985, p. 2023.

escalated from 2.5% of all such revenue to 58.1% in 1970, to 93.6% in 1975, and to 98% and more through the first half of the 1980s.[2]

The growing centrality of oil revenues correlates with the rapid decline of agriculture (from *circa* two-thirds of GNP at independence to less than one-fifth in the 1980s, and from more than four-fifths of export receipts to practically no receipts at all) as well as with a gradual rise in industrial output from perhaps 7% in the mid-1960s to more than 10% of total economic output in recent years. These latter developments will be examined presently.

Table 11.2 *Oil's share in Federal Government revenue, 1961–85 (Nm.)*

Year	Oil Revenue	Total Revenue	Oil Revenue as % of Total Revenue
1961	17.1	223.6	7.6
1962	16.9	238.8	7.1
1963	10.1	249.0	4.1
1964	16.4	277.6	5.9
1965	27.1	321.0	8.4
1966	37.7	339.2	11.1
1967	41.2	300.0	13.7
1968	23.3	299.9	7.8
1969	72.5	435.9	16.6
1970	196.4	759.1	25.9
1971	740.1	1,410.9	52.5
1972	576.2	1,389.9	41.5
1973	1,461.6	2,171.3	67.3
1974	4,183.8	5,177.1	80.8
1975	4,611.7	5,861.6	78.7
1976	5,548.5	7,070.3	78.5
1977	5,821.5	8,251.3	70.6
1978	4,654.1	7,371.1	63.1
1979	8,880.9	10,913.1	81.4
1980	13,630.0	15,513.1	75.1
1981	10,540.0	12,980.3	83.3
1982	8,580.0	10,204.0	80.0
1983	4,590.0	6,080.0	75.6
1984	5,950.0	n/a	n/a
1985*	6,730.0	8,024.0*	84.0

* = estimated.
Source: Compiled from a variety of sources by Leo Ogba, *Emerging Patterns of Conflict Management in Africa: The Role of Nigeria, 1960–1983*, doctoral thesis, University of Toronto, 1986, p. 172.

Thus, the Nigerian economy has come to conform to the classic profile of a mono-mineral, dependent enclave economy resembling, in Crawford Young's metaphor (1982:219), 'an inverted pyramid, teetering precariously on a hydrocarbon pinnacle'. As such, it has evolved into a *rentier state*.[3] The essential feature of the rentier state in the world market is that it severs the link between production and distribution. State revenues accrue from taxes or 'rents' on production, rather than from productive activity. This production depends, however, on techniques, expertise, investments – and markets – generated outside the territory controlled by the state. For this reason, practically all aspects of exploration, production and marketing are dominated by international capital, typically in the form of the transnational corporation. For the transnationalised state, rents derive from local ownership of the areas and/or resources of extraction. The Nigerian state exacts its share of oil revenues by means of 'joint ventures' with oil multinationals within which it assumes an increasing equity over time (Table 11:3).

Table 11.3 *Participation by the Nigerian Government in the oil industry*

Company	Participation (%)	Date Acquired
ELF	35	1 April 1971
	55	1 April 1974
	60	1 July 1979
AGIP/PHILLIPS	33 1/3[a]	1 April 1971
	55	1 April 1974
	60	1 July 1979
SHELL BP	35	1 April 1973
	55	1 April 1974
	60	1 July 1979
	80	1 August 1979
GULF	35	1 April 1973
	55	1 April 1974
	60	1 July 1979
MOBIL	35	1 April 1973
	55	1 April 1974
	60	1 July 1979
TEXACO	55	1 May 1975
	60	1 July 1979
PAN OCEAN	55	1 January 1978
	60	1 July 1979
ASHLAND[b]	n.a.	1 June 1973

Notes: a = Equity participation.
          b = NNPC/Ashland arrangement is a production-sharing agreement.
Source: *NAPETCOR*, quarterly magazine of the Nigerian National Petroleum Corporation, Vol. 2, No. 1, January–March, 1981.

The rentier state in the world market exhibits several important characteristics.

It is, first, and almost by definition, *crisis-susceptible* and hence tendentially unstable. Fluctuation in global demand, after-effects of world-wide recessions, technical break-downs, even labour disputes may reduce the flow of rents and thus undercut national plans, intricate budgets and the entire 'development' process. The unpredictability and volatility of the rentier economy has been shown, in preceding chapters, to have been a central factor in all regime changes and political developments since Independence. Civilian and military governments alike have been forced to take account of its spasmodic, boom-and-bust cycles. When in 1977–8, for instance, crude oil production dropped from 2.23 bn b/d to 1.57 bn b/d, the Nigerian economy immediately entered into a minor crisis. The production cutbacks, resulting from the 1981 'oil glut', from 2.23 bn b/d in January to 0.64 bn b/d in August (though again rising consistently to over 1 bn b/d since then) shook the Second Republic, undermined its Fourth National Development Plan and caused a US $1.5 bn cut in planned expenditures.[4] In times of sharply declining revenue a fiscal crisis in the rentier state is practically inevitable because of the continued outflow of revenues in the form of 'capital drain' – persistence of obligation to pay for vital *and* luxury imports, ongoing net outflow of transnational corporation profits, interest payments on foreign loans, upsurge in 'flight capital' etc. – upon which the existence of the rentier economy absolutely depends. Table 11:4 illustrates certain macro-economic fluctuations in the oil-centred economy beset by crisis. The Nigerian situation demonstrates again, and more urgently, the absence in the political lexicon of an 'oil' equivalent of the 'banana republic' to describe the post-OPEC-induced mono-mineral dependencies in certain areas of the Third World.

Table 11.4 *Some key economic indicators (Nm.)*

	1970	1980	1983
Money Supply	608.3	9,226.8	11,282.4
Federal Budget Revenue	365.3	12,138.7	6,791.4
Expenditure (current and capital)	838.8	14,113.9	11,664.6
Public Debt	1,215.4	9,785.3	40,466.6
External	175.4	1,866.8	18,466.6
Internal	1,040.0	7,918.5	22,224.3
External Assets	176.7	5,655.0	798.5

Source: Adapted from *West Africa*, 30 September 1985, p. 2023.

Second, the rentier state at the periphery of the world capitalist system is locked into, and *dependent upon, North–South trade patterns*. Trade links, for both imports and exports, are overwhelmingly with the advanced capitalist areas of the OECD, between 80 and 90% in each category. Table 11:5 sums up Nigeria's main trading partners.

Table 11.5 *The directions of Nigerian trade*

Import partners — % of total imports		Export partners — % of total exports	
UK	22.0	USA	44.3
FRG	14.0	Netherlands	12.1
USA	11.2	France	11.2
Japan	10.8	FRG	6.6
France	7.1	Italy	2.8
Italy	6.7	ECOWAS	2.8
Netherlands	4.1		

Source: New African, January 1982, p. 59.

Third, the oil-dominated economy is an enhanced *enclave economy*. Oil production is necessarily a high-technology, capital-intensive enterprise which cannot generate either jobs or direct ('forward' and 'backward') linkages with the other sectors of the economy. Thus in total the industry employs about 30,000 workers (made up of some 24,000 junior and senior oil industry staff and *circa* 6,000 non-unionised auxiliary workers (Turner, 1985b:10)), representing perhaps 5% of workers in the *formal* wage structure and far less than 1% of the total working population, while all the essential steps in the production and consumption of oil, from exploration to drilling, refining and distribution, are carried out by the multinational partners and therefore hardly affect the national economy at all, beyond the massive influx of rents at the top.

Fourth, then, the oil economy *perpetuates* and *deepens* patterns of *economic disarticulation* generated in the colonial phase and reinforced by neo-colonial petty commodity production. Oil revenues, as it were, overwhelm and eclipse the other sectors of the dependent economy, so that balanced, autocentric development becomes an even more remote prospect than during the colonial era. This Moloch-like quality of the oil sector is apparent in the parallel *underdevelopment* of agriculture and the distortion of industry and manufacturing.

Developments in the agricultural sector are particularly instructive. Even before the rise of oil dependency, Nigerian agriculture was beset by a structural crisis. Corresponding to colonial patterns of surplus extraction, post-colonial elites derived revenues for their own capital formation and luxury consumption mainly by exploiting the peasantry. Between 1960 and 1974, agriculture contributed more than 50% of Regional/State governmental revenue, while only about 20% of total government expenditures actually returned to the peasants (Olatunbosun, 1975:22). Colonial priorities in the areas of cash-cropping (cocoa, palm oil, rubber, coconuts, etc.) and peasant commodification as the foundation of the labour reproduction process were simply taken over intact. Despite colonial and neo-colonial deformations, however, so long as agriculture remains the primary source of accumulation in a peripheral economy, its inner dynamic produces a certain transformational logic. Employing now roughly 70% of the work force, it represents the source of livelihood for the majority of the population. With population growth, urbanisation and the progress of industry and manufacturing, agriculture could – and in a non-mono-mineral economy, *must* – increase production to feed the growing population, produce cash crops for export revenues to be utilised productively in the economy, rationalise techniques to free labour for the 'modern' sectors, produce profits for further investment, create a network of infrastructures to facilitate trade and commerce, and thus act as the motor of development. But where this classical accumulation and rationalisation strategy is precluded by massive 'unearned' revenues, agricultural development stagnates. The availability of huge quantities of foreign exchange and the relatively low cost (due in part to the overvalued naira) of importing North American grains and cereals – especially when spurred by droughts like that of 1973/4 – permit the rentier state to import large quantities of food, thus alleviating short-term crises and undermining price and productivity structures in local agriculture. At the same time the construction boom and the vastly more profitable commercial and service opportunities in other sectors have led to an exodus of peasants into the more attractive urban and industrial areas, which results in the decay of the labour-intensive agricultural sector.

The high-technology, capital-intensive nature of the import-based 'new' economic sector, however, proved to have a very limited absorptive capacity, so that unemployment rose even while food dependency increased. This 'modernising' syndrome extended into agricultural production as well. Rather than encourage small-scale peasant production (which even today produces 90% of Nigeria's food), government policy consciously favoured the development of capitalist agriculture. The 1976 Operation Feed the Nation, the Green Revolution of 1979, and the agricultural revolutions proclaimed by Buhari and Babangida rest on the assumption that money and technology are the keys to agrarian development. Such a strategy entails: first, a heavy reliance on foreign consultants whose knowledge of local conditions is not always as adequate as that of those who have worked the land for generations; second, huge investments in administrative and technical infrastructures which are rarely productive, given the 'pathologies' of the Nigerian State bureaucracy;[5] third, massive infrastructural provisions (such as the Kano River Project, the Sokoto Rima Project or the Chad River Basin Development Project), also involving great expenditures; fourth, high debt burdens on the part of the individual farming enterprises to pay for the imported inputs of technology and machinery; and fifth, therefore, intricate credit-granting schemes which almost invariably work to the advantage of already wealthy and well-connected commercial-farming elites, both foreign and domestic, and discriminate against small producers. Thus Tina Wallace concludes her careful analysis of Nigerian agriculture with the observation (1981:258):[6]

> While the rhetoric is that these policies are designed to help the small farmer, improve life in the rural areas and increase food production, the reality is that Nigeria's agricultural policy primarily places reliance on the largest farmers, agricultural companies, foreign consultants, agricultural technicians and bureaucrats in order to achieve a rise in food production. These policies ignore or even undermine the mass of the rural population.

The point is not that small-scale production is intrinsically superior to large-scale capitalist agriculture. North American agribusiness stands as a refutation of any such assertion. Rather, it is that in Africa, and most notably in Nigeria, massive agricultural schemes relying on bureaucratic management, advanced technology and capital investments have been and remain far less productive than peasant production. Their failure is due mainly to the absence of appropriate socio-economic preconditions as well as the structure of elite rule and surplus appropriation. Analagous to import-substitution strategies in the manufacturing sector, such schemes deepen dependency and further widen the elite-mass gap. Thus, despite all government exhortations, the agricultural sector has decayed, during the past decade and a half, both in production for domestic consumption (where Nigeria has moved from a food exporter to importer and its index of food production dropped from 100 in 1975 to 74.3 in 1983[7]) and for cash crops for export (cocoa has declined by 43%, rubber by 29%, cotton by 65% and groundnuts by 64%[8]).

The 'petro-naira syndrome' also affects the manufacturing and industrial sector. This sector has in fact grown in both relative and absolute terms. If the index of manufacturing production was 100 in 1972, then by 1982 it had increased to 446 before dropping off in 1983 and 1984,[9] representing an average annual growth rate of 12% throughout the 1970s. Yet much of this growth is either state-sponsored or foreign-controlled, and almost all of it has been the result of 'import-substituting' policies formulated and executed largely *ad hoc* during temporary ebbs in the flow of oil revenues. As elsewhere in the Third World, Nigerian 'import-substitution' strategies substitute mainly labour in the final stages of production. Assembly, packaging and licence-manufacture therefore are the central features of Nigerian manufacturing, while technologies and other inputs are mainly provided by transnational corporations. Moreover, such arrangements are largely subsidised or indeed owned by the state. The local contribution to the value-added of such products is very low, and they are almost exclusively geared to domestic consumption. Foreign investment is concentrated in vehicle components, agriculture and food processing, building materials, household goods, chemicals, telecommunications equipment and electrical goods, while domestic investment is focussed on such light consumer goods industries as cigarettes, detergents, beer, soft drinks, and, of course, textiles. The latter is the only self-sufficient Nigerian manufacturing industry and employs about one quarter of the total manufacturing labour force.[10] Since manufacturing cannot be internationally competitive under such conditions, the state is left to promote it, in part by means of state ownership or shares (especially following from indigenisation policies) and in part by certain fiscal incentives (tariff protection, tax holidays, accelerated depreciation, loans, start-up allowances, provision of industrial estates, etc.).

The image of a highly dependent, disarticulated political economy which emerges from the analysis so far, is however mainly descriptive and one-sided. As such it corresponds with Sayre P. Schatz's conception of an *inert economy*, or one 'which has reacted passively, to the increased revenues, but which has no growth-generating power of its own outside the crude-oil producing sector' (1984:45), a phenomenon which he attributes to a high marginal propensity to spend or transfer funds abroad and to the inelasticity of domestic supply. Framed in these terms, the argument too readily lends itself to an interpretation of the rentier state as an essentially passive object in the grip of transnational forces, as locked into problems and contradictions whose solutions lie mainly outside the domain of the Nigerian state. Yet oil revenues, however massive, do not in themselves *cause* dependency and produce a rentier state; and there is nothing inevitable about the growing domination of foreign capital. Indeed, the massive increase in state-collected revenues and the broader range of trading partners associated with the transnationalisation of the post-colonial economy also present potential new opportunities to reduce dependency by instigating local capital accumulation and initiating autocentric development. Dependency and disarticulation, stunted agriculture and underdeveloped industry are as much functions of political will as of external exigencies. To assume that the latter constitute the sole explanation (rather than the general context) is to abandon the analysis to an unsustainable determinism and, moreover, to ignore the active role of Nigerians in these processes:[11]

> Africans are not the mute objects of the manipulation of colonialism. They are, through their states, its *active* partners. Not to recognize this is to deny the historical agency of Africans.

The question of 'Nigerian agency' is best addressed via the special nature, class composition and beneficiaries of the Nigerian state, a theme which underlies the remaining sections of this chapter.

State capitalism at the periphery

The concept of state capitalism has been introduced and developed in previous chapters, notably chapter 4. There, it was defined as the appropriation and deployment of public resources for private ends. The relationship might also be expressed as: a capitalist economy operated by non-capitalists. Like capitalist states at the core, the peripheral capitalist state exists mainly to guarantee the conditions for the reproduction and expansion of capitalist property relations and mode(s) of production. But unlike them, it lacks the socio-economic 'base' to sustain and develop a relatively autochthonous capitalism and so intervenes in the economy, in collaboration with the external elements of this economic 'base', to create the preconditions for, and to promote, private accumulation. The role of the state is therefore determining, and includes (i) the creation of a bourgeoisie (or 'state class' – see below), (ii) the organisation of distribution (because production is pre-organised externally) in the interests of this bourgeoisie, (iii) the management of investment, accumulation and hence capital formation, (iv) the continuous negotiation and renegotiation of the relative positions of domestic capital and foreign capital, (v) the co-optation, buying-off or suppression of opposition, and (vi) mediation between fractions (or segments) of domestic capital.

The core of Nigerian state capitalism is as follows: the oil revenues enter the political economy, virtually intact, via the central government of the rentier state. The central government, military or civilian, itself spends well over.half these revenues and distributes the rest to State and local governments (for whom centrally distributed funds make up over 90% of all income). This accounts in large measure for the increasing centralism of the rentier state, particularly under military hegemony (see especially chapter 3). Thus, the state has functioned mainly as a 'collective capitalist', providing about two-thirds of all production capital outlays and investing in sectors and enterprises where local capital lacked adequate funds or know-how (especially in strategic economic sectors such as iron and steel, petrochemicals, fertiliser and oil). It has also renegotiated and redefined the relationship between foreign and domestic capital, as will be discussed in the next section. But by far the greatest area of state expansion has been in the state apparatus itself. The number and size of federal offices and officials, of State and local governments, of parastatals (now more than 800) and quasi-government firms, and of the small army of state-dependent contractors, suppliers, agents, advisers and consultants – to say nothing of infrastructural agencies engaged in education, transportation, construction, etc. – have increased to such an unchecked extent that it has become impossible to quantify and classify them.

In a sense, therefore, the state becomes the 'means of production' in peripheral society insofar as it monopolises the means of exploitation, appropriates a large part of the surplus value, and acts as the fundamental source of accumulation and hence of class formation. This direct, unmediated link between economics and politics is in fact a major distinguishing feature of the peripheral state. If in the core country the state has historically evolved some measure of distance or 'relative autonomy' from the economically dominant classes and fractions, the peripheral state fuses class power and political power. The classical distinction between governing class and ruling class is rendered irrelevant at the periphery where the 'governing class' amounts to the coalition of elite groups and segments able to achieve hegemony over the state at a given time. The ongoing struggle for state power is therefore simultaneously a struggle for the means of distribution and consumption which only control of state power can confer. In other words, the mediating and regulatory role foreseen for the state is supplanted by a state that is at once the arena and object of particularist conflicts. The state is politicised and instrumentalised into a partisan state.

Since the state therefore cannot in some measure stand above society, it becomes a broker among the structurally heterogeneous parts or segments of the society. Competition among and between individual (all more or less state-dependent) capitals becomes a complex series of fractional struggles within and for the state. Although this competition takes place within the framework of the nation-state, the relative strengths of the contenders are defined by their sectoral, ethnic or fractional constituencies. Since no clear, permanent alignment of forces can emerge, it is useful to conceptualise the state as 'pre-hegemonic'. But the moment state power is captured by a coalition of particularised segments, it becomes 'their' (provisional) property. This very process of 'privatisation' of state power, however, negates the central state function of system-maintenance. Instability is its corollary.

Paradoxically, however, the more the state is 'privatised' in this way, the greater is its propensity to grow. The inflating peripheral state is a direct consequence of its particularist nature. From below, pressures to expand are generated by popular needs, demands and expectations. The provision, for instance, of jobs, public works projects or social welfare measures lends the state an image of provider and developer and thus enhances its legitimacy. And, from above, aspiring elite members pressure the state to create opportunities for accumulation, new positions and new areas of investment. By conceding to these demands in the form of expanding state involvement in the administration and economy, the state broadens the range of its beneficiaries and creates firmer links of patronage and clienteles.

Yet this state expansion occurs upon the foundation of an unmodified neo-colonial capitalist mode of production. Public sector growth is not supported by changes in the accumulation or distribution processes, as, for example, a modified taxation system or new allocative priorities might represent, but is simply transposed into existing social relations. Profligate and ruinous elite consumption patterns, based on expensive imports, are perpetuated. Or, as just discussed, agriculture is allowed to stagnate while manufacturing, as the object of strategies of import-substitution, is further incorporated into, and dependent upon, the world capitalist economy. Within the context of the oil economy, this merely exaggerates certain well-developed tendencies of the Nigerian post-colonial state (G. Williams, 1976:13):

> . . . the state has promoted the development of capitalism, foreign and domestic, by shifting resources from more competitive to less competitive producers, from craft to factory production, from agriculture to industry, from rural to urban areas, from the poor to the rich, and from Nigerians to foreigners. It has hardly given free rein to the ability of people to produce goods. It has promoted the 'wealth of the nation' but only by the impoverishment of the people.

Williams's observation suggests perhaps the fundamental weakness of 'the' African state operating according to the principles of state capitalism. It is that such a state is and remains a foreign imposition in both its conception and organisation. It derives its logic from the colonial state, not from the real, material conditions of African societies. It serves not the interests of the society in which it remains in some measure a foreign, alienated entity, but the interests of groups and segments whose 'strength' is a function of external conditions and classes. A somewhat different perspective on the same phenomenon is furnished by James Petras who postulates (1984:117) that 'the growth of the state apparatus is directly proportional to the weakness of the local ruling classes in exercising hegemony'. This apparent paradox permits us to bypass the still unresolved, and basically unresolvable, debate about whether the state in the Third World is an 'overdeveloped' (in relation to the society it dominates) or 'underdeveloped' (vis-à-vis external political and economic power) one.[12] For the 'strength' of a state (still following Petras) is only measurable in terms of its capacity to maintain existing social relations of production and to control counter-hegemonic class power within, while exerting sufficient power externally to realise a surplus in the world market and convert it into productive capacity. Since these indicators of 'strength' normally contradict one another – for instance, state power at home is generally built up on the strength of an international class alliance – the problem of 'strength' actually translates into a problem of definitional relativity. State capitalism is merely the domestic correlate of the peripheral state's marginal, subordinate status in the world capitalist system.

To concretise the point for the Nigerian context, the further the rentier state pursues the strategy of state capitalist development, the more it precludes internally-generated, self-centred development. For Watts (1984:409), the rentier state is 'simultaneously enabling and constraining; an avenue to personal accumulation and yet a barrier to industrial growth'. It is not only that the mono-mineral dependency distorts and deforms the other economic sectors, although this is a crucial aspect. It is also that the particularisation of the political economy transforms it into an active *obstacle* to universal development. Its symptoms include, *inter alia*:[13] (i) resource wastage by the principal state actors (imports of luxury goods, arms purchases, prestige construction and infrastructural projects); (ii) administrative incompetence, lack of leadership, corruption and other manifestations of non-rational rule; and (iii) instrumentalisation of the state and its resources by unproductive, parasitical class interests and/or consumption-oriented, particularist interests. More than that, the peripheral state, by its nature, prevents the processes of commodification and creation of relations of exchange (that is, the 'capitalisation' of society, as has happened in the advanced capitalist countries) from penetrating throughout the peripheral society. These processes have been halted by the persistence of the subsistence (or dual) economy, of socio-economic marginalisation and of quasi-feudal relations of production, which they in fact reinforce. Hence the basic contradiction of peripheral capitalism may be expressed as follows:[14]

> The dependent, deformed and heterogeneous relations of production at the periphery limit the growth of the intrinsically heterogeneous forces of production which are only relatively developed and dependent. This contradiction emerges as a threefold structural crisis: as an economic crisis in the form of limited industrialization, as a social crisis in the form of marginalization, and as a political crisis in the form of the 'weak state' [in the sense of low legitimacy, fractionalized class structures, etc.].

Whose state?

This issue of peripheral capitalism as an obstacle to further development brings the discussion back to a central premise of the preceding two sections. It is now evident that peripheral capital stands in a subordinate relationship to capital at the centre and that reproduction processes at the periphery, mediated by the world market, are overwhelmingly determined by valorisation processes emanating from the centre. Peripheral capitalism, in a word, functions as an aspect of surplus production at the core. The reality of these tendencies is not in dispute, at least not among those who adopt a political economy approach in the study of contemporary Nigeria. Controversy arises from their evaluation and projection, and the implications of the debate address the issue of the control over, and beneficiaries of, the Nigerian state.

The neo-colonialism-dependency interpretation has evolved mainly within Nigeria during the past decade.[15] Proponents of this paradigm rightly observe that the fact of foreign ownership and control has persisted into the post-colonial phases, that the essential mode and relations of production remain, that the patterns of trade exchange continue and that the post-colonial political economy is still dependent and extroverted – a mere extension of the colonial international division of labour. It is important to add that these theories almost always contain a strong polemical intent. Like Nkrumah's neo-colonialism framework of two decades earlier, therefore, these works must also be considered as attempts to generate a mobilising, counter-hegemonic ideology against the dominant notions of modernisation and capitalist development. As such, however, they are, in Björn Beckman's words (1985:97), too generalised 'to allow us to see the specific economic and political forms of imperialist domination and how they link up with class struggle'.

The neo-colonial-dependency argument thus tends to deprive the peripheral state of any independent power or will. Certainly the operation of the world market constrains independent development and reduces the scope of state action at the periphery. But even within these parameters, a variety of options and possibilities presents itself to peripheral states. The existence within the world system of Newly Industrialising Countries and Newly Influential Countries, of an OPEC or a G-77, of export-led developers and negative-growth states, refutes any monolithic, undifferentiated explanation based on the constraints of the world system. How these restrictions are coped with and opportunities perceived, seems to be rather more a function of the peripheral political system and its social structure. 'Not the growing importance of the state in the economies of the Third World leads to "dependent development",' Hartmut Elsenhans argues, 'but the relative successes achieved by Third World countries by means of extending state intervention into the international struggle for distribution.'[16] In other words, there is nothing intrinsically necessary about Nigerian dependency; the growth of the state, its appropriation of an increasing share of capital surplus and its stronger role in the international system endow it with the pre-requisites for a strategy of autocentric or basic-human-needs development. Rather, the state 'chooses' – for reasons which will be analysed in the following section – to take the line of least resistance towards economic development. Technology imports, foreign investment, luxury consumption, maintenance of post-colonial class structures and disarticulation are, of course, the milestones on this path.

Nevertheless, irrespective of the development strategy adopted, the Nigerian state, by virtue of oil revenues and state expansion, has embarked on the process of what Bill Warren long ago defined as dependent development:[17] some industrial growth has taken place and some of that growth is based on home market consumption, leading to the creation of certain intermediate sectors and the beginnings of indigenous technological development. For Paul Collins (1983:421) in fact, the image of the Nigerian state as rentier or comprador no longer reflects its real position. For him, the growing power of the Nigerian state – its ability to create a national bourgeoisie within while forcing economic concessions from foreign capital – qualifies it as something like Warren's dependently developing state. Peter Evans' observations on the Brazilian and Nigerian states reinforce Collins's thesis:[18]

> The internationalization of imperialism has given the [peripheral] state a new position of power from which to bargain with the multinationals. If classic dependence was associated with weak states, dependent development is associated with the strengthening of "strong" states in the semi-periphery.

Thus, the growth of state power at the periphery is, in this model, the *sine qua non* of dependent development. The analytical problem is to comprehend a state power which, even as it expands and asserts itself, by definition grows more distorted and dependent. The process of further integration into, and reliance on, the world market economy somehow correlates with greater domestic control and relative international autonomy.

In this context it is purposeful to examine some further implications of indigenisation policy as described in chapter 4. Indigenisation or 'economic nationalism' policies are implemented in consequence of always latent and frequently manifest conflicts of interest between foreign and domestic capital. Within the symbiotic relationship between core capital and the peripheral state, the former has a permanent interest in cheap raw materials, in minimal restrictions on its profit-generating activities, and in withholding the advanced technology and know-how that underpins its economic power. But the peripheral state (or at least its leading elements; see next section) wants the very reverse: higher prices for primary products, strong controls over trans-national corporations' operations at home, and ready access to modern technology. The necessary symbiosis comes about in the form of a provisional pact or alliance, the conditions of which are determined by the relative strengths of the peripheral state classes and the international capitalist classes. Indigenisation, as a central prop of this relationship, is designed to regulate and canalise potentially debilitating competition and to give each of the two parties a permanent – though fluctuating – stake in the prosperity of the other. It is therefore a means, in Claude Ake's words, (1978:49) 'of rationalizing the relationship between the Nigerian bourgeoisie and its patron, international capital'. Contrary, then, to popularised notions of economic sovereignty and the progressive nature of economic nationalism, it is evident that indigenisation furthers collaboration rather than conflict between the two, it does not seek to change the prevailing mode of production but merely to legitimate it. It also, as Sanousi rightly notes, does away with any justification for the notion that the primary contradiction of Nigerian society is that between foreign and domestic capital; the real contradiction is between the combination of Nigerian and foreign owners on the one hand, and the propertyless within Nigerian society on the other, that is, between capital and labour.[19]

Conceptualised in this way, the Nigerian state appears unambiguously as the (national and international) 'collective capitalist' of Marxist theory. For Beckman this 'transnational alliance of international capital backed at both ends by the power of the state' operates in the interests of capital as a whole, that is as a 'unity of capital vis-à-vis the social forces which are opposed to it'. Thus 'the primary role of the Nigerian state is to establish, maintain, protect and expand the conditions of capitalist accumulation in general, without which neither foreign nor Nigerian capital can prosper' (1985:108, 101).

While this conceptualisation is extremely important heuristically, in itself it says little about the composition and interaction of the two sets of capital. Of the two, foreign capital is the most readily comprehended at least at the level of analysis required here. Resting on its own autocentric basis of reproduction and occupying the role of subject in the international capitalist system, it enters, in monopoly form, into the peripheral state through the agency of the transnational corporation or large commercial venture, facilitated by, and organically linked to, the aggregating institutions of international capital such as the World Bank and the International Monetary Fund. But this capacity for self-generating reproduction is not present in peripheral societies whose reproduction is dependent on the superordinate forces of the world market. In other words, the political structures in the peripheral society are not congruent with its economic processes. The peripheral state specialises in the political regulation and ordering of the conditions of production which are initiated and sustained by external economic forces. Market relations, as it were, are controlled by the core, social relations by the periphery. Local state power thus attends to labour discipline, political stability and the politics of distribution within the state. Its task is to ensure the totality of the conditions of capitalist relations of production for which it receives a negotiated share of the surplus, which it facilitates. The more it furthers exploitation within, therefore, the 'stronger' the state stands to become.

This disjuncture between politics as the means of control at the state level and economics as the means of development at the international level can, however, lead to an all too dogmatic insistence on the separation and inversion of 'base' and 'superstructure'. Yet, as Hanisch and Tetzlaff argue, the peripheral state is in many ways a 'territorial incongruence' between the inter-linked processes of 'national' politics and the international economy. Both the state at the core and the state at the periphery are characterised by:[20]

> central decision-making authorities with their far-reaching monopoly of force which operates as a 'superstructure' within the parameters of one and the same social formation, and at the base of which lies the same dominant mode of production – capitalism. The individual components of this system – constituted as states – are linked by chains of interdependence and processes of exchange in a world market arising from the international division of labour, and make up what may be termed the (capitalist) 'world society'.

Elites and underdevelopment

In their by now classical analyses, both Terisa Turner (1976) with her concept of the commercial triangle (between state officials, local middlemen and foreign suppliers) and Peter Evans with his triple alliance (of state, local and international capital) underline the collaborator and auxiliary quality of the local ruling classes of the peripheral state. In chapters 1 and 2 such terms as 'intendant classes' (Cohen) and 'organizational bourgeoisie' (Markovitz) were invoked to account for the crucial role of the state in elite formation. And class interests and alliances constitute the central explanatory variable advanced – in chapters 3, 4, 5 and 8 – for the fractional elite shifts leading to every regime change in Nigeria since independence. These analytical approaches, together with the account of peripheral capitalism in the preceding sections of this chapter, suggest certain features characteristic of the Nigerian ruling classes.

(i) *They necessarily cohere around the state apparatus.* Since the rentier state derives its saleable resource from a single, transnationalised economic sector and since the state, by means of state capitalism, appropriates these revenues and determines their distribution, access to and position in the state are the determining criteria of elite formation. Unlike the bourgeoisie in the advanced capitalist state, the Nigerian state-centred elites have practically no basis outside the state political economy. Where the market – or a common hegemonic class interest deriving from the market-place – does not govern the process of accumulation and surplus appropriation, then this process must be in the outcome of a given political power constellation. As the state expands its role in organising and managing the domestic economy, and given the (historically conditioned) weakness of the local bourgeoisie, the bureaucracy itself evolves into an identifiable class – held together by its relationship not to the means of production, but of distribution. Thus an initially functional corporate group is transformed into a social class whose class power derives from the state. Yet in view of the economic strength of the 'external estate' (foreign collaborator classes), state power is in some measure separated from class power. The bureaucratic-political stratum, whose domestic power stems mainly from its mandate 'to provide invitation, insurance and expeditor'[21] functions for transnational capital, has been variously conceptualised as a 'state bourgeoisie' or 'administrative bourgeoisie', in addition to the notions, mentioned earlier, of organisational bourgeoisie and intendant classes. A more recent, and perhaps more useful coinage is Hartmut Elsenhans' 'state class',[22] a term which has become more or less standard in the peripheral state debate in continental Europe. The value of the state class construct is that it is more inclusive than the other terms, since it takes in those employed directly in the state and those who, though formally independent of it (contractors, agents, consultants, etc.), nevertheless owe their livelihood to it. It also allows for the inclusion of those factions described in chapters 1 and 2 as the political class. And it implies a centralised class which collectively expropriates 'its' share of society's surplus (the other share being that of transnational capital) and, relatively unfettered by either market or popular forces, disposes of it in its own interests, that is, for consumption, prestige projects or private accumulation. Thus the state class takes on the role of the collective owner of the national economy, its resources and its expanding public sector. In the interstices of foreign ownership and the disarticulated economy, as it were, 'the techno-economic autonomy of the oil sector transforms itself into the [relative] socio-economic autonomy of the state'[23] as a function of the latter's monopoly in collecting and distributing its percentage of oil revenues. The state class emerges as a network of clients and patrons linked to the state as the principal supplier of the means of consumption, and economic power is determined by proximity to the state hierarchy itself.

(ii) *They are essentially non-productive,* dependent and hence in large measure parasitical. If the state class's central concern is the expansion of its scope for distribution, as just argued, then its major activity is the inflation of the state's functions and agencies. It utilises resources, expands the state bureaucracy, imports and exports, signs contracts and engages in state enterprise, not in order to realise any longer-term goals, but simply as ends in themselves, i.e. for self-aggrandisement. The purchase of capital-intensive, high-technology machinery and luxury goods, financed entirely by 'unearned' public revenues, both enhances the prestige of the state class and permits private capital accumulation in the form of fees, commissions and bribes – despite the fact that such inputs often exceed the country's absorptive capacity, are accompanied by incredible wastage, lead to indebtedness, and preclude expenditures for welfare and other popular needs. It also produces a broad, *nouveau-riche* series of sub-classes and fractions based on import licences, government contracts, tax evasion scams, subsidies, licences, credit allocation preferences, import–export trade, bureaucratic offices – in short, on rents. The 'nurture capitalism' (Schatz) which the state practises on behalf of the individually weak local bourgeoisies is most clearly expressed through indigenisation policy, where the state selects and promotes the local bourgeoisie through all manner of grants, subsidies, quotas, cheap credit, licence allocations, etc. (see chapter 4).

Middlemanship for Terisa Turner is in fact the driving force and dominant quality of the rentier economy. In terms of her commercial triangle construct, the Nigerian political economy is essentially government by contract in which the foreign supplier operates through local middlemen, who receive kickbacks for their services, in dealings with the state official or comprador, who also receives a commission on the purchase of goods from abroad or the sale of resources on behalf of the state. The state here is the regulator of, or gatekeeper to, commercial opportunities. The foreign partner is the seller, inventor, supplier or purchaser and therefore main beneficiary. And (1985b:23):

> The other side of government by contract is the expansion of a huge army of middlemen, commission-takers, import-export agents, facilitators and contact men. This group links international suppliers or lenders with the state. In the period to 1980 many projects intended to increase production in Nigeria were started but because they were controlled by the private-public comprador alliance, these projects were ill-organized, except to achieve the sponsors' real objective of primitive accumulation.

(iii) *They are fragmented and segmented*. The Turner model, just outlined, has required some modifications in the face of the quantitative changes in the Nigerian political economy since the rise of oil dependency, and these modifications underlie the growing complexity and contradictory nature of the class structure. For one, the growing scope of state enterpreneurial activity frequently eclipsed the middleman in the private sector and permitted state officials to assume a more lucrative, direct comprador role. In addition, state capitalist production in the 1970s threw up a new group of what Turner calls 'state technocrats' who advanced state intervention into the economy and whose rational management role placed them in conflict with existing commercial triangles. Their outlook and interests correspond in many ways with those of the ruling military class who, as has been shown, are also productively and 'rationally' oriented. Moreover, the several generations of middlemen that have operated the state as the means of distribution have blurred these 'ideal-type' categories. Over time middlemen have used part of their cut to enter into import-substituting industry, for example; retired military officers have invested in agrobusiness; and state compradors have become private-sector consultants and fixers. Any combination of these activities may be carried on simultaneously by the same individual.

From these developments, is it possible to infer a movement toward a 'hegemonic bloc' on the part of the Nigerian elite? Only a very substantial leap of logic would permit such a conclusion. The Nigerian ruling classes have so far not collectively managed to establish their hegemony, either by imposition or persuasion, upon the remaining social classes. In part this is due to the absence of a 'historical mandate' such as that accruing to the Western bourgeoisie in overcoming feudalism. In part there is no functional basis for the Nigerian ruling class as the initiator and bearer of development (however defined). And in part this class lacks a basis in national cohesion, since it owes its existence in large measure to an external bourgeoisie with whom it collaborates to the detriment of any 'national interest'. The one possibility for the state class to escape from this cycle of delegitimation – namely, to deliver material progress via economic development – is inhibited by the fact of dependent development.

In the absence of a unifying hegemonic basis of elite rule, access to the ruling class – the state class – is determined by sectoral, ethnic, sectional and therefore particularist factors. The more these particularist enablements are reinforced, paradoxically, the stronger are the respective elites' claims on and influence in the central government, and the greater is their negotiating power vis-à-vis the external bourgeoisies. At the same time, the state-centred accumulation strategy stunts the development of the Nigerian bourgeoisie into a universal hegemonic class in the economic sphere, because state ownership and faulty utilisation of the means of production prevent its evolution into a broadly based, self-aware class in and for itself.

Particularised and segmented in these ways, the only realistic 'hegemony' attainable by the state class is a temporally limited pact based on concrete mutual interests. This 'hegemony' correlates with the concept of intra-class and inter-class struggle developed in chapter 4 insofar as it relates merely to the provisional attainment of class solidarity attendant upon the realisation of specific interests vis-à-vis the popular classes. Here again, indigenisation policy illustrates the point:[24]

> Indigenization as partial ownership of partial sections of business enterprises, by partial sections of the bourgeoisie, was thus essentially a compromise formula, aimed at reconciling the technocratic cadre within the state – who favored state capitalism – [with] the Nigerian owning class – who favored the promotion of private and indigenous enterprise – and foreign capital, which both the state and private Nigerian investors saw as constituting an external estate in the Nigerian economy.

Similarly, the allocation of positions in the state bureaucracy is a tried instrument to ensure intra-elite cohesion. Thus perhaps the most important tactic contributing to 'national reconciliation' after the civil war was the federal government's readiness to restore the 'Biafran' political class to its former positions in the state hierarchy, irrespective of their behaviour during the attempted secession.[25] Or the vast planning process, with its input from all sectors and levels of the state bureaucracy, binds the state elite into the process of systematised public plunder.

Otherwise, however, the Nigerian class structure, like class structures in similar peripheral capitalist states, reflects the structural heterogeneity of its political economy. It is at once more complex than that of core states, while the classes themselves are much weaker and the ultimately dominant class is external; it is thus more factionalised and characterised by a variety of more or less unstable alliances.[26] Since this prehegemonic quality of elite segments has been discussed in some detail in chapter 8, particularly with reference to factional alignments surrounding the polarising issues of OPEC membership, the IMF loan and privatisation of the parastatals, it need not be further elaborated here. It is important to recall, however, that the fact of elite segmentation renders the political economy unstable, crisis-susceptible and unbalanced.

(iv) And, finally, *they underdevelop Nigeria*. Because the state class in its own interest deploys the powers and institutions of the state in order to maintain the basically mercantilist and export-trade orientation of the economy and in so doing ensures the pre-eminence of foreign capital in the peripheral state, it precludes any strategy of autocentric development. As a sectionalised, segmented, tribalised and therefore divided class, it possesses no historical *raison d'être* capable of mobilising the popular classes for social goals. Because it is particularised and self-centred, it is incapable even of creating a broad, universally accessible infrastructure to underpin its continued domination. If the rising Western bourgeoisie once created generally beneficial systems of transport and communications, of health care and education, of social amenities and state services, the Nigerian state class in a sense fashions its 'private' infrastructure, endowing itself with expensive cars and private jets, with individual generators and water tanks, with fenced compounds and private armies – all paid for with surpluses realised at the expense of society as a whole. Economic decision-making is accomplished not in accordance with economic rationality but on the basis of prevailing power relations among segments of the elite. Despite the inpouring of oil revenues during the 1970s, a 1981 ILO study pointed out that for the majority of the Nigerian people (especially rural dwellers and those in big-city slums) living conditions had grown considerably worse.[27] The state class's internecine rivalries and perpetual conflicts undermine political and economic stability, and create a Hobbesian war of all (factions and interests) against all. Ministries, parastatals and other state institutions, each sectionally, ethnically or personally demarcated, engage in unremitting struggle for a share of society's surplus rather than integrating and co-ordinating their operations in the interest of society as a whole. This structurally conditioned self-centred behaviour justifies the most cynical interpretation of the elites' role in the dysfunctioning of the Nigerian political system.

A central, crisis-producing contradiction of the peripheral economy arises from the conflict, alluded to in previous chapters, between the need to maintain a balanced, integrated economy in the interests of capital as a whole, and the continued instrumentalisation of the state in order to realise particularised group interests. In times of economic prosperity conflicts are generally submerged under an intra-elite pact (if not conspiracy) to carry on parallel self-enriching activities. This is particularly so where, as in the case of oil, the surplus need not be extracted directly from the popular classes and where the required inputs can be obtained from without. But in periods of economic crisis, which can be drastic and unpredictable in the mono-mineral economy, intra-elite struggles may be bitter, protracted and systemically debilitating, especially as more and more surplus must be generated from within (austerity measures, wage freezes, rollbacks of public services, etc.). Even in such situations, the peripheral state class cannot ally itself, either totally or as a combination of segments, with the popular classes – as once the European bourgeoisie and proletariat joined in the anti-feudal struggle – since any strategy promoting mass economic well-being or development would *ipso facto* undermine the basis and rationale of the peripheral state. The state class, in a word, has a vested interest in the suppression of basic human needs and in perpetuating economic underdevelopment, and this interest is most evident in times of economic crisis. For instance, the austerity measures proclaimed by both the Shagari and Buhari regimes in the face of the oil glut of the early 1980s not only weighed most heavily on the popular classes (see chapters 6, 8), they were both bypassed (smuggling, immoderate consumption) and in fact capitalised upon (hoarding, trade in import licences, price-gouging) by factions of the state class. Thus, following Petras, the state class may usefully be regarded as a coalition of 'collaborator classes whose function is to organize the state and economy in accordance with core definitions of the international division of labour'. Theirs is a 'double role – exploitation within the society and exchange outside the society'.[28] As such it remains the pivotal link in the nexus of underdevelopment.

To sum up this section, it is evident that the state class, embedded in a peripheral and exploitative role in the world capitalist economy, is structurally underdeveloping Nigeria. Since the point applies to civilian and military fractions alike, a major premise of this book – namely, that the political system is a function of the development of the political economy and state class over time – is vindicated. If the international market and the local state with its ruling classes collectively constitute the determining factors (or independent variables), the form in which they are expressed (dependent variable) is the political system with all its structures and processes.

In one of the most perceptive remarks attributed to Shehu Shagari, the former president was said to have observed that in Nigeria there exist only two parties – the civilians and the military. The alternation of civilian and military regimes must now be seen as the norm, rather than an aberration, of Nigerian politics. And, given the peculiarities of the Nigerian political economy, this pendulum-movement may be the adequate (or least inadequate) political 'form' of system maintenance.

The question of whether or not this is the case may be addressed in terms of James O'Connor's thesis that any capitalist state, core or peripheral, must in the long term perform the two contradictory functions of (particularist) accumulation and (universal) legitimation.[29] In the peripheral state, not only are these functions distorted and transnationalised, as has just been discussed, but political power is not separated, as it largely is in the West, from ownership of the means of production (or distribution). Because this is so, neither elections nor *coups* in Nigeria can effect a real transfer of power from one social class to another; they merely exchange sets of factions of the state class. Only where there exists a (relative) separation between 'bourgeois society' and 'the state' in capitalist societies, Elsenhans argues, can mass interests be articulated via the institutions of the state. Without the prospect of a real power transfer, political parties (or, by extension, military-led factions) can at best perform a brokerage function within the state class.[30] In the absence of countervailing forces, groups or powers, therefore, the formal classification of party systems or military regime-types is practically irrelevant. The state, rather than the individual parties, is the instrument of economic development and source of leading cadres, and it encompasses and adjusts the various particular interests.

Nevertheless, the state must master the conflicting pulls of accumulation and legitimation. Again and again it has been demonstrated throughout this book that every factional combination of the state class, where it retains political hegemony for an extended period, has a propensity to lapse into dysfunctional self-aggrandisement. The dynamics of the respective regimes may differ somewhat – the military tending toward excessive repression and narrowing of the state classes, the civilians tending to surrender entirely to middleman-comprador elements – but both precipitate a crisis of legitimation over time, because of their preoccupation with accumulation. Where 'public opinion' cannot foresee an end to the self-enriching activities of the particular elite coalition in power at the moment (as after Gowon's retraction of his promise to recivilianise), mass disaffection is the result. But where the next factional realignment can be expected or at least realistically considered a possibility, the current regime is legitimised and stabilised in some measure. General Babangida's pledge to recivilianise in 1992 may be seen in this context. By the same token, the deprivations of the Second Republic were rendered more bearable by the awareness that the military could choose to intervene if the situation became intolerable. The longer more or less regular regime turnover continues, the more salient will its legitimating role become. In other words, government-form rotation in itself, rather than constitutional norms and political continuity, becomes the 'principle' of government and the means by which individual regime contradictions are alleviated.

The alternation of regime types also relates to particular conjunctures. As the peripheral state is beset by, and forced to adjust to, fluctuations in the world capitalist system, it is better served by different governing forms. Again following Elsenhans, shifting conjunctures generate various pressures:[31]

> Where pressure for an expansion of capitalist relations of exchange emanate from the highly monopolistic, hegemonial economic sectors, threatening the existence of weaker capital fractions [or for that matter, when economic shrinkage threatens the same fractions from a different side – W. G.], these correspond to authoritarian forms of politics. On the other hand, phases of the socio-economic status quo are more appropriate to 'democratic' forms.

To conceptualise the problem in a somewhat related perspective, it can be argued that the chronic legitimacy crisis of the peripheral state can only be countered – failing any prospect of broad, human-needs-oriented development – by *repression* and *populism*,[32] which are therefore two sides of the same phenomenon. Populism, broadly defined as the complex of measures adopted by the state elite to create system legitimacy (nationalist rhetoric, co-optation, corruption, etc.) roughly corresponds to the paradigm of elite consolidation (or 'agglutination') developed in previous chapters and is best expressed in a liberal-democratic structure. Repression occurs where a dominant (usually military-led) faction imposes solutions on society and restricts the number and strength of ruling elite factions; it correlates with the military regime. Of course both regime types employ varying degrees of repression and populism but, with the passage of time, the escalating dialectic of rapid (though fitful) economic growth and elite self-enrichment, on the one hand, and the increasing marginalisation and pauperisation of the popular classes, on the other, favours the former.

Excursus on foreign policy

In the mid-1970s, a particularly auspicious conjuncture developed within which Nigerian foreign policy was able to move beyond its rather inward pro-Western posture of the First Republic and the undistinguished conservative image of the Gowon years. National reconciliation following the civil war, massive oil revenues after the formation of OPEC, and the apparent consolidation of the state class on the strength of indigenisation and recivilianisation policies coincided with the emergence of a new 'corrective' military government whose self-image and popular legitimacy rested on its 'dynamic' and 'reforming' ethos. Nigerian foreign policy became assertive and in some measure progressive. Simultaneously, the country became a leader in the search for regional unity and development (formation of the Economic Community of West African States – ECOWAS), a force for pan-African co-operation (activities in the Organisation of African Unity – OAU) and a leading voice in the liberation of African territories under colonial rule or direct neo-colonial domination (support for the MPLA in Angola, aid to the frontline states in Southern Africa). In pursuit of these policies, Nigerian foreign policy occasionally came up against, and overrode, certain Western interests: those of the USA in Angola, of France in the formation of ECOWAS and opposition to the former colonial power's military involvement in the Shaba Province of Zaïre, of the West as a whole in the establishment of the OPEC cartel, and – most dramatically – of Britain when Nigeria unilaterally decided in 1979 to nationalise BP because of its violations of the international oil embargo against South Africa.

These developments fed a veritable cottage industry of scholarly works focussed on

Nigerian foreign policy. Insofar as this literature went beyond descriptive accounts of individual policies or simple adulatory paeans to the country's new-found power and prestige, it focussed on Nigeria's evolution into a 'regional power' (Aluko, 1981:1) or its entry into the 'semi-periphery' (Shaw and Fasehun, 1981:209) of the world system or the ranks of 'sub-imperialist' powers. The aspiring political class and its allies in the media appropriated this ethos and converted it into such bombastic claims as 'Nigeria's Leadership Role in Africa',[33] or Nigeria's manifest destiny 'to lead Africa and the Black race'.[34] The limits of this rhetoric were probably reached with the agitation for nuclear weapons for Nigeria. Foreign Minister Iya Abubakar argued that, since Nigeria had become 'a great country', it needed a strong defence capacity; it must therefore become a nuclear power – 'at any price' – in order to challenge the South African *apartheid* regime.[35]

Today, from the perspective of the foreign policy failures in Chad and Cameroon, the winding down of ECOWAS, the disunity in the OAU over the Libyan and Western Saharan issues and the 'return' of Nigeria to the (unprefixed) periphery, it is perhaps too facile to denigrate all these inflated expectations. More to the point, these fluctuations afford an opportunity to 'locate' foreign policy as a function and product of the domestic political economy rather than as a quasi-autonomous area of state policy.

One of the central tasks of foreign policy in a peripheral state is, not unlike indigenisation in the domestic sphere, to define and redefine the relationship between the internal and external dominant classes in the light of the evolving international division of labour. Thus the 'golden era' of Nigerian foreign policy, roughly from 1975 to 1980, coincides with the peaking of the state class's relative economic power on the strength of its control over a strategic resource and its share of oil revenues. Apart from the BP nationalisation (and even then only tendentially, since the state-owned firm still depends on multinational inputs), none of the economic measures of this period posed a threat to the domination of the multinational corporations; they merely renegotiated certain terms and conditions within the international division of labour. On the other hand, the active Nigerian part in the formation of ECOWAS and its concern with preserving stability within the OAU could equally be interpreted as an attempt to establish spheres of economic influence for Nigerian export sales which were supposed to follow from increasing import-substituting manufactures. In any case, Nigerian influence in ECOWAS and among the frontline states was based almost entirely on grants, donations, soft loans, technical assistance, preferential oil allocations and other material aid, rather than any moral force or ideological appeals. When oil revenues diminished, so did Nigeria's influence in these councils.

Activist foreign policy was thus conducted on the strength of the country's growing integration into the world capitalist economy. Well over 90% of its trade was with, and almost all its imports came from, the advanced capitalist countries. Yet in order to enhance its credibility and influence in the African area, it felt constrained to articulate a foreign policy that supported liberation movements and radical regimes (Patriotic Front, MPLA), which, by virtue of their anti-imperialist aims, negated the international economic 'base' on which Nigerian rested. So long as these causes are relatively remote and long-term, and the targets more or less 'soft', their looming contradiction can be averted. But when the issue presents a direct threat to the state class's interests, anti-imperialism yields to self-preservation. For instance, where the Doe and Rawlings *coups* raised the spectre of a 'contagion effect', Nigeria became a leader in the movement to bar Liberia from representation in ECOWAS, while Nigerian oil to Ghana was embargoed. Under the Second Republic, the gap between rhetoric and foreign policy reality became especially wide. The ideals of West African unity were set back for generations as a result of the precipitate, arbitrary and brutal expulsion of immigrant workers at the first sign of economic crisis. When in 1980 the United States failed to support Namibian independence, despite earlier pledges, Shagari nevertheless concluded a series of agricultural agreements with President Carter. Or when in March 1981 Britain rejected a series of Nigerian proposals concerning reform of the Commonwealth, Shagari publicly advocated an open-door policy for British imports.[36] Many more similar examples could be cited.

The second major function of Nigerian foreign policy is its domestic use as an *ersatz* ideology, analogous to the mixed economy or liberal democracy. Foreign policy is a principal area of elite consensus-formation. Formulated entirely by elites and presented intact to the population, it is the one ideological area relatively removed from domestic interest-conflict. Particularly in times of economic prosperity, concepts such as Africa's giant or Nigeria's leadership role in Africa, coupled with anti-imperialism, anti-racism and black solidarity, can exert a certain integrative or pacifying effect. But, like the socio-economic provisions of the 1979 Constitution, they are not justiciable; nothing actually has to be done about realising them. For these reasons, Nigerian foreign policy is best analysed in terms of its *class content*, an approach which helps to overcome the regime-by-regime focus alluded to earlier. Military governments, as self-proclaimed 'correctives' without revolutionary missions, tend to rely on the instant legitimacy deriving from their self-image of efficiency, probity and rationality. Their activist ethos and heterogeneous mass basis almost compel a radically phrased foreign policy, not least as a substitute for the lack of fundamental reforms which is a necessary consequence of that 'corrective' function. Civilian regimes, based on political party hegemony and dominated by a comprador/middleman-centred set of factions, tend to be more inwardly oriented, concerned with producing consensus in regulating access to the troughs of state patronage, and hence more 'moderate' in foreign-policy behaviour. Different constellations of class interests explain much about different foreign policy approaches.

The point of this excursus is evident: the study of Nigerian foreign policy as though it were somehow detached from the domestic political economy is a barren undertaking. In the context of peripheral capitalism, the class links, commercial interdependencies and economic dependencies which characterise and define Nigeria's political economy are the more salient analytical focus.

Incomplete hegemony

The peripheral capitalist state in Nigeria is thus permanently beset by a series of interrelated structural contradictions. As so far depicted, these include contradictions (i) between domestic political sovereignty and international economic dependency, (ii) between segments and factions of the elite stratum, (iii) between capabilities and aspirations, and (iv) between the exigencies of accumulation and legitimation. Though these are all determining contradictions which deeply affect the Nigerian political economy, they are nevertheless secondary. The primary contradiction of the Nigerian state – and this too has already been outlined – is that between capital and labour. The peripheral state is governed by and subject to the (transnationalised) processes of capitalism. It is the product and agent of 'capital as a whole' and socio-economic relations within it are in the main thoroughly 'capitalised' or, perhaps better, commodified.

The existence of a large public sector, of vast clientele networks and of a strong pre-capitalist sector does not change the fact of capital domination; they are merely its peripheral manifestations. 'Peripheral capitalism' remains the predominant mode of 'production' and the most adequate (least inadequate?) characteristic feature of the Nigerian state formation. The structural heterogeneity of post-colonial society, however, reproduces the capital–labour contradiction in a 'distorted' – that is, different from the West – form. Capital enters the colonial society in the form of imperialist monopolies; Nigerianisation of the political structure and indigenisation of parts of the economy replace colonial monopolies with transnational monopolies. Capital is preorganised and internationalised, and maintains a 'base' inside and outside the territorial shell called 'Nigeria'. Labour, on the other hand, not only organises *ex posto facto*, but is confined in its scope to, and is a function of, the structurally heterogeneous society. 'Labour' in Nigeria has therefore not emerged as a large, conscious and organised 'proletariat' but instead – corresponding to the segmented economy and factionalised elite – has been sectoralised, tribalised and hence instrumentalised by colonial and post-colonial elites alike. By far the largest component of labour is a peasantry which, as a relatively amorphous, isolated, impoverished, quasi-subsistent social group comprising perhaps seven in ten Nigerians, is scarcely organisable and mobilisable for sustained social change. The urban 'masses' too, as a category of mainly first- and second-generation peasants engaged in economic activities (portering, touting, petty trade, casual labour, domestic service and the like) and also not conducive to political organisation and class politics, do not constitute a permanent, consistent countervailing force to state-class power.

The situation of the trade unions is rather more ambiguous. On the one hand, the relatively small size of local organised labour is a direct reflection of an international division of labour which locates much of the dynamic, employment-generating 'base' of the economy outside the country's national territory. The formal waged sector therefore represents only a minuscule percentage of the workforce, while the existence of a massive 'reserve army' of unemployed and semi-employed acts as a powerful disincentive to militancy. Since most jobs are concentrated in the extractive, service and simple processing industries, and – with the notable exception of the oil industry – are practically interchangeable,

> the power of management to hire and fire is substantially increased. The union in an underdeveloped country is, in short, in an inherently unequal position. To rely solely on collective bargaining in these circumstances is simply unproductive. (Cohen, 1974:147–8)

'Management' here refers mainly to government which, employing between three-fifths and four-fifths of organised labour, acts as the main determiner of wage levels and working conditions, as well as the central agency for labour control and discipline. Moreover, the interaction between the state class and the trade union elite has frequently led to the incorporation of parts of the latter into the former, while intra-union power and jurisdictional struggles have reproduced segmentation and, in particular, ethnicity within the movement itself. On the other hand, precisely the trade unions' weaknesses explain much of their potential strength in the peripheral economy. Since wage levels are not determined in the market-place in accordance with the factors of supply and demand, they must be set through organised political action by the workers against the state itself. Concentrated in the urban areas and in the strategic economic sectors, led by a multi-ethnic leadership cadre, more organised than any other group among the popular classes, still linked directly to the countryside by a multiplicity of ties and sentiments, and most directly affected by shifting government policies and omissions, the trade unions – somewhat analogous to the middle ranks of the military – remain a permanent, though mainly latent and numerically small, class-based challenge to the ruling classes of the peripheral state. In this context, James Zasha's conclusions about industrial workers of the Middle Belt are of more general applicability:[37]

> [they are] neither a revolutionary proletariat nor a labour aristocracy; rather the incorporation of politicized ethnicity in class formation renders revolutionary conceptions of the Nigerian working class premature.

The broader phenomenon, of which these developments are essentially symptoms, is the peculiar nature of peripheral accumulation. At the core, in early modern Europe, the goods for the rulers' luxury consumption were created within (court handicraftsmen, tailors, etc.; later, suppliers of uniforms and guns) so that the workforce's organisation and power evolved abreast of the development of the economy. The resistance of the underprivileged to exploitation and the registering of their collective demands forced the ruling classes continually to make material concessions to them. The resultant redistribution of incomes and services flowed back into an expanding and productive domestic market. In the industrialisation phases, mass social democratic parties and trade unions formed a counterhegemonic class power in the liberal-capitalist state. But at the periphery, the luxuries and goods for elite-consumption are produced abroad, with few 'backward linkages'. They are paid for with raw materials and minerals, which drains capital surplus without much affecting the class structure at the bottom, though enhancing elite power above. When such imports become too expensive, the peripheral state resorts to (dependent) import-substitution behind protective walls. Since the capital-intensive technology employed in both types of economic policy limits the expansion of the wage force, no real proletariat – to say nothing of a 'national' middle class – is able to emerge. Thus class formation and class conflict are inhibited by the operation of peripheral capitalism. One searches in vain for a concrete, structural alliance among the subordinate classes which might be capable of seizing state power and transferring it from one combination of social classes to another.

Does this mean, then, that despite its fragmentation and segmentation, the ruling class in the Nigerian peripheral state has achieved a permanent hegemony? The beginnings of an answer to this rather rhetorical question are contained in the Marxian concept of contradictions, namely 'the tendency inherent within a specific mode of production to destroy those very preconditions on which its survival depends'.[38] The Nigerian mode of 'production' – peripheral capitalism – has been shown to have 'developed' in such a way as to produce disjunctures between a substantially foreign economic ruling class (with its junior partner, a comprador-middleman local elite) and a domestic, overpoliticised state-centred class. While it has not produced an organised, class-based, countervailing opposition, it has created an internally contradictory, unproductive and pre-hegemonic ruling class whose fragmentary nature prevents it from establishing control and direction in the political economy, but whose narrow interests, both long- and short-term, preclude an alliance between any combination of its segments and the popular classes.

The 'fragile equilibrium' posited in chapter 8 is therefore a function of the pre-hegemonic quality of the state-centred elite whose elaborate, chop-based coalitions can be rent and shaken, for instance over the issues of OPEC solidarity, IMF conditionalities or countertrade. Economic crisis in particular threatens intra-elite stability, since, for reasons explained above, it leads to instant delegitimation. When the 'inverted pyramid resting on a hydrocarbon pinnacle' teeters, the entire socio-economic edifice is put in jeopardy. In mid-1986, for instance, it was impossible for the government to formulate a national budget in the face of low and unpredictable oil rents. A remark by the AFRC President captures the contingent nature of the Nigerian economy: 'Whenever the market settles down, we will reassess the situation and decide whether or not a review of the budget will be necessary.'[39] Without a budget, the planning process also ran aground, and the Fifth National Development Plan had to be deferred until 1987. This produced repercussions throughout the economy. When in the rentier state foreign revenues decline, elite luxury consumption is cut and essential imported inputs for agribusiness and manufacturing cannot be obtained, Government revenues from profit taxes, import levies and the like decline apace, and state subsidies and services cannot be delivered. Unemployment rises. External debts must then be postponed or renegotiated, thus necessarily conceding to creditors (World Bank, IMF, EEC, transnational banks) an enhanced influence on domestic politics. The way out of such crises is invariably sought by increasing the rate of exploitation at home (austerity, wage reductions, welfare rollbacks, etc.).

It is the drastic nature of economic crises at the periphery – or better: margin – of the world market and their sharp denial of the promise of 'development' that instigates a critical awareness on the part of the popular classes. If populism and repression are the twin props of elite domination, as has been argued above, then popular disaffection and spontaneous militancy are their counterparts in the counter-hegemonic struggle. For Peter Gutkind (1975:30), the consciousness of the African poor is 'spontaneous, sporadic and localized rather than predictable and consistent'. Popular opposition – which, despite the lack of empirical studies, can certainly be said to have increased rapidly in recent years – is typically unorganised, unco-ordinated and therefore relatively short-lived. But it is also normally intensive. Ostensibly religiously motivated mass uprisings have occurred in the course of the Maitatsine riots in Kano in 1980, in Yola and Maiduguri in 1982 and in Gombe in 1985, with huge losses in lives and property. In rural areas there have been many cases of peasant resistance to specific state policies, notably the villagers' sustained opposition to their relocation in order to make way for the Bakalori dam. And organised labour, though subject more frequently and more intensively than other popular sectors to state repressive measures and, since September 1978, decreed into a National Labour Congress with its 42 constituent unions under state control, has continued to act at crucial conjunctures as a militant opposition, characterised by walkouts, sabotage, stoppages and, in particular, nationwide general strikes in 1964, 1971, 1975 and 1981.

An emergent 'counter-hegemonic bloc' is thus discernible among the so-called masses of Nigeria. *Objectively*, the groups and interests that constitute this bloc are united in their common exploitation. M. Watts nicely captures their commonality in terms of the concept of exclusion. He posits (1984:423):

> the oil boom systematically excluded what one might call the 'popular classes' from any significant material benefits, at the same time that they were exposed to the radical social and economic dislocation of urban explosion, new forms of rural intervention by the state, and the cargo cultism of the privileged elites. It is precisely this exclusion – from access to state patronage, to the market, to new internationalized styles of consumption, and so on – that asserts a class unity to these 'popular' assemblages of informal sector commodity producers, poor peasants, low-level industrial workers, and lumpen elements. And it is, of course, from within these excluded ranks that resistance to rapidly changing material circumstances actually surfaced.

But *subjectively*, the lack of organisational coherence within and among the excluded popular classes is reflected in the absence of an encompassing political movement with a unifying strategy for the realisation of long-term goals. Because the resentments and cynicism[40] of the popular classes are both intense and inchoate, they lend themselves to 'hijacking'[41] by aspiring politicians or military officers seeking mass legitimacy for their current intra-elite factional realignment.

Beyond peripheral capitalism?

Quite obviously then, any prospects for overcoming underdevelopment and capital domination in Nigeria will hinge in large measure on whether and to what extent the popular classes are capable of effecting a qualitative link between their objective situation and their subjective awareness, perhaps achieving the kind of insight once formulated by Bala Usman:[42]

> It is not as individual persons, or as Katsinawa or Zazzagawa, Daurawa or Kaje, Gwari or Katab, Northerners or Southerners, Ibos or Igalas, Muslims or Christians, that we become unemployed, fail to get paid wages and salaries or become unable to afford to buy Omo, groundnut oil and sugar. It is not even simply because we are teachers, drivers, steel or textile workers, market labourers, students, peasant farmers, carpenters or petty traders that we are subjected to this hardship. The root causes of our suffering and hardship go beyond our individual, sectional or even sectoral role.

How these 'root causes of suffering and hardship' may evolve into an anti-imperialist organisation and strategy, remains a matter of projection and indeed speculation at this juncture.

In the longer term – and the analysis so far practically compels this conclusion – peripheral capitalism in Nigeria cannot be overcome without the active involvement of the popular classes in a form of government related to their fundamental needs and interests, one which would *ipso facto* depend on more autocentric articulated development. Such arrangements would have to exclude the dominant elite stratum – in both its military- and civilian-led variants – not only because it is hopelessly compromised by its complicity in organising the local state, on behalf of international capital, in pursuit of its own ends, but because the interests of the popular classes can only be realised *in direct and fundamental opposition* to those of the state-centred classes. At present it is difficult to foresee how counter-hegemonic power might evolve out of the current cynical and critical ethos. The trade unions, with their relatively coherent anti-imperialist programmes, their supra-ethnic composition, their multiple links – via individual workers – to the urban masses and the peasantry, might, under propitious conditions, develop into an organisational and ideological centre of a mass oppositional movement. This is particularly true of the well organised and highly conscious oil workers' union. But, by itself, the labour movement remains too small and divided to constitute such a movement. Given the distribution of coercive power in Nigerian society, no revolutionary bloc could sustain itself against the international and local elite forces without support in the military. The increasingly radicalised cadre of junior officers (see chapters 3 and 8), backed perhaps by elements among the rank and file, would at the very least have to ensure the military's neutrality in such an event. Concerning the canalisation of peasant opposition, there is at present no broader agency to link their individual struggles and uprisings. Here local governments – if freed from State domination and democratised in ways suggested in chapter 9 – might eventually provide the nucleus of an adequate organisation. This would be especially so, if rural peoples had adequate material enablements (literacy, education) and appropriate organisational forms (rural co-operatives) to participate in governing themselves. Beyond these, the appropriate forms might develop in the course of the struggles themselves. Turner and Baker, for instance, are most optimistic about the development of 'popular committees' of workers and peasants as an 'alternative thrown up by those on the receiving end of commercial capitalism'.[43] Like similar committees in Ghana and Upper Volta, they would be locally focussed and would resemble the communes, soviets and shop-floor organisations generated by analogous struggles in other parts of the world.

In the short term, however, the question posed in this section is more realistically addressed in terms of how best to foster the *preconditions* for the eventual transformation of Nigerian peripheral capitalism. At this conjuncture, two broad immediate possibilities are worth mentioning.

From the analysis of military government, first, it is evident that a junior-officer or rank-and-file military *coup* is a permanent and increasingly likely possibility. Both the Buhari and Babangida interventions have been shown to have been, at least in part, pre-emptive *putsches*. Though it is impossible to determine the degree of consciousness and the goals of these intermediate military groups, available evidence suggests growing dissatisfaction with the cycle of *coups* and counter*coups* and the performance of the Nigerian state. In this, the military undoubtedly shares the feelings of the growing lower middle classes of professionals, teachers, administrators and technocrats who once supported liberal democracy but who defected in large numbers from the comprador-led Second Republic. Moreover, it is generally known that much of the recruitment into the armed forces nowadays derives from critical, conscious young people who regard the military as the only realistic basis from which to effect social change and who see themselves as carrying out a revolutionary role within it. The military is thus tendentially becoming a vanguard of popular struggles. The difficulties which might arise should such a scenario be enacted relate to the fact that there is no necessary link between the sub-officer class in the military and the popular classes. Such a *coup* could produce a Rawlings or a Doe, a Sankara or a Bokassa, and in any case runs the constant danger of being 'hijacked' by the ruling military elite, as Nzeogwu was by Ironsi. A revolution effected in the absence of the popular classes – though it be proclaimed to be 'on their behalf' – will always be subject to the exigencies of 'voluntarism' and 'substitutionism'.

Second, the Babangida exercise in recivilianisation, which is to culminate in October 1992, suggests itself as an opportunity to look beyond peripheral capitalism. The salient motive force of this process has already been set out in chapter 8: it is in the first instance a legitimacy-producing device for the current military regime and a renewed attempt to find a permanent, functional means of welding the segments and fractions of the state class into an hegemonic bloc. Its medium, the Political Bureau, has been shown to have been established by, and constituted of, members of the elite groups – though this time, compared to the CDC, with a more radical component. Indeed, in the words of its Marxist-oriented member, Eddie Madunagu, 'those who actually produce the wealth of the nation don't really participate in the debate'.[44]

It is not surprising, in this context, that much of the debate surrounding the appropriate form of government for Nigeria concerns the old Azikiwean notion of a civilian–military diarchy or, more recently, 'cimilcy'.[45] S. E. Oyovbaire, whose position as a member of the Political Bureau makes his views particularly relevant, has provided a concise rationale for a diarchy. Since the 'military factor' has proved to be a central aspect rather than a brief deviation in Nigerian politics, he wonders:[46]

> How did Nigeria, in the first place, become entangled with the burden of 'liberal democracy' when, as a matter of historical fact, we have been ruled much more peacefully, both in time and quality of social life, by 'coercion' than by 'consensus'? I am saying that this regime together with historical and social scientists should address itself not to some idea of a return to a democracy which has had no Nigerian history – 'the democracy of Tafawa Balewa,

Benjamin Azikiwe, Shehu Shagari, Augustus Akinloye, Umaru Dikko, Uba Ahmed and Joseph Wayas' – but the one which has historical contents and authenticity (pre-colonial, colonial and post-colonial), the one in which the so-called separate civil order and military order are structurally and normatively fused in one social order.

As this quotation implies, any prescription of diarchy for Nigeria – or, for that matter, any ruling form that prescribes bureaucratic authoritarianism borne by presumed 'universal classes' – rests, in its ultimate effect, on three presumptions, namely (a) that, as hitherto, the popular classes must be excluded from a share of intra-societal decision-making, (b) that the 'historical content' and 'authenticity' of colonial and post-colonial reality are immutable and must simply be incorporated into the political system rather than being overcome, and (c) that peripheral capitalism, presided over by the state class, is the proper form of government for Nigeria. For diarchy amounts to a new, even more comprehensive scheme of elite consolidation and hence of popular exclusion. Assuming that it could be successfully implemented, it might well initially derive some legitimation from its novelty value and the semblance of national unity which it would exude. But as an even broader coalition of the various segments and fractions of the ruling class, it would be subject to and would magnify all the contradictions and conflicts that beset more modest elite groupings. The intra-military and military-civil-service conflicts of the purely military regime would enter into and infuse the comprador-national and middleman-producer conflicts of the civilian regime, and the conglomeration would be undermined by the external estate, the world market and the rentier economy. The legitimacy-producing effect of regime rotation would of course be forfeited, and the state-centred classes would appear even more like a monolithic ruling class from the perspective of the popular classes. Diarchy would thus heighten class consciousness in the longer term and would ensure that the populist strategy of elite domination would more and more yield to a strategy of repression.

For these reasons a strategy aimed at overcoming peripheral capitalism in Nigeria could usefully start from a critique of the diarchy proposition as a diarchy of state plunder on behalf of capital as a whole. This strategy could monitor and check the essentially intra-elite debate which all such regime turnovers evoke. In so doing it might succeed in forging a minimal programme for popular-class consolidation corresponding to that of the ruling classes. Although the formulation of such a programme is beyond the scope and mandate of this book, it is worth considering some possible elements of it here.

(i) Following Claude Ake, 'defensive radicalism' has been seen to be an essential feature of elite domination. In chapter 4 the concept was linked expressly to the Fundamental Objectives and Directives of State Policy of the 1979 Constitution. It was argued that, in the absence of a binding mandate on government to realise these social rights, they remained mere ideological obfuscation. The anti-imperialist forces ought to agitate for the inclusion of the same set of principles in the 1992 political order, but this time they should be made justiciable. Such laws would, of course, penetrate into the hard core of elite legitimacy and highlight the chronic discrepancy between theory and praxis that characterises successive Nigerian regimes.

(ii) Given the diversity and strength of sectoral interests in Nigeria, the various governing forms have had to allow for a variety of minority, regional and even ethnically based interests. While the 'federal character' of Nigeria in part reinforces aspects of separatist or communal consciousness, it has also prevented an outright military or civilian dictatorship from imposing itself on society. This explains, for instance, why Nigeria has not been subject to a Banda-like single-party dictatorship, or to any of the forms of 'personal rule' examined by Jackson and Rosberg;[47] its extreme regional, ethnic, cultural and economic heterogeneity virtually compels some form of federalism and institutionalised compromise at the centre. A strategy centred around the minorities might therefore be an auspicious cornerstone for the coming Third Republic (or however it may be designated). After all – and this has also been shown in previous chapters – the minority ethic groups have been the most consistent supporters of national unity and democratic rights, since they have a permanent vested interest in upholding liberal rights and state safeguards.

(iii) Although it is evident that federalism is a vital necessity for the Nigerian state irrespective of which hegemonic fractional grouping may be leading it, it is also apparent that the appropriate balance has not been found. From the analyses developed in this book, the sub-federal units – Regions, then States – clearly emerge as the greatest obstacle to the realisation of democracy. It is here that one-party sub-states, moves to undermine local government, and the worst forms of oppression appear to be enacted – albeit frequently in reaction to prior oppressive measures and policies at the centre. If central power were held constant (but subject to firmer popular controls) and (reorganised) local government powers greatly enhanced at the expense of State governments, a much more adequate combination of central leadership and popular mobilisation at the 'grass-roots' could be achieved. The solution of the extremely ambiguous problem of the appropriate role for traditional rule could be incorporated into the local government's mandate.

(iv) The role of the military needs to be fundamentally re-examined and redefined. The existing military apparatus can only be justified in terms of domestic repression. Inadequately trained, poorly equipped and top-heavy with a bloated officer corps, it serves virtually no military purpose within the context of West African geopolitics. If it is seen, as is sometimes argued, as an absorber of surplus manpower, then it could be more usefully trained and deployed for specifically domestic productive functions, such as harvesting, dam construction, road-building and the like. In place of an entrenched, corporate officer corps and a massive standing army (now totalling about 185,000 persons), a reserve militia with constant rotation of personnel at the top and bottom might be considered. A supra-ethnic, democratised, developmentally-oriented and relatively open military structure would be a strong force for the democratisation of society. Its creation would, of course, make the diarchy proposition irrelevant.

(v) Olusegun Obasanjo, in his Ibadan speech (discussed in chapter 8) just before the fall of the Second Republic, rightly argued that not the form of civilian government, but the negative qualities of those who operated it, were responsible for its collapse. As a result, 'ordinary Nigerians' were more concerned with the substance rather than the form of 'their' government, and therefore future governments must meet people's basic needs, strengthen the social fabric and enhance the country's credibility abroad. Now in the long term, as this book argues, the realisation of these and related goals is not possible within the peripheral state. But in terms of short-term prescriptions for the coming Third Republic, the popular class's interests would be best served by specific means of regulating, checking, controlling and canalising dysfunctional elite behaviour. An enhanced code of conduct, as suggested in chapter 10, would be a minimal requirement here. Avenues would have to be found to extend popular control into the real sources of elite accumulation and formation. Participation in determining the generation and distribution of oil revenues would be a crucial provision. So would greater accountability on the part of the entire state bureaucracy – real accountability in the form of assets declaration, an enforceable code of conduct and clear norms of service which, when violated, would result in appropriate sanctions. Key areas of past deficiencies, including the issuance of import licences, allocation of foreign exchange, the whole indigenisation exercise, the awarding of contracts and all buying and selling on behalf of the state, would have to be made subject to public scrutiny and responsive to public needs.

(vi) The historical opportunity afforded by a ruling class temporarily prepared to grant specific concessions within the framework of defensive radicalism might be utilised to end the systematic exploitation of Nigerian women. Polygamy, clitorectomy and purdah – all of which have, following colonial and post-colonial deformations, forfeited their once organic roots in traditional society – could be abolished or at least discouraged. If oppression based on gender can be reduced, then such aberrations as Buhari's anti-women campaign (chapter 8) stand to be averted and important liberating tendencies released into the larger society.

(vii) Much has been said about the need for a 'national ideology' for Nigeria which might unite the people behind shared goals, discipline and motivate the population for further development, shape and constrain the behaviour of leaders and followers alike, and underpin all political discourse. While this thesis is most compelling, the prospect of substitutionism, already alluded to, arises in a situation in which the 'national' ideology is formulated and imposed from above. Precisely this is inherent in the re-thinking exercise conducted by the Political Bureau. Although no doubt more socially-minded and containing more concessions to what are thought to be popular needs than its predecessor, the post-1990 constitutional order is likely to be a mainly elite affair. Again, ways and means must be found to enter mass concerns into the debate.

To sum up: the present historical conjuncture, despite obstacles, presents opportunities in both the short and long terms for countering the domination of peripheral capitalism and the state classes in Nigeria, and these opportunities are a function of the contradictions and dysfunctions of that system itself. There is, however, nothing inevitable about these developments, and only deliberate, determined and patient counter-hegemonic work in all spheres of politics, society and the economy, by and for the popular classes, stands to propel the Nigerian political economy beyond peripheral capitalism.

Notes

1. Extrapolated from statistics given in Dudley, 1982, p. 113. It is worth reiterating that virtually all statistics relating to Nigerian economic development are, for various reasons, tenuous, suspect and rarely reliable. All figures cited here should therefore be considered merely as illustrative and tendential.
2. From tables reproduced in Terisa Turner and Arnold Baker, 'Soldiers and Oil: The 1983 Coup in Nigeria', Montreal: McGill University Centre for Developing Area Studies, Discussion Paper No. 28, 1985, pp. 25–8.
3. A concept first employed in the African context by Ruth First (*Libya: The Elusive Revolution*, London, 1971) and adapted to the Nigerian situation by Tom Forrest ('Notes on the Political Economy of State Intervention', *IDS Bulletin* 9, 1, 1977) and Turner, 1976.
4. On these developments, see Robert Shenton, *The Development of Capitalism in Northern Nigeria*, London and Toronto, forthcoming, here cited from ms.
5. See, for instance, Nick Van Hear's account of the profligate jurisdictional clash between the Agricultural Development Projects (ADPs) and the River Basin and Rural Development Authorities (RBRDAs) in *African Business*, July 1985.

6. Further see Gavin Williams, 1980a.
7. *West Africa*, 7 October 1985, p. 2093.
8. *West Africa*, 22 April 1985, p. 784.
9. *West Africa*, 30 September 1985, p. 2024.
10. On all this, see Forrest, *op. cit.*
11. Maimire Mennasemay, 'Political Theory, Political Science and African Development', *Canadian Journal of African Studies*, Vol. 16, No. 2 (1982), p. 236.
12. The debate, with the contributions of its main protagonists (Alavi and Saul) is recreated in H. Goulbourne (ed.), *Politics and State in the Third World*, London, 1979, chapters 4 and 5.
13. On these, see Rolf Hanisch and Rainer Tetzlaff's introduction to their edited volume, *Historische Konstitutionsbedingungen des Staates in Entwicklungsländern*, Hamburg, 1980, pp. 2–5.
14. Wolfgang Hein and Georg Simonis, 'Entwicklungspolitik, Staatsfunktionen und Klassenauseinandersetzungen im peripheren Kapitalismus', in Alfred Schmidt (ed.), *Strategien gegen Unterentwicklung: Zwischen Weltmarkt und Eigenständigkeit*, Frankfurt and New York, 1978, pp. 223–4.
15. And has been most consistently articulated by such scholars as Okwudiba Nnoli, Eddie Madunagu, Eskor Toyo, Yolamu Barongo, Bala Usman, Ola Oni, Bade Onimode, Wang Metuge, Toyin Falola, Julius Ihonvbere and Segun Osoba – see bibliography. The dependency perspective is most explicitly stated by B. C. Sullivan, 'Structural Dependency: The Nigerian Economy as a Case Study', *Journal of Asian and African Studies*, Vol. XIV, No. 1–2, pp. 44–54.
16. Hartmut Elsenhans, 'Peripherer Staat und abhängige Entwicklung', in Institut fur Auslandsbeziehungen (ed.), *Kolonialismus und Kolonialreiche*, proceedings of the 5th Tübingen conference, 11–12 May 1984, reproduced as special issue of *Zeitschrift fur Kulturaustausch*, Vol. 34, No. 4 (1984), p. 347; on all this see also Ulrich Menzel, 'The Differentiation Process in the Third World and its Consequences for the North–South Conflict and Development Theory', *Law and State*, Vol. 30 (1984), pp. 52–83.
17. Bill Warren, 'Imperialism and Capitalist Industrialization', *New Left Review*, No. 81 (Sept.–Dec.) 1973, pp. 3–45; further see his posthumous *Imperialism: Pioneer of Capitalism*, London, 1982, which reproduces this and several related articles.
18. Peter Evans, *Dependent Development: The Alliance of Multinational, State and Local Capital in Brazil*, Princeton, 1979, p. 11.
19. H. Sanousi, 'State and Capitalist Development in Nigeria: A Political Economy', unpublished doctoral thesis, Northwestern University, 1982, p. 452.
20. Rolf Hanisch and Rainer Tetzlaff, 'The State in Developing Societies as an Object of Social Science Research', *Law and State*, forthcoming, here quoted from ms., p. 5.
21. James Petras, *Class, State and Power in the Third World, with Case Studies on Class Conflict in Latin America*, Montclair, 1981, p. 125.
22. Hartmut Elsenhans, *Abhängiger Kapitalismus oder bürokratische Entwicklungsgesellschaft: Versuch über den Staat in der Dritten Welt*, Frankfurt and New York, 1981, chapter 1.
23. Homayoun Katouzian, 'Die politische Ökonomie der ölexportierenden Lander – ein analytisches Modell', in *Revolution in Iran und Afghanistan. Jahrbuch zur Geschichte und Gesellschaft des Mittleren Orients*, Frankfurt, 1980, pp. 34–5.
24. Sanousi, *op. cit.*, pp. 432–3.
25. A point made by Elsenhans, *Abhängiger Kapitalismus*, *op. cit.*, pp. 157–8.
26. See Ian Roxborough, *Theories of Underdevelopment*, London, 1979, pp. 72–3.
27. International Labour Organization, *First Things First: Meeting the Basic Needs of the People of Nigeria*, Addis Ababa 1981, introduction.
28. James Petras, *Critical Perspectives on Imperialism and Social Class in the Third World*, New York, 1978, p. 36.
29. James O'Connor, *The Fiscal Crisis of the State*, New York, 1973.
30. Elsenhans, *Abhängiger Kapitalismus*, *op. cit.*, pp. 185–6.
31. *Ibid.*, p. 204.
32. On this, see Hein and Simonis, *op. cit.*, pp. 228–9.

33. Which is, of course, the title of Joseph Wayas's (the erstwhile Senate President and now 'wanted' ex-politician) book; London, 1979.
34. A. B. Ahmed, 'Dynamism and Foreign Policy in Nigeria's Second Republic', *New Nigerian*, 6 March 1980.
35. As quoted in interview with *West Africa*, 19 May 1980. This was no isolated assertion: the Nigerian Society of International Affairs put forward a similar argument (see the Society's communiqué, reproduced as a supplement to *New Nigerian*, 23 February 1980), as did much of the press.
36. These last two examples are cited in Stephen Wright, 'Limits of Nigeria's Power Overseas', *West Africa*, 27 July 1981, p. 1685.
37. James Zasha, 'Class Formation, Ethnicity and Politics Among Industrial Workers in the Nigerian Middle Belt', paper presented to Canadian Association of African Studies, Antigonish, Nova Scotia, May 1984, mimeo., p. 47.
38. As formulated by Claus Offe, *Contradictions of the Welfare State*, London, etc. 1985, p. 132.
39. Quoted in *West Africa*, 24 March 1986.
40. On this aspect of popular cynicism, S. E. Oyovbaire perceptively writes (1982b:25) 'Because the practices [of corruption, favouritism, discrimination, etc.] are pervasive and are generally officially approved, promoted and rationalized, their victims as well as their victors have taken them for granted. The phrase 'This is Nigeria' is an instructive daily summary of the sense of resignation or alienation. Negativity has been internalized as a powerful cultural element. As a result, people no longer have qualms and reservations in this connection: they do not feel they owe much obligation to the civic public vis-à-vis the primordial public. Personality in Nigeria has deeply internalized the elements of a dog-eat-dog society.'
41. A point which Julius Ihonvbere uses to explain the anti-Shagari military *coup* carried out by Buhari; see his 'The 1983 Elections and the Buhari Coup in Nigeria: Contradictions in a (Semi-) Peripheral Political Economy', Dalhousie University African Working Papers No. 3, April 1985, p. 7.
42. Yusuf Bala Usman, May Day 1983 public lecture at Katsina, reproduced as 'The Nature and Causes of the Current Economic Crisis in Nigeria', *Nigerian Tribune*, 31 May 1983.
43. Turner and Baker, 'Soldiers and Oil', *op. cit.*, p. 21.
44. Quoted in *West Africa*, 28 April 1986, p. 901.
45. Zik's original proposal is formulated in the booklet, *The Fourth Arm of Government*, 1972. The concept of diarchy is advocated by Ikoku, 1985. And cimilcy, which enhances the military's positive democratic role, is the concern of Nwankwo, 1986.
46. Sam Egite Oyovbaire, 'Leadership in Nigeria: The Living Legacy of the Late Murtala Mohammed', ASUU Guest of the Month Lecture, University of Benin, 13 February 1984, mimeo., p. 11. In a letter of 1 December 1986 to the author, Professor Oyovbaire writes: 'I do not agree with you in your interpretation . . . that I was advocating a diarchy. In fact, my position is far removed from diarchy, at least as it was propounded by Azikiwe. If anything, what I have in mind is that the arbitrary gap between civil and military society as it was notionally inherited at Independence needs to be studied and possibly bridged. This is not diarchy or the collaboration of soldiers and civilians in government.'
47. R. H. Jackson and C. G. Rosberg, *Personal Rule in Black Africa: Prince, Autocrat, Prophet, Tyrant*, Berkeley, 1982. For a critique of this work with reference to its inapplicability to Nigeria, see my review in *International Journal of African Historial Studies*, Vol. 17, No. 1 (1984) pp. 165-7.

Bibliography

Aboyade, O. (1969) 'The Economy of Nigeria' in: P. Robson and D. A. Lury, *Economics of Africa*. Evanston (Ill.): Northwestern University Press.

Aboyade, Ojetunji (1966) *Foundations of an African Economy. A Study of Investment and Growth in Nigeria*. New York/Washington/London: Praeger.

Aboyade, O. (1965) *Nigeria 1965: Crisis and Criticism*. Ibadan.

Aboyade, O. and A. Ayida (1971) 'The War Economy in Perspective', *Nigerian Journal of Economic and Social Studies*, Vol. 13, No. 1, March.

Abu, Joseph (1979) 'A Review of the Local Government Reforms', *New Nigerian*, 27 September.

Abumere, S. (1981) 'Multinationals, Import Substitution and Export Valorisation in Nigeria', in M. J. Taylor and N. J. Thrift (eds): *The Geography of Multinationals*, London: Croom Helm.

Achike, Okay (1973) *Groundwork of Military Law and Military Rule in Nigeria*. Enugu: Fourth Dimension.

Adamolekun, Ladipo (1985) *The Fall of The Second Republic*. Ibadan: Spectrum Books.

Adamolekun, Ladipo (1982) *Public Administration: A Nigerian and Comparative Perspective*. London: Longman.

Adamolekun, Ladipo (1982) 'Nigerian Constitution', Part 3, *West Africa*, 1 November.

Adamolekun, Ladipo and Alex Gboyega (1979) *Leading Issues in Nigerian Public Service*. Ile-Ife: University of Ife Press.

Adamolekun, L. and L. Osunkunle (1982) *Nigeria's Ombudsman System. Five Years of the Public Complaints Commission*. Ibadan: Heinemann.

Adamu, H. A. (n.d.) *The North and Nigerian Unity: Some Reflections on the Political, Social and Educational Problems of Northern Nigeria*. Zaria: Ahmadu Bello University, Department of Government (mimeo.).

Adebayo, Augustus (1979) 'Policy-Making in Nigerian Public Administration', *Journal of Administration Overseas*, Vol. 18, No. 1, January: 4–14.

Adebayo, Augustus O. (1973) 'The Problem of the Administrator and the Professional Expert in the Public Service of Nigeria', *Quarterly Journal of Administration*, July: 343–59.

Adebiyi Report (1977) *Report of the Tribunal of Inquiry into the Activities of the Trade Unions*, Lagos.

Adebo Report (1970) *First Report of the Wages and Salaries Review Commission*, Lagos.

Adedeji, Adebayo (ed.) (1968) *Nigerian Administration and its Political Setting*. London: Hutchinson Educational.

Adedeji, Adebayo (ed.) (1981) *The Indigenization of African Economies*. London: Hutchinson University Library.

Adedeji, Adebayo (ed.) (1969) *The Future of Local Government in Nigeria. The Report of the National Conference on Local Government*. Ile-Ife: University of Ife Press.

Adedeji, Adebayo and L. Rowland (1976) *Local Government Finance in Nigeria: Problems and Prospects*. Ile-Ife: University of Ife Press.

Adejugbe, Michael (1984) 'The Myths and Realities of Nigeria's Business Indigenization', *Development and Change*, Vol. 15: 577–92.

Adekson, J.'Bayo (1973) 'Nigerian Military and Social Expenditures 1970–1976', *New Nigerian*, 5 and 6 May.

Adekson, J.'Bayo (1981) *Nigeria in Search of a Stable Civil-Military System*. Boulder, Col.: Westview Press.

Ademoya, Adewale (1981) *Why We Struck: The Story of the First Nigerian Coup*. Ibadan: Evans.

Adeniji, Kola (1978) 'Government Regulation of Business in Nigeria: A Case Study of Regulatory Administration in a Mixed Economy', *Quarterly Journal of Administration*, July: 409–29.

Adeniran, Tunde (1982) 'Three Years of Nigeria's New Constitution, Part II', *West Africa*, 28 October: 27–68.

Adeniyi, Emola Oloruntobi (1975) 'Administrative Framework for Physical Planning in Nigeria', *Journal of Administration Overseas*, Vol. 14, No. 3, July.

Adeogun, A. A. (1979) 'Strikes and the Institutionalisation of Labour Protest: The Case of Nigeria' in P. Waterman (ed.) *Third World Strikes* Zug: Interdocumentation Co. Microfiche.

Adeogun, A. A. (1980) 'Strikes, the Law and the Institutionalisation of Labour Protest in Nigeria', *Indian Journal of Industrial Relations*, Vol. 16, No. 1: 1–23.

Adu, A. (1969) *The Civil Service in Commonwealth Africa: Development and Transition*. London: George Allen & Unwin.

Afigbo, A. E. (1972) *The Warrant Chiefs: Indirect Rule in South-Eastern Nigeria 1891–1929*. Bristol: Western Printing Services.

Africa Research Group (1970) *The Other Side of Nigeria's Civil War*. Cambridge, Mass.

Aguda, T. Akinola (1980) *Practice and Procedure of the Supreme Court, Court of Appeal and High Courts of Nigeria*. London: Sweet & Maxwell.

Aina, S. (1982) 'Bureaucratic Corruption in Nigeria: The Continuing Search for Causes and Cures', *International Review of Administrative Science*, No. 1: 70–76.

Aina, Tade Akin. (1982) 'The State, Industrial Policy and Industrial Transformation: The Nigerian Experience and its Problems, 1946–1979'. Paper presented at the 9th Annual Conference of the Nigerian Political Science Association, July.

Ajaegbu, Hyacinth I. (1976) *Urban and Rural Development in Nigeria*. London: Heinemann.

Ajayi, J. F. Ade and B. Ikara (1985) *Evolution of Political Culture in Nigeria*. Ibadan: University Press.

Ajibola, W. A. and T. A. Oyejide (1975) 'Local Government System in Western Nigeria: A Comparative Evaluation Performance under Civilian and Military Regimes', *Indian Journal of Political Science*, Vol. XXXVI, No. 2, April–June: 123–36.

Akande, Jadesola O. (1982a) *Introduction to the Nigerian Constitution*. London: Sweet & Maxwell.

Akande, Jadesola O. (ed.). (1982b) *The Constitution of the Federal Republic of Nigeria*. London: Sweet & Maxwell.

Ake, Claude (1973) 'Explaining Political Instability in New States', *Journal of Modern African Studies*, XI, 3:347–59.

Ake, Claude (1976) 'Explanatory Notes on the Political Economy of Africa', *Journal of Modern African Studies*, 4:1–23.

Ake, Claude (1978) *Revolutionary Pressures in Africa*. London: Zed Press.

Ake, Claude (1979) *Social Science as Imperialism: The Theory of Political Development*. Ibadan: Ibadan University Press.

Ake, Claude (1981) *A Political Economy of Africa*. London: Longman.

Ake, Claude (1986) *The Political Economy of Nigeria*. London: Longman.

Akeredolu, Ale (ed.) (forthcoming) *Social Development in Nigeria: Readings on Policy and Research*. Ibadan.

Akinbode, Ade (1978) 'The Implications of Land Reforms for Socio-Economic Development in Nigeria', *The Bureaucrat*, Vol. 6, No. 2, April/June.

Akinsanya, A. (1977a) 'Federalism and Military Rule in Nigeria, 1966–1975', *Indian Journal of Public Administration*, Vol. 23, No. 1, January/March.

Akinsanya, A. (1977b) 'The Machinery of Government during the Military Regime in Nigeria', *Africa Quarterly*, Vol. XVII, No. 2: 32–54.

Akinsanya, A. (1979) 'The Count-Down to Civil Rule in Nigeria: The Constituent Assembly', *Journal of Administration Overseas*, Vol. 18, No. 1: 34–45.

Akinsanya, A. (1983) 'State Strategies Toward Nigerian and Foreign Business' in I. William Zartmann (ed.) *The Political Economy of Nigeria*. New York: Praeger.

Akinyemi, A. B. (1971) 'Nigeria: What Should Follow Army Rule – and When?' *Africa Report*, 16.

Akinyemi, Bolaji (ed.) (1978) *Nigeria and the World: Readings in Nigerian Foreign Policy*. Ibadan: Oxford University Press.

Akinyemi, Bolaji (1979a) *Foreign Policy and Federalism*. Ibadan: Oxford University Press.

Akinyemi, Bolaji (1979b) *Foreign Policy and the Constitution*. Lagos: Nigerian Institute of International Affairs.

Akiwowo, Akinsola (1964) 'The Sociology of Nigerian Tribalism' *Phylon*, 25, Summer: 155–63.

Akiwowo, Akinsola (1971) 'The Performance of the Nigerian Military from 1966 to 1970' in M. Janowitz and J. van Doorn (eds) *On Military Ideology*. Rotterdam: Rotterdam University Press.

Akpan, Moses E. (1977) *Nigerian Politics: A Search for National Unity and Stability*. Washington, D. C.: University Press of America.

Alabi, Mac (ed.) (1981) *The Constitution on Trial: Balarabe Musa vs. The Assembly*. Lagos: Nigerian Daily Times.

Alavi, H. (1973) 'Peasant Classes and Primordial Loyalties', *Journal of Peasant Studies*, Vol. 1, No. 1, 23–62.

Aliyu, A. T. (1982) *The Role of Local Government in Social, Political and Economic Development in Nigeria, 1976–9*. Zaria: Ahmadu Bello University Press.

Aliyu, A. Y. (1978/9) 'The Nature and Implications of Local Government Reform in Nigeria', *Nigerian Journal of Public Affairs*, Vol. VIII: 131–43.

Aliyu, A. Y. (1980) 'The Nature and Composition of the Legislature, Parts I and II' *New Nigerian*, 6 and 7 June.

Allan, Keith (1978) 'Nation, Tribalism and National Language', *Cahiers d'Études Africaines*, Vol. 18, No. 3: 397–415.

Allen, C. and R. W. Johnson (eds) (1971) *African Perspectives*. Cambridge: Cambridge University Press.

Almond, G. (1970) *Political Development: Essays in Beuristic Theory*. Boston, Mass: Little, Brown.

Almond G. and J. S. Coleman (eds) (1960) *The Politics of the Developing Areas*. Princeton, N. J.: Princeton University Press.

Almond G. and B. Powell (1966) *Comparative Politics: Developmental Approach*. Boston, Mass: Little, Brown.

Aluko, Olajide (1976) *Ghana and Nigeria, 1957–70*. New York: Barnes & Noble.

Aluko, Olajide (ed.) (1981) *Essays in Nigerian Foreign Policy*. London: George Allen & Unwin.

Aluko, S. A. (1965) *Federal Election Crisis 1964 – An Analysis*. Onitsha: Etudo.

Amadi, Elechi (1982) *Ethics in Nigerian Culture*. Ibadan: Heinemann.

Amin, Samir (1973) *Neo-Colonialism in West Africa*. New York: Monthly Review Press.

Anadozie, G. O. (1980) 'Current Trends in the Industrial Relations Scene in Nigeria', Seminar Paper, Nigerian Employers' Consultative Association. Lagos.

Anamaleze, John (1979) *The Nigerian Press: The People's Conscience?* New York: Vantage.

Ananaba, Wogu (1969) *The Trade Union Movement in Nigeria*. London: Hurst.

Ananaba, Wogu (1979) *The Trade Union Movement in Africa: Promise and Performance*. London: Hurst.

Andrae, Gunilla and Bjorn Beckman (1986) *The Wheat Trap: Bread and Underdevelopment in Nigeria*. London: Zed Press.

Anon (1978) 'The Politics of Transition to Civilian Rule in Nigeria: The National Bourgeoisie Comes of Age', *Positive Review*, No. 1.

Anyanwu, K. C. (1982) 'Bases of Political Instability in Nigeria', *Journal of Black Studies*, 13, Summer 101–17.

Apter, David E. (1965) *The Politics of Modernization*. Chicago: University of Chicago Press.

Arikpo, Okoi (1967) *The Development of Modern Nigeria*. Baltimore: Penguin.

Armstrong, Robert G. (1967) *The Issues at Stake: Nigeria 1967*. Ibadan: Ibadan University Press.

Arnold, Guy (1977) *Modern Nigeria*. London: Longman.

Arrighi, G. and J. S. Saul (1973) *Essays on the Political Economy of Africa*. New York: Monthly Review Press.

Asika, Ukpabi (1970) 'A Social Definition of the African Intellectual' in W. Cartey and M. Kilson (eds) *Independent Africa: The Africa Reader*. New York: Vintage.

Asiodu, P. C. (1967) 'Industrial Policy and Incentive in Nigeria', *Nigerian Journal of Economic and Social Studies*, Vol. 9, No. 2, July.

'Aspects of the Draft Constitution'. (1977) Special Issue of *Quarterly Journal of Administration*, Vol. XI, No. 4, July.

Atta, Abdul (1971) *The Rule of Civil Service in the Development Process*. Economic Development Seminar. Lagos: Nigerian National Press.

Auma-Osolo, Agola (1980) 'Objective African Military Control: A New Paradigm in Civil–Military Relations', *Journal of Peace Research*, Vol. XVII, No. 1: 29–46.

Awa, Eme O. (1964) *Federal Government in Nigeria*. Berkeley: University of California Press.

Awa, Eme O. (1964) 'High Level Administration in the Public Services of Nigeria', *Nigerian Journal of Economic and Social Studies*, Vol. 6, No. 1 March: 43ff.

Awa, Eme O. (1974) 'The Place of Ideology in Nigerian Politics', *African Review*, Vol. 4, No. 3.

Awolowo, Obafemi (1966) *Thoughts on the Nigerian Constitution*. Ibadan: Oxford University Press.

Awolowo, Obafemi (1968) *The People's Republic*. Ibadan: Oxford University Press.

Awolowo, Obafemi (1970) *The Strategy and Tactics of the People's Republic of Nigeria*. London: Macmillan.

Ayandele, Emmanuel A. (1974) *The Educated Elite in the Nigerian Society*. Ibadan: University of Ibadan Press.

Ayida, A. A. (1976) *Economic Survey of Nigeria 1960–1975*. Ibadan: University of Ibadan Press.

Ayida, A. A. and H. M. A. Onitiri (eds) (1971) *Reconstruction and Development in Nigeria: Proceedings of a National Conference*. Ibadan: Ibadan University Press.

Ayoade, J. A. A. (1975) 'Federalism and Wage Politics in Nigeria', *Journal of Commonwealth and Comparative Politics*, Vol. 13, No. 3: 282–9.

Ayoade, J. A. A. (1978) 'Electoral Laws and National Unity in Nigeria'. Paper presented at the Conference of the Nigerian Political Science Association.

Ayorinde, J. A. (1957) *History of Cocoa in Nigeria*. Ibadan: Ministry of Agriculture and Natural Resources.

Azikiwe, N. (1937, 1963) *Renascent Africa*. London: Cass. repr.

Azikiwe, N. (1961) *Zik: A Selection of the Speeches of Dr. Nnamdi Azikiwe*. London: Cambridge University Press.

Azikiwe, Nnamdi (1974) *Democracy with Military Vigilance*. Nsukka: African Book Company.

Azikiwe, Nnamdi (1982) *Ideology for Nigeria: Capitalism, Socialism or Welfarism*. Ibadan: Afrografika.

Babatope, Ebenezer (1976) *Student Power vs. Militarism (1971–1975)*. Lagos: Deto Deni (Educational) Publications.

Baker, Colin (ed.) (1975) *Ife Essays in Administration*. Ile-Ife: University of Ife Press.

Baker, Pauline H. (1971) 'The Politics of Nigerian Military Rule', *African Report*. February: 18–21.

Balewa, Sir Abubaker Tafawa (1966) *Nigeria Speaks: Speeches Made Between 1957–1964: by Sam Epelle* Lagos: University of Lagos Press.

Balogun, M. J. *et al.* (1979) *Managerial Efficiency in the Public Sector: Patterns and Problems*. Ile-Ife: University of Ife Press.

Balogun, Ola (1973) *The Tragic Years: Nigeria in Crisis 1966–1970*. Benin City: Ethiope.

Bamisaiye, A. (1971) 'Ethnic Politics as an Instrument of Unequal Socio-Economic Development in Nigeria's First Republic', *African Notes*, Vol. 6, No. 2: 94–106.

Bangura, Y. (1982) 'The Payments Crisis of the Nigerian State'. Ahmadu Bello University, Zaria: Department of Political Science, Staff Seminar Paper, June.

Banks, Ferdinand (1981) *The Political Economy of Oil*. Aldershot: Gower.

Barbour, Kenneth M. (1972) *Planning for Nigeria*. Ibadan: Ibadan University Press.

Barker, Jonathan (ed.) (1984) *The Politics of Agriculture in Tropical Africa*. Beverly Hills: Sage.

Barongo, Yolamu R. (1980) 'The Political Economy of Foreign Private Investments in Nigeria'. Paper presented to the 7th Annual Convention of the Nigerian Political Science Association, University of Port Harcourt, March (mimeo.).

Barrett, Stanley R. (1977) *The Rise and Fall of an African Utopia: A Wealthy Theocracy in Comparative Perspective*. Waterloo: University of Waterloo Press.

Barrows, Walter L. (1976) 'Ethnic Diversity and Political Instability in Black Africa', *Comparative Political Studies*, Vol. 9, No. 2, July: 139–70.

Bates, Robert H. (1974) 'Ethnic Competition and Modernization in Contemporary Africa', *Comparative Political Studies*, Vol. 6, No. 4: 457–84.

Beckett, Paul and James O'Connell (1977) *Education and Power in Nigeria: A Study of the University Students*. New York: Holmes and Meier.

Beckman, Björn (1976) *Organising the Farmers. Cocoa Politics and National Development in Ghana*. Uppsala: Scandinavian Institute of African Studies.

Beckman, Björn (1981) 'Oil, State Expenditure and Class Formation in Nigeria'. Paper presented to the Conference of the Nordic Association of Political Scientists. Turku: August.

Beckman, Björn (1982) 'Imperialism and the "National Bourgeoisie" '. *Review of African Political Economy (R.O.A.P.E.)*, No. 22, Oct./Dec.: 5–19.

Beckman, Björn (1985) 'Neocolonialism, Capitalism and the State in Nigeria' in Henry Berstein and Bonnie Campbell (eds) *Contradictions of Accumulation in Africa*. Beverly Hills: Sage.

Beer, C. E. F. (1975) *The Politics of Peasant Groups in Western Nigeria*. Ibadan: Ibadan University Press.

Belasco, Bernard (1980) *The Entrepreneur as Culture Hero: Preadaptations for Nigerian Development*. New York: Praeger.

Bello, Ahmadu (1962) *My Life*. London: Cambridge University Press.

Benemy, F. W. G. (1968) *Constitutional Government and West Africa*. London: Harrap.

Berg, Elliot (1964) 'Socialism and Economic Development in Tropical Africa', *Quarterly Journal of Economics*, Vol. 67, No. 4.

Berger, Manfred (1975) *Industrialisation Policies in Nigeria*. Munich: Weltforum Verlag.

Berry, S. F. (1975) *Cocoa, Custom and Socioeconomic Change in Rural Western Nigeria*. Oxford: Oxford University Press.

Bienen, Henry (1978) 'Military Rule and Political Process', *Comparative Politics*, January: 205–25.

Bienen, Henry (1983) 'Income Distribution and Politics in Nigeria', in I. William Zartman (ed) *The Political Economy of Nigeria*. New York: Praeger.

Bienen, Henry (1985) *Political Conflict and Economic Change in Nigeria*. London: Frank Cass.

Bienen, Henry and V. P. Diejomah (eds) (1981) *The Political Economy of Income Distribution in Nigeria*. New York: Holmes & Meier.

Biersteker, Thomas J. (1978) *Distortion or Development: Contending Perspectives on the Multinational Corporation*. Cambridge, Mass.: MIT Press.

Biersteker, T. J. (1983) 'Indigenization in Nigeria: Renationalization or Denationalization?' in I. William Zartman (ed.) *The Political Economy of Nigeria*. New York: Praeger.

Binder, Lloyd (ed.) (1971) *Crises and Sequences in Political Development*. Princeton: Princeton University Press.

Blitz, L. Franklin (1965) *The Politics and Administration of Nigerian Government*. London: Sweet & Maxwell. Lagos: African University Press.

Bowden, E. (1976) 'Maladministration: A Thematic Analysis of Nigerian Case Studies in the Context of Administrative Initiative', *Human Organization*, 35, Winter 391–4.

Bozeman, A. (1976) *Conflict in Africa: Concepts and Realities*. Princeton: Princeton University Press.

Bray, T. M. and G. R. Cooper (1979) 'Education and Nation Building in Nigeria since the Civil War', *Comparative Education*, Vol. 15, No. 1, March: 33–41.

Bretton, Henry L. (1962) *Power and Stability in Nigeria: The Politics of Decolonization*. New York: Praeger.

Brockway, Fenner (1973) *African Socialism*. London: Bodley Head.

Buijtenhuajs, Robert (1978) 'Les Potentialités Révolutionnaires de l'Afrique Noire: Les Elites Dissidentes', *Cahiers des Études Africaines*, Vol. 18, Nos. 1–2.

Burns, Sir Alan (1955) *History of Nigeria*. 5th edn. London: George Allen & Unwin.

Buttner, T. (1970) 'The Economic and Social Character of Precolonial States in Tropical Africa',

Journal of the Historical Society of Nigeria, 5, 2: 275–90.

Callaghy, Thomas M. (1980) 'The Rise of the African State', *Problems of Communism* Sept./Oct.

Callaway, Barbara (1975) 'The Political Economy of Nigeria', in Richard Harris (ed.) *The Political Economy of Africa*. New York: Halstead Press.

Campbell, Ian (1975) 'The Nigerian Census: An Essay in Civil–Military Relations' *Journal of Commonwealth and Comparative Politics*.

Carlston, Kenneth S. (1968) *Social Theory and African Tribal Organization*. Urbana: University of Illinois Press.

Carter, G. M. (ed.) (1966) *National Unity and Regionalism in Eight African States*. Ithaca: Cornell University Press.

Carver, Richard and Brian Slocock (1969) 'Will the Transfer to Democracy Destabilise Africa's Heavyweight? Regionalism Reemerges', *New Statesman*, 10 August.

Cervenka, Zdenek (1971) *The Nigerian Civil War 1967–1970*. Frankfurt/Main: Bernard & Graek.

Cervenka, Zdenek (1972) *A History of the Nigerian War 1967–1970*. Lagos: Onibonoje Press.

Chinweizu (1985) 'Debt Trap Peonage', *Monthly Review*, Vol. 37, No. 6.

Chukumerije, Uche *et al.* (1980) 'Report of the Committee of Inquiry on the Party's Problems', Lagos: PRP, 16 July.

Chukunta, N. K. Onuoha (1978) 'Education and National Integration in Africa: A Case Study of Nigeria', *African Studies Review*, Vol. 21, No. 2, 67–75.

Cohen, R. (1972) 'Class in Africa: Analytical Problems and Perspectives', *Socialist Register*, 230–56.

Cohen, R. (1977) 'Michael Imoudu and the Nigerian Labour Movement', *Race and Class*, Vol. 3, Spring, 345–62.

Cohen, Robin (1974) *Labour and Politics in Nigeria 1945–71*. London: Heinemann.

Cohen, R., P. Brazier and P. C. W. Gutkind (1979) *Peasants and Proletarians: The Struggle of Third World Workers*. New York: Monthly Review Press.

Coleman, J. S. (1960) *Nigeria: Background to Nationalism*. Berkeley: University of California Press.

Coleman, J. S. and C. G. Rosberg (1964) *Political Parties and National Integration in Tropical Africa*. Berkeley and Los Angeles: University of California Press.

Collins, Paul (1975) 'The Policy of Indigenization: An Overall View', *Quarterly Journal of Africa*, Vol. IX, No. 2 *et seq.*

Collins, Paul (1976) 'The Political Economy of Indigenisation: The Case of the Nigerian Enterprises Promotion Decree', *African Review*, 4: 491–503.

Collins, Paul (1977) 'Public Policy and the Development of Indigenous Capitalism: The Nigerian Experience', *Journal of Commonwealth and Comparative Politics*, Vol. XV, No. 2.

Collins, Paul (ed.) (1980) *Administration for Development in Nigeria*. Lagos: African Education Press.

Collins, Paul (1983) 'The State and Industrial Capitalism in West Africa', *Development and Change*, Vol. 14, 403–28.

Collis, Robert (1970) *Nigeria in Conflict*. London: Secker & Warburg.

Cook, A. N. (1964) *British Enterprise in Nigeria*. London: Frank Cass.

Cookey, S. J. S. (1982) 'Colonialism and the Process of Underdevelopment in Nigeria', *Journal of Asian and African Studies*, Vol. XIV, Nos. 1–2.

Cooper, F. (1981) 'Africa and the World Economy', *Africa Studies Review*, 24 (15).

Copains, Jean, 'Conscience Politique ou Conscience de la Politique', *Cahiers des Études Africaines*, 57, XV.

Cowan, L. Gray (1968) *The Dilemmas of African Independence*. New York: Walker.

Cox, Robert W. (1981) 'Social Forces, States and World Orders: Beyond International Relations Theory', *Millenium: Journal of International Studies*, X, 2, 126–55.

Crowder, Michael and Obaro Ikime (1970) *West African Chiefs. Their Changing Status Under Colonial Rule and Independence*. New York: Africana Publishing Corporation.

Crowder, Michael (1971a) *West Africa Resistance – The Military Response to Colonial Occupation*. New York: African Publishing Corporation.

Crowder, Michael (1971b) *West Africa Under Colonial Rule*. Evanston: Northwestern University Press.

Dada, Akinremi (1975) *Nigeria in Intra-African Politics, 1960–1970: A Linkage Analysis*. Washington, D. C.: unpublished Ph. D. thesis, American University.

Damachi, U. G. and H. D. Seibel (eds.) (1973) *Social Change and Economic Development in Nigeria*. New York: Praeger.

Damachi, U. G. *et al.* (eds) (1976) *Development Paths in Africa and China*. London: Macmillan for International Institute for Labour Studies.

Damachi, Ukandi Godwin (1972) *Nigerian Modernization*. New York: The Third Press.

Dare, Leo O. (1974) 'The Dilemma of Military Disengagement: The Nigerian Case', *Nigerian Journal of Economic and Social Studies*, Vol. 16, No. 2.

Dare, Leo O. (1981) 'Military Withdrawal from Politics in Nigeria', *International Political Science Review*, Vol. 2, No. 3.

Davidson, Basil (1978) *Africa in Modern History – The Search for a New Society*. Harmondsworth: Penguin.

Davidson, John Biggs (1972) *Africa – Hope Deferred*. London: Johnson.

Davis, Morris (1977) *Interpreters for Nigeria: The Third World and International Public Relations*. Urbana: University of Illinois Press.

de St. Jorre, John (1972) *The Nigerian Civil War*. London: Hodder & Stoughton.

Dean, Edwin (1974) *Plan Implementation in Nigeria, 1962–1966*. Ibadan: Oxford University Press.

Decalo, Samuel (1973) 'Military Coups and Military Regimes in Africa', *Journal of Modern African Studies*, 11: 1.

Decalo, Samuel (1976) *Coups and Army Rule in Africa: Studies in Military Style*. New Haven and London: Yale University Press.

Dennis, Carolynne (1978) 'Nigeria Economy and Society – a Review Article', *Quarterly Journal of Administration*, Vol. 12, No. 3, April.

Dent, M. J. (1969) 'The Military and Politics: A Study of the Relation between the Army and the Political Process in Nigeria', St. Antony's Papers 21, *African Affairs*, No. 3.

Dent, M. J. (1977) *Improving Nigeria's Draft Constitution: A Constructive and Detailed Study with Suggestions for Amendment and Improvement in the Constituent Assembly* Keele: Dark Horse Publications.

Dent, Martin (1978) *Nigeria: The Politics of Military Rule*. London: Frank Cass.

Deutsch, Karl (1961) 'Social Mobilization and Political Development', *American Political Science Review*, Vol. LV, No. 3.

Deutsche Bank (1975) *Nigeria*. Frankfurt: Deutsche Bank.

Diaku, I. (1972) 'A Capital Surplus Illusion – The Nigerian Case Revisited', *Nigerian Journal of Economic and Social Studies*, XIV, 1.

Diamond, Larry (1980) *The Social Foundations of Democracy: The Case of Nigeria*. Vols. 1–2, Unpublished Ph.D. thesis, Vanderbilt University.

Diamond, Larry (1982) 'Cleavage, Conflict and Anxiety in the Second Nigerian Republic', *Journal of Modern African Studies*, Vol. 20, No. 4.

Diamond, Larry (1983) 'Social Change and Political Conflict in Nigeria's Second Republic', in I. William Zartman (ed.) *The Political Economy of Nigeria*, New York: Praeger.

Diamond, Larry (1984) 'Nigeria in Search of Democracy', *Foreign Affairs*, Spring.

Diejemah, V. P. (1979) 'Industrial Relations in a Development Context: The Case of Nigeria', in U. G. Damachi, H. D. Seibel and L. Trachtman (eds) *Industrial Relations in Africa*. London: Macmillan.

Dikshit, R. D. (1976) 'Nigeria: From Federation to the Civil War – A Study in the Dynamics of Federalism', *Political Science Review*, Vol. 15, No. 1.

Dofny, Jacques and Akiwowo Akinsola (1980) *National and Ethnic Movements*. Beverly Hills: Sage.

Doob, Leonard W. (1962) 'From Tribalism to Nationalism in Africa', *Journal of International Affairs*, 16.

Doro, M. and N. Stultz (1970) *Governing in Black Africa: Perspectives on New States*. Englewood Cliffs: Prentice Hall.

D'Silva, B. and M. Raza (1980) 'Integrated Rural Development in Nigeria', *Food Policy*, Vol. 5.

Dudley, B. J. (1969) 'The Military and Politics in Nigeria', in J. van Doorn, (ed.) *Military Profession and Military Regimes*. The Hague: Mouton.

Dudley, B. J. (1971) 'The Military and Development', *Nigerian Journal of Economic and Social Studies*, Vol. 13, No. 2.

Dudley, B. J. (1973) *Instability and Political Order: Politics and Nigeria in Crisis*. Ibadan: Ibadan University Press.

Dudley, B. J. (1974) 'Demilitarization and Civilianization', *Quarterly Journal of Administration*, Vol. 9, Oct.

Dudley, B. J. (1980) *Murtala Muhammed*. London: Frank Cass.

Dudley, B. J. (1982) *An Introduction to Nigerian Government and Politics*. London: Macmillan.

Dudley, Billy (1981) 'The Nigerian Elections of 1979: The Voting Decision', *Journal of Commonwealth and Comparative Politics*, XIX: 3.

Duignan, Peter and L. H. Gann (eds) (1970) *Colonialism in Africa 1870-1960*. 2 vols. Cambridge: Cambridge University Press.

Durotoye, Oluyomi Oluokun (1978) *The Role of the Nigerian Legislature in National Integration, 1960-1966*, unpublished Ph.D. thesis, Duke University.

Economist Intelligence Unit London (1982) *Quarterly Economic Review of Nigeria*. London: EIU.

Edogun, Clifford Ikponmwosa (1978) *Federalism, Public Finance and Development Policy in Nigeria: An Anatomy of Public Policy and Structural Change*, unpublished Ph.D. thesis, Rutgers University, State University of New Jersey.

Efrat, Edgar Shlomo (1960) *The Application of Federalism to Emergent States in Central Africa*. Austin, Texas.

Egwurube, J. O. (1982) 'Local Government under the Second Republic – Some Problems of Definition'. Paper presented at National Conference on Problems of Political Stability and the Future of the Second Republic. Ahmadu Bello University, Zaria, 26–9 April, mimeo.

Ehrlich, Stanislaw and Graham Wootton (eds) (1980) *Three Faces of Pluralism*. London: Gower.

Eicher, Carl K. and Carl Liedholm (eds) (1970) *Growth and Development of the Nigerian Economy*. Ann Arbor, Michigan: University of Michigan Press.

Ejiofor, P. (1978) 'Indigenisation Programme Revisited', *Management in Nigeria*, July.

Ekeh, Peter P. (1975) 'Colonialism and the Two Publics in Africa: A Theoretical Statement', *Comparative Studies in Society and History*, Vol. 17.

Ekekwe, Eme (1983) 'State and Economic Development in Nigeria'. Paper presented to the 5th Bi-annual Conference, African Association of Political Science, Dakar, 27–9 June.

Ekong, Ekong E. (1976/7) 'The Fictiveness of Class Analysis in Contemporary Nigerian Society', *West African Journal of Sociology and Political Science*, Vol. II, Nos. 1 and 2.

Ekundare, R. Olufemi (1972) 'The Political Economy of Private Investment in Nigeria', *Journal of Modern African Studies*, Vol. 10, No. 1.

Ekundare, R. Olufemi (1973) *An Economic History of Nigeria 1860-1960*. London: Methuen.

Ekwe-Ekwe, Herbert (1985) 'The Nigerian Plight: Shagari to Buhari', *Third World Quarterly*, Vol. 7, No. 3.

Elaigwu, J. I. (1976) 'The Political Trio in Nigeria's Military Government: The Dynamics of Inter-Elite Relations in a Military Regime, 1967-1975', *Nigerian Journal of Public Affairs*, Vol. V, No. 2.

Elaigwu, Jonah Isawa (1976) 'Subnational Units and Political Development in New States: An African Experience', unpublished Ph.D. thesis, Stanford University.

Elazar, D. J. (1976) 'Federalism vs. Decentralization: The Drift from Authenticity', *Publius: The Journal of Federalism*, Fall.

Eleazu, Uma O. (1973) 'The Role of the Army in African Politics: A Reconsideration of Existing Theories and Practices', *Journal of the Developing Areas*, Vol. 7, January.

Eleazu, Uma O. (1977) *Federalism and Nation-Building: The Nigerian Experience 1954-1964*. Ilfracombe: Stockwell.

Elias, T. O. (1967) *Nigeria: The Development of its Laws and Constitution*. London: Stevens & Sons.

Elias, T. O. (ed.) (1972) *Law and Social Change in Nigeria*. Lagos, University of Lagos. London: Evans.

Elias, T. O. (1973) *Law in a Developing Society*. Benin City: Ethiope.

Elsenhans, Hartmut (1983) 'Capitalist Growth and Mass Incomes', *International Organization*, 37, 1, Winter.

Emezi, C. E. (1977) 'Development of Administration in Nigeria', *Africa Quarterly*, Vol. 16, No. 4.

Enteng, Inya A. (1977) 'The Nigerian Draft Constitution, Foreign Economic Domination and National Development', *The African Review*, Vol. 7, No. 2.

Epelle, Sam (ed.) (1964) *Nigeria Speaks: Speeches of Alhaji Sir Abubakar Tafawa Balewa*. London: Longman.

Esinulu, K. 'Nigerian Foreign Policy: Social Roots, Ideological Expression and Political Practice', unpublished MSS thesis, Institute of Social Studies, The Hague.

Essien-Udom, E. U. (1974) 'The Study of Nigerian Politics: Tribalism and Politics', *Theory and Practice*, Vol. 1.

Eteng, Inya A. (1977) 'The Nigerian Draft Constitution, Foreign Economic Domination and National Development', *The African Review*, Vol. 7, No. 2.

Etim, B. A. and F. N. Erontini (1979) 'Personal Income Distribution in Nigeria 1960–70 to 1971–72', in *Poverty in Nigeria*. Ibadan: Nigerian Economics Society.

Evers, Tilman (1977) *Bürgerliche Herrschaft in der Dritten Welt. Zur Theorie des Staates in ökonomiscb unterentwickelten Gesellschaftsformationen*. Cologne and Frankfurt: Europäische Verlagsanstalt.

Evers, Tilman T. and von Wagau, Peter (1973) ' "Dependencia": lateinamerikanische Beitrage zur Theorie der Unterentwicklung', *Das Argument*, Vol. 15, No. 416.

Ewing, A. F. (1963) *Industry in Africa*. London: Oxford University Press.

Eze, Pius (1971) 'Political Integration and Societal Instability: the Case of Nigeria'. Eugene, Oregon: University of Oregon, unpublished Ph.D. thesis.

Ezera, Kalu (1960) *Constitutional Developments in Nigeria*. Cambridge: Cambridge University Press.

Faculty of Law, University of Ife (1975) *Integration of Customary and Modern Legal Systems in Africa*. Ile-Ife: University of Ife Press.

Fadahunsi, Akin (1979) 'A Review of Nigeria's Public Sector Industrial Development Policy: 1960–78', *CSER Reprint Paper, No. 6*. Centre for Social and Economic Research, Ahmadu Bello University, Zaria.

Fadahunsi, Isaac Olusanya (1972) 'Bureaucratic Development in a Period of Change: The Case of the Nigerian Federal Bureaucracy'. Kent, Ohio: Kent State University, unpublished Ph.D. thesis.

Fadahunsi, Olu (1976) 'Local Government Reform in Western Nigeria: A Preliminary Assessment', *Greenhill Journal of Administration*, Achimota, Ghana, January/March.

Falola, Toyin (ed.) (1985) *Britain and Nigeria: Exploitation or Development?* London: Zed Press.

Falola, Toyin and Julius Ihonvaire (1985) *The Rise and Fall of Nigeria's Second Republic, 1979–1984*. London: Zed Press.

Fashoyin, Tayo (1980) *Industrial Relations in Nigeria: Development and Practice*. London: Longman.

Fawehinmi, Gani (1981) *Nigerian Constitutional Law Reports: 1981*, Vol. 1. Lagos: Nigerian Law Publications.

Federal Electoral Commission (1979) *The General Elections 1979*. Lagos: Federal Electoral Commission.

Federal Ministry of Information (1963) *The Constitution of the Federal Republic of Nigeria*. Lagos.

Federal Ministry of Information (1976) *Federal Military Government White Paper of Panel on Creation of New States*. Lagos.

Federal Ministry of Information. *Nigeria Handbook 1980*. Lagos.

Federal Republic of Nigeria (1962) *National Development Plan 1962–68*. Lagos: Federal Ministry of Economic Development.

Federal Republic of Nigeria (1974) *Public Service Review Commission's Main Report*, September.

Federal Republic of Nigeria (1975) *Government Views on the Report of the Public Service Review Panel*. Lagos: Federal Ministry of Information, September.

Federal Republic of Nigeria (1976) *Guidelines for Local Government Reform*. Kaduna: The Government Printer.

Federal Republic of Nigeria (1976) *Second National Development Plan 1970-74*. Federal Government Printer.

Federal Republic of Nigeria *Third National Development Plan 1975-80*. Vol. 1. Lagos: Ministry of Economic Development.

Federal Republic of Nigeria (n.d.) *Nigeria: A Guide to Understanding*. Lagos: Federal Ministry of Information.

Federal Republic of Nigeria (1977) *Report of the Technical Committee on Revenue Allocation* (2 vols). Lagos: December.

Federal Republic of Nigeria (1980) *The Presidency in Nigeria*. Lagos: Executive Office of the President, Department of Information.

Federal Republic of Nigeria (1982) *Economic Stabilization Temporary Provisions Act 1982*. Lagos.

Federal Republic of Nigeria Views (1977) *The Federal Military Government's Views on the Tribunal of Inquiry into the Activities of the Trade Unions*.

Federal Republic of Nigeria White Paper (1971) *White Paper of the Second and Final Report of the Wages and Salaries Review Commission, 1970-1971*.

Federal Republic of Nigeria. Constituent Assembly (1978) *Proceedings of the Constituent Assembly*. Lagos: Federal Ministry of Information, Printing Division.

Federal Republic of Nigeria. Federal Ministry of Information (1978) *Nigeria Handbook*. Lagos.

First, Ruth (1970) *The Barrel of a Gun*. London: Allen Lane Penguin Press.

First, Ruth (1972) *Power in Africa*. Baltimore: Penguin.

Fletcher, F. J. and S. U. Ifejika (1976) *Mass Media and National Integration in Nigeria: A Development Approach*. Paper given at Canadian Association of African Studies 6th Annual Conference, Victoria, 18-21 February.

Focus (1975) *Investment in Nigeria*. London: Focus Research.

Forrest, T. (1980) 'Agricultural Policies in Nigeria', in J. Heyer, P. Roberts and G. Williams (eds), *Rural Development in Tropical Africa*. New York: St Martin's Press.

Forsyth, Frederick (1970) *The Biafra Story*. Harmondsworth: Penguin.

Forsyth, Frederick (1983) *Emeka*. Ibadan: Spectrum Books.

Fortes, Meyer and E. E. Evans-Pritchard (1940) *African Political Systems*. London: Oxford University Press.

Foster and Sullivan Inc. (1985) *Country Political Risk Analyses: Nigeria*. New York: Foster and Sullivan Inc.

Frank, Lawrence P. (1979) 'Ideological Competition in Nigeria: Urban Populism versus Elite Nationalism', *The Journal of Modern African Studies*, Vol. 17, No. 3.

Fransmann, Martin (ed.) (1982) *Industry and Accumulation in Africa*. London: Heinemann.

Free, Lloyd A. (1964) *The Attitudes, Hopes and Fears of Nigerians*. Princeton, N. J.: Institute of International Social Research.

Freedman, David H. (1981) 'Work in Nigeria: A Cornerstone of Meeting the Needs of the People', *International Labour Review*, Vol. 120, No. 6.

Freund, Bill (1978) 'Oil Boom and Crisis in Contemporary Nigeria', *Review of African Political Economy*, 13 May-August.

Freund, Bill (1981) *Capital and Labour in the Nigerian Tin Mines*. London: Longman.

Gambari, I. A. (1975) 'Nigeria and the World: A Growing Internal Stability, Wealth and External Influence', *Journal of International Affairs*, 29, 2, Fall.

Gambari, I. A. (1980) *Party Politics and Foreign Policy: Nigeria under the First Republic*. Zaria: Ahmadu Bello University Press.

Gana, A. I. (1982) 'Local Government, or Local Self-Government: Some Theoretical Considerations'. Paper presented to National Conference on Problems of Political Stability and the Future of the Second Republic, Ahmadu Bello University, Zaria, 26-9 April, mimeo.

Garba, Brigadier Joseph (1979) 'The Military Regime and the Nigerian Society'. Address to a seminar 'Nigeria in Transition', 11 September. Reprinted in *New Nigerian*, Supplement on Nigeria in Transition, 28 September.

Garba, Joe (1982) *Revolution in Nigeria: Another View*, London: Africa Books.

Gbulie, Ben (1982) *Nigeria's Five Majors*. Africana Educational Publishers.

Ghai, D. P. (ed.) (1973) *Economic Independence in Africa*. Nairobi: East African Literature Bureau.

Gibson, Richard (1972) *African Liberation Movements*. London: Oxford University Press.

Giwa-Amu, S. I. C. (1982) 'Bourgeois Law: Instrument for Oppression'. Paper to Conference of Civil Servants' Technical Workers Union of Nigeria, Benin City, 19 June.

Goody, Jack (1977) *Technology, Tradition and the State in Africa*. London: Oxford University Press.

Goonsekere, R. K. W. (1973) 'Land Tenure Law and Land Use Decree (II)', *New Nigerian*, 24 June.

Graf, William D. (1979) *Elections 1979: The Nigerian Citizen's Guide to Parties, Politics, Leaders and Issues*. Lagos: Daily Times Press.

Grant, Ronald and E. Spencer Welhofer (1978) *Ethno-Nationalism, Multinational Corporations and the Modern State*. Denver: University of Denver Press.

Green, Reginald and Ann Seidman (1968) *Unity or Poverty: The Economics of Pan-Africanism*. Baltimore: Penguin.

Grundy, Kenneth W. (1964) 'The Class Struggle in Africa – An Examination of Conflicting Theories', *Journal of Modern African Studies*, 2 November.

Guardian, The (1982) *Nigerian Handbook 1982–83*. Glasgow and London: Collins.

Gutkind, P. C. W. (1975) 'The View from Below: Political Consciousness of the Urban Poor in Ibadan', *Cahiers*, Vol. 15, No. 1.

Gutkind, P. C. W. (1978) 'From the Energy of Despair to the Anger of Despair: The Transition from Social Circulation to Political Consciousness among the Urban Poor in Africa', *Canadian Journal of African Studies*, Vol. VII, No. 2.

Gutkind, P. C. W. and Immanuel Wallerstein (eds) (1976) *The Political Economy of Contemporary Africa*. Beverly Hills: Sage.

Gutteridge, W. F. (1975) *Military Regimes in Africa*. London: Methuen.

Hannan, Michael T. (1979) 'The Dynamics of Ethnic Boundaries', in John W. Meyer and Michael T. Hannan (eds) *National Development and the World System*, Chicago: University of Chicago Press.

Harrell-Bond, Barbara (1978) *Freedom of the Press in Nigeria: The Debate*. Hanover, NH, Aufs.

Harris, Richard (ed.) (1975) *The Political Economy of Africa*. New York: Halstead Press.

Hatch, John (1971) *Nigeria*. London: Heinemann.

Hazlewood, Arthur (ed.) (1967) *African Integration and Disintegration – Political and Economic Case Studies*. London: Oxford University Press.

Helleiner, G. K. (1966) *Peasant Agriculture, Government and Economic Growth in Nigeria*. Homewood: Richard D. Irwin.

Herskovits, Jean (1977/8) 'Dateline Nigeria: A Black Power', *Foreign Policy*, No. 29, Winter.

Herskovits, Jean (1979/80) 'Democracy in Nigeria', *Foreign Affairs*, Vol. 58, No. 2, Winter.

Hicks, Ursula (1979) *Federalism: Failure and Success*. London: Macmillan.

Hill, P. (1977) *Population, Prosperity and Poverty: Rural Kano 1900 and 1970*. Cambridge: Cambridge University Press.

Hilton, Andrew C. E. (1973) 'Foreign Investment in Nigeria: Perceptions and Reality'. Philadelphia: Pennsylvania State University, unpublished Ph.D. thesis.

Himmelstrand, Ulf (1978) 'Tribalism, Regionalism, Nationalism and Secession in Nigeria' in S. N. Eisenstadt and S. Rokkan (eds), *Building States and Nations: Analyses by Region*. Beverly Hills: Sage.

Hogben, P. (1967) *An Introduction to the History of the Islamic States of Northern Nigeria*. Oxford: Oxford University Press.

Hoogvelt, Ankie (1979) 'Indigenisation and Foreign Capital: Industrialisation in Nigeria', *Review of African Political Economy*, No. 13.

Horowitz, D. L. (1979) 'About-face in Africa: the Return to Civilian Rule in Nigeria', *Yale Review*, Winter.

Hughes, A. (1977) 'The Army as "Social Engineers" in Nigeria', *Contemporary Review*, No. 231.

Hutchenreuter, Klaus (1980) 'Einige Grundzüge der Fortbildung der poitischen Systeme sowie des Staats-und Verfassungsrechts in Landern Afrikas und Asiens mit kapitalistischer Entwicklung', *Asien-afrika-Lateinamerika*, Vol. 8, No. 3.

Idang, Gordon (1971) *Nigerian Internal Politics and Foreign Policy 1960–66*. Ibadan: Ibadan University Press.

Idemudia, Taiwo Donatus Ayomwan (1978) *An Inquiry into the Performance of Nigerian Indigenous Entrepreneurs*. Buffalo: unpublished Ph.D. thesis, State University of New York.

Igbozurike, Martin (1976) *Problem-Generating Structures in Nigeria's Rural Development*. Uppsala: Scandinavian Institute of African Studies.

Igiehon, Noser (1975) *To Build a Nigerian Nation*. Ilfracombe: Stockwell.

Igun, Adenola A. (1972) 'The Collection of Demographic Statistics for Reconstruction and Development in Nigeria', A. A. Igun and G. T. Acsadi (eds), *Demographic Statistics in Nigeria*. Proceedings of the Symposium on Technical and Practical Problems in the Collection of Demographic Statistics for Reconstruction and Development in Nigeria. Ile-Ife, 3–5 August 1970. University of Ife (photo-mechanical repro.).

Ihonvbere, Julius O. (1983) *The Oil Industry in Nigeria: An Annotated Bibliography*. Montreal: Bibliography Series, Centre for Developing Area Studies, McGill University.

Ijere, M. O. (1980) *Labour and Management Problems in Nigeria*. Enugu: Fourth Dimension.

Ike, V. C. (1976) *University Development in Africa: the Nigerian Experience*. Ibadan: Oxford University Press.

Ikime, O. (1969) *Niger Delta Rivalry*. London: Longman.

Ikoiwak, Ebong Abasi (1979) *Bureaucracy in Development: The Case of the Nigerian Federal Civil Service*, unpublished Ph.D. thesis, Atlanta University.

Ikoku, S. G. (1980) *Building the New Nigeria. A Collection of Essays*. Enugu: Fourth Dimension.

Ikoku, S. G. (1985) *Nigeria's Fourth Coup: Options of Modern Statehood*. Enugu: Fourth Dimension.

Imoagene, O. (1976) *Social Mobility in Emergent Society: A Study of the New Elite in Western Nigeria*. Canberra: Australian National University Press.

Imoagene, O. (1976/7) 'Extended Family Detachment among the New Elite in Nigeria', *West African Journal of Social and Political Science*, Vol. II, Nos. 1 and 2.

Inanaga, Eno. I. (1978) 'The First "Indigenisation Decree" and the Dividend Policy of Nigerian Quoted Companies', *Journal of Modern African Studies*, Vol. 16, No. 2.

Inkles, A. (1969) 'Participant Citizenship in Six Developing Countries', *American Political Science Review*, 63, No. 4.

International Bank for Reconstruction and Development (1974) *Nigeria: Options for Long-Term Development*. World Bank Country Report No. 5. Baltimore: Johns Hopkins University Press.

International Labour Organization (1982) *Nigeria: First Things First*. Addis Ababa: International Labor Office.

Iroh, Eddie (1981) 'Radicals', *Africa*, No. 118, June.

Ituen, Edet Bassey (1971) *Nigeria's Foreign Relations: A Study of the Factors Influencing Nigeria's Foreign Relations After Independence*. St. Louis, MO.: unpublished Ph.D. thesis, St. Louis University.

Jackson, R. H. (1978) 'Political Stratification in Tropical Africa', *CJAS*, Vol. 7, No. 3.

Jakande, L. K. (1975) *Role of the Mass Media in a Developing Country*. University of Ife, Faculty of Arts Lecture Series.

Jemibewon, David M. (1978) *A Combatant in Government*. Ibadan: Heinemann.

Jinadu, L. Adele (1978) 'Notes for a Discussion of the Relationship between Federalism and Democracy'. Paper presented to the Nigerian Political Science Association Ile-Ife, 3–6 April.

Jones, G. I. (1957) *Report of the Position, Status and Influence of Chiefs and Natural Rulers in the Eastern Region of Nigeria*. Enugu: Eastern Region Government Printer.

Jordan, Robert S. (1969) *Government and Power in West Africa*. London: Faber & Faber.

Joseph, R. A. (1978) 'Affluence and Underdevelopment', *Journal of Modern African Studies*, No. 16, June.

Joseph, Richard (1979) 'Political Parties and Ideology in Nigeria', *Review of African Political Economy*, No. 13.

Joseph, Richard (1981) 'Democratization under Military Tutelage: Crisis and Consensus in the 1979 Elections', *Comparative Politics*, Vol. XIV, No. 1.

Joseph, Richard (1981a) 'The Ethnic Trap: Notes on the Nigerian Elections, 1978–79', *Issue*, XI, 1/2.

Joseph, Richard A. (1981b) 'The Ethnic Trap: Notes on the Nigerian Campaign and Elections, 1978–79', in C. S. Whitaker Jr. (ed.) *Perspectives on the Second Republic*. Brandeis University, Mass.: Crossroads Press.

Joseph, Richard A. 'Class, State and Prebendal Politics in Nigeria', *Journal of Commonwealth and Comparative Politics*. Vol. 21, No. 3.

Joseph, Richard (1984) 'The Overthrow of Nigeria's Second Republic', *Current History*, March.

Journal of African Studies (1979) Special Issue on 'Nigeria and Dependency Theory', Jan. and April.

Jouve, E. (1979) 'Nigeria: de la chute de Gowon à la présidence du Gen. Obasanjo', *RFEPA*, No. 157.

Joye, E. Michael and Kingsley Igweike (1982) *Intrduction to the 1979 Nigerian Constitution*. London: Macmillan.

'Judgement of the Special Tribunal, The', *New Nigerian*, 16 October 1979.

Kadzai, Ayuba (1976) *Nigeria's Global Strategy*. Lagos: The Nigerian Institute of International Affairs.

Kamarck, Andrew W. (1971) *The Economics of African Development*. New York: Praeger, rev. edn.

Kasunmu, A. B. (1973) 'Nigeria', in A. P. Blaustein and G. H. Flaz (eds) *Constitutions of the Countries of the World*, New York: Oceana Publications.

Kasunmu, A. B. (1977) *The Supreme Court of Nigeria 1956–70*. London: Heinemann.

Kay, G. B. (1972) *The Political Economy of Colonialism in Ghana*. Cambridge: Cambridge University Press.

Kay, G. B. (1975) *Development and Underdevelopment: A Marxist Analysis*, London: Macmillan.

Kilby, Peter (1969) *Industrialization in an Open Economy: Nigeria, 1945–1966*. Cambridge: Cambridge University Press.

Kilson, Martin L. (1958) 'The Analysis of African Nationalism', *World Politics*, April.

King, Mae C. (1976/7) 'State Creation in Federal Systems: A Quest for Unity', *West African Journal of Political Science*, Vol. II, Nos. 1 and 2 (1976–1977).

King, Mae C. (1977) 'Executive Leadership and Political Development: The Nigerian Proposal of 1976'. Paper delivered to the fourth Annual Conference of the Nigerian Political Science Association. Reprinted in: *Political Issues of the Draft Constitution*. Zaria: NPSA.

King-Akesode, Mae C. (1980) 'The Dynamics of Localism in National Development'. Paper presented to the Nigerian Political Science Association Annual Conference, Port Harcourt, March (mimeo.).

Kirk-Greene, A. H. M. (1971) *Crisis and Conflict in Nigeria. A Documentary Sourcebook*. (2 vols.) London: Oxford University Press.

Kirk-Greene, A. H. M. (1981) *West African Portraits*. London: Frank Cass.

Kirk-Greene, Anthony (1981) 'The Making of the Second Republic', in Anthony Kirk-Greene and Douglas Rimmer (eds) *Nigeria Since 1970: A Political and Economic Outline*. New York: Holmes and Meier (London: Hodder & Stoughton).

Kirk-Greene A. H. M. (1983) *African Administrators in Action*. London: Frank Cass.

Kirk-Greene, Anthony and Douglas Rimmer (eds) (1981) *Nigeria Since 1970: A Political and Economic Outline*. London: Hodder & Stoughton.

Klein, Martin A. (ed.) (1980) *Peasants in Africa*. Beverly Hills: Sage.

Knight, C. Gregory (1976) 'One Nigeria? A Regional View from the Western State', *African Studies Review*, Vol. 19, No. 2.

Koehn, Peter (1981) 'Prelude to Civilian Rule: The Nigerian Elections of 1979' *Africa Today*, Vol. 28, No. 1.

Koehn, Peter (1983) 'State Land Allocation and Class Formation in Nigeria', *Journal of Modern African Studies*, Vol. 21, No. 3.

Kolawole, A. (1982) 'The Role of Grassroots Participation in National Development. Lessons from the Kwara State of Nigeria', *Community Development Journal*, April.

Kraus, J. (1979) 'From Military to Civilian Regimes in Ghana and Nigeria', *Current History*, March.

Kraus, J. (1982) 'Nigeria under Shagari', *Current History* Vol. 76, No. 445.

Kulp, Philip Masterton (1975) 'The Role of Education in Political Socialization and its Implications for Foreign Policy: A Comparison of the Balewa and Gowon Governments in Nigeria'. Washington, D. C.: unpublished Ph.D. thesis, American University.

Lagos Programme. 1st vol. of 6 (1976) FESTAC '76 Programme of Action for Black Revolution. Lagos: Federal Commission for Education.

Laidi, Z. (1979) 'Le Nigeria, ou l'emergence d'un nouveau centre de pouvoir?', *L'Afrique et L'Asie*, 122.

Langley, J. Agodele (1973) *Pan-Africanism and Nationalism in West Africa*. London: Oxford University Press.

Lawson, C. D. (1974) *The Role of Civil Servants in a Military Regime*. Lagos: Federal Ministry of Information.

Lawson, Kay (1976) 'Nigeria's Future Constitution: Academic Hopes vs. Military Intentions', *Journal of African Studies*, Vol. 2, Spring.

LeFever, Ernest W. (1970) *Spear and Sceptre: Army, Police and Politics in Tropical Africa*. Washington, D. C.: Brookings Institution.

Lewis, A. (1973) *Nigeria's Exports: Problems, Prospects and Implications for Economic Growth*. Budapest: Magyar Tudomanyos Akademia Studies on Developing Countries, No. 68.

Leys, Colin (1977) 'Underdevelopment and Dependency: Critical Notes', *Journal of Contemporary Asia*, Vol. 7, No. 1.

Liedholm, Carl (ed.) (1970) *Growth and Development of Nigeria's Economy*. Ann Arbor: University of Michigan Press.

Lipset, S. M. (1963) *The First New Nation: The United States in Historical Comparative Perspective*. New York: Basic Books.

Lloyd, Peter C. (1967) *Africa in Social Change: Changing Traditional Societies in the Modern World*. Baltimore: Penguin

Lofchie, M. F. (ed.) (1971) *The State of the Nations: Constraints on Development in Independent Africa*. Berkeley: University of California Press.

Lozoya, J. (ed.) (1980) *Africa, the Middle East and the New International Economic Order*. New York: Pergamon Policy Studies.

Lubeck, Paul (1978) 'Labour in Kano Since the Petroleum Boom', *Review of African Political Economy*, No. 13.

Lubeck, Paul (1979) 'The Value of Multiple Methods in Researching Third World Strikes: A Nigerian Example', *Development and Change*, Vol. 10.

Lubeck, Paul (1981) 'Class Formation at the Periphery: Class Consciousness and Islamic Nationalism Among Nigerian Workers', in R. L. and I. H. Simpson (eds) *Research in the Sociology of Work. Worker Consciousness*, Vol. 1. Greenwich: JAI Press.

Lubeck, Paul (1981/2) 'Islamic Networks and Urban Capitalism', *Cahiers d'Études Africaines*, Vol. XXVI.

Lubeck, P. and J. Walton (1979) 'Urban Class Conflict in Africa and Latin America', *International Journal of Urban and Regional Studies*, Vol. 3, No. 1.

Luckham, Robin (1971) *The Nigerian Military: A Sociological Analysis of Authority and Revolt 1960-1967*. Cambridge: Cambridge University Press.

Mabogunje, Akin L. (1969) *Urbanization in Nigeria*. New York: Africana.

Mabogunje, Akin L. (1971) *Growth Poles and Growth Centres in the Regional Development of Nigeria*. Geneva: United Nations Research Institute for Social Development.

Mackay I. K. (1964) *Broadcasting in Nigeria*. Ibadan: Ibadan University Press.

Mackintosh, J. P. (1962) 'Federalism in Nigeria', *Political Studies*, Vol. 10.

Mackintosh, J. P. (ed.) (1966) *Nigerian Government and Politics*. London: George Allen & Unwin.

Madanugu, Eddie (1982) *Problems of Socialism: The Nigerian Challenge*. London: Zed Press.
Madanagu, Eddie (1984) *Nigeria: The Economy and the People*. London: New Beacon Books.
Maddocks, K. P. and D. A. Pott (1960) *Report on Local Government in Northern Provinces of Nigeria*. Kaduna: Government Printing Offices.
Madiebo, Major Gen. Alexander A. (1980) *The Nigerian Revolution and the Biafran War*. Enugu: Fourth Dimension.
Madujibeya, S. A. (1976) 'Oil and Nigeria's Economic Development', *African Affairs*, 75, 300, July.
Mafeje, Archie (1971) 'The Ideology of "Tribalism" ', *The Journal of Modern African Studies*, Vol. 9, No. 2.
Mamdani, Mahmood (1976) *Politics and Class Formation in Uganda*. New York: Monthly Review.
Maquet, Jaques (1971) *Power and Society in Africa*. London: Weidenfeld & Nicolson.
Marenin, Otwin (1978) 'Class Issues and Democratic Institutions'. Paper presented at the Conference of the Nigerian Political Science Association, Ife, April.
Marenin, Otwin (1979) 'National Service and National Consciousness in Nigeria', *Journal of Modern African Studies*, Vol. 17.
Markovitz, I. L. (1976) 'Bureaucratic Development and Economic Growth', *Journal of Modern African Studies*, 14 June.
Markovitz, Irving L. (1977) *Power and Class in Africa*. Englewood Cliffs, N. J.: Prentice Hall.
Markovitz, Irving Leonard (ed.) (1970) *African Politics and Society: Basic Issues and Problems of Government and Development*. New York: Free Press.
Mazrui, Ali (1976) 'Soldiers as Traditionalizers: Military Rule and Re-Africanization of Africa', *World Politics*, Vol. 23, January.
Mazrui, Ali A. (1978) *Africa's International Relations*. London: Heinemann/Westview.
Mbadinuju, Clement Chinweoke (1973) 'Domestic Factors Shaping Nigeria's Foreign Policy'. Ithaca, N. Y.: unpublished Ph.D. thesis, Cornell University.
McEwan, Peter and Robert B. Sutcliffe (eds) (1965) *Modern Africa*. New York: Thomas Crowell.
Melson, R. (1967) 'Marxists in the Nigerian Labor Movement: A Case Study in the Failure of Ideology'. Cambridge, Mass.: unpublished Ph.D. thesis, Massachusetts Institute of Technology.
Melson, R. and Harold Wolpe (1970) 'Modernization and the Politics of Communalism: A Theoretical Perspective', *American Political Science Review*, Vol. 64, No. 4.
Melson, R. and Harold Wolpe (eds) (1972) *Nigeria: Modernization and the Politics of Communalism*. East Lansing: Michigan State University Press.
Miller, R. A. (1974) 'Elite Formation in Africa', *Journal of Modern African Studies*, 12, December.
Miller, Robert A. (1975) 'The Party-State and Bureaucratic/Political Relations in Africa', *Comparative Political Studies*, Vol. 8, No. 3.
Miners, N. J. (1971) *The Nigerian Army 1956–1966*. London: Methuen.
Minogue, Martin and Judith Molloy (eds) (1974) *African Aims and Attitudes: Selected Documents*. Cambridge: Cambridge University Press.
Morgan, E. Phillip (ed.) (1974) *The Administration of Change in Africa: Essays in the Theory and Practice of Development Administration in Africa*. New York and London: Dunellen.
Morgan Report (1964) *Report of the Commission for the Review of Wages, Salaries and Conditions of Employment of the Junior Employees of the Governments of the Federation and in Private Establishments*.
Morris-Jones, W. W. (ed.) (1982) *Decolonisation and After*. London: Frank Cass.
Munoz, Louis J. (1980) 'Traditional Participation in a Modern Political System – The Case of Nigeria', *Journal of Modern African Studies*, Vol. 18, No. 3.
Murray, D. J. (1969) *The Work of Administration in Nigeria*. London: Hutchinson for the Institute of Administration, University of Ife.
Murray, D. J. (ed.) (1970) *Studies in Nigerian Administration*. London: Hutchinson.
Murray, David J. (1975) 'Nigeria: The Experience of Military Rule', *Current History*, May.
Nafziger, E. Wayne (1977) *African Capitalism: A Case Study in Nigerian Entrepreneurship*. Stanford: Hoover Institution Press.

Nduka, R. (1964) *Western Education and the Nigerian Cultural Background*. Ibadan: Oxford University Press.

Nelson, Harold D. *et al.* (1972) *Area Handbook for Nigeria*. Washington, D. C.: U. S. Government Printing Office.

Neu, John Howard (1972) *Ethnic Politics and Political Integration in Nigeria and Sudan: A Comparative Study*, unpublished Ph.D. thesis: University of Nebraska.

New Nigerian National Day Supplement, Monday, 1 October 1979.

Nicolson, I. F. (1969) *The Administration of Nigeria 1900-1960*. London: Oxford University Press.

Nigerian Economic Society (1974) *Nigeria's Indigenisation Policy*. Proceedings of the November 1974 Symposium. Ibadan: Nigerian Economic Society.

'Nigeria: Impact of the Oil Economy', *Africa Today*. Oct./Dec. 1977.

'Nigeria: Regionalism Re-emerges', *The New Statesman*, 10 August 1979.

'Nigeria: What Ideology for 1979?', *African Mirror*. New York: November 1978.

Nigeria Year Book (1975, 1982) Lagos: Daily Times of Nigeria.

'Nigeria Extra', in *New African Development*, London, July 1977.

Nigeria, Ministry of Information (1977) *Report of the Tribunal of Inquiry into the Activities of the Trade Unions*. Lagos.

Nigerian Institute of Management (1971) *Indigenization and Management in Nigeria*. Enugu, mimeo.

Nigerian Economic Society (1975) *Nigeria's Indigenisation Policy*. Lagos: Nigerian Economic Society.

'Nigeria Surveys 1977', in *New African Development*, June 1977.

'Nigerian Socialists Speak (Documents)', (1975) *Review of African Political Economy*, No. 4.

The Nigerian Academy of Arts, Sciences and Technology (1974) *The Nigerian People's Manifesto*. Ibadan: The Nigerian Academy of Arts, Sciences and Technology.

Nigeria's New Government: A Confidential Report on the Structure, Policies, and Personalities of the Babangida Administration (1985) Washington, D. C.: Defense and Foreign Affairs Publications.

Niven, Sir Rex (1970) *The War of Nigerian Unity 1967-1970*. Ibadan: Evans Brothers.

Nixon, C. R. (1974) 'Adaptation of Cultural Ties to Economic Development', *American Behavioral Science*, 13, Summer.

Nkemnacho, G. B. 'The Land Use Decree' 1 and 2, *The Bureaucrat*, Vol. 6, No. 4 (Oct–Dec 1973); and Vol. 7, No. 1 (Jan–March 1979).

NLC (1981) *The Need to Sustain One Central Labour Organisation (NLC) in Nigeria*. Lagos: Nigerian Labour Congress.

Nnoli, Okwudiba (1967) *Economic Decolonization and Inter-state Politics in Africa: A Study of Ghana, Guinea, Ivory Coast, Mali, Nigeria and Senegal*. Stanford, California: unpublished Ph.D. thesis, Stanford University.

Nnoli, Okwudiba (1974) 'Socio-Economic Insecurity and Ethnic Politics in Africa', *The African Review*, Vol. 4, No. 1.

Nnoli, Okwudiba (1978) *Ethnic Politics in Nigeria*. Enugu: Fourth Dimension.

Nnoli, Okwudiba (1981) *Path to Nigerian Development*. London: Zed Press.

Nwabueze, B. O. (1968) *The Machinery of Justice in Nigeria.* London: Hurst.

Nwabueze, Benjamin Obi (1973) *Constitutionalism in the Emergent States*. London: Hurst.

Nwabueze, B. O. (1974) *Presidentialism in Commonwealth Africa*. London, Enugu: Fourth Dimension.

Nwabueze, B. O. (1982a) *A Constitutional History of Nigeria*. London: Hurst.

Nwabueze, B. O. (1982b) *The Presidential Constitution of Nigeria*. London: Hurst.

Nwabueze, B. O. (1982c) *The Individual and the State Under the New Constitution* (together with *Government Powers in Relation to Economic Affairs and the Economy Under the Constitution*). Lagos: NIIA Lecture Series No. 25.

Nwabueze, B. O. (1985) *Nigeria's Presidential Constitution 1979-1983: The Second Experiment in Constitutional Democracy*. London: Longman.

Nwabueze, R. O. (1981) 'Impact of Military Rule on Nigerian Trade Union Movement (1966–73)', *Indian Journal of Industrial Relations*, Vol. 16, No. 4.

Nwala, U. (1979) 'Ideological Dependency and the Problem of Autonomy in Nigeria', *Journal of Asian and African Studies*, Vol. 14, Nos. 1–2.

Nwankwo, A. A. (1972) *Nigeria: The Challenge of Biafra*. London: Rex Collings.

Nwankwo, A. A. (1981) *Can Nigeria Survive?* Enugu: Fourth Dimension.

Nwankwo, A. A. (1985) *Nigeria: My People, My Vision* Enugu: Fourth Dimension.

Nwankwo, A. A. (1986) *Civilianized Soldiers: Army/Civilian Government for Nigeria*. Enugu: Fourth Dimension.

Nwankwo, G. O. (1977) *Ideology for Accelerated Development in Nigeria*. The Hague: International Institute for Labour Studies.

Nwankwo, G. O. (1979) *The Nigerian Financial System*. London: Macmillan.

Nwanko, Jason Chibueze (1983) 'Agrarian Policy Implementation in a Cocoa Producing Region of Nigeria: The Analysis of Agrarian Class Relations and Participation in Policy Benefits', unpublished Ph.D. thesis, University of Wisconsin-Madison.

Nwanze, Michael C. (1979) 'Nigeria 1979: Problems and Prospects of Civilian Rule', *Journal of Social and Political Studies*, Vol. 4, No. 1.

Nwatu, D. N. (1979/80) *The Development of Parliamentary Democracy in Nigeria*. Enugu: Fourth Dimension.

Nwigwe, H. E. (n.d.) *Nigeria: The Fall of the First Republic*. London: Ebony Press.

Nwomonoh, Jonathan N. (1978) 'The Role of Local Government in Nation Building: The Nigerian Case', unpublished Ph.D. thesis, Claremont, California: Claremont Graduate School.

Nwosu, E. J. (1980) 'Rural Development as a Factor in National Development', in E. C. Amucheazi (ed.) *Readings in Social Sciences: Issues in National Development*, Enugu: Fourth Dimension.

Nwosu, Humphrey (1980) *Problems of Nigerian Administration: A Book of Readings*. Enugu: Fourth Dimension.

Nwosu, Humphrey N. (1977) *Political Authority and the Nigerian Civil Service*. Enugu: Fourth Dimension.

Nzimiro, Ikenna (1972) *Studies in Ibo Political Systems, Chieftaincy and Politics in Four Nigerian States*. London: Frank Cass.

Nzimiro, Ikenna (1977) 'The Crisis in the Social Sciences: the Nigerian Situation', *Third World Forum*, Mexico.

Nzimiro, Ikenna (1979) *The Nigerian Civil War: A Study in Class Conflict*. Enugu: Fourth Dimension.

Obasanjo, General Olusegun (n.d.?1980) *A March of Progress: Collected Speeches of His Excellency General Olusegun Obasanjo*. Lagos: Federal Ministry of Information.

Obasanjo, General Olusegun (1981) *My Command. An Account of the Nigerian Civil War 1967–70*. London: Heinemann.

Obichere, Boniface (ed.) (1981) *African States and the Military*. London: Frank Cass.

Obilade, Akintunde Olusegun (1979) *The Nigerian Legal System* London: Sweet & Maxwell.

Obinna, O. E. (1982) *An Introduction to Nigerian Budget Policy*. Winchester, MA: George Allen & Unwin.

O'Brien, D. C. (1972) 'Modernization, Order, and the Erosion of a Democratic Ideal: American Political Science 1960–1970', *Journal of Development Studies, 1970*, Vol. 8, No. 4.

O'Connell, J. (1967) 'Political Integration: The Nigerian Case', in A. Hazlewood (ed.) *African Integration and Disintegration*, London: Oxford University Press.

O'Connell, James and Paul A. Beckett (1975) 'Social Characteristics of an Elite-in-Formation: The Case of Nigerian University Students', *The British Journal of Sociology*, Vol. XXVI, No. 3.

Odetola, T. O. (1978a) *Military Politics in Nigeria*. New Brunswick, N. J.: Transaction Books.

Odetola, T. O. (1978b) 'National Integration and the Creation of States in Nigeria', *Journal of Black Studies*, Vol. 9, No. 2.

Odetola, Theophilus Olatunde (1980) *Military Politics in Nigeria: Economic Development and Political Stability*. Eastbourne: Transaction Books.

Odife, D. Onyema (1976) 'The 1977 Budget and the Second Phase of Indigenisation: A Note', *Nigerian Journal of Economic and Social Studies*, Vol. 18, No. 3.

Odinegwe, Godwin A. (1957) 'The Constitutional Development in Nigeria: The Origins of Federalism, 1862–1954', unpublished Ph.D. thesis, Clark University, Worcester, Mass.

Odogwu, Bernard (1985) *No Place to Hide: Conflicts and Crises Inside Biafra*. Enugu: Fourth Dimension.

Odumosu, Oluwole Idowu (1963) *The Nigerian Constitution: History and Development*. London: Sweet & Maxwell; Lagos: African University Press.

Odunkele, Feme (ed.) (1983) *Nigeria: Development in Corruption*. Ibadan: Ibadan University Press.

Offiong, Daniel (1980) *The Role of Organised Labour and Political Development in Nigeria*. Enugu: Fourth Dimension.

Offiong, Daniel A. (1982) 'The Dilemma of Traditional Rulers in a Changing Nigeria'. Paper presented to the twelfth annual conference of the Canadian Association of African Studies, Toronto, 10–14 May, mimeo.

Ofiaja, Nicholas D. (1979) *Stability and Instability in Politics: The Case of Nigeria and Cameroon*. New York: Vantage Press.

Ofonagoro, Walter Ibekwe (1979) *The Story of the Nigerian General Elections, 1979*. Lagos: Federal Ministry of Information.

Ohonbamu, O. (1969) *The Psychology of the Nigerian Revolution*. Ilfracombe: Stockwell.

Ojigbo, A. O. (1972) 'On the Advantages of a No-Party State', *Journal of Modern African Studies*, Vol. 10, No. 1.

Ojigbo, Okion (1980) *Nigeria Returns to Civilian Rule*. Lagos: Tokion (Nigeria) Company.

Ojo, F. (1975) *Economic Integration: The Nigerian Experience Since Independence*. The Hague: Institute of Social Studies, Occasional Paper 54.

Ojo, Folayan (1976) 'Economic Integration: The Nigerian Experience Since 1966', *Nigerian Journal of Economic and Social Studies*, Vol. 18, No. 2.

Ojo, J. D. (1976) 'The Changing Role of Traditional Rulers in the Nigerian Political Set Up', *Indian Journal of Political Science*, Vol. 37, No. 4.

Ojo, Olatunde J. B. (1974) 'Nigeria's Foreign Policy 1960–66: Politics, Economics and the Struggle for African Leadership', unpublished Ph.D. thesis, Storrs, Conn.: University of Connecticut.

Ojo, Olatunde J. B. (1976) 'Federal-State Relations [in Nigeria] 1967–1974', *Quarterly Journal of Administration*, Vol. 10, January.

Ojo, Olatunde J. B. (1980) 'Nigeria and the Formation of ECOWAS', *International Organization*, Vol. 34, No. 4.

Ojo, Olatunde J. B. (1981) 'The Impact of Personality and Ethnicity on the Nigerian Elections of 1979', *Africa Today*, Vol. 28, No. 1.

Okadigbo, Chuba *The Mission of the NPN*. Ejike: R. Nwankwo Associates, undated.

Okafor, F. C. (1977) 'Political Development and the Modernization Process in Nigeria', *Civilisations* (Brussels), Vol. 112.

Okafor, F. C. (1982) 'Rural Change in Contemporary Nigeria: Implications for Development'. Paper presented at twelfth Annual Conference of the Canadian Association of African Studies, University of Toronto, May.

Okafor, Samuel D. (1972) 'Ibo Chiefs and Social Change', *Journal of Modern African Studies*, Vol. 10, No. 1.

Okediji, F. Olu (1975) 'Indigenization Decree and Income Distribution: The Social Implications', *Quarterly Journal of Administration*, Vol. IX, No. 2.

Okigbo, P. N. C. (1982) *Nigeria's Financial System*. London: Longman.

Okoli, Ekwueme Felix (1978) 'Institutional Structure and Conflict in Nigeria: A Case Study of Conflict in a Multi-Ethnic State from 1946–1966', unpublished Ph.D. thesis, New York New School for Social Research.

Okolo, Amechi Peters Adolf (1978) 'International Political Economy and Nigeria's Development:

1945–75', unpublished Ph.D. thesis, Purdue University, Lafayette, Indiana.

Okonjo, I. M. (1972) *Some Aspects of Public Administration in a Developing Economy*. Benin City: Ministry of Home Affairs and Information, Information Division.

Okonjo, Isaac M. (1974) *British Administration in Nigeria 1900–1950: A Nigerian View*. New York: NOK Publishers.

Okonkwo, Cyprian (1980) *Introduction to Nigerian Law*. London: Sweet & Maxwell.

Okoye, Mokwugo (1975) *Politics and Problems of the First Republic of Nigeria*. Ile-Ife: University of Ife Press (published for the Faculty of Arts).

Okpaku, Joseph (ed.) (1972) *Nigeria: Dilemma of Nationhood: An African Analysis of the Biafran Conflict*. New York: Third Press.

Okpu, U. (1977) *Ethnic Minority Problems in Nigerian Politics, 1960–1965*. Uppsala: Uppsala University.

Ola, Opeyemi (1968) 'The Study of West African Local Government', *Journal of Modern African Studies*, Vol. 6, No. 2.

Ola, Robert F. (1984) *Local Administration in Nigeria*. London: Hutchinson.

Olaloku, F. A. *et al.* (1979) *Structure of the Nigerian Economy*. London and Ibadan: Macmillan/ University of Lagos.

Olatunbosun, Dupe (1975) *Nigeria's Neglected Rural Majority*. Ibadan: Oxford University Press.

Ollawa, P. E. (1981) 'The Nigerian Elections of 1979: A Further Comment', *Journal of Commonwealth and Comparative Politics*, Vol. XIX, No. 3.

Olorunsola, V. A. (1978) *Social Reconstruction in Two African States*. Washington: University Press of America.

Olorunsola, Victor (1972) *The Politics of Cultural Sub-Nationalism in Africa*. New York: Doubleday.

Olorunsola, Victor A. (1968) 'Patterns of Interaction between Bureaucratic and Political Leaders: A Case Study', *The Journal of Developing Areas*, Vol. 3, No. 1.

Olorunsola, Victor A. (1977) *Soldiers and Power*. Stanford, Cal.: Hoover Institution Press.

Olowu, Dele (1983) 'The Nature of Bureaucratic Corruption in Nigeria', *International Review of Administrative Sciences*, 3.

Olugbemi, Stephen Oluwole (1978) 'Military Leadership and Political Integration in Nigeria 1966–76: A Policy Approach to the Study of the Developmental Performance of the Military in a New and Plural Society', unpublished Ph.D. thesis, State University of New York.

Oluleye, James J. (1985) *Military Leadership in Nigeria 1966–1979*. Ibadan: University Press.

Olusanya, G. O. (1975) *The Evolution of the Nigerian Civil Service 1861–1960*. Humanities Monograph Series No. 2. Lagos: Lagos University Library Press.

Olutala, Aderemi (1981) 'Education and Elections in Nigeria', *The Round Table*, No. 281. January.

Oluwide, Baba (Baba Omojola) (1970) *Agbe-Ko-Ya (Farmers Against Oppression)*. Peasant Movements South of the Sahara Series. Research Unit of the Young Toilers Brigade. Lagos: International Press.

Omer-Cooper, J. D. *et al.* (1964) 'Nigerian Marxism and Social Progress', *Nigerian Journal of Economic and Social Studies*, July.

Omo-Ananigie, P. I. (1957) *The Life History of M. A. O. Imoudu: Coeur de Lion*. Lagos.

Omonina, Moses Adekunle (1981) *Party Politics and the Transition from Military to Civilian Rule in Nigeria*. Zaria: Ahmadu Bello University.

Oneyewu, Nicholas D. Ukachi (1966) 'Nation-Building in Nigeria 1900–1960', unpublished Ph.D. thesis, Washington D.C.: American University.

Oni, O. (1966) 'Features of Nigeria's Financial Institutions: A Marxist Approach', *Nigerian Journal of Economic and Social Studies*, Vol. 8, No. 3.

Oni, Ola and Bade Onimode (1975) *The Economic Development of Nigeria: The Socialist Alternative*. Ibadan: Ibadan University Press.

Onibonoje, G. O. (1959) *Civics for Nigerians*. Ibadan: Onibonoje Press.

Onimode, B. (1976) 'Towards New Orientations for Economics in Developing Countries', *Nigerian Journal of Economic and Social Studies*, Vol. 18, No. 3.

Onimode, B. (1978) 'Economic Development and Class Struggle in Nigeria', *Nigerian Journal of Economic and Social Studies*, Vol. 20, No. 3.

Onimode, Bade (1978) 'Exploitation in the Theory of Political Economy', *The African Review*, Vol. 3, No. 3.

Onimode, Bade (1982) *Imperialism and Underdevelopment in Nigeria*. London: Zed Press.

Onitiri, O. and B. Ayida (eds) (1972) *Reconstruction and Development in Nigeria*. London: Oxford University Press.

Onoge, Omafume F. (1974) 'The Indigenisation Decree and Economic Independence: Another Case of Bourgeois Utopianism', in *Nigeria's Indigenisation Policy*. Proceedings of the Symposium organised by the Nigerian Economic Society. Ibadan: University of Ibadan.

Onoh, J. K. (1983) *The Nigerian Oil Economy*. London: Croom Helm.

Onokerhoraye, A. G. (1973) 'The Urban System and National Integration in Nigeria', *Journal of Black Studies*, Vol. 3, No. 2.

Onokerhoraye, A. G. (1984) *Social Services in Nigeria*. London, etc.: Kegan Paul.

Onu, P. E. (1977) 'Mass Media in the Dependency Syndrome: An Exploratory Case Study of the Nigerian Daily Newspaper'. Paper presented to 7th Annual Conference, Canadian Association of African Studies, Sherbrooke, Que., 3–6 May.

Onwubu, Chukwuemeka (1975) 'Ethnic Identity, Political Integration, and National Development: the Igbo Diaspora in Nigeria', *Journal of Modern African Studies*, Vol. 13, No. 3.

Onwuejeogwu, M. Angulu (1975) *The Social Anthropology of Africa. An Introduction*. London/Ibadan: Heinemann.

Onyejekwe, Lawrence Okey (1978) 'The Role of the Military in Economic and Social Development: An Analysis of Regime Performance in Nigeria', unpublished Ph.D. thesis, Ohio State University.

Onyemelukwe, Clement (1969) *Problems of Industrial Planning and Management in Nigeria*. New York: Columbia.

Osoba, O. (1979) 'The Nigerian Constitution and the Nigerian Working Class', *Positive Review* (Ile-Ife), Vol. 1, No. 3.

Osoba, Segun (1979) 'The Deepening Crisis of the Nigerian National Bourgeoisie', *R.O.A.P.E.*, No. 13.

Osoba, Segun (1979) 'Trade Unions: Does the New Constitution Discriminate?' *New Horizon*, Vol. 4, No. 4.

Osolo-Auma, A. (1980) 'Objective African Military Control; a New Paradigm in Civil-Military Relations', *Journal of Peace Research*, Vol. 17, No. 1.

Ostheimer, J. M. (1973) *Nigerian Politics*. New York: Harper & Row.

Osuntokun, Akinjide (1982) *Expansion of University Education in Nigeria*. Occasional publication of the Nigerian University Commission in Washington, Vol. 1, No. 1.

Otite, Onugu (1975) 'Resource Competition and Inter-Ethnic Relations in Nigeria', in Leo A. Despres (ed.) *Ethnicity and Resource Competition in Plural Societies*. The Hague/Paris: Mouton.

Otobo, Dafe (1982) 'The Nigerian General Strike of 1981', *Review of African Political Economy*, No. 22.

Ottah, Nelson (1981) *Rebels Against Rebels*. Ikeja: Manson & Co.

Owona, J. (1979) 'Le processus de retour des civils au pouvoir: le projet de constitution de l'Assemble constituante', *R.F.E.P.A.*, 157.

Oyediran, Oyeleye (1977) 'Council Manager Plan: The Experience of Western Nigeria', *Philippine Journal of Public Administration*, Vol. 21, No. 1.

Oyediran, Oyeleye (1974a) 'Local Government in Southern Nigeria: The Direction of Change', *African Review*, Vol. 4, No. 4.

Oyediran, Oyeleye (1974b) 'Reorganization of the Nigerian Federation: Its Background and Administrative Problems', *Philippine Journal of Public Administration*, Vol. 18, No. 3.

Oyediran, Oyeleye (1979) *Nigerian Government and Politics under Military Rule 1966–79*. London: Macmillan.

Oyediran, Oyeleye (1980) 'Leadership in Nigeria's New Constitution', *Presence Africaine*, No. 115.

Oyediran, Oyeleye (1982) *The Nigerian 1979 Elections*. London: Macmillan.

Oyejide, T. A. 'Patterns of Economic Growth in Nigeria 1957–67' in *Tariff Policy and Industrialization in Nigeria*.

Oyenuga, V. A. (1967) *Agriculture in Nigeria*. Rome: Food and Agriculture Organization of the U.N.

Oyewole, Anthony (1970) 'Judicial Review of Administrative Action in Nigeria: A Study in National Integration', unpublished Ph.D. thesis, Durham, N.C.: Duke University.

Oyewole, Major Fola (1977) *Reluctant Rebels*. London: Rex Collings.

Oyinbo, John (1971) *Nigeria: Crisis and Beyond*. London: Knight.

Oyovbaire, S. E. (1978) 'The Context of Democracy in Nigeria'. Paper présented to the 5th Annual Conference of the Nigerian Political Science Association, University of Ife, 3–6 April, mimeo.

Oyovbaire, S. E. (1979) 'The Theory of Federalism: A Critical Appraisal', *Nigerian Journal of Political Science*, Vol. 1.

Oyovbaire, S. E. (1980) 'The Nigerian State as a Conceptual Variable'. Paper delivered at the Seventh Annual Conference of the Nigerian Political Science Association. University of Port Harcourt, 25–8 March.

Oyovbaire, S. E. (1982) 'Politics and Development Planning', in M. Dent and D. Austin (eds) *Operation of the Nigerian Political System under the Second Republic*, Manchester: Manchester University Press.

Oyovbaire, S. E. (1982a) 'Towards a Critical Realignment of the Nigerian Party System'. Paper delivered at the ninth Annual Conference of the Nigerian Political Science Association, 1–3 July.

Oyovbaire, S. E. (1982b) 'The Nigerian Political Process and the Crisis of Personality'. Revised version of paper presented at National Seminar on Culture and Personality in Nigeria, organized by the Kaduna State Council of Arts and Culture, 13–16 September.

Oyovbaire, S. E. (1983) 'Structural Change and Political Processes in Nigeria', *African Affairs*, Vol. 82, No. 326.

Oyovbaire, S. E. (forthcoming) *Democracy in Nigeria: Interpretative Essays*. Benin City: Koda Publishers.

Padmore, G. (1956) *Pan-Africanism or Communism: the Coming Struggle for Africa*. New York: Denis Dobson.

Panter-Brick, S. K. (ed.) (1970) *Nigerian Politics and Military Rule: Prelude to the Civil War*. London: Athlone Press.

Panter-Brick, S. K. (ed.) (1973) *Soldiers and Oil: The Political Transformation of Nigeria*. London: Frank Cass. •

Panter-Brick, S. K. (1980) 'Nigeria and the Uncertainties of Pluralism' in Stanislaw Ehrlick and Graham Wootton (eds), *Three Faces of Pluralism*, London: Gower.

Panter-Brick, S. K. (1981) 'Nigeria: The 1979 Elections', *Afrika Spektrum*, Vol. 3.

Park, A. E. W. (1973) *The Sources of Nigerian Law*. Lagos: African University Press; London, Sweet & Maxwell, 3rd impression.

Park, Sang-Seek (1977) 'Political Systems in Black Africa: Toward a New Typology', *Journal of African Studies*, Fall.

Peace, Adrian (1974) 'Industrial Protest in Nigeria' in E. DeKadt and G. Williams (eds) *Sociology and Development*, London: Tavistock.

Peace, Adrian (1979) *Choice, Class and Conflict: A Study of Southern Nigerian Factory Workers*. Brighton: Harvester Press.

Peace, A. (1980) 'Social Mobility in Emergent Society: Western Nigeria', *Oceania*, Vol. 51, No. 1.

Pearson, Scott R. (1970) *Petroleum and the Nigerian Economy*. Stanford: Stanford University Press.

Peel, Quentin (1984) 'Nigeria: Economic Options and Political Constraints', *World Today*, Vol. 40, June.

Peil, Margaret (1978) *Consensus and Conflict in African Societies: An Introduction to Sociology*. London: Longman.

People's Redemption Party. *Who is Responsible? The Nigerian Workers and the Current Economic Crisis. May Day Speeches and Statements, Kaduna, May 1, 1982*. PRP National Research Directorate, POB 522, Kaduna.

Perham, Margery (1937) *Native Administration in Nigeria*. London: Oxford University Press.

Perlmutter, Amos (1980) 'The Comparative Analysis of Military Regimes: Formations, Aspirations, and Achievements', *World Politics*, Vol. 33, No. 1.

Petras, James F. (1983) *Capitalist and Socialist Crises in the Late Twentieth Century*. Totowa, N.J.: Rowman & Allanheld.

Phillips, Claude S. (1980) 'Nigeria's New Political Institutions 1975-9', *The Journal of Modern African Studies*, Vol. 18, No. 1.

Pollet, M. (1978) 'Le Nigeria, de l'independence a la guerre civile', *R.F.E.P.A.*, Vol. 152, No. 3.

Post, K. W. J. (1963) *The Nigerian Federal Elections of 1959: Politics and Administration in a Developing Political System*. Published for the Nigerian Institute of Social and Economic Research by the Oxford University Press.

Post, K. W. J. and M. Vickers (1973) *Structure and Conflict in Nigeria 1960-65*. London: Heinemann.

Post, Kenneth W. J. (1964) 'Nationalism and Politics in Nigeria: A Marxist Approach', *Nigerian Journal of Economic and Social Studies*, 6.

Post, Kenneth W. J. (1966) 'National Movements in West Africa', in J. C. Anene and Godfrey Brown (eds) *Africa in the 19th and 20th Centuries*, London: Nelson.

Prescott, John (1973) *The Evolution of Nigeria's International Boundaries, 1861-1971*. Vancouver: Tantalus Research Ltd.

Pribitkovskij, L. and I. Sledzevskij (1978) 'New Phenomena and Tendencies in Nigeria's Social and Political Development' in *Economic Relations of Africa with the Socialist Countries*. Vol. 2. Budapest.

Proceedings of the Constitutional Assembly (1977/8) Official Report. Lagos: Government Printer.

Proehl, B. (1965) *Foreign Enterprises in Nigeria: Laws and Policies*. Chapel Hill: University of North Carolina Press.

Quarterly Journal of Administration (1978) Special Issue on 'The Public Policy Making Process in Nigerian Administration', Vol. XII, No. 2.

Quarterly Journal of Administration (1979) Special Issue on 'Nigerian Higher Civil Servants', Vol. XIII, Nos. 3 and 4.

Randle, J. K. (1985) *Who is Fooling Who?* Winchester, Hampshire: West African Book Publishers.

Ranson, Brian H. A. (1972) 'Northern Nigerian Managers – An African Commercial Elite', *Journal of Administration Overseas*, Vol. II, No. 1.

Reed, Wm. Cyrus (1982) *The Role of Traditional Rulers in Elective Politics in Nigeria*. Paper produced by African Studies Program, Indiana University.

Report of the Constitution Drafting Committee Containing the Draft Constitution, 2 Vols. Lagos: 1976.

Riggs, Fred W. (1984) *Administration in Developing Countries: The Theory of Prismatic Society*. Boston: Houghton Mifflin.

Rimi, Mohammed Abubakar (1981) *Struggle for Redemption*. Selected Speeches of Mohammed Abubakar Rimi. Zaria: Northern Nigerian Publishing Co.

Rimlinger, Gaston V. (1976) *Communalism and the Gains from Development*. Houston, Texas: Program of Development Studies, William Marsh Rice University.

Rivkin, Arnold (1969) *Nation-Building in Africa*. New Brunswick: Rutgers University Press.

Rodney, Walter (1972) *How Europe Underdeveloped Africa*. Washington: Howard University Press.

Roth, David F. and Frank L. Wilson (1980) *The Comparative Study of Politics* (2nd edn.). Englewood Cliffs, N.J.: Prentice Hall.

Rustow, Dankwart A. (1967) *A World of Nations: Problems of Political Modernization*. Washington, D.C.: Brookings Institution.

Sahlin, Michael (1977) *Neo-authoritarianism and the Problem of Legitimacy*. Stockholm: Raben and Sjogren (Hist.).

Sahota, Gian S. (1980) 'The Distribution of the Benefits of Public Expenditure in Nigeria'. Report for the World Bank.

Salomone, Frank A. (1975) 'Becoming Hausa: Ethnic Identity Change and its Implications for the Study of Ethnic Pluralism and Stratification', *Africa*, Vol. 45, No. 4.

Salomone, Frank A. (1976) 'Ethnicity and the Nigerian Civil War', *L'Afrique et L'Asie Modernes*, No. 111.

Salomone, F. A. and C. H. Swanson (1979) 'Identity and Ethnicity: Ethnic Groups and Inter-actions in a Multi-Ethnic Society', *Ethnic Groups*, Vol. 2, No. 2.

Samoff, J. (1979) 'The Bureaucracy and the Bourgeoisie: Decentralization and Class Structure in Tanzania', *Comparative Studies in Sociology and History*, January.

Sanda, A. O. (1974) 'Ethnicity and Intergroup Conflicts: Some Insights from Non-Elite Actors in a Nigerian City', *Nigerian Journal of Economic and Social Studies*, Vol. 16, No. 3.

Sanda, A. O. (1982) 'Economic Nationalism: The Nigerian Experience, 1972–1982'. Paper presented at the twelfth Annual Conference of the Canadian Association of African Studies, University of Toronto, 10–14 May.

Sanda, Akinade Olumuyiwa (ed.) (1976) *Ethnic Relations in Nigeria: Problems and Prospects*. Ibadan: Caxton Press/University of Ibadan.

Sandbrook, R. and R. Cohen (1978) *The Development of an African Working Class – Studies in Class Formation and Action*. London: Longman.

Sano, Han-Oto (1983) *The Political Economy of Food in Nigeria 1960–82: A Discussion on Peasants, State and World Economy*. Uppsala: Scandinavian Institute of African Studies Research Report No. 69.

Schatten, F. (1966) *Communism in Africa*. London: George Allen & Unwin.

Schatz, Ludwig H. (1973) *Industrialization in Nigeria*. Munich: Weltforum Verlag.

Schatz, Sayre P. (1984) 'The Inert Economy of Nigeria: From Nurture-Capitalism to Pirate Capitalism', *Journal of Modern African Studies*, Vol. 22, No. 1.

Schlechter, Stephen L. (1972) 'International Dependence Relations: A Study of the Transnational Ties of the Former British and French Dependencies', unpublished Ph.D. thesis, University of Pittsburgh.

Schwarz, Frederick A. O., Jr. (1965) *Nigeria: The Tribes, the Nation or the Race: The Politics of Independence*. Cambridge, Mass. and London: MIT Press.

Schwarz, Walter (1968) *Nigeria*. New York: Praeger.

Seifert, J. (1981) 'Der Einfluss einiger traditioneller Faktoren auf den Formierungsprozess der Arbeiterklasse in Afrika am Beispiel Nigerias', *Asien Afrika Latein-Amerika*, Vol. 9, No. 1.

Selassie, Bereket H. (1974) *The Executive in African Governments*. London: Heinemann.

Silver, J. (1982) 'West African Workers', *Canadian Journal of African Studies*, Vol. 16, No. 2.

Simmons, Michael and Ad'Obe Obe (gen. eds) (1982) *The Guardian Nigerian Handbook 1982–3*. London: Collins.

Segun, Mabel (1978) *Friends, Nigerians, Countrymen*. Ibadan: Oxford University Press.

Shagari, Shehu (1982) *My Vision of Nigeria*, Aminu Tidjani and David Williams (eds) London: Frank Cass.

Shaw, Timothy (1979) 'The Semi-periphery in Africa and Latin America: Sub-imperialism and Semi-industrialism', *Review of Black Political Economy*, Vol. 9, No. 4.

Shaw, Timothy (1979) 'EEC-ACP Interactions and Images as Redefinitions of Eur-Africa', *Journal of Common Market Studies*, Vol. 18, No. 2.

Shaw, Timothy (1980) 'Foreign Policy, Political Economy, and the Future: Reflections on Africa in the World System', *African Affairs*, 75, 315.

Shaw, Timothy (1981) 'Class, Country and Corporation: Africa in the Capitalist World System', in *Into the 80s: Proceedings of the 11th Annual Conference of the Canadian Association of African Studies*, Vol. 2. Vancouver: Tantalus.

Shaw, Timothy (ed.) (1981) *Alternative Futures for Africa*. Boulder: Westview Press.

Shaw, Timothy and Olajide Aluko (eds) (1982) *Nigerian Foreign Policy: Alternative Perceptions and Projections*. London: Macmillan.

Shaw, Timothy M. and Orobola Fasehun (1981) 'Nigeria in the World System: Alternative Approaches, Explanations and Projections', *Journal of Modern African Studies*, Vol. 19, No. 1.

Shaw, Timothy and Malcolm Grieve (1979) 'Dependence as an Approach to Understanding Continuing Inequalities in Africa', *Journal of the Developing Areas*, Vol. 13, No. 3.

Shaw, Timothy M. (1980) 'Nigeria's Political Economy: Capitalism, Constitutions and Contra-dictions', *ODI Review*, No. 2.

Shenton, Bob and Bill Freund (1977–9) 'The Incorporation of Northern Nigeria into the World Capitalist Economy', *Review of African Political Economy*, No. 13.
Shils, Edward (1966) *Political Development and New States*. The Hague: Mouton.
Sithole, Ndabaningi (1968) *African Nationalism*. New York: Oxford University Press, 2nd edn.
Sklar, R. L. (1963) *Nigerian Political Parties: Power in an Emergent African Nation*. Princeton, N.J.: Princeton University Press.
Sklar, R. L. (1967) 'Political Science and National Integration – A Radical Approach', *Journal of Modern African Studies*, Vol. 5, No. 1.
Sklar, R. L. (1972) 'Nigerian Politics in Perspective', in R. Melson and H. Wolpe (eds), *Modernization and the Politics of Communalism: A Theoretical Perspective*. East-Lansing, Michigan State University Press.
Sklar, R. L. (1975) *Corporate Power in an African State*. Berkeley: University of California Press.
Sklar, R. L. (1979) 'The Nature of Class Domination in Africa', *The Journal of Modern African Studies*, Vol. 17, No. 4.
Sklar, R. L. (1981) 'Democracy for the Second Nigerian Republic', *Issue*, Vol. 11, No. 1/2.
Sklar, R. L. and C. S. Whitaker, Jr. (1966) 'The Federal Republic of Nigeria', in Gwendolen M. Carter (ed.) *National Unity and Regionalism in Eight African States*, Ithaca, N.Y.: Cornell University Press.
Smith, B. C. (1982) 'The Revenue Position of Local Government in Nigeria', *Public Administration and Development*, Vol. 2.
Smith, Brian (1981) 'Federal-State Relations in Nigeria', *African Affairs*, Vol. 80, No. 320.
Smith, M. G. (1960) *Government in Zazzau*. London: Oxford University Press.
Smith, Robert S. (1989) *Warfare and Diplomacy in Pre-Colonial West Africa*. London: Currey.
Smith, Sheila (1979) 'Colonialism in Economic Theory: the Experience of Nigeria', *The Journal of Development Studies*, Vol. 15, No. 3.
Smock, Audrey C. (1971) *Ibo Politics: The Role of Ethnic Unions in Eastern Nigeria*. Cambridge, Mass.: Harvard University Press.
Smock, D. (1969) *Conflict and Control in an African Trade Union: A Study of the Nigerian Coal Miners Union*. Stanford: Stanford University Press.
Smock, David R. (1972) *Cultural and Political Aspects of Rural Transformation: A Case Study of Eastern Nigeria*. New York: Praeger.
Smock, David and K. Bentsi-Enchill (eds) (1976) *The Search for National Integration in Africa*. New York: Free Press.
Smythe, Hugh H. (1962) *The New Nigerian Elite*. Stanford, California: Stanford University Press.
Socialist Forum (1982) 'On Working Class Consciousness', *Socialist Forum* (Ile-Ife), No. 5.
Sokari, George E. (1979) 'Centralization in Nigeria as it Relates to Economic Development Policy', unpublished Ph.D. thesis, Florida State University.
Sonaike, Olayinka and Bode Olowoporoku (1979) 'Economic Dependence: The Problem of Definition', *Journal of Asian and African Studies*, Vol. XIV, No. 1–2.
Sorkaa, Akase Paul (forthcoming) 'Democratic Values and Limitations of Local Government Reforms', in S. E. Oyovbaire (ed.) *Democratic Experiment in Nigeria: Interpretative Essays*. Benin City.
Spiro, Herbert J. (ed.) (1966) *Africa, The Primacy of Politics*. New York: Random House.
Spiro, Herbert J (ed.) (1967) *Patterns of African Development*. Englewood Cliffs N.J.: Prentice Hall.
Stokke, Olav (1970) *Nigeria: An Introduction to the Politics, Economy and Social Setting of Modern Nigeria*. Uppsala: Scandinavian Institute of African Studies.
Stremlau, John J. (1977) *The International Politics of the Nigerian Civil War 1967–1970*. Princeton: Princeton University Press.
Taiwo, Olufemi (1984) 'The Political Thought of Obafemi Awolowo'. Paper presented at the Fourteenth Annual Conference of the Canadian Association of African Studies, held at St. Francis Xavier University, Antigonish, Nova Scotia, 9–12 May.
Taiwo Williams, S. K. (1974) *Rural Poverty to Rural Prosperity: A Strategy for Development in Nigeria*. Ile-Ife: University of Ife Press.

Takaya, Bala J. (1979) 'The Role of Legislation in an Executive System of Government', *New Nigerian*, 5 October.

Talbot, Percy A. (1966) *The Peoples of Southern Nigeria*. London: Frank Cass.

Teriba, O. and M. O. Kayode (eds) (1977) *Industrial Development in Nigeria: Patterns, Problems and Prospects*. Ibadan: Ibadan University Press.

Teriba, O., E. C. Edozien and M. O. Kayode (1972) 'Some Aspects of Ownership and Control Structure of Business Enterprise in a Developing Economy. The Nigerian Case', *Nigerian Journal of Economic and Social Studies*, Vol. XIV, No. 1.

'The Texts of the Supreme Court Opinions (majority and dissenting)', *New Nigerian*, 26 October and 3 November 1979.

Thomas, B. D. (1975) *Capital Accumulation and Technology Transfer: A Comprehensive Analysis of Nigerian Manufacturing Industries*. New York: Praeger.

Tilman, Robert O. (ed.) (1962) *The Nigerian Political Scene*. Durham N.C.: Duke University Press.

Tims, Wouter (1974) *Nigeria: Options for Long Term Development*. Baltimore: Johns Hopkins University Press.

'Towards a New Political Realignment', *Africa*, No. 118 (June 1981).

Toyo, Eskor (1967) *The Working Class and the Nigerian Crisis*. Ibadan: Sketch Publishing Co.

Toyo, Eskor (1982) *Storms in the Nigerian Polity. The Process of Bourgeois Ascendancy and its Conflicts*. Kano: Triumph Publishing Co.

Tseayo, P. (1975) *Conflict and Incorporation*. Zaria: Gaskiya.

Tuden, Arthur (1970) *Social Stratification in Africa*. New York: Free Press.

Tukur, M. (ed.) (1971) *Reform of the Nigerian Public Service*. Zaria: Ahmadu Bello University.

Tukur, M. and T. Olagunju (eds) (1977) *Nigeria in Search of a Viable Polity*. Zaria: Institute for Administration, Ahmadu Bello University.

Tukur, Mahmud (ed.) (1970) *Administrative and Political Development - Prospects for Nigeria*. Report of a Conference held at the Institute of Administration, Zaria, 24–27 August.

Turner, Terisa (1976) 'Multinational Corporations and the Instability of the Nigerian State', *Review of African Political Economy*, Vol. 5.

Turner, Terisa (1980) 'Nigeria: Imperialism, Oil Technology and the Comprador State' in P. Nore and T. Turner (eds) *Oil and Class Struggle*. London: Zed Press.

Turner, Terisa (1985a) 'Oil and Instability: Class Contradictions and the 1983 Coup in Nigeria', *Journal of African Marxists*, No. 7.

Turner, Terisa (1985b) 'Petroleum, Recession and the Internationalization of Class Struggle in Nigeria', *Labour, Capital and Society*, Vol. 18, No. 1.

Turner, Terisa (1985c) 'Experiences of Oil Research in Africa: The Energy and Social Development Research Group', (University of Port Harcourt, Nigeria). Paper presented to A.A. Annual Meeting, New Orleans, 23–26 November.

Udo-Aka, Udo, Hayford I. Alile and M. Kayode (eds) (1977) *Management Development in Nigeria: The Challenge of Indigenisation*. Ibadan: Oxford University Press.

Udo-Aka, Udo, Hayford I. Alile and M. Kayode (1980) 'Management Development in Nigeria: The Challenge of Indigenisation' (book review). *The Journal of Economic Literature*, Vol. 18, No. 4.

Udoji Report (1974) *Public Service Review Commission: Main Report*.

Ugboajah, Frank Okwu (1980) *Communication Policies in Nigeria*. Paris: Unesco.

Ukaeje, Inno (1978) 'The Influence of Civilian–Military Relations/Interaction on the Tendency/Frequency of the Military Institution to Intervene in Civilian Politics in Nigeria', unpublished Ph.D. thesis, State University of New York at Binghampton.

Ukpu, U. (1979) 'Ethnic Minority Problems in Nigerian Politics (1960–65)' (book review), *Journal of Asian and African Studies*, Vol. 14, No. 3–4.

Ukpu, Ugbana (1977) *Ethnic Minority Problems in Nigerian Politics 1960–65*. Uppsala: Studia Historica Upsaliensia 88.

UNESCO (1956) *Social Implications of Industrialization and Urbanization in Africa South of the Sahara*. Paris: UNESCO.

UNIDO (1978) *Country Industrial Development Profile of the Federal Republic of Nigeria*. Vienna, Doc. no. UNIDO/ICIS. 78 ISN 8246.

Unongo, Paul I. (1968) *The Case of Nigeria*. Lagos: Town and Gown.

Urhobo, Emmanuel (1979) 'The Increase of Inequality in Nigeria, 1960–77', unpublished Ph.D. thesis, Washington, D.C.: American University.

Usman, Y. B. 'Behind the Oil Smokescreen: The Real Cause of the Current Economic Crisis', in *Who is Responsible?* Kaduna: PRP National Research Directorate, POB 522, Kaduna.

Usman, Y. B. (ed.) (1982) *Political Repression in Nigeria*. Kano: Bala Mohammed Memorial Committee.

Usman, Yusuf Bala (1979) *For the Liberation of Nigeria*. London: New Beacon.

Usoro, Eno J. (1974) 'Government Policies, Politics and Industrial Development Strategy in Nigeria 1947–1974', *Nigerian Journal of Economic and Social Studies*, Vol. 16, No. 2.

Uwechue, R. (1969) *Reflections on the Nigerian Civil War. A Call for Realism*. London: OITH International Publishers.

Uzoaga, W. O. and J. U. Alozienwa (1974) 'Dividend Policy in an Era of Indigenization', *New Journal of Economic and Social Studies*, Vol. 16, No. 3.

Van de Walle, Etienne (1970) 'Who's Who and Where in Nigeria', *African Report*, No. 1.

Van Den Berghe, Pierre L. 'Nigeria and Peru: Two Contrasting Cases in Ethnic Pluralism', *International Journal of Comparative Sociology*, Vol. XX, 1–2.

Various Authors (1985) *The Nigerian Economic Crisis: Causes and Solutions*. Zaria: Academic Staff Union of Universities of Nigeria. Gaskiya.

Wai, Dunstan M. (ed.) (1980) *The Search for Political Legitimacy in Africa*. London: Frank Cass.

Wallace, T. (1980) 'Agricultural Projects and Land in Northern Nigeria', *Review of African Political Economy*, No. 17.

Wallace, T. (1981) 'The Challenge of Food: Nigeria's Approach to Agriculture 1975–80', *Canadian Journal of African Studies*, Vol. 15, No. 2.

Walleri, R. Dan (1978) 'Trade Dependence and Underdevelopment – A Causal Chain Analysis', *Comparative Political Studies*, Vol. 11, No. 1.

Wallerstein, Immanuel (1960) 'Ethnicity and National Integration in West Africa', Sociologie Politique de l'Afrique Noire, *Cahiers d'Études Africaines*, Vol. 3.

Wallerstein, Immanuel (1966) *Social Change, The Colonial Situation*. New York: Wiley.

Wallerstein, Immanuel (1973) 'Class and Class Conflict in Contemporary Africa', *Canadian Journal of African Studies*, Vol. 7, No. 3.

Waterman, P. (1979) 'Consciousness, Organisation and Action Amongst Lagos Portworkers', *Review of African Political Economy*, No. 13.

Waterman, P. (1982) *Division and Unity amongst Nigerian Workers: Lagos Port Unionism 1940s–1960s*. The Hague: Research Report 11, Institute of Social Studies.

Waterman, P. (1983) *Aristocrats and Plebians in African Unions? Lagos Port and Dock Worker Organisation and Struggle*. The Hague.

Waterman, P. (1982) *Wage Labour Relations in Nigeria: State, Capitalists, Unions and Workers in the Lagos Cargo-Handling Industry*. Zug: Interdocumentation Co. Microfiche.

Waterman, Peter (1973) 'Communist Theory in the Nigerian Trade Union Movement', *Politics and Society*, Vol. 3, No. 2.

Waterman, Peter (1983) 'International Labour Studies: A Third World and Labour-Oriented Bibliography', 'Special theme: Contemporary Nigerian Labour Studies' The Hague: Institute of Social Studies, 17.

Watts, M. (1984) 'State, Oil and Accumulation – From Boom to Crisis', *Society and Space, Environment and Planning*, Vol. 2, No. 4.

Watts, R. L. (1966) *New Federations: Experiments in the Commonwealth*. London: Oxford University Press.

Wayas, Joseph (1979) *Nigeria's Leadership Role in Africa*. London: Macmillan.

Welch, Claude E. Jr. (ed.) (1976) *Civilian Control of the Military: Theory and Cases from Developing Countries*. Albany: State University of New York Press.

Welch, Claude Jr. (ed.) (1970) *Soldier and State in Africa: A Comparative Analysis of Military Intervention and Political Change*. Evanston: Northwestern University Press.

Welch, Claude Jr. (1974) 'The Dilemma of Military Withdrawal from Politics. Some Considerations from Tropical Africa', *African Studies Review*, Vol. 17.

Wells, Frederic Arthur (1974) *Agricultural Policy and Economic Growth in Nigeria 1962–1968.* Ibadan: Ibadan University Press.

Wells, Frederic Arthur (1963) *Studies in Industrialization in Nigeria and Cameroon.* London: Published for the Institute of Social and Economic Research by the Oxford University Press.

Wesson, Robert G. (1981) *Modern Governments: Three Worlds of Politics.* Englewood Cliffs, N.J.: Prentice Hall.

Wey, S. O. (1971) *Socio-Economic Problems in Political Regimes.* Lagos: Federal Ministry of Information.

Wey, S. O. and E. Osagie *An Ideology for Social Development*, Lagos: Academy Press, n.d. (1977).

Whitaker, C. S. (1981) 'Second Beginnings: The Political Framework', *Issue*, Vol. 11, No. 1/2.

Whitaker, C. S. (ed.) (1981) *Perspectives on the Second Republic in Nigeria.* Los Angeles, Cal.: Crossroads Press, (UCLA).

Whitaker, C. S. (1970) 'Traditional and Modern Styles Leadership: Northern Nigeria', in Eric A. Nordlinger (ed.) *Politics and Society* Englewood Cliffs, N.J.: Prentice Hall.

Whitaker, C. S. Jr. (1970) *The Politics of Tradition: Continuity and Change in Northern Nigeria 1946–1966.* Princeton N.J.: Princeton University Press.

Widstrand, Carl (ed.) (1975) *Multi-National Firms in Africa.* Uppsala: Scandinavian Institute of African Studies.

Williams, Babatunde (1976) 'The Prospect for Democracy in New Africa', *African Spark*, February.

Williams, Babatunde A.(1968) 'Constitutions and National Unity in Nigeria: A Historical and Analytical Study', *Journal of Business and Social Studies*, No. 1.

Williams, David (1982) *President and Power in Nigeria: the Life of Shehu Shagari.* London: Frank Cass.

Williams, Gavin (1980a) 'Inequalities in Rural Nigeria'. Report prepared for the International Labour Organization, Oxford University Press.

Williams, Gavin (1980b) *State and Society in Nigeria.* Idanre: Afrografika Publishers.

Williams, Gavin (n.d.) 'Class Politics and the State in Nigeria' (Politics Seminar Paper). London: Institute of Commonwealth Studies.

Williams, Gavin (1979) 'Editorial: Nigeria', *Review of African Political Economy*, No. 13.

Williams, Gavin (ed.) (1976) *Nigeria: Economy and Society.* London: Rex Collings.

Williams, Gavin (1974) 'Political Consciousness Among the Ibadan Poor', in Gavin Williams and Emanuel de Kadt (eds) *Sociology and Development.* London: Tavistock Publications.

Williams, Gavin (1970) 'The Social Stratification of a Neo-Colonial Economy: Western Nigeria', in Christopher Allen and R. W. Johnson (eds), *African Perspectives: Papers in the History, Politics and Economics of Africa.* Presented to Thomas Hodgkin. Cambridge: Cambridge University Press.

Williams, Gavin (1982) 'Equity, Growth and the State', *Africa* Vol. 52, No. 3.

Williams, Gavin and T. Turner (1978) 'Nigeria' in John Dunn (ed.) *West African States: Failure and Promise*, Cambridge: Cambridge University Press.

Wilmot, Patrick (1979) *In Search of Nationhood: The Theory and Practice of Nationalism in Africa.* Ibadan: Lantern.

Wilson, Ernest James III (1978) 'The Political Economy of Public Corporations in the Energy Sector of Nigeria and Zaire', unpublished Ph.D. thesis, University of California at Berkeley.

Wilson, Henry S. (1969) *Origins of West African Nationalism.* New York: St. Martins Press.

Wirz, Albert (1982) *Krieg in Africa: Die nachkolonialen Konflikte in Nigeria, Sudan, Tschad und Konge.* Wiesbaden: Steiner.

Wolff, Hans (1967) 'Language, Ethnic Identity and Social Change in Southern Nigeria', *Anthropological Linguistics*, January.

Wolpe, H. (ed.) (1971) *Nigeria: Modernization and the Politics of Communalism.* Ann Arbor: University of Michigan Press.

World Bank (1978) *Report on Economic Conditions in Nigeria.* Washington: World Bank (mimeo.).

World Bank (1981) *World Development Report 1981.* New York: Oxford University Press.

Wright, Stephen (1979) *Africa's Emergent Super-Power: the Resource Dimension of Nigerian Foreign Policy*. Keele: British International Studies Association, December.

Wright, S. (1982) 'Nigeria: A Mid-Term Assessment', *World Today*, March.

Wright, S. (1979) 'Towards Civilian Rule in Nigeria', *World Today*, March.

Yahaya, A. D. (1975) 'Enhancing Local Government Performance: The Udoji Recipe', *The Nigerian Journal of Public Affairs*, Vol. V, May/October.

Yannapolous. T. and D. Martin (1972) 'Regimes militaires et classes sociales en Afrique', *Revue Française de Science Politique*, Vol. 22, No. 4.

Yesufu, T. M. (1962) *Manpower Problems and Economic Development in Nigeria*. London: Oxford University Press.

Yesufu, T. M. (1980) 'Industrial Relations in the '80s', *Management in Nigeria*, June.

Young, Crawford (1976) *The Politics of Cultural Pluralism*. Madison: University of Wisconsin Press.

Young, Crawford (1982) *Ideology and Development in Africa*. New Haven: Yale University Press.

Index

Abacha, Sanni, 149
Abiola, M.K.O., 80, 98
Aboyade Committee, 173
Abubakar, Iya, 236
Abuja, 47
Achebe, Chinua, 111
Action Group (AG), 31, 33–6, 188
Ad Hoc Constitutional Conference, 43
Adebayo, Maj.-Gen., 80
Adebo Salaries and Wages Review Commission, 208
Adelakun, Busari, 98
Ademola, Adetokunbo, 165
Aderemi, Adesoji, 9
Afolabi, Sunday, 98
African personality, 15
Aguiyi-Ironsi, Johnson, see Ironsi
Ajasin, Michael, 98, 137, 169
Ajibola, Bola, 168
Ake, Claude, 32, 74, 111, 228, 243
Akeem, Habeeb, 98
Akinrinade, Alani, 168
Akintola, Samuel, 35, 36, 39, 82
Akinyemi, Bolaji, 168
Aku, Aper, 100
Alhaji, Abubakar Alhaji, 166–7
Ali-Akilu Memorial Fund, 80
Alli, Ambrose, 128, 135, 136–7, 138, 190
American structural-functionalism, 203
Aminu, Jabril, 168
Anikulapo-Kuti, Fela, 166
Anglo-Nigerian Defence Pact, 35
Anti-woman campaign, 165–6, 245
Armed Forces Ruling Council (AFRC), 127, 168, 175, 239
Attah, Adamu, 99
Atukum, Samuel, 150
Audu, Ishaya, 90, 169
Auxiliary bourgeoisie, 57
Awo, see Awolowo
Awolowo, Obafemi, 13, 35, 43, 65, 71, 82, 83, 84, 85, 91, 93, 123, 145, 188, 211, 212

Azikiwe, Nnamdi, 31, 35, 46, 82–4, 87, 91, 93, 94

Babangida, Ibrahim, 133, 134, 141, 155, 160, 167, 169, 171, 194, 199, 242
Balanced development, 25
Bali, Domkat, 174
Ballot-rigging, 108, 154
Balogun, Kola, 92
Barde, Abubakar, 92, 100
Barewa Old Boys' Association, 80
Beckett, Paul, 111
Beckman, Bjorn, 227, 229
Bendel Igbo, 22
Bey, Shitta, 98
Biafra, 12, 43, 232
Biersteker, Thomas, 58
Braithwaite, Tunji, 96
British Petroleum (BP), nationalisation of, 235, 236
Broker parties, 80
Buhari, Mohammed, 133, 134, 141, 149–67, 194, 199, 213, 242

Calabar-Ogoja-Rivers State Union (COR), 31
Callaway, Barbara, 32
Cement scandal, 46, 63
Census – of 1962/63, 36, 47; – of 1973, 46, 47, 63
Centrifugal (cf. centripetal) federalism, 17, 29, 47, 117, 133
Churches and missions, 11
Ciroma, Adamu, 163, 172
Civil service, 46–7, 49, 54–5, 57–8, 61, 159–60, 171, 203–16
Civil war, Nigerian, 43–4, 50
Class conflict, xiii
Class formation, xiii
Club 19, 82
Club 400, 82
Code of Conduct/Bureau/Tribunal, 213, 214, 244

Cohen, Robin, 17, 20, 32
Coker Commission, 35
Coleman, James S., 11, 31
Collins, Paul, 58, 183, 207–8, 228
Colonial Administration, 7, 10, 11, 23, 28, 203
Colonial Elite, 12
Colonial statism, 18
Colonialism, 22, 25; – impacts of, 7–9
Command federalism, 134
Commercial triangle, 229, 231
Committee of 111, 80
Communalism (*see also* tribalism), 30–1
Comprador/bourgeoisie, 59, 161
Conglomerate society, 1, 5
Consolidated Revenue Fund, 127
Constitutent Assembly (CA), 47, 66–7, 196
Constitution of 1979, 29, 41, 65–74, 108, 115, 117, 123, 128–9, 152, 189, 198, 204, 205, 211–12, 237, 243
Constitution-Drafting Committee (CDC), 47–65, 68, 69, 80, 116, 126, 176, 177, 196, 206; – Minority Report, 69
Constitution Suspension and Modification Decree, 41, 152
Corrective, military as, 41, 44, 63, 157–60, 162, 167–9, 175, 200, 235, 237
Council of State, 206
Countertrade, 167, 168, 172–3, 239
Coup – of 1966, 33, 36, 42, 48; – of 1975, 46; – of 1976, 47; – of 1983, 54, 65, 70, 100, 108, 123, 129, 149 *et seq.*, 192; – of 1985, 54, 167 *et seq.*, 174–5
Crown Colony of Lagos, 7
Customary Appeal Court, 210
Customary Law, 210–11

Daily Sketch, 126
Daily Standard, 126
Danjuma, Theophilius, 46, 155
Daura, Mamman, 172
David-West, Tam, 160, 168
Davies, H.O., 31
Decampees, 98–100
Decolonisation, 26–7, 126
Defensive radicalism, 74, 243, 245
Democratic humanism, 83
Dent, Martin, 45, 61
Development administration, 208–9
Diamond, Larry, 92
Dikko, Umaru, 52, 163, 172
Dimka-Bisalla conspiracy/coup, 47, 60, 169, 170, 174
Distributive Pool Account, 139, 145
Divide and rule, 15
Doe, Samuel K., 63, 112, 156, 164, 236, 242

Diya, Oladipo, 151
Dosunmu, Wahab, 153
Dual executive, 28 (*see also* Westminister Model)
Dudley, Billy J., 21, 84
Dyarchy (or Diarchy), 46, 242–3
Dynamic Party, 35, 38

Eastern Consultative Assembly, 143
Economic Community of West African States (ECOWAS), 235–6, 237
Economic nationalism – *see* Indigenisation
Egbe Omo Oduduwa, 22, 31
Ekpu, Ray, 174
Ekwueme, Alex, 74, 98, 142, 175, 190
Elections – of 1964, 38, 39; – of 1979, 85–90, 109, 123; – of 1983, 96–106
Electoral Decree, 78, 198
Elites, 10–12, 19, 53–9, 68–9, 71, 77, 79, 107, 109, 118, 141, 156, 174, 182–4, 189, 191–2, 200, 229–35, 244–5
Elsenhans, Hartmut, 227, 230, 234–5
English language, role of, 5
Engineered democracy, 78
Essang, Sunday, 153
Esuene, Jacob, 99
Ethical revolution, 95
Ethnicity, 13, 19 (*see also* Tribalism)
Ethnic plurality/groups, 5–7
Etiebet, Donald, 99
Evans, Peter, 228, 229
Evers, Tilman, xi
Executive-legislative relations, 127 *et seq.*
Eze, Nduka, 92

Federal Capital Territory, 47, 140
Federal character, 77–8, 80, 116, 124–5, 141
Federal Civil Service Commission, 206
Federal Court of Appeal, 210
Federal Election Commission (FEDECO), 64, 92, 93, 96, 97, 107, 123, 143
Federal Executive Council, 46, 48, 150
Federal High Court, 210
Federalism, 28–34, 39, 43, 49, 55–6, 63, 116–7, 126, 133–47, 180, 191, 207, 212, 244
Federated Igbo State Union, 31
First Republic, xii, 19, 21, 26, 28, 29, 33
Fundamental objectives (and directives) of state policy, 67, 70, 73, 152, 243

Gambari, Ibrahim, 160
Garba, Joseph, 57
Gentlemen farmers, 158, 171
Golden era of Nigerian foreign policy, 236
Gomwalk, Joseph, 46

Gorsuch Commission, 203, 208
Gowon, Yakubu, 42, 43, 44–5, 54, 57, 60, 61, 205, 234
Gratien, F.E.N., 35
Great Nigerian People's Party (GNPP), 82, 83–5, chs. 6–7, 199
Green Revolution, 196, 222
Gwandu, Emir of, 166

Halpern, Manfred, 22
Haruna, Mohammed, 197
Hausa-Fulani oligarchy, 2, 30, 31, 33, 36, 87
Hegemonic bloc, 231
House of Assembly, 26, 134–6
House of Representatives, *see* National Assembly

Ibibio State Union, 22
Ibrahim, Awwal, 99
Ibrahim, Waziri, 82, 83, 91
Ideology crisis, 163
Idiagbon, Tunde, 160, 163, 167, 173
Igbo State Union, 22
Ige, Bola, 137, 199
Ikoku, Samuel G., 35, 82, 83, 90, 92, 93, 98, 152
Ikoli, Ernest, 31
Imoudou, Michael, 37, 83, 87
Impeachment, 135–6
Independence Constitution, 27, 30
Indigenisation/Decree, 20, 26, 47, 53–9, 228–9, 231, 232
Indirect rule, 7–8, 15
Inert economy, 224
Institutionalised bargaining, 88
Integration, 12–14
Intendent classes, 21, 48, 55, 203, 230
Inter-class and intra-class struggle, 70, 232
International Monetary Fund (IMF), 158, 160–2, 167, 170–1, 229, 239
Intra-military dynamics, 105, 110, ch. 8
Irabor, Nduka, 159
Irikife Report/Panel, 117
Ironsi, Johnson Aguiyi-, 42, 54, 242
Isong, Clement, 99, 169

Jaguar deal, 155
Jakande, Lateef, 35, 137, 169
Jam'iyyar Mutanen Arewa, 31
Janowitz, Morris, 158
Jibil, Leme, 172
Johnson-Matthey Bank Affair, 151
Joint Action Committee (JAC), 37
Joint Finance Committee, 140, 212

Joseph, Richard, 77, 78, 84
Judiciary/Judicature, 118, 209–13

Kadiya, John Jato, 100
Kaduna Mafia, 172–3, 174
Kaita, Lawal, 99
Kalu, Kalu Idika, 168, 171
Kano, Aminu, 38, 83, 87, 92, 93, 99
Koehn, Peter, 196–7

Land Use Decree, 67, 70, 158, 194–7
Language differences, 5–6
Lar, Solomon, 100
Leaders of Thought, 55
Legitimacy crisis, 166–7
Level-of-development thesis, 107
Liberal democratic forms, 41, 62, 77, 136, 154
Local government/reform/councils, 28, 140–1, 181, 183, 184, 188, 189–90, 192, 193
LOOB States, 82, 87, 194
Lyttelton Constitution, 27, 187

Macauley, Herbert, 31
Macebuh, Stanley, 74, 122
Macpherson Constitution, 27
Madanugu, Eddie, 83, 176, 242
Maitatsina movement/incidents/riots, 95, 240
Mark, David, 150
Markovitz, I.L., 187
Masses, 10–12, 110, 130, 240, 243, 245
Mbadiwe, Kingsley, 80, 98
Mbu, Matthew, 90
Middle Belt, 4–5
Middle Zone League (MZL), 31
Mid-West Region, 36
Midwest State Movement, 31
Miliband, Ralph, xi, 189
Military officer caste, 156
Minorities Commission Report, 29
Mixed economy, 57, 71–2
Mobilisation crisis, 164
Modernization theory, 22–3
Mohammed, Murtala, 42, 46, 54, 63, 65, 119, 150, 168, 183, 205
Moore, Barrington jr., xii
Morgan Commission Report, 37
Musa, Balarabe, 83, 92, 99, 118, 127–8, 135–6, 169
Musawa, Musa, 99
Muslim Sudanic culture, 3
Mustapha, Shettima, 94

National Assembly, 118–22, 125, 127, 128, 212, 215

National character, *see* Federal character
National Concord, 95, 108, 126, 151
National Council of Ministers, 168
National Council of Nigeria and the Camerouns/National Council of Nigerian Citizens (NCNC), 31–3 *et seq.*, 188
National Council of States, 48, 168
National Development Plans (First-Fourth), 44, 53, 125, 184, 207, 220, 240
National Economic Council, 120
National Movement, 80
National Party of Nigeria (NPN), 80–82, 84–90, chs. 6–7, 199
National Security Organisation (NSO), 67, 166–7, 212
National Union of Nigerian Students (NUNS), 69
National Universities Commission (NUC), 65
National Youth Service Corps (NYSC), 44, 67
Native administration/courts, 34
New feudal elite, 158, 160
Niger Delta Congress (NDC), 38
Nigerian Advance Party (NAP), 96 *et seq.*
Nigerian Chamber of Commerce and Industry, 49
Nigerian Elements Progressive Union (NEPU), 31
Nigerian Employers Consultative Association, 49
Nigerian Enterprises Promotion Decree, 56 – *see also* Indigenisation
Nigerian Institute of Management, 119
Nigerian National Alliance (NNA), 37
Nigerian National Democratic Party (NNDP), 31, 36
Nigerian National Supply Company (NNSC) scandals, 151–2
Nigerian People's Congress (NPC), 30–33, 80
Nigerian Tribune, 125
Nigerian Youth Movement, 31
Nkrumah, Kwame, 227
Nnoli, Okwudiba, 14, 21, 73, 166
North, the, 2–3, 29–30, 34, 39, 42–3, 145, 172–3, 181
NPN-NPP Accord, 88, 90
Nurture capitalism, 231
Nwobodo, Jim, 84
Nzeribe, Ben, 92, 98

Obasanjo, Olusegun, 46, 63–4, 67, 78, 112, 150, 154, 167, 195, 196, 244
Obi, Chike, 35, 211
Obih, Collins, 98
O'Connor, James, 234
Odetola, T.O., 51

Odunjo, Soji, 98
Offodile, Chike, 165
Ogbemudia, Samuel, 100, 154
Ogundipe, Brigadier, 42
Ojo, O.J.B., 87
Ojukwu, Chukwuemeka, 42, 43, 98, 154, 155
Okeowo, Segun, 69
Okigbo Commission, 117, 140
Okilo, Melford, 100, 135
Okpara, Michael, 98, 187
Oluleye, James, 167, 171
Omeruah, Group Captain, 164
Omoboriowo, Akin, 98
Omokhodian, Lawson, 98
Omoruyi, Omo, 84
Omotoso, Kole, 109
Onimode, Bade, 73
Onoh, Chris, 98
Opara, Okey, 108
Operation Feed the Nation (OFN), 222
Organisational bourgeoisie, 230
Organisation of Islamic Conferences (OIC), 175
Organisation of Petroleum Exporting Countries (OPEC), 160, 161, 221, 227
Osamor, Emmanuel, 153
Oshinwo, Oladosun, 98
Otiko, Commodore, 150
Ovie-Whiskey, Victor, 96, 190
Oyovbaire, Sam Egite, 79, 163, 176, 192, 204, 242

Panter-Brick, Keith, 145
Parties, 77–112, 129
Passive consensus, 130
People's Redemption Party (PRP), 83–4, chs. 6–7, 199
Peripheral accumulation, 239
Peripheral capitalism, 53, 227, 232, 238, 241
Peripheral state xi, xiv, 224–30
Petro-Naira syndrome, 223
Phillips, Claude, 64
Police controversy, 138–9
Political Bureau, 175, 176, 242, 245
Political Class, 32, 48, 111, 118, 150, 196
Political justice, 35, 211
Political parties decree, 152
Political tycoon class, 110
Popular classes, *see* Masses
Post-independence elite, 18
Presidency, 123–5, 206
Presidential Liaison Officers (PLOs), 91, 138
Privatization of parastatals, 171
Progressive Party Alliance (PPA), 92, 93, 108
Progressive People's Party (PPP), 94, 108

Public Complaints Bureau/Commission, 47, 67

Radicalism, in political economy, xiii
Rafindadi, Lawal, 166
Ransome-Kuti, Olukoye, 168
Ransome-Kuti, Beko, 168
Rawlings, John Jerry, 63, 112, 156, 164, 236, 242
Recivilianisation, 60–3, 175, 182, 198, 207, 242
Regionalism/regionalisation, 26–34
Rentier state, 218–9, 220
Representation, 68–9, 119–20; see also Federal character
Representative bureaucracy, 125, 203, 204
Republican Constitution, 27
Revenue Allocation Bill (1981), 91
Revenue-sharing, 139–41
Richards Constitution, 26, 27, 29
Rimi, Abubakar, 83, 92, 198, 199
Rimi, Musa, 99
Rimini, M.A., 184
Robertson Constitution, 27, 29

Sabiya, Wilson, 100
Sabon gari, 15
Samoff, Joel, xiii
Saraki, Olusola, 99
Sardauna of Sokoto, 39
Schwarz, Walter, 37
Sectoralisation of the national economy, 9
Segmentation, 9
Senate, see National Assembly
Shagari, Shehu, 82, 85, 95, 100, 118, 123, 124, 138, 154, 161, 175, 197, 215, 234, 237
Shaib, Bukar, 160
Sharia Appeal Courts, 66–7, 70, 119, 212
Sharia controversy, 71
Sharia law, 210
Sklar, Richard, 55, 62
Shugaba, Alhaji, 91
Social contract, Nigerian version of, 166
Socialism, 71–2, 74
South, the, 3–4, 39, 43–4, 145, 172, 181
State and Boundary Adjustment Bill, 143
State bureaucracy, xii, 203–16, 230, 232, 244
State capitalism, 53–9, 224–7
State class, xiii,, 109, 224, 230, 232–5, 245
State-creation, 139, 141–7
State High Court, 211
Structural factionalism, 7, 107
Sub-imperialism, 236
Successor elites, 25, 29, 117, 203
Super lobbies, 139

Supra-ethnic associations/groups, 88, 94
Supreme court, 211, 212
Supreme Military Council (SMC), 47–8, 69–70, 150, 151, 160

Tafewa Balewa, Abubakar, 27, 28, 35, 39
Taiwo, Olufemi, 54
Talakawa, 87, 92
Tarka, Joseph S., 34, 35, 38, 46, 80, 82
Thomas, Clive, xi
Thompson, Tunde, 159, 160
Trade unions, 47, 49, 64, 69, 170, 238–9, 240, 241–2
Traditional rule/rulers, 7–9, 160, 163, 180–200, 244
Triangular elite alliance, 54–5
Tribalism, 13–14, 19, 21, 55, 64, 107; see also Ethnicity
Tukur, Bamanga, 100, 169
Tukur, Mahmud, 160, 167, 172, 173
Turner, Terisa, 158, 229–30, 231, 241
Twelve and two-thirds clause, 123–4, 131n10
Twelve Progressive Governors, 91, 93, 138, 140
Tycoon class, 110–111, 164, 173

Udoji Report, 46, 181, 208
Udoma, Udo, 66
Uhuru, 12
Ujamaa, 12
Ukiwe, Ebitu, 168
Umar, Abubakar, 168
Umeadi, Phillip, 98
Ume-Ezeoke, Edwin, 122
Unequal development/exchange, 9
United Middle Belt Congress (UMC), 31, 38
United People's Party (UPP), 36
United Progressive Grand Alliance (UGPA), 38, 39
Unity in diversity, 1, 29, 117, 138, 198–9, 204
Unity Party of Nigeria (UPN), 82 et seq., chs. 6–7, 198, 199
Universal Primary Education (UPE), 46, 194
Unongo, Paul, 100
Urhobo Progressive Union, 22
Uwaifo Panel, 175

Vatsa, Mamman, 174
Vertical-horizontal mosaic, 1

Wali, Aminu Bashir, 99
Wallace, Tina, 223
War Against Indiscipline (WAI), 95, 164–5, 166
Warren, Bill, 228

Waterman, Peter, xii, 53
Wayas, Joseph, 99
Waziri, Mahmud, 90, 92
West African Students' Association, 31
Westminister Model/Westminster Constitution, 27, 28, 29, 116, 188
Williams, Babatunde, 26
Williams, Gavin, 36
Williams, Rotimi, 155

World-systems theory, xi

Yar'Adua, Shehu, 47, 71, 78, 112, 158, 172
Yusuf, Hassan, 93

Zik, *see* Azikiwe, Nnamdi
Zoning system (NPN), 81–2
Zuwo, Sabo Bakin, 93, 99, 100